1980

ari and Paul begin a conversation about how ann arbor could use a traditional Jewish deli like the ones they grew up with in detroit (Paul) and chicago (ari).

november 1981

Paul notices that the building on the corner of kingsley and detroit is available. he calls ari to see if he's ready to open the deli that they had talked about.

1986

the 700-square-foot addition to the original zingerman's building is completed. the pie-shaped wedge houses the sandwich line and provides expanded room for dry goods.

march 15, 1982

zingerman's opens its doors for the first time. ari and Paul are behind the counter making sandwiches and cutting bread and cheeses.

"America's very best rye? No contest. We found it in Ann Arbor, Michigan ... It comes from Zingerman's Bakehouse, which makes loaves of rugged rye that are dense and springy, laced with the taste of hearth smoke."

jane and michael Stern, saveur

1996

zingerman's catering, famous for extraordinary deli trays and for bringing "the zingerman's experience" beyond the deli's doors, and into Southeast michigan, is launched.

1998

food gatherers delivers over 2,000,000 pounds of food to help feed those in need in washtenaw county.

after three years of

1997

the new bread bag from zingerman's bakehouse earns national design recognition from "Print" magazine. zing artists become "Print" favorites, receiving similar recognition the next three years in a row for four other zingerman's design projects.

mail or

D1218310

Zingerman's

Guide to Good Leading, Part 3

A Lapsed Anarchist's Approach to

MANAGING
OURSELVES

Ari Weinzweig

PRESS

Ann Arbor

2013

Published in the United States of America by Zingerman's Press
Manufactured in Michigan, United States of America

First Edition, Second Printing

2018   2017   2016   2015   4   3   2

Cover illustration: Ian Nagy
Cover design: Nicole Robichaud
Interior illustrations: Ian Nagy and Ryan Stiner
Text design: Raul Peña
Text font: Adobe Caslon Pro

ISBN: 978–0–9893494–2–0

www.zingermanspress.com

Printed, bound, and warehoused locally, in southeastern Michigan.

Printed on FSC certified paper with a recycled content of 100 percent post-consumer waste.

BEFORE WE COMMENCE

Someone—a very successful entrepreneur, actually—asked me the other day if, after all these years in business, I was still afraid. Although I waited a few seconds before I responded, his question wasn't really all that hard to answer. "The truth is I'm almost always afraid," I said. "It's just that I've learned to go ahead with things anyway." Which in a sense, I suppose, sums up both this book and my whole life. A bit of fear, some uncertainty, and a good dose of self-doubt are standard elements of my everyday existence. I think it's been that way since I was a kid. For a long time, I allowed fear to hold me back. Though it's still there today, far more often than not, I'm able to work through it to get where I want to go anyway.

Entering new emotional territory—like the writing of this book—is still sort of scary. But it's a good kind of scary. It's a lot like what Wendell Berry wrote: "Always in the big woods when you leave familiar ground and step off alone into a new place there will be, along with the feelings of curiosity and excitement, a little nagging of dread. It is the ancient fear of the Unknown, and it is your first bond with the wilderness you are going into." With that in mind, here are a few small warnings, a bit of context I want to clarify, before you commence your reading:

For openers, I want to be clear that I'm not positioning myself as the paragon of perfect self-management. While I stand strongly behind everything in this book, I still manage to mess up most of it with far more frequency than I'd like to admit. My apologies if you're one of the people I've cut off in a meeting, failed to listen to well enough, or lost patience with prematurely. My intentions are always good, but the implementation is ever imperfect.

Secondly, I want to stress that what follows are my own thoughts, not an official statement of certified Zingerman's policy that every person who works here has signed off on. Not long ago I was presenting to a group of business leaders when one man raised his hand. "So, can your employees all recite your mission statement?" I was caught off guard, but that answer was easy as well. "No, I doubt it," I said. I paused for a minute to process. "The thing is I don't really care if they've memorized it. What I do care about it is that, in their own ways, each of them actually lives it. They can't recite the mission by rote, but they definitely make it come alive every day." The same goes for this book—while I'm pretty sure that it reflects the spirit of most everyone who's been a part of Zingerman's, it is not *meant to represent a scientifically arrived at average of the views of all six hundred people who are part of our organization. Everyone from Paul Saginaw, my partner of 30-plus years, to the 30-plus people we've only recently hired will surely have their own intelligent, informed perspectives which is as it ought to be—individuality and freethinking are at the core of what we do!*

As with Parts 1 and 2 *of this series, I've endeavored to put together* Part 3 *so that you can start reading it wherever you want. If you're feeling more orderly, read the series from the first page of* Part 1 *until the last page of this one. Feeling feisty? Flip straight to page 95 and read the essay about Free Choice—or enter at whatever Secret strikes your fancy. Some of you are starting your Zingerman's Experience here and have little context for it; if I've failed to give enough background or if you're just interested to know more, feel free to email me with questions any time at ari@zingermans.com. Others of you might well have read everything I've ever written, been eating our food for three decades, and seen me at the Deli, Roadhouse, or Bakehouse the day before yesterday. For you, my fear is that I'll be repeating too much. If I am, just take charge—make your way a few paragraphs or so ahead until you get to something you didn't already know.*

Lastly, while all of what follows is about free choice, I know full well that the work outlined in this book will be many times harder for those who are living in poverty, or are victims of abuse, natural disaster, or violence, than it might be for those of us who are more fortunate. I know that my own experience is anything but average. I've been blessed with a middle-class upbringing, a pretty high-end education, good partners, thousands of great people to work with and an Ann Arbor community that I love. I get to eat and sell really delicious food every day and be part of a learning organization and an industry that's generally given to high levels of sharing, caring, and creativity.

There are hundreds of millions of people, I know, who don't get all those things, who don't even have enough to eat, let alone the chance to work on something like self-management. It's hard to own your own life when you have little support. But I do believe that the experiences, insights, and approaches that follow can be of some help, regardless of the circumstances in which we find ourselves. As Holocaust survivor Viktor Frankl wrote in Man's Search for Meaning, *"Everything can be taken from a human being but one thing: the last of the human freedoms—to choose one's attitude in any given set of circumstances, to choose one's own way."*

Since so much of this book, though, is about collaboration, I would love to hear about what you learn, what resonates, and what you put into practice. Please, by all means, email away with anecdotes and stories, struggles and successes, or better still come by for coffee and a bit of conversation.

Ari

maggie stiffler working on the patio at the deli on a beautiful summer day

CONTENTS

PREFACE

"We Carry a New World, Here in Our Hearts"

In his essay "Politics Within Limits," philosopher, playwright, poet, and anarchist Paul Goodman wrote that "Having a vocation is somewhat of a miracle, like falling in love and it works out." His supposition fits me to a T. Thirty or so years ago I fell in love with my work. This book is about how that love story came to happen.

I'm also in full agreement with what an elderly French farmer told food writer Patricia Wells, as quoted in her fine book *A Food Lover's Guide to France*. "We love our work," he said. "We don't count our hours. We think our work has value." Those two quotes—one from a well-known New York intellectual, the other from an unnamed Provençal peasant—sum things up for me: the wonders of hard work (rather than wondering why we "have" to work hard), never counting hours (while mindfully making every hour count), the power of a poet (and the poetry of power used in positive ways), working out (in both senses of the word), making a difference in the world, anarchists' insights, old-fashioned farming, and falling in love. All are essential elements in what's made my life so seriously rewarding.

They are also, I believe, a big part of what's made Zingerman's so successful. The basic premise of this book is that *if we want to run a great business, then the place to start is inside ourselves.*

Like most real-life love stories, mine is as much about messing up and trying to make peace as it is about pursuing passion and gaining great success. Getting to greatness and finding one's way in the world is not an overnight activity; for me at least, experiencing meaningful miracles, true vocation, and lasting love all take time and a lot of work. While the relationship has, of course, had its difficult days, it's most definitely worked out wonderfully well; my life and I have had a very good time of it together. When all is said (though still not all done), it's been a rewarding, positive, and hugely productive journey, one that feels, as Paul Goodman puts it, like something of a miracle.

Imperfectly as I've lived it, I wouldn't trade my life for any other. It's a life that I own free, fully, and clear, one that I've worked hard for many decades now to construct. Whether it's great partners, great problems, a great piece of cheese, an incredible slice of country bread that Patricia Wells's farmer would surely appreciate, an amazing insight from a little known anarchist, a smile from a coworker, a sip of delicious tea, or a compliment from a customer, I'm grateful for it all every day. To say that I feel lucky is an incredible understatement. I have a meaningful opportunity to contribute to thousands of customers and coworkers. I get to learn and love and write and taste and talk and teach and travel, all with great regularity. I freely choose to work long hours and spend them with pretty wonderful people and really fine foods. I get to make lots of mistakes, most of which, fortunately, take place in the presence of people patient enough to put up with me.

Not that long ago a friend of mine asked me, "What is it that drives you so hard to do, well, everything that you do? What motivates you? You work so much, you're writing these books, you're pouring water in the restaurant, you're picking up paper off the floor, you're traveling to teach, you make time for nearly everyone who asks. You've been doing it for thirty-one years now. So what drives you?" Her question felt more like a throw-down than a compliment, though I know she meant it more as the latter. Her curiosity was understandable but she'd caught me off guard. I stared back at her. "I know it's not money," she continued. "So what is it? Is it fear?" I responded slowly, trying to avoid overreacting. "I don't know. I have many fears but they're definitely not what drive me." I was trying not to sound defensive. "I don't know. I need to think about it."

My partner, Paul Saginaw, long ago shared a hugely helpful phrase with me: "When furious, get curious." I use his saying so regularly it's become almost a ritual, a helpful little regimen that keeps me on track when I'm struggling to make sense of things. I've since added a similar saying of my own: "When in doubt, sort it out." While there's a lot to be said for the unexplained mysteries of the universe, in general I like to understand what's going on. Sorting it out, for me, almost always starts with looking inward; it's about entering the unknown in the interest of greater understanding. When I don't have the answer, I wait, wonder, and try to work my way back to what's happening inside my head.

In this case, it only took a few days before it occurred to me that I'd actually known the answer to my friend's question all along. I was, it turns out, what the training world would call "unconsciously competent" about the essential underpinnings of my own existence; although I was *very* motivated to make great things happen and pretty darned good at managing myself, I wasn't very good at explaining to others what I was doing and why it was effective.

The essays that follow are an effort to move myself into "conscious competence"—to sort out what's worked well in my own life, and here at Zingerman's organizationally, so that I can then share it with anyone who's interested. My commitment is to make sense out of all of that's gone on in my own error-filled, educationally oriented, fun- and food- and philosophy-focused life. I'm determined to figure out what's contributed to the thousands of constructive and creative products, projects, and people who are part of our world here at Zingerman's; to explore and explain what it is we've done that's enhanced the lives of so many staff members, suppliers, customers, readers, and writers; and to convert all of that into a form that others can learn from.

My hope is that the things that have helped me over the last twenty or thirty years will also aid others who are interested and eager to work as hard—in their own ways—to make miracles of their lives. To help others make a life that they also own, that they too can fall in love with, and have it all work out. If we want to get to greatness, then self-management, not strategic planning, is the place to start. And, with a few breaks, a lot of support from colleagues and community, family and friends, and a whole lot of hard work on ourselves, *anyone who wants can start working on making their life pretty miraculous, as well.*

It's not an overnight activity. I am still, to be clear, often in doubt. The thing I'm most certain about is that I'm living my life with uncertainty, indecision, and confusion. This book is about how I've been learning to move through that uncertainty, to sort things out successfully. It's about taking stock of what I've done, understanding how I've gotten to where I am, and being mindful about what I've learned. It's about how all of that, in turn, has helped me to change my ways and make my life about eight hundred times more satisfying than it was thirty years ago.

As Drs. Bob and Judith Wright confirmed in their work, *Transformed!*, "We can literally change our brains and our minds, and what we believe, who we are, and how we live. We can transform." *And when we do what the Wrights are talking about, we can significantly alter our organizations as well.* That's certainly been the case for us here at Zingerman's. While we are true to who we were when we first opened, we have clearly come a long, long way over the last three decades. I doubt that we'd be remotely close to what we are now (or, for that matter, even still in business) if Paul and I and so many others here hadn't worked so hard at self-improvement. It's not the glamorous, one-good-idea-solves-all, strategically brilliant solution that so many people are searching for. But if we've contributed positively to our community, the lives of our coworkers, and the food world at large over the years, it's mostly because we've managed to get a lot better at managing ourselves.

From Corner Deli to a Dream of Community

If by chance this book is your first entrée into the world that makes up the Zingerman's Community of Businesses today, welcome. The business story begins on March 15, 1982—just me and Paul and a pair of employees (Marci Fribourg and Ricky Cohen, to give credit where it's clearly due), 29 seats, 25 sandwiches, some specialty foods, and a commitment to doing something special and constructive in the community. Fast forwarding to 2013, that commitment is now a Community with a capital C. The Zingerman's Community of Businesses employs nearly 600 people (and another 300 at the holidays for Mail Order) and achieves sales of over $46,000,000. The little Deli on the corner is now about eight times as big as it was when we began—as I write, we're almost finished with a nearly seven-year-long construction project to renovate our original building on Detroit St. and add more space so that all those food lovers who line up to get in for lunch can do it less stressfully and have more room to shop and eat. We've also started a Candy Manufactory and a full-service sit-down restaurant called Zingerman's Roadhouse that serves traditional American food and includes a 47-acre sustainable farm. There's an amazing Bakehouse turning out thousands of loaves of beautiful artisan bread and almost as many pieces of traditionally made pastry. There's a Creamery that makes cheese and gelato, and a Coffee Company that sources, roasts, and brews some great beans. We have a Mail Order business that ships traditional foods all over the country. And there's ZingTrain, our training business, that teaches what you could call the Zingerman's way of working to interested folks in both businesses and not-for-profits around the country, and even around the world.

That's a fairly good synopsis of the surface-level business story. If you wanted a few hundred words to stick in a short article, it would probably suffice. But this, you'll recall, is really a love story, and love stories are always about a lot more than a set of staid statistics. What writer Wendell Berry calls "good work," as I've experienced it, is a far richer, more holistic existence than can be explained with numbers alone—there are people and problems and ideas and struggles and successes and a thousand other things at play at the same time. It is, after all, all one life.

Our work at Zingerman's is far more than a business school case study. It's about lovingly made traditional food, old-style agriculture, artisan craftsman-ship, caring for people, and creatively making a difference. It's about freshly cut corned beef, excellent handmade candy bars, beautiful custom-made wedding cakes, and hand-crafted breads and cheeses. It's about sustainable farming and sustainable families. It's about learning (as Paul taught me twenty-something years ago) to "disagree without being disagreeable." It's about collaboration and community. It's about self-reflection and learning to slice smoked salmon. It's about food writing and philosophy, good finance and good fun, and getting a heckuva lot done while still feeling good about what we're doing. It's about a workplace in which everyone is encouraged to be themselves and invited to get involved, in which information flows liberally and new dreams develop daily.

But What Is Zingerman's All About?

When people come to visit and ask me to describe what we do at Zingerman's, I usually just turn to someone else nearby and say, "Why don't you ask *them*." It could be a customer, a coworker, a cop on our beat, a truck driver who came in the back door, or a busboy who just cleared a table. "How do *you* describe what we do?" I'll ask. It's a marvelous thing really—the most meaningful comments come from frontline folks who are unrehearsed, who haven't formally prepared themselves to put forward an opinion. It's remarkable how much our customers pick up on the nuances of what we do, how the people who work here realize the way their work fits into the bigger picture, and how much they all seem to understand what it takes to run a successfully sustainable business.

At times I refer my questioners to what others have put in print. Most recently, we've been featured rather prominently in Michael Paterniti's best-selling, truth-is-seriously-stranger-than-fiction book *The Telling Room*. It's a tantalizingly true mystery story that—as some have said about Zingerman's—seems so amazing you think it must be made up, but actually isn't. *The Telling Room* tale begins back in 1991 when we hired Michael to proof the Zingerman's newsletter I was writing. We've both, I'm sure, come a long way in our writing skills since then—I was nine years into owning a Deli that was just starting to gain national acclaim, and he was a grad student at the University of Michigan.

The second set of essays we sent Michael to edit included a couple paragraphs that I'd put in about a Spanish cheese I'd fallen in love with, one of the best I'd ever tried. The article caught his attention and stayed with him, both in his soul and in his wallet, for many years. A decade down the road he decided to go to the source in Spain to find the man who made this amazing cheese.

The Telling Room traces that journey, from Mike's first awkward editing days at the Deli to the village of Guzman, where both the cheese and its maker had their home. That the tale, Mike's travels, and his passionate pursuit of a great product and the people who make it started here at Zingerman's is emblematic of what we do—help people discover their dreams, which they then go out and live. Because he's been around us in one form or another for so long, and has experienced amazing things in his travels, Michael's description of what we do means a lot to me. "In the days before the rise of gourmand culture," he explains, "before our obsession with purity and pesticides . . . Zingerman's preached a new way of thinking about food: Eat the best, and eat homemade." He goes on, "If Zingerman's preached a new way of thinking about food, it was by practicing the old ways, by trying to make latkes as they'd been made a hundred years ago, by returning to traditional recipes."

If you ask a dozen other people what it is we do, you'll get at least that many answers. Mario Batali says we're "the center of [his] gastro-deli universe." *Inc.* magazine called us the "coolest small company in America." And the other day an eight-year-old, out for dinner at the Roadhouse, wrote us a message on the kids' menu. In green crayon he'd circled "macaroni and cheese" and then written "is the best!" Down the side of the menu, he'd added a bit more. "But only at this restaurant." My favorite Zingerman's quote of the moment comes from Gary Snyder, Beat poet, Pulitzer Prize winner, and author of an essay called "Buddhist Anarchism." After visiting us for the first time a few months ago, Gary wrote me that, "Zingerman's is a remarkable synthesis of the old and the new, the elite and the populist. I loved it!"

An Anarchist Approach to the Work World

Anarchist writers from Gary Snyder back to Emma Goldman have been a big part of my life for many years now, since I started reading and falling in love with their work when I was a student at the University of Michigan. In truth, their approaches have been part of my spirit since I was about six. As will come up many times in the course of the book, the ways we're wired early in our lives will almost always have a big impact on how we interact many years later as adults. As a kid I was drawn to independence, to free choice, to going my own way and resisting being forced into the same path everyone around me was on. When I was in college, I was probably one of only a tiny handful of people that regularly used the reading room at the Labadie Collection (the country's largest collection of anarchist and radical material, located on the 7th floor of the University of Michigan's Graduate Library). What they were saying was drastically different from everything else I'd read; the little pamphlets, long essays, provocative poetry, and beautifully illustrated books all caught—and kept—my attention.

For the most part, though, I left the anarchists behind, or at least stacked on my bookshelves, while we worked to make Zingerman's an ever-more effective organization. Thirty-plus years after I graduated with my BA in history, I started studying them again. I reread a bit of Emma Goldman's work for the first time in decades and was shocked (in a good way) to find so many surprisingly strong parallels between anarchist approaches and the way we were working to run our organization.

Four years later there are probably a hundred books by or about anarchists now stacked on my living room shelves, with more piled up on the floor nearby. The ideas of Goldman, Gustav Landauer, Murray Bookchin, Colin Ward, Voltairine de Cleyre, and their colleagues that caught my attention when I was eighteen have now inspired me anew. Their insights are integrated into the essays that follow. The key concepts they wrote about are all here: be yourself; make your choices mindfully; contribute positively to the community; be kind, creative, and caring; help others to live their dreams; respect and assist everyone you can, including yourself; develop your spirit; support those in need; honor the planet and the amazing collection of people, plants, and animals that are on it. Be daring and do the right thing for yourself and the world.

All this has been at the core of the organizational culture we've been creating at Zingerman's for three decades. While we don't directly sell any of those approaches by the pound, they underlie everything we do. Without them, without our efforts at self-reflection and mindful management, we wouldn't be what we are. Our customers know us for our food and our service, the informative and entertaining nature of our marketing, and the energy of the men and women who work here. But I would argue it's the far-from-glamorous activity outlined in this book that makes all that more visible, and edible, activity possible. I believe that our internal work makes all the difference. And I believe, in the words of Buenaventura Durutti, an anarchist who died in the Spanish Civil War: "We carry a new world, here in our hearts. That world is growing in this [very] minute."

Pouring goat milk into the cheese vat from old-style milk cans

Into the Looking Glass, the Leader's Imperative

I consider Ari and his partner Paul to be among those rare business people who earn the title of transformational leader. Transformational leaders display integrity, vision, intellectual engagement, and a dedication to the well-being of all their staff members. They are people others want to be like. But you should know that no one becomes a leader like that without doing a great deal of work. Transformational leaders, Ari and Paul included, look deeply and honestly at themselves, at what they do well and what they can do better. They embark on a lifelong mission to become the leaders they want to be.

When we choose to lead in this way, consciously, leadership becomes a dangerous occupation. It is especially dangerous to our cherished, long-held ideas of who we are. If we are going to do more than simply make a lot of money (the easy part) and impress others with our donations to charitable organizations (the guilt salving), we need to look into the mirror of our organization and take stock of how it reflects us. We want to appreciate what we do best—our passion, our commitment to quality, etc. But we also want to take an honest look at what we don't do as well, to study the parts of ourselves that we never wanted to see. The ways we don't really listen or show respect, the ways we didn't want to ever be like our father, mother, or someone else whose behavior disturbed us. When we pay attention, we're all too often shocked to discover that the words that come out of our mouths are the same ones our parents used, the words we swore would never cross our lips. And to top it all off, we are embarrassed all over again when our employees (and kids) start saying those exact same things back to us.

This book is about making changes in the way we work by looking into the mirrors of those we lead, and then using the feedback we receive to see how our thoughts, feelings, and actions need to change to reflect our higher ideals. Ari shares techniques for building the inner discipline necessary for us to responsibly look into those mirrors and make the adjustments that will bring us to our better selves. With this approach, we don't get to just criticize others and complain about their shortcomings. Instead, we need to ask how the mirror reflects lessons for us to learn, to confront aspects of ourselves that we often deny. Only when we *do* look and take responsibility for what we see can we adjust, learn, grow, and even transform. Ari's personal disciplines of self-management take us to ever-new levels of development and greatness.

Ari could have called this book *Into the Looking Glass, the Leader's Imperative.* He shows us here how great leadership begins with great leaders who are willing to peer into the looking glass of their companies and adjust themselves rather than gripe, or attempt to buy themselves a "better" mirror. As he writes:

> *The buck that comes back to us is almost always a reflection of what's happening in our heads and hearts. Our product quality, service, systems effectiveness, operating profit, organizational culture, etc. begin not in the kitchen or on the factory floor, but with us. The buck at Zingerman's then, my buck at least, starts here with me.*

In reading Ari's words, I admonish you, as well as myself, to look if we dare. And if we don't, we'd better buckle up and prepare for a rocky ride as our unconscious pain and the parts of ourselves we try to avoid are reflected back, and carried forward by others in our lives. The technical term is displacement. Let me give you an example. I once coached a widely respected CEO. Men and women he had led went on to become highly respected top executives in their own right throughout the business world. This man, however, did not look into the mirror very much. He was on his fourth marriage, and his most recent ex-wife died, alone, of an addictive disorder. For this CEO, the pain he denied was displaced onto others, inherited by his wives and children. The same thing happens in companies.

When we don't dare to look, our denial hurts our organizations. If we deny our fear, we will instill that fear in others or fail to plan adequately for potentially difficult situations. If we deny our hurt, our leadership will be unnecessarily hurtful or too passive. If we deny our own disorganization, we will decry it in those we lead or drown in the ensuing chaos. And our employees will suffer since we cannot guide them to do what we do not know how to do ourselves.

Denial and displacement on the part of leaders doesn't necessarily mean that a business will fail, but there inevitably will be consequences.

Over the years, I've coached brilliant strategists, finance whizzes, and driving producers who are considered great leaders in manufacturing, service, and retail. One CEO was sitting on billions of dollars to invest but complained regularly about how much his team members complained all the time while doing their work. I asked him what he thought about the fact that he was grousing to me about the problem rather than strategizing a change to the culture that needed to begin with him. He kept me in the meeting another 45 minutes, adding further complaints about his wife and how she constantly complained about him. Despite the fact that his firm continued to retain our services, that was the last time we saw him. Like so many "successful" CEOs, his values started and ended at the cash bottom line. He simply did not want to look into the mirror to discover how he was displacing his pain onto his wife and the people he led.

Another leader came to see me when his manufacturing business was just a struggling startup. He took my coaching very well . . . *until* the company was consistently profitable. When he had bought out his former partners, paid off all his debts, purchased his mansion with cash, and was swimming in money, I asked him what he was going to do for the low-paid hourly people he employed. He responded to my suggestion that he consider sharing the company wealth with those who did the daily labor as if it were heresy. Ultimately, it became clear that he had no interest in helping the hourly workers at his company deal with their own and their families' aspirations. And, thus, he completely missed the chance to help them and get help from them in return. Instead, he continued to complain about the problems of finding good employees. Despite four years of very successful individual and group coaching, he never came back to see me or to participate in his leadership group after that conversation. He continues to operate under the illusion that he's "helping" those in need when he donates significant sums to local charities, while neglecting to offer healthcare programs for his hourly staff or educational support for their children.

Unfortunately, he is one of many leaders I've met who have failed to embrace a win-win approach. Ari, on the other hand, gives us an intimate glimpse into the inner world of a truly transformational leader. He not only focuses on the win-win-win approach for owners, management, and employees, but he also adds two additional wins for both his suppliers and the community.

Leadership from this point of view is an inside job. Ari's techniques for the inner game of management will help any leader be more effective. His commitment to physical and mental health is inspirational—from the daily regime he follows to keep his body fit to the regular therapeutic personal coaching he maintains to keep his psyche in shape.

Another leader I recently coached, who heads a fast-growing international tech firm, also complained of his staff's complaints. But this leader, like Ari, *was* willing to look into the mirror. As he looked, he discovered that his resentment of his employees' concerns was really a projected reflection of his failure to adequately take care of his own needs. He felt himself to be on a thankless mission of extreme hours and travel. He hadn't learned to take care of himself, so he resented his staff's desires to take care of themselves. Looking further, he found significant leadership challenges he needed to face to help his people reorient to their own vision of a robust, nourishing life and to shift the company's vision to be inspiring for all involved. He has since set about doing the personal work to change himself and his organization for the better.

These leaders, the ones who care about their customers *and* their employees, whether they lead eight or 80,000, are the kind I end up caring the most about. Like Ari, many of these leaders came up through the ranks and know what it is like to be in the employee position. They consistently lean towards mutuality and embedded empathy. They are big advocates for the needs and dreams of their staff. No softies, however, they expect a great deal from their employees, who must earn the right to participate in corporate bounty. No fuzzy humanitarians, they are stark realists with a pragmatic understanding of their responsibility to protect and value the individual employees as critical elements of company success. Like Ari, they look directly into the mirror while honoring individual freedom and expression, values Ari describes as those of the anarchists as well. They understand that "good" business is only truly good if it contributes to all concerned.

I saw these values in action when I took a couple of my staff up for one of ZingTrain's two-day seminars. There were four Zingerman's employees among the 25 attendees that day. The four were a diverse lot, working in areas from food service to shipping. One nineteen- or twenty-year-old young man who worked at Zingerman's Mail Order proved to be the most articulate on the Zingerman's experience. As he spoke, he seemed to be as comfortable with a room full of executives as I imagine he would be with his peers. His sense of belonging spoke volumes to me about a transformational leader's ability to empower employees at every level.

After this young man offered praise, Ari was quick to point out that Zingerman's still has many imperfections and talked about the ever-evolving nature of the business. In doing this, he was inviting the staff to join him in honestly pointing out company flaws and to engage in constructive self-criticism as well—all of them were then able to learn and grow together as a team.

What Ari demonstrated then, and what he provides in this book, is a very useful guide for the leader who yearns for a company community, engaged shoulder-to-shoulder in a worthy pursuit. It speaks to what leaders must do internally to cultivate fantastic businesses of fantastic individuals, to be transformational leaders. These leaders aren't ensconced in a fortified executive suite but rather are hungry to be out among the people that represent their firm. It is here, among the people, where all of us who aspire to be transformational leaders get to look in that mirror and discover both the problems—and the solutions to those problems—to which we, as leaders, may be temporarily blind.

It seems that every retiring CEO I know eventually decides to write a leadership book. These "last hurrahs" risk becoming apologetic justifications for all the leaders did or did not do. This book, on the other hand, is no navel-gazing retrospective. It is a glimpse into the inner workings of a practicing CEO who shares what he learns so he can learn even more. Enjoy the inner disciplines of a transformational leader who invites us into a celebration of our humanity while we explore its fullest potential.

Dr. Bob Wright is a Chicago-based educator and proponent of transformational leadership. He and his wife, Judith, write, teach, and run the Wright Graduate University, with the stated goal of helping their degree and non-degree students "bring out their best and live spectacular lives." The Wrights have authored many books, the most recent of which is Transformed! The Science of Spectacular Living.[1]

a toasted sesame bagel from the bakehouse topped with handmade
traditional cream cheese from the creamery, served up at the deli

INTRODUCTION

Leading the Life We Want to Lead

This book is the third in the *Zingerman's Guide to Good Leading* series that explains the strangely odd, but apparently very effective, style we use in our work. What you hold in your hands is reflective of our inverted, Zingerman's, way of working. To wit, most business books focus on the big stuff—vision, mission, strategy, systems, beating the competition, making money, making it big. Many other books, looking through a leadership lens, focus on ways to get staff members to do better work, motivating them, applying new management techniques, etc. All of this, of course, is important. I've shared my own thoughts on many of these subjects in *Parts 1* and *2* of the series.

Part 3 goes in a different direction. It's not about big headlines, hard-to-top organizational visions, or bold strokes of business genius. Nor is it really about how and why other people do what they do, or how to get them to do something different. It is, instead, all about *us;* it addresses the ways in which you and I, as leaders of our organizations, deal not with others but with ourselves. It's all about looking inward—finding how we can make quiet but meaningful improvements in the way we think, live, and work. It's about our biases and beliefs, how we spend our time, and how we treat ourselves. It's about how we can teach all those same things to the people we care about and work with every day. It's based on the firm belief that the way we manage ourselves will have a hugely positive impact on our lives, our families, our friends, and our organizations, and even, in the end, on the entire planet.

The "Secrets" that follow are anything but secrets—we teach them to everyone who works here and share them regularly through ZingTrain. They're all about life, about business, about art, about finding a vocation, about falling in love, and about having it all work out. As with *Parts 1* and *2,* you can read the Secrets in any order you like; of course, I've placed them in the order that makes the most sense to me. I hope they help, and make you think, and wonder, and work hard to live the life you want to live. Not long ago I met with a new U of M graduate who'd heard me speak a few days earlier. About ten minutes into our meeting, he sighed and said, "You make it sound like it's so easy." I smiled. "It's simple," I said. "But it's definitely *not* easy. It's mostly a lot of work. And fun and fulfilling."

How you use this book is, of course, your call. Writing it—both learning the material by means of personal, sometimes painful, experience, and then sorting out how to share it constructively with others—has helped me to be more in synch with myself, to be a better leader, to run a better business, and to live a more rewarding life. Having taught much of what follows here at Zingerman's and around the country (through ZingTrain, our training business), I know these approaches have helped many others to do similarly positive things. They will at the least, I hope, make you take pause and reflect. As Wendell Berry writes in *The Unforeseen Wilderness,* "the world cannot be discovered by a journey of miles, no matter how long, but only by a spiritual journey, a journey of one inch, very arduous and humbling and joyful, by which we arrive at the ground at our own feet, and learn to be at home."

Ultimately, it comes down to the directive my friend Daphne Zepos shared only a few weeks before she died, at the far-too-young age of 53: "Own your life." The work this book details is not likely to get a lot of attention in the mass market. Introspection hardly makes for sensational headlines. But I'm convinced that the ideas and approaches that follow can change the lives and organizations of others as it has mine. I believe that that work is about bringing out the best in everyone, ourselves and those around us. The other way, the more mainstream model—focusing on fitting in and following other people's recipe for living your life—for me, at least, doesn't work. As 19th century philosopher and Christian anarchist Søren Kierkegaard said, "The most common form of despair is not being who you are."

It's my belief that we don't need to go down that dark road. Given a strong commitment to self-growth, a clear vision of the future, and a willingness to work long and hard to get there, we can definitely find constructive and creative ways to be ourselves while still contributing to the community that we're a part of. This book is based on my belief that business and life can be as artistically conceived as any of Gary Snyder's great poems. Counter to common wisdom, business doesn't have to be about downgrading our spirits in the interest of increasing sales. It can be as creative, innovative, and thought-provoking as anything Picasso ever painted. When we align our passions, dreams, values, and desires, we can do great things. As lyricist and novelist Paulo Coehlo says, "wherever your heart is, there you will find your treasure."

In a little book that might well be considered a minor masterpiece, *Life Is a Miracle,* Wendell Berry explains the art of self-management. "Good artists," he argues, "are people who can stick things together so that they stay stuck. They know how to gather things into formal arrangements that are intelligible, memorable, and lasting. Good forms confer health upon the things that they gather together. Farms, families, and communities are forms of art just as are poems, paintings, and symphonies. None of these things would exist if we did not make them. We can make them either well, or poorly; this choice is another thing that we make."

That choice is, ultimately, where it all begins. "To be free," anarchist author Howard Ehrlich explains, "people must liberate themselves." It's rarely easy but it's almost always effective. I believe, as Gary Snyder says, "We are all capable of extraordinary transformations." The Secrets in this series have helped me to get moving on mine. I hope they're of help to you in yours. *It's up to each of us to choose the lives we want to lead, to emancipate ourselves, and to go for the greatness we dream about.* The words that follow are mine, but the thoughts and insights they evoke are all yours. Together, I'm confident, we can make great things happen.

jelly bean attentively watching the author at work

Cast of Characters

What follows is intended to help you keep track of the characters I reference regularly in the book. If you're starting the series here with Part 3, *you may not be familiar with them all. I like to think of it also as a nod to my roots as a student of Russian history—these sorts of character lists are commonly found in the front matter of 19th century Russian novels.*

Abraham Maslow: Pioneering twentieth century psychologist best known for his theory about a "hierarchy of needs." He was known for teaching his students to focus on the positive. His work around self-actualization is very much in line with the idea of "owning your life."

Alexander Berkman: Late 19th and early 20th century anarchist. Born in Russia, lived for twenty years in the US before being expelled in 1917 along with his colleague, friend, and former lover, Emma Goldman.

Amanda Palmer: American musician, poet, and performer, known by her fans for using a common swear word that starts with "F" as her middle name.

Amin Maalouf: Lebanese-born French contemporary writer of insightful fiction and nonfiction, including one of my favorite books, *In the Name of Identity.*

Ammon Hennacy: Author of *Autobiography of a Catholic Anarchist* and *The One-Man Revolution in America.* Folk singer Utah Phillips called him "a Catholic, Anarchist, Pacifist, Draft Dodger of two World Wars, Tax Refuser, Vegetarian, One Man Revolution in America."

Amy Emberling: Co-managing partner of Zingerman's Bakehouse, along with Frank Carollo. Amy started with us as a baker in 1992 after getting her undergraduate degree in social movements from Harvard and a pastry degree in Paris. She later went back to school to get her MBA at Columbia, before returning to Zingerman's.

Anaïs Nin: 20th century American poet and writer, her most famous published works were probably her journals and her erotica. Much of her work, including *Little Birds,* was published posthumously.

Anders Ericsson: Swedish-born psychologist, now professor at Florida State. His research on the development of expertise (he authored the 10,000 hour theory) has led the way to many insights about self-management.

Anese Cavanaugh: Leadership coach and promoter of positive organizational culture, Anese is the woman who first taught me about the idea of energy management. Anese refers to her work as "bootist leadership," a tribute to her love of boots and belief in the importance of good grounding and congruence in all we do. You can check out her work at anesecavanaugh.com.

Bo Burlingham: Business writer and editor-at-large for *Inc.* magazine. His articles and books have been a big influence on us. He coauthored the seminal work on open book finance, *The Great Game of Business,* with Jack Stack, and also wrote *Small Giants: Businesses that Choose to Be Great Instead of Big.*

Bob Wright: Educator and proponent of transformational leadership. He and his wife, Judith, write, teach, and run the Wright Graduate University with the stated goal of helping their degree and non-degree students "live spectacular lives."

Brenda Ueland: A formidable feminist, writer, and free thinker. Born in 1891 in Minnesota, her best-known book is *If You Really Want to Write: A Book about Art, Independence and Spirit.* This book changed my writing and my life. Brenda lived by two rules: "To tell the truth and to not do anything she didn't want to."

Buenaventura Durutti: A central figure of Spanish anarchism, he died in battle in 1936 at the age of 40 during the Spanish Civil War.

Chaim Weinberg: Late 19th and early 20th century anarchist. Born in Russia to a Jewish family, immigrated to the US (via London) in 1881.

Chris Peterson: A leading proponent of positive psychology, working here at the University of Michigan prior to his untimely death in October of 2012.

Colin Ward: One of the most prominent of late 20th century British anarchist writers. His best know work is *Anarchy in Action.*

Daniel Goleman: Psychologist, science journalist, Pulitzer Prize winner, and author of *Emotional Intelligence.*

Daphne Zepos: One of my best friends, Daphne was born in Greece, lived in half a dozen countries in Europe, and settled in the US in the early 1990s. Her work helped to change the way millions of people in the US think about traditional cheese. She died of cancer on July 3, 2012.

David Whyte: Poet and writer of British and Irish heritage, his insightful books about progressive approaches to business center on collaborative conversation. He runs the Institute for Conversational Leadership.

Emma Goldman: Known by the tongue-in-cheek title of "Queen of the Anarchists," Emma arrived in the US from her native Lithuania in 1885, at the age of 16. She became one of the world's most renowned anarchists, an outspoken advocate for freedom, women's rights, and social equality. Her creative thinking was, I believe, far ahead of its time.

Edward Carpenter: Late 19th and early 20th century British anarchist, gay rights advocate, poet, and philosopher.

Edward Sapir: Born in Prussia in 1884, Sapir came to the US as a child. He went on to become a prominent and pioneering linguist and anthropologist, and probably the first person to study the connection between the two.

Errico Malatesta: Late 19th and early 20th century Italian anarchist who later immigrated to Britain.

Frank Carollo: Co-managing partner at Zingerman's Bakehouse. Frank first trained me in how to cook the line back in my early restaurant days. Without his patient guidance, I don't think the *Guides to Good Leading* would have come to be.

Gary Snyder: Pulitzer Prize–winning poet, whose friends and fellow writers included Allen Ginsberg, Jack Kerouac, and others. Gary has studied and practiced Buddhism extensively, and in 1961 he published the essay "Buddhist Anarchism." Lawrence Ferlinghetti called him "the Thoreau of the Beat Generation."

George Woodcock: A Canadian-born anarchist who wrote extensively throughout the 20th century; his best-known work is *Anarchism: A History of Libertarian Ideas and Movements.*

Gustav Landauer: A pacifist anarchist from Germany whose late 19th and early 20th century writings have been hugely inspirational to me and many others. He is quoted throughout the *Guides to Good Leading*. One of his most inspiring insights (to me) is this belief: "The State is not something which can be destroyed by a revolution, but is a condition, a certain relationship between human beings, a mode of human behaviour; we destroy it by contracting other relationships, by behaving differently."

Henry David Thoreau: 19th century poet, abolitionist, anarchist, and one of the great American thinkers. I think of him as the Gary Snyder of his era.

Howard Ehrlich: Anarchist writer, former professor at University of Iowa, and founder of the journal *Social Anarchism*.

Hugh MacLeod: British author, cartoonist, and author of one of my favorite books, *Ignore Everybody*.

James C. Scott: History professor at Yale and author of an array of interesting texts, many of which look at the past through an anarchist lens, such as *Seeing Like a State* and *The Art of Being Ungoverned: An Anarchist History of Southeast Asia*.

Jack Stack: CEO of Springfield Remanufacturing and the man behind open book management.

Jelly Bean: My much loved little dog. Mostly Corgi with a bit of something else that enables her to run with me; we've spent thirteen years enjoying life together.

Jim Munroe: Canadian cartoonist and author of *Time Management for Anarchists*.

Jon Kabat-Zinn: Professor of medicine at the University of Massachusetts Medical School, founder of the Center for Mindfulness in Medicine, and author of many books on mindfulness.

Joseph Ishill: Rumanian-born Jewish anarchist who immigrated to the US in 1909 and went on to start Oriole Press. Ishill published some of the most beautiful books I've ever seen, all hand-printed and bound and reflecting the anarchist ethos in both their aesthetic sense and their provocative content.

Julia Cameron: Author, poet, playwright, filmmaker, and more, best known for her book on creative recovery, *The Artist's Way*.

Lex Alexander: My good friend in North Carolina, Lex started the natural foods–oriented Wellspring Grocery in Durham in 1981 and later sold it to Whole Foods. I've learned many things from Lex, including our now well-established ritual at Zingerman's of ending every meeting with appreciations.

Maggie Bayless: Managing partner at ZingTrain, our training business. Maggie's passion for training and her insight into our ways of working and learning are embedded in the materials in this book.

Maia Genisio: A lifelong Zingerman's customer, colleague, and friend. My conversations with Maia have inspired many insights over the years. At the time of this book's publication, Maia will be six years old.

Marcus Graham: Born Shmuel Marcus in Romania in the late 19th century, he immigrated to the US, changed his name, and began to actively write about and advocate for his anarchist beliefs.

Martin Seligman: Generally acknowledged as the father of positive psychology, his books and articles on the subject offer great insight into how to build a positive workplace.

Meg Noodin: Ojibwe language teacher, poet, writer, editor, and all-around insightful leader here at the University of Michigan for many years, now at the University of Wisconsin, Milwaukee.

Michael Paterniti: After getting his masters in English at the University of Michigan and working part-time for us here at Zingerman's editing our newsletter, Mike went on to win the 1998 National Magazine Award for his article "Driving Mr. Albert." His most recent work is *The Telling Room*, which begins right here at Zingerman's.

Michel de Montaigne: 16th century French writer, often credited as being the first author of the personal essay form. He was a friend and supporter of early anarchist thinker, Étienne de La Boétie, and then an advocate after La Boétie's untimely death.

Mikhail Bakunin: One of the great figures of Russian anarchism, he lived, wrote, spoke, and preached revolution with great passion.

Mohammed Bamyeh: Anarchist-oriented professor of sociology, with a specialty in Islamic studies, at the University of Pittsburgh.

Murray Bookchin: A mid-to-late 20th century American anarchist and radical advocate for positive ecology and the environment.

Nikolai Berdyaev: Late 19th and early 20th century Russian philosopher and Christian anarchist.

Olu Dara: American cornetist, born Charles Jones in Natchez, Mississippi, his music is a mix of jazz, gospel, African rhythms, and R&B.

Osho: An Indian mystic, guru, professor of philosophy, and spiritual teacher. His many books present intriguing ideas about managing ourselves.

Paul Goodman: 20th century American anarchist, poet, playwright, philosopher, and creative antagonist.

Paul Hawken: Founder of the Smith & Hawken, and author of many books, including one of my favorites, *Growing a Business.*

Paul Saginaw: The co-founding partner of our organization, Paul and I have worked together for 35 years, the last 31 of them as partners at Zingerman's. Paul's insight, guidance, patience, generosity of spirit, and everything else are imprinted all over our organization and this book.

Peter Drucker: Probably the most prolific and insightful 20th century business writer.

Peter Kropotkin: Born a Russian prince, he later renounced his royal birthright and went on to become an internationally recognized scientist and one of the world's most mindful anarchists. His work on Mutual Aid (the belief that Natural Selection favors the most collaborative, not the most competitive) and his advocacy for local agriculture were well ahead of his time.

Ram Dass: Born Richard Alpert, he's a long time spiritual leader in the US. His most famous written work is *Be Here Now,* on the subject of mindfulness.

Robert Greenleaf: The author of *Servant Leadership* and one of the great business thinkers of the 20th century.

Ron Lippitt: A social scientist who joined the Institute for Social Research at the University of Michigan. His pioneering work on what he called "positive futuring" is at the core of what we do with visioning here at Zingerman's.

Rosabeth Moss Kanter: Michigan MBA, a former editor of the *Harvard Business Review,* and author of many books and articles including one of my favorites, *Confidence.*

Rudolf Rocker: Born in Germany, he spent much of his life in London, where he came to be known as the Anarchist Rabbi for his work with the community of Jewish anarchists in the East End. He referred to himself as an "anarchist without adjectives."

Sam Keen: Author, poet, psychologist, and philosopher, his writings have been a major influence on my thinking over the years. Among his many insightful works are *Hymns to an Unknown God*, *To Love and Be Loved*, *Inward Bound*, and *Fire in the Belly*.

Stas' Kazmierski: Recently retired as co-managing partner at ZingTrain. Paul and I first engaged Stas' in the early '90s to help us write our mission statement and guiding principles. The vast majority of what we know about visioning has come from what Stas' has taught us over the years.

Seth Godin: Writer and major source of wit in the American business world. He's written many excellent books, one of the most recent of which is *The Icarus Deception*.

Siegfried Kracauer: German-Jewish writer, cultural critic, film critic, and anarchist.

Søren Kierkegaard: One of the 19th century's most compelling philosophers, a Christian existentialist and anarchist.

Steven Johnson: Creative business thinker and author of *History of Ideas: A Natural History of Innovation*.

Tamar Adler: Food writer, chef, and author of the excellent *An Everlasting Meal*.

Voltairine de Cleyre: Late 19th and early 20th century American poet, feminist, and passionate believer in anarchism.

Viktor Frankl: Austrian psychologist and neurologist who was sent to the concentration camps after Germany took control of Austria. His book, *Man's Search for Meaning*, is one of the great books about self-study and self-management.

Wendell Berry: Born in 1934, he's been writing insightfully and often controversially about America's rural heritage, ecological preservation, and traditional agriculture for over 60 years.

Ursula K. Le Guin: American science fiction writer and anarchist.

zingerman's delicatessen. est. 1982

The "Secrets"

The essays that follow aren't really secrets, but they are, in essence, the "secrets" that so many people have been asking us for. Secrets #1–18 were all in Zingerman's Guide to Good Leading, Part 1. *Secrets #19–29 follow in* Part 2. *Below are Secrets #30–39. Each is an important element of what makes Zingerman's Zingerman's. Read and use each on its own, or adapt them all to your organization. Many thanks to all the insightful folks—both within our organization and without—who have contributed ideas, comments, stories, edits, and advice!*

courtney suciu happily opening up a trio of gift boxes
from zingerman's mail order

SECRET #30

Why Managing Ourselves Well Matters

*Four Reasons Why I Work So Hard
to Make It Happen*

Author Simon Sinek says, "It doesn't matter what you do, it matters why you do it." I agree. Knowing why I'm doing something makes all the difference. I've long believed that managing myself more effectively would have a positive impact on my life. Per Simon's suggestion, it's worth reflecting on why it's so important. Self-management, it turns out, is at the core of everything I'm trying to do. Here are four benefits to effective self-management that have me fired up.

1. The Better We Manage Ourselves, the Better Our Businesses Will Be

I was sitting at the Deli one day, sharing thoughts with a big Zingerman's fan. A businessman from Canada, Brian's read most of what I've written and has been actively bringing it back to his own business. Under the guise of going to a Michigan football game, he explained, he'd convinced his family to come down to Ann Arbor for the weekend. He'd been once before on his own, had become a big believer in what we do, and wanted his family to have the Zingerman's Experience for themselves. It's really not the food that he finds so fascinating. He likes to eat, of course, and by his own admission has learned a lot from us about the importance of good ingredients and just how great great food can taste. But it's our organizational work, not our culinary offerings, that's gotten him going. "Every single person we talk to," he told me, "is so excited about what they're doing. It's fantastic! What you do is so amazing." He smiled, then shook his head and chuckled. "The thing is, the way you work is 180 degrees opposite of what everyone else does."

It's a point I've heard many times from people who work elsewhere, but it still gets me thinking. What is it that we've done that's put us on the positive side of the looking glass when so many others out there are struggling to stay afloat? Why are our sales strong and our staff more energized than most? And how, I wonder, did we get here? Where does the creativity come from? Where did the sustainability start? How did all the teaching take hold? And how did we blend a seriously out-of-the-box, anarchistic approach to organizational life with solid old-school business sense to build such a great success? The answers, I would argue, don't lie in economic cycles, secretive strategies, subversive political campaigns, really good trend watching, or feats of entrepreneurial brilliance. While most start by studying the marketplace, making macro predictions, and musing about what might happen out in the world, *we start by looking internally.*

Over the years, I've started to see business as a mirror. Our organizations say a lot about our hopes and dreams, about the way we think, what we believe, what we do well, what we work at and how hard we work at it, what we get wrong, how we handle struggle, and how we celebrate success. What we see around us, the way our organizations operate, how much our customers care, the kind of community connections we've created, the quality of our products and services, are all, more likely than not, a realistic, if not always all that pleasant, reflection of who we are as leaders. More than anything, I'll argue, our businesses manifest the way we feel about, relate to, and manage ourselves. All of which means that if we want to improve our organizations, the best place to begin is by reading our emotions, investigating our instincts, owning our biases, and being mindful of our moods. As Patti McGraw, the very wise woman who runs our Department for People, is wont to say, "If you're focusing on what the other person is doing wrong, you're probably focusing on the wrong person."

The "right person" in Patti's model is, of course, each of us. The outcomes we get originate in our spirit, soul, psyche, centeredness, self-management, or whatever else you'd like to call it. The buck that comes back to us is almost always a reflection of what's happening in our heads and hearts. Our product quality, service, systems effectiveness, operating profit, organizational culture, etc. begin not in the kitchen or on the factory floor, but with us. The buck at Zingerman's then, my buck at least, *starts* here with me. (I should better say "me and my partners" to be accurate, but you get the point.) If we want our organizations to improve, the work we need to start with is more effectively managing our own minds. If we want a respectful organization, the place to start is with the way we treat ourselves. If we want to be more in touch, we need to listen more closely to our subconscious. If we want a more even-keeled company, we'd do best to explore how we each manage our own anxiety. If we want more creativity, we need to get more connected with our inner artist, let our edginess emerge, and put our natural wildness—productively—to work.

To be clear, though, this isn't just about us as leaders—it's about every single person who's a part of our organization. Part of what makes us so different here at Zingerman's is that we encourage everyone to think, and act, like a leader. The material in this book about effective self-management is what we teach to *everyone* in our organization. I regularly hear from folks who love the way we work at Zingerman's but are frustrated because their boss doesn't believe in working as we do. Here, anyone can step up and make a difference. As Gandhi said so beautifully, "We need not wait to see what others do." You don't, after all, need anyone's permission, a new corporate strategy, a better boss, or a big rebranding to treat yourself with more respect, to be more mindful of what's going on around you, to inspire hope, or to live the spirit of generosity.

This inside-out approach seems to be working. While a big part of our success surely comes from the quality of our food and service, our work with visioning, creative marketing, open book finance, and Servant Leadership, it's clearer to me more now than ever that we'd never have come remotely close to where we are had we not pursued a path of positive self-management. Whether your organization is small or large, for- or not-for-profit, in India or Indiana, the time to start doing this internal investigation is probably now; an increase in self-awareness is *always* appropriate. If you've gone so far as to buy this book, then clearly something about self-management is calling out to you. The sooner you start this work, the sooner you'll arrive successfully at your vision. No matter where we are on an org chart, no matter how young or old or odd or well-outfitted we may be, the change we want to see needs to start with us.

It is my strong belief that successful, sustainable organizations always start with self-aware and self-reflective people. Leaders who are respected are almost always those that respect themselves. Entrepreneurs who inspire creativity are themselves inspired and creative. Collaborative, cooperative, caring organizations are led by collaborative, cooperative, caring individuals. Passionate people produce passionate organizations. If, then, you're up for some introspection, for finding some (free) ways to work more effectively, for fine-tuning your own temperament in the interest of improving your entire organization, then settle in and start working on more effective self-management. What you discover en route will, I guarantee, be of great value. If you put what you learn to work, it will help you be a better leader and build a better, more sustainable business to boot.

2. Successful Self-Management Is About Living your Dream

People tell me all the time: "You're living the dream!" In all honesty, I kind of cringe every time I hear it. They mean well, I know, but it sounds so superficial, so overly idealized, and almost cynical that it raises my anxiety every time. By society's more superficial standards, I'm hardly the golden boy. I've done well, I know, but I'm far from the richest person around. I haven't won a lottery, I've never bought a boat, and I have a TV with a smallish screen that's not flat and cost me about $200. I've had four surgeries, screwed up all sorts of things, struggled for many years to make peace with myself, and worked hard and long to find my place in the world. While I feel very lucky, and I'm not complaining in the least, it's not like my life has been a cakewalk, let alone some made-for-TV dream.

And yet, there is some merit to what they say—unlike so many people I meet, who long for a life they don't have, I love what I do. There's a lot I don't know, but I do know that I'm having fun, I'm learning a lot, I'm eating (very) well, and I believe from the heart that I'm helping a lot of other people in the world do the same. After a bit of self-reflection, I realized the reason people think I'm "living *the* dream" is that I'm actually living *my* dream. Or in our language here at Zingerman's, I'm actively making my personal vision into a vibrant and rewarding—if ever imperfect—reality. Mine is a vision in which I learn to work through my missteps while moving a bit closer to the sustainable business and positively focused personal life I so strongly believe in. In the process, I've learned, I'm infinitely more able to assist others around me to live their dreams as well. How much more win-win could the world be?

The way I live and lead today has come a long, long way from where I was when we opened the Deli. Mindful management, treating myself with respect, observing my own emotions, paying close attention to the way my beliefs and biases impacted our business, thinking through the way my own thinking was affecting the organization—none of these practices were on my radar or in my management repertoire back in 1982. I had no personal vision to speak of, I wasn't very mindful in my management, I was out of touch with my emotions, and, I'm sure, made others around me pay the price for my poor preparation. Today, though, mindfulness and self-management are at the core of everything I do. Without them, we might never have made it through our first decade at the Deli. If we had, I'm sure I'd be struggling to survive the stress, taking pills to fight high blood pressure, and wondering if I should sell the business to reclaim my sanity the way so many entrepreneurs I meet do.

Living *my* dream means that I'm working a lot. But, because I've spent three decades designing a job in which I feel fulfilled, and because I freely choose it all, I have a good time doing what I do. People who see me working the floor on Saturday night at the Roadhouse, and then again early Sunday morning at the Deli, ask me regularly and a bit worriedly, "What do you do for fun?" The question makes me smile every time. Whether I'm at work or on my own reading or writing, cooking each evening, spending time with friends, or reflecting each morning in my journal, I enjoy almost everything. I'm working hard to have fun in all I do, and I have fun when I'm working hard. It's not quite a palindrome, but it is very positive, and it's definitely productive.

It wasn't always that way though—I've worked hard to come clean with myself about what I want, what my dreams are, what my vision is, and a very large part of my life is now made up of doing those things. At the same time, I've learned to have fun, to find the joy, to appreciate the insights I can gain and the good things I can contribute even while doing things that others might write off as mundane. The "Secrets" of self-management that follow are the most important elements of that work. While this stuff isn't easy to do well every day, the concepts are actually surprisingly simple. Anyone whose mind is open to learning new approaches can, and will, get them. And when we do them well, many great things are possible. Amin Maalouf writes in *In the Name of Identity*, "If you believe in something and have enough energy, passion and love of life, you can find among the resources of the world of today the means to make some of your dreams come true."

When I first saw the title of anarchist Emma Goldman's autobiography, *Living My Life*, I didn't realize the right place to put the emphasis. Working on this third installment in the *Guide to Good Leading* series, it's become clear to me that her (and my) anarchist orientation ought, by all rights, to put the emphasis on the "My" in the middle. It's Living *My* Life that's at the core of all this—not in an exclusive, elitist, or adversarial way, but in the belief that each of us is a unique, creative individual with our own history, dreams, and hopes. And that respectfully and caringly living our lives—mindfully making appropriate compromises in the interest of assisting others in our community—helps to make things right with the world. Anarchist and artisan printer Joseph Ishill wrote: "I wish always to live my own life and by myself to create things which appeal to my taste. I am bound to confess that this is a hard road but it is an honest one and I propose to end my days in this manner."

3. Successful Self-Management Puts Anarchism into Action

If the idea of anarchists in your boardroom, or in your brain, causes you anxiety, just skip ahead to the safety of the next Secret on page 51. But if you're up for the odd ideas of a history major turned modern day business person, read on. This is not a call for extreme political action or for overturning our government. My approach is aligned with that of author Ursula K. Le Guin, who asked, "What is an anarchist?" And then answered, "One who, choosing, accepts the responsibility of choice."

Although anarchists get little attention from anyone other than those considered extreme social outliers, concerned law enforcement officers, or on-the-edge history professors, I think they had a lot to say that's worth studying. Of course, if you're like most Americans, the image you probably have of anarchists is of bomb- and rock-throwing crazy people. My anarchism has no bombs and no bombast. It really just comes down to the fact that I'm a big believer in human ability.

My version of anarchism, at least, is about honoring every individual for who they are and helping them to get to the greatness they desire. It's about setting aside authority and hierarchy unless we absolutely have to use them. It's about free choice, freethinking, and freely deciding to work in the best interests of everyone around us, all the while respecting ourselves and our dreams. It's about caring collaboration between equals, treating everyone with dignity, consciously doing the right thing for the community, believing that everyone in an organization has something significant to contribute. It's about the belief that if we encourage everyone we work with to share their insights and then collaboratively build our community, we can each become our own best boss. *Anarchism, in practice, is really all about effective self-management.*

It only makes sense—if you remove all forms of formal, external authority (as is the anarchist way), then the only tool really left to us is better self-management by each and every member of the community. Anarchism, at its core then, is really a declaration of responsible and caring, community-minded, personal independence. It is, in essence, a commitment to working—imperfectly, of course—to find a reasonable balance between the good of the group and what's best for ourselves. It is, per Emma Goldman's urging, to "give what we have of ability and talent to educate and to help others. It is only through this that we will realize the true aim of life."

Anarchism, in this sense, is actually quite simple and down to earth. As Howard Ehrlich explains, it "begins with the transformation of our everyday lives." Or as Englishman Colin Ward puts it in *Anarchy in Action,* "Anarchism in all its guises is an assertion of human identity and responsibility. It is not a program for political change but an act of social self-determination."

When all else is said and done, anarchism is about each of us going after our dreams, caringly and respectfully, and supporting others around us in doing the same. It's about finding one's own unique and creative way in the world, while working with others who support that effort. As Gustav Landauer suggests, "To me, someone without a master, someone who is free, an individual, an anarchist, is one who is his own master, who has unearthed the desire that tells him who he truly wants to be. This desire is his life." To take it even further, Marcus Graham asserts in the first ever issue of the anarchist journal, *Man,* on New Year's Day, 1933, "One who understands fully the meaning of the term [anarchism]—cannot act irresponsibly."

From a business standpoint, the anarchist angle is all about building healthy, respectful workplaces where we honor and benefit from differences, in the interest of helping everyone to live the life they want to lead and, at the same time, getting to a shared vision of organizational greatness.[2] While most of the world is working on what everyone else is doing wrong, this application of effective anarchist self-management means taking the lead on making ourselves more effective, not looking for a quick fix or a free pass. "The way to create a community that encompasses the entire world," Landauer says, "leads not outward, but inward." If we want to make a better business, or a better community in which to work, the place to start is pretty surely in our own souls.

Whatever we dream of, whatever we want, whatever we believe in, *it's up to us to get it going*. As the writer Peggy Kornegger argues, "Anarchism provides a framework for this [personal] transformation. *It is a vision, a dream, a possibility which becomes 'real' as we live it.*" The emphasis is mine. What appeals to me so strongly is that this anarchism is not about *waiting* for utopia to arrive, or critiquing others en route. It is, to the contrary, about taking action to directly improve what we do every day, and helping everyone around us to do the same. It's all about getting our (anarchist) act together and then working constructively and collaboratively to create a truly great, mutually rewarding reality for ourselves, our families, our organizations, and our communities.

4. Caring Self-Management Could Lead to a Creative Revolution

This one is, I know, a bold statement. But take or leave it, I believe it's true—the essays in this book have the power to start a revolution. The changes that revolution would bring about would be quiet ones: calmness, centeredness, mindfulness, caring, and creative generosity get a tiny fraction of the attention that goes to violence, chaos, and competitive destruction. But nevertheless the approaches I'm referring to have the power to alter the way we work, to improve the effectiveness of our businesses, and, ultimately, to change our lives and the lives of everyone we work and live with.

It would be, as per the legacy of the late Gustav Landauer, a "revolution of spirit." No rocks will get thrown, no governments will fall, no heads will roll, and no windows will be broken. The revolution I'm writing about won't include any incitement to riot nor is it likely to be noted in history books. In its early days, only you will know with certainty that it's even begun. But don't let the silence of the situation fool you. That quiet, effective, internal work is where it's at. As anarchist musical artist, pre-punk prophet, and poet Jim Morrison said: "There can't be any large-scale revolution until there's a personal revolution on an individual level. It's got to happen inside first."

The world around us, I know, may not cooperate. Positive change, inevitably, provokes pushback. As Ursula K. Le Guin observes, "It's always easier not to think for oneself. Find a nice safe hierarchy and settle in." Harder still may be the work of those who have little support to help them in their efforts. There are millions of caring people out there with few resources, very limited funds, little education, and, in many cases, nowhere to sleep or to get a good meal. Part of the anarchist ideal that interests me is the belief that each of us will be best, and do best, when we freely and actively choose to help those around us in need. I believe that if we work together in the interest of group success, everyone in our communities—even those who have little—can make a positive move forward. Which is why, at its core, even when we're dealing with very difficult socioeconomic contexts, this is still very much about politely and purposefully taking back personal power. I know that many have staggering obstacles to overcome. But whether the revolution actually takes hold is, of course, up to each of us. "You cannot buy the revolution," Le Guin says. "You cannot make the revolution. You can only be the revolution. It is in your spirit, or it is nowhere."

I wish I could assure you of life satisfaction in the same way I guarantee our sandwiches. But ultimately the success of this work is about what each of us does with the ideas, insights, and essays that follow. History, after all, is full of failed rebellions—uprisings that came close but didn't stick, and resulted only in the return of the old regime. The nine essays on self-management that follow are, after all, only tools, and the effectiveness of even the best tool is contingent on the hands that hold it. On the other hand, if a whole lot of people were to commit to implementing more effective self-management, to cultivating caring self-respect, to pursuing their passions in community-oriented ways, then the outcome could not help but be meaningful change, both personal and social.

It's just that in this case the change comes not from a big legislative body or some famous leader, but rather from somewhere deep within each one of us. The revolution I'm thinking about grows from respect for ourselves, and for others around us; it's work that's nurtured by our sensitive spirits, by focusing on giving rather than taking. Rather than engaging in unconstructive conflict around difficult issues, this is about working through them in caring and collaborative ways. This revolution is about respecting others, rather than always needing to be right. It's about getting back the natural energy, creativity, spirit, and sense of fun that I believe is inside everyone but is so frequently forced into hiding by social pressures and ineffective leadership.

It is, as Catholic anarchist Ammon Hennacy said in 1970, "We really can't change the world. We really can't change other people! The best we can do is to start a few thinking here and there. The best way to do this, if we are sincere, is to change ourselves!" I'm with Ammon. "[T]he only revolution worthwhile," he writes, is "the one-man revolution within the heart. Each one could make this by himself and not need to wait on a majority."

What Motivates *You* to Study Self-Management?

You now have a pretty good sense of why this work has been so important to me. But motivation is, of course, most effective when it's intrinsic—the more you know about what drives *you* (or doesn't), the more meaningful the material that follows will be. To wit, Virginia Woolf once wrote, "The only advice . . . that one person can give another about reading is to take no advice, to follow your own instincts, to use your own reason, to come to your own conclusions. And always ask good questions."

Speaking of which, I'd advocate for anarchist Peter Kropotkin's admonition in *Memoirs of a Revolutionist:* "One must have some question addressed to the book one is going to read." What you want to know will, of course, alter what you take away as you read. If you're up for the challenge, take twenty or thirty minutes to write a list of your own motivations. As Simon Sinek says, it all starts with why. So why then is more effective self-management so meaningful to you?

Shalette Mays, Production Supervisor, Zingerman's Mail Order

I have worked at Zingerman's since I was a teenager, and let's just say I feel as if I'm spoiled. I did not have many jobs before working at Zingerman's, but looking back, I really dreaded going to work every day. Then I found

Zingerman's. I remember my first week of working here, and my managing partner worked beside me on numerous occasions. That spoke volumes because he isn't the "big guy" sitting in his office just watching us work or coming through criticizing our work—he truly cares about us and the work that is being done. Employees here feel like our voices are heard. It's very inspiring working for a company that creates a Vision, and you actually see the Vision come true! It has been a pleasure to be a part of the Zingerman's family. We make sure that every last customer that we interact with gets the Zingerman's experience, and we also give it to each other as well.

Nathan Koorhan, Retail Staffer, Zingerman's Delicatessen

Throughout my life, I've struggled when confronted with things that are unexpected or don't necessarily go the way I've planned. I'm extremely cerebral (as most artists are) and I have often wasted time dwelling on things that have happened in the past and things that *could* happen in the future. It's cost me valuable time with the people I care about most. It's part of the reason I left teaching once before: I had expectations for my students that they didn't always meet and I took it personally. It stripped away my confidence.

What Zingerman's has provided me are tools that have made it easier for me to *respond* to the unexpected rather than *react*. I find myself using the 3 Steps to Great Service away from work. It's not that I'm treating the people in my life as customers, but listening, responding, and doing one better than people expect. It makes me feel good. It makes me confident. It also has the power to turn a potentially negative situation into a positive one.

I can never thank the ZCoB enough for not only hiring me when I needed a job, but positively affecting the way I live my life. Even though I'll be teaching and unable to work during the week, I'm hoping to find a way to stay involved in the Zingerman's community in some capacity. Please let me know if you have any ideas.

My favorite memories with my grandpa are of eating pastrami sandwiches and drinking Dr. Brown's Cel-Ray at the Deli. Thank you for making those old favorite moments possible and allowing me the opportunity to make new memories as a member of the team.

I'm forever grateful.

craig rominski, i.t. guy, doing a bit of computer maintenance
at zingerman's mail order

Managing Ourselves

Inside Out Insights
That Can Change Your Life

People who pay attention to business take great delight in speculating as to what the "secret" is behind our success here at Zingerman's. Our service, product quality, or staff selection are probably the three that are put forward most frequently. "It's because you're in Ann Arbor," others argue. Others still alternately attribute what we've achieved to visioning, Servant Leadership, open book finance, or our training systems. They are all correct, of course, even if partially so—each of these pieces clearly contributes to making Zingerman's what it is. Interestingly, the one thing I don't think I've ever heard anyone offer up as a speculative "secret" behind our success is the intensive work we've put into improving the way we manage ourselves. And yet, I would argue that the work that Paul and I and most everyone else here at Zingerman's has invested in learning to do so—summed up in the "Secret" that follows—is actually one of the single most important elements in helping us create what we've created.

Don't let the fact that so many experts miss the point send the wrong message. When all the big business stuff is said and done—missions and visions written, strategies and systems set, values and cultures established—our long-term success still really comes down to this: the effectiveness with which we manage ourselves will almost always make or break the rest of the work we do. While it's true that a once-in-a-lifetime innovation or a quickly implemented stroke of genius might bring us success in spite of ourselves, 98 times out of 100 the effectiveness with which our organizations operate will depend on the way we work within ourselves. The better we manage ourselves, the better we, and everyone around us, will do.

If you mention the word "manager," most folks probably think first about someone in power, a "boss," who's out in the world making waves by effectively managing his or her "employees." "Management," many will say, "is about getting other people to do their work." Personally, I think the place to start our leadership work is not in learning more about how to get others going; it's about getting our own internal act together. As 16th century French proto-anarchist author Michel de Montaigne wrote, "Learned we may be with another man's learning: [but] we can only be wise with wisdom of our own."

What would good self-management look like? I think it's about doing for ourselves what every progressive business leader will most likely say they want for their most valuable staff members—being in touch with our hopes, owning both our dreams and our self-doubts, getting clear on a vision of greatness and going steadily after it, keeping our energy high and staying productively focused on even the most difficult of days, making sure that what we're saying and doing is in synch with our values, keeping the power of our passion at the center of what we do every day, and creating peaceful and positive energy in the midst of chaos.

Learning to lead others effectively has been no small feat for me—even after working hard at it for thirty years now, I have loads more to learn and I still, unintentionally, let others and myself down more times than I'd like to admit. I am, much to my perfectionist heart's frustration, as flawed and human as the next person. But as challenging as learning leadership has been, the truth is that managing others has been easy compared to the challenge of really effectively managing myself. Doing it well requires great diligence, a challenge that I, for one, had little practice with growing up. Accepting myself as I am, understanding how I fit into the world, and being in touch with where I want to go and how I want to get there were hardly subjects anyone taught me either at home or at school.

For me, self-management has meant making peace with my past and finding ways to feel good about my future. More often than not, effective self-management has meant changing behavioral patterns I've built up over a lifetime of unconscious learning. It's meant being willing to push myself to move past limits I'd long ago accepted, leaving my comfort zone to enter areas of emotional and intellectual existence with which I was never previously familiar. And it's pushed me to go for greatness in my internal work in much the same way that I'd decided, far earlier, to pursue excellence in more easily identified categories like food quality, customer service, and financial performance.

It's definitely not glamorous work. Like email, payroll systems, and health care, we generally remark upon self-management mostly when something goes awry. Fall off the wagon, act in anger, say the wrong thing at the wrong time, and you'll get more attention than you ever imagined possible. Doing the right thing every day, being at peace with your possibilities, celebrating the small stuff, and staying mindful of the moment are seldom noticed, let alone actively appreciated. Unlike major marketing initiatives, exciting entrepreneurial ventures, or progressive new product rollouts, making improvements in the way we manage ourselves is barely visible. It's only later, after we've done significant work on ourselves, that someone might say, "You know, you really have changed the way you . . ."

The Importance of Being Introspective

The ability to stay centered as we work our way through the world hardly comes naturally for most adults. Self-knowledge isn't all that easy to come by. In *Good to Great,* author Jim Collins writes about how great leaders need to be "born twice"—they need to struggle through some stage of personal crisis and emerge successfully on the other side to really develop the level of self-understanding, humility, and insight that's imperative if one wants to lead an organization to greatness. Nearly a century earlier, anarchist Gustav Landauer wrote, "Those who want to create life must also embrace it and be reborn from within." And, he added, "Those whom I call true anarchists no longer deceive themselves; they have been able to remold themselves through the experience of a deep existential crisis; they can act in the way which their most secret nature demands."

Calling my own screw-ups and life lessons "deep" and "existential" seems a bit self-centered, but I definitely went through some serious struggles around the time that I hit thirty. I'll spare you all the details; I'm confident that my experience was comparable to that of millions of others who hit hard times somewhere around midlife. The bad news is that I probably naively passed up plenty of previous opportunities I'd had to get right with myself and the world. If I'd paid attention to them, I would have saved myself and others a lot of aggravation. That said, making peace with one's past is part of this process, so it doesn't really matter that much now what I did wrong. The point is that I screwed up—we all do. It's part of being human.

The good news is that, through whatever combination of internal wiring, karma, and coincidence, I eventually got going. I took action to bring the somewhat disjointed segments of my mind into alignment. For the first time in my life, I took self-learning seriously. And, probably much to the surprise of those around me who'd seen me misfire so many other times, I started the work to really dig deep into my own mind. The idea of studying with great intensity in order to make something special wasn't new to me. I'd been doing it for years with cheese, sandwiches, olive oil, and organizational behavior. The difference was that I was now actively examining my own uncertain existence. This time around my self-assigned project was to study myself with the same sense of purpose and dedication that I'd applied to so many other things over the years, and then to apply that learning to every element of my life.

It's possible, I suppose, that one can arrive at this sort of rebirth, higher level of leadership effectiveness, and anarchist emergence *without* a crisis. I can hardly recommend intentionally wreaking havoc on your life solely for the purpose of getting to the next level. Sam Keen says, "The best of life begins after the worst of life has been accepted," but it's possible that you could be the exception. I know that I (mistakenly) thought I was. Maybe I've spent all these years getting the equivalent of the advanced degree I never got at school. A master's degree in *ariology*, or something of that sort. Not that I've totally mastered myself. I'm studying as hard now, I think, as I ever was.

The work was well worth it. As one gets better at self-management, stress goes down, dreams unfold, and fun quotients increase. Internal and external achievement, it turns out, are very closely correlated. The calmer and more grounded my energy is, the more effectively everyone around me is going to work. The more I'm able to avoid getting stuck on rocky emotional shoals, the more effectively everyone at Zingerman's can focus on quality and customer service. The better I manage my self-doubt, the more quickly I can say what I truly believe to be correct even when others think I'm crazy. And as everyone in the organization follows suit and self-manages more successfully (see the Secret on Anarcho-Capitalism in *Part 2* of the Series), so too will the business get to greatness. One feeds the other; it's a virtuous, *self*-sustaining cycle.

Self-Management Leads to Organizational Success

If you didn't already know it, let me say here again—*I'm all about finding free space for people to be themselves so that they can then choose, consciously, to contribute to others around them.* When people are learning to be self-aware, to be reflective, to treat themselves and then everyone around them in more appreciative and supportive ways, great things are almost certain to happen. Positive energy will always go up in the process. As Gustav Landauer writes, "During revolution, everyone is filled with the spirit that is otherwise reserved for exemplary individuals; everyone is courageous, wild and fanatic and caring and loving at the same time." What Landauer is describing, I think, is the kind of organization that we're committed to creating. It's definitely the kind of organization I want to be a part of. And to the credit of all the cool people around me who help make it happen every day, I think I already am.

Max Baginski and Emma Goldman wrote back in 1907, "An organization, in the true sense of the word, cannot be the product of a union of pure nothingness. It must be made up of self-conscious and intelligent persons." Or you might want to rely more on modern business writers like Robert Greenleaf, who, writing on Servant Leadership, says, "The aim of [leadership] is not to motivate people. Motivation ceases to be what is done to people. Motivation becomes what people generate for themselves when they experience growth." Peter Koestenbaum, in *Leadership: the Inner Side of Greatness, A Philosophy for Leaders,* puts it this way: "Business, as commerce, is above all a vehicle for achieving personal and organizational greatness. It is for accomplishing something worthy and noble . . . It is important that you connect your work with your personal depth. In fact, you must learn to value the pain of growing. And the significance of your job is not that it offers you security but that it demands from you personal growth."

We can't change our organizations without us, ourselves, changing. Chaim Leib Weinberg, a late 19th century Philadelphia-based anarchist said, "One cannot remake the world without starting with the individual. And if one is starting with the individual, one must indeed begin with oneself." What follows is a list of the practices that have helped me to manage myself with ever-greater effectiveness over the years. Pick and choose what you like (or if you'd rather, poke holes in it all). All I can say is that this stuff has surely helped me enormously—I hope it gets similarly good results for you and yours.

Twelve Tips for More Effective Self-Management

1. GET TO KNOW YOURSELF

If I told you that I had an applicant for you, someone smart, reasonably resilient, capable, and exceptionally hardworking, and that if you would just commit to getting to know this applicant, setting aside maybe an hour or two a week to work with them diligently on self-awareness and all-around self-improvement, then this person would most certainly stay with you and give it their all for as long as you were around, you'd probably consider hiring this person, right? Well, I have good news and not-so-good news. The-not-so-good news is that I don't actually have such an applicant to send you. The good news, though, is that this person exists—it's the one staring down at this page right now. It is, of course, you.

We all know it—the more we know those we manage, the better our odds of effectively managing them. The same goes for a coach with a player, a service provider with a customer, a teacher with a student: the more we know about those around us, the better we're going to be able to help them arrive effectively at all they aspire to do. In this case, that "someone" is each of us. Getting to know ourselves is always the first and most foundational step towards effective self-management. Like it or not, for better and for worse, wherever we go in our lives, we're basically stuck with ourselves. Other people may come and go, economic cycles will ebb and flow, equipment will wear out, customers may move away, but you, alone, are sure to still be there. To quote Charles Handy in his excellent book *The Hungry Spirit:* "We must know ourselves to be of any use to others." I'm not talking here about looking in the mirror in the morning, reading your own resume, keeping up with social media, or other surface-level stuff. The work is about really getting to know the way our minds operate, to know our biases, our beliefs, our backgrounds, and all the other filters through which we experience the world. Although as leaders we're all charged with "being objective," the truth is that's pretty much an impossibility—the ideal of objectivity is alluring, but the reality of life is that we all look out at the world from our own perspectives.

Our perceptions are, by definition, skewed by our own prejudices, our own views, our own experiences. As Sam Keen writes in *Inward Bound,* "The first task of introspection is to examine how we've been programmed by the shoulds and should nots of others." Self-awareness is where the improvement begins. If you don't know that you're leaning over 45° all the time, then how do you know what's actually straight up and down? You don't. In fact, everyone who's actually standing up straight will start to look like they're the ones out of alignment. And, FYI, the problem isn't that we're bent over, nor is the answer that we need to try to conform and stand straight like everyone else. What does matter is that we're aware and ever-more mindful of what's really going on. Only then can we make effective decisions about how to move forward.

Our challenge then is to get to know ourselves—to really understand our strengths and weaknesses, what inspires us and what shuts us down, how we like to learn and what makes us burn with anger, the stuff that lights up our intellectual lights and the stuff that sinks our spirits. The quicker we can recognize trouble lights coming on, the more we learn to trust our guts, the more effective we can be in leading others. When all else is said, and at least somewhat done, if we don't know and understand our own internal workings, we have little chance of achieving greatness in anything that we're after.

Side View Victories

You know what it says on the passenger's side mirror on your car, right? Those little white letters: "Warning: objects in the mirror are closer than they appear." I use it as an emotional touchstone every time I get in the car. Looking at it helps me keep things in perspective; the message reminds me that the way things look is rarely the way they really are. As Susan Cain writes in *Quiet: The Power of Introverts in a World That Can't Stop Talking*, "Whoever you are, bear in mind that appearance is not reality." The likelihood is that left to our own unwittingly devilish devices, *each of us will consistently misread the same situations over and over again, almost always in the same way.* The better we know ourselves, the more we'll be able to spot the warning signs in our own brains, and the better we can train those around us to help us succeed.

It's even harder to get others to live as we'd like if we ourselves aren't modeling the behaviors we're asking them to adopt. My partner Paul points out that when we're out of touch with ourselves, we project our insecurity out into the world. "Your actions, how you behave in situations, need to be congruent with how you see yourself in the world," he says. "It is very hard to consistently behave in a way that is not in line with your values. The resulting inconsistency will have people confused and feeling that they can't trust you." Congruence is critical; if we *believe* that our work is in synch with what we've said but we're misreading reality, then trouble, diminished integrity, and an ever-stronger sense of self-doubt are sure to follow.

How do we find out how things "really are"? Gathering input from others, tracking the effectiveness of our decisions and the impact of our actions, journaling, setting aside regular time for reflection, and the like can at least give us a sense of what's really going on.

A Few Tips for Self-Monitoring

Engage in 360° reviews where you gather performance feedback on a regular basis from your colleagues. Inevitably, you will hear many positives and also plenty of opportunities to improve. Although the latter can, at times, be hard to hear, we've found them effective.

Use the Decision Log (see page 455) to see how effectively your decisions pan out once you announced them to the world. I learned about this method from Peter Drucker and it's helped me straighten myself out many times.

Schedule regular sessions of reflection to monitor your emotional swings, watching for patterns and problems and uncovering helpful self-management techniques.

Monitor your mental state throughout the day. A couple of days of tracking emotions in your journal, noting the setting and situation in which they were triggered, what you did in response, and how it all worked out, can be very helpful.

Go to counseling, either individually or in a group. It can provide a really helpful "mirror," in which objects might be reflected more realistically than in our own "side mirrors."

Check relevant data, which may reflect a different reality from your emotionally charged hunches. While I can often trust my intuition, there are plenty of times that my initial reaction is really off base. For instance, almost every year at the holidays I feel like sales seem flat. I almost immediately start to stress. But when I check the actual numbers at the end of the month, we're almost always where we'd hoped to be.

All that, I know, may seem like it'll take way too much time. How can you fit in the time to take stock of yourself when your schedule is already overloaded? Fair enough. But the better question to ask might be this: If you won't spend a few hours a week getting to know yourself, who will?

When I presented on self-management at a business conference a couple months ago, I asked the audience how many of them would be willing to spend a couple hours a week to connect with and coach a new long-term employee who might become a key staff member for many years to come. Nearly everyone raised a hand in the affirmative. Then I asked them, "What if I introduced you to a new customer, one who was probably going to buy $100,000 or $200,000 a year from your business? What's the first thing you'd want to do?" Many called out answers, almost all along the lines of "Get to know them!" "Learn about what they do." "Find out what they want."

I followed up with another question: "And how many of you would spend an hour or two a week with them to make sure you gave them great service so that you could land and then keep their account?" Again, nearly everyone raised a hand in the affirmative. "So," I continued, "if you'd do that for a customer who was going to buy a good bit from your business, why would you not do the same for yourself, knowing full well that the level of self-knowledge you can develop is going to have a huge impact, not just on a single high-end client, but on everything that happens in your organization every single day?"

I think most of them got the point. I had more than a few emails later that day confirming that the questions had brought them a new sense of clarity. If you're trying to run your business better but you barely know yourself, you're going to have a very hard time getting to greatness.

2. HONOR YOUR EMOTIONS

Whether we want to admit it or not, we all have emotions. Learning to read, accept, and manage through them is one of the most important elements of effective self-management. There's no such thing as effective leadership without them. For those who would rather focus their attention almost exclusively on facts and figures, emotional activity, I would argue, is data too.

Though I suppose the standard business line is to leave your feelings at home (along with your problems, right?), that approach is impossibly absurd. Our feelings come with us wherever we go; all we can do is learn to monitor them and manage ourselves so they don't get in the way of what we're trying to do. The act of acknowledging our emotions—even if only to ourselves—is a big step in the right direction. As Sam Keen says, "We can only choose *whether* we will feel and not *what* we will feel."

The most effective leaders in any field are exceptionally self-aware. Pick your area of study and you'll find your own examples. All are imperfect, but all are introspective and perceptive about their own strengths, weaknesses, limitations, and opportunities. Most excel at reading their own emotions and then mindfully managing their reactions. A thousand images of what that looks like come to mind, but for the moment let's say that great leaders learn to read their own emotions the way an all-pro quarterback reads defenses. Or the way an experienced Ojibwe elder might walk the north woods of Wisconsin. Neither controls what's coming at them, but they're able to anticipate, prepare, mindfully process their own reactions, self-manage, and then respond in ways that are respectful of themselves and their surroundings. That sort of self-management reduces stress, increases both personal and organizational effectiveness, improves our ability to appreciate what's around us, and makes it much more likely that we're going to get done what we want to get done and go where we want to go.

Just to be clear, when I talk about managing our emotions, I don't mean that we should never be spontaneous or act in the moment. As wild as our emotional swings may be, it's not really our emotions that get us in trouble. Hugging someone we feel affection for, showing excitement after getting some great news, celebrating a big success right when it happens, letting tears flow when we're suddenly saddened, or high-fiving someone who just experienced some sort of big win are probably all really positive decisions made in the moment. Those, I love. Bring them on!

Rather, it's the unmindful and not very responsible decisions that come as a *response* to our emotions that cause problems. Are you familiar with the feeling? The reactive, potentially big consequence stuff, like firing an employee in the moment because they pissed you off, giving someone a raise on the spot because they did one really great thing, shouting at a supplier who seriously screwed up, or shooting your mouth off in a meeting. While these responses may feel fantastic in the moment, they will rarely beget brilliant, big picture results. More likely, they'll just cause problems that will take days, weeks, or even months to mend. If all you take from this essay is the idea that when the emotions feel particularly strong, that's almost always the worst possible time to make a big decision, I would feel like the time I've spent on it has been well worth it. Action spurred solely to relieve anxiety is rarely effective. When in doubt, I come back to the saying of 13th century Persian philosopher Rumi: "When you're drunk and near a cliff, sit down."

Just as a single leader who acts all-knowing and dominates decision making in an organization will almost always end up leading others astray, so too one emotion imposing itself above and beyond all others will lead to poor decisions and perpetual, self-created problems. I come from a family of worriers, and I've seen worry take over and undermine the lives of many good men and women. In *Emotional Intelligence*, Daniel Goleman calls it "emotional hijacking." While it's only one emotion, worry will lead the rest of the mind, and the body too, into situations where it would never otherwise go. Honoring our concerns—but at the same time not letting them take over our lives—is one of the most important pieces of self-management I know.

All this, of course, is easier said than done. Others often don't do what we want; coworkers can't comprehend what we're trying to communicate; the world throws things like hurricanes, tornadoes, and floods at us; we slip, we fall, and we fail when we least want to. There are days, I know, where the best I can do is to avoid acting out—sometimes not doing something stupid is a really big achievement! Learning to read the pressures that life is throwing at us and responding with grace and good will is hard to do, but I find that increased self-awareness always gets better results. I make fewer bad decisions and my energy is less dissonant, which means that by helping myself, I'm simultaneously helping increase the effectiveness of everyone around me.

Engaging with our emotions also opens us up to a kaleidoscope of cool stuff that we totally miss when we close off access to them. "Feeling," Sam Keen conveys, "opens us to intercourse with the world. We agree to be engaged to enter into life—for better, for worse, for richer, for poorer. There is no guarantee that by deciding to feel you will feel *better*. Only that you will feel *more*— more of everything." For me at least, feeling *more* is generally a more rewarding and much richer, more interesting way to live. Knowing how we feel won't stop the pain, frustration, anxiety, anger, or any of the other challenging emotions that emerge every day. It just lets them into the room with us where we can quietly and constructively coexist.

For others, of course, the issue is the opposite. Even small surprises and disappointments can overwhelm them with emotion. Managing that intensity isn't easy, but it's definitely doable. Feeling immersed in anger or overcome with worry makes it hard, if not impossible, to function effectively in the world. Finding ways to defuse that naturally occurring, but nevertheless destructive, state is a significant step towards success. Emotional awareness is an important element of that work. Optimism, mindfulness, working to overcome worry, getting clear on what's triggering the emotional "takeovers" that occur when things feel out of control—all can help us find a bit of balance and peace within the powerful winds of the emotional storms. Talking or writing (or drawing) about what we're feeling is even more effective. As one of my favorite authors of all time, Henry Roth, wrote in his great 1934 novel, *Call It Sleep,* "If you could put words to what you felt, it was yours."

When we make peace with our emotional swings, when we accept what is (even if we don't always like it), we can move effectively towards a more positive tomorrow. To quote Sam Keen again: "When anger becomes an occasional, welcomed visitor, and we accept the inevitable ambivalent love-hate of intimacy, the real alchemy of emotion begins. . . . Only you can decide to convert your anger from a reactive to a creative force." Anger is a normal emotion—it's how we handle it and what we do with it that takes it from destructive to productive. If you were to survey people on which emotion was the most difficult to manage effectively in the workplace—so that you were neither denying its existence nor letting it take over your life—anger would surely score very high. Dealing with either our own or that of others can be very difficult. I'd advocate for the advice of the Indian mystic Osho. In *Life, Love, Laughter,* he says, "When anger comes you are not to do anything; just sit silently and watch it. Don't be against it, don't be for it. Don't cooperate with it, don't repress it. Just watch it, be patient, just see what happens . . . let it rise."

Managing our anger well means both owning that we have it and finding effective ways to manage through it. Denial never helps. We need to accept that anger has a cause and that this cause is well worth exploring. The direct object of my anger, I've learned, frequently has little to do with the issues I need to address. I may have been set off by something someone said, but the root cause is generally much deeper. We also need to develop the ability to manage ourselves well enough never to act in anger—making decisions out of anger and/or acting in anger always gets us in trouble. The challenge is to set our egos aside and just sit with things until the situation mellows. "Just as night becomes day if you can wait a little," Osho says, "in the same way, anger becomes compassion."

While being mindful of one's emotions generally gets short shrift in the work world, it turns out to be an essential element of effective management. As Daniel Goleman says, "Even mild mood changes can sway thinking." When we're in the flow of positive emotion, we're more likely to see the upside of an idea. When we're angry or afraid, we're far more likely to identify with the downsides—risks loom larger when we're feeling fear. We all have either worked with, or heard of, the manager whose moods swing drastically from day to day or hour to hour. The staff members learn when it's the right time to pitch a new idea, and when it isn't. They're doing a grassroots application of Goleman's well-researched observation. When someone is in a better mood, they're more likely to think big and take chances on positive, focused projects. And at the opposite end—you probably don't need me or Daniel Goleman to tell you, but he says it succinctly: "Emotions out of control impede the intellect."

In their insightful book, *Transformed!,* Bob and Judith Wright teach a model of emotional management that they call "The Ins, Ups, Downs of Emotional Faculty." It's easy to remember, very practical, and not all that hard to put into use. To do this well, you'll want to work in all four directions:

In means being in touch with how we're feeling.

Out refers to our ability to express to others what we're experiencing.

Up is about increasing our engagement with our emotions,

heightening our awareness to experience them fully rather than living in denial or skimming the surface.

Down means learning to own and then manage our emotional swings, so that we can effectively stay away from extremes.

Why Extra Virgin Olive Oil Is a Lot Like Effective Emotional Expression

Bob and Judith Wright compare emotions to a couple of subjects close to my heart—olives and olive oil. The oil, they opine, "is contained within the olives but it has to be ex-pressed, or pressed out, in order for you to enjoy the wonders of olive oil. The same is true of your feelings. They need to be expressed in order for you to fully experience their trans-formational power." Building on the Wrights' reasoning, I'll add that, while all olives can be crushed to get olive oil, getting the best, most complex, richly flavored, and balanced extra virgin olive oil is a very complex pro-cess that takes great care and superior skill. The same is true of emotions. Learning to express them productively takes practice. When done well, expression yields a wonderfully balanced blend of bitter and sweet, spicy and savory, lending its richness to pretty much anything it's added to.

Following this food metaphor further, I'll add that whole olives need to be cured to bring them into the form in which they can be eaten and most fully enjoyed. In their raw state—like raw emotion—they're hard to handle. Take note, too, that many commercial olives are pasteurized, mini-mizing many of the flavor nuances that make traditionally cured olives more interesting. I'll compare that here to depending on pills to "take the edge off," medicating one's way through life rather than feeling emotions as we naturally experience them. Living too safely, without letting your emotions out at all, might then be the equivalent of those canned, "black-ripe" olives you may likely have tasted—inoffensive, but totally bland.

Mind you, no matter how much we might want to, we can never really "control" our emotions; whether we like them or not, they are, like the weather, what they are. What we do have, though, is a high degree of influence over how we respond to them when they come up.[3] Here's a small personal story to illustrate the point. As much as I like to travel, I am pretty much *always* sad when I leave home to head out of town. Even today, after decades of traveling all over the world, when I pull out of the driveway, and when I'm on the plane waiting for it to take off, I get very sad. It's not as bad as having severe claustrophobia or an all-out panic attack. But it is there, and it's not insignificant. In that moment, I almost never want to leave.

Twenty years ago, the sadness made me think twice about taking the trip—I wondered if there was something wrong with me, or with travel, or with my work that it was bringing out such strong, almost scary, emotions. But, having spent a good bit of time getting to know myself, I know that *this feeling actually requires no action at all.* It comes up, and then just as quickly goes away. The best thing I can do, I've learned, is just to smile to myself, reflect a bit, and then go ahead and go. I know now that it's going to be fine, that once I get to my destination, I'm going to enjoy the travel. And I know that if I change my plans and decide to stay home, I'll be frustrated later for having succumbed to the sadness.

Whether it's this or any of the other wacky ways my mind works, I've just learned to let the feelings be, knowing from experience that if I do that, they will return to whatever corner of my mind they quietly live in most of the time. The most powerful reflection I've ever read in this regard is in Viktor Frankl's *Man's Search for Meaning.* If you don't already know his writing, I'd recommend making time for it. The few sentences I'm sticking in here do little justice to the depth of his wisdom and his life experience. Frankl was a brilliant neurologist and psychiatrist, born and raised in Austria, who, at the age of 37, was sent to the concentration camp at Theresienstadt. I've heard this quote a thousand times, but I still pause to process it anew every time: "Between stimulus and response, there is a space. In that space lies our freedom and power to choose our response. In our response lies our growth and freedom." It's the influence we have over that space that gives us the chance to choose freedom—the internal component, incidentally, of the freedom that the anarchists were all writing about, the freedom everyone wants but so many of us opt not to take.

The Pause That Keeps You Productive

Learning to respond to extreme emotional pressure with wisdom and self-awareness rather than taking immediate action in the moment is no small achievement. When the emotional intensity is at its highest is when things like breathing deeply, making a conscious effort to slow one's mind down, taking a long walk, calling a trusted colleague or friend, or going for a run—as I do a lot—can only help. To quote Gay Hendricks and Kate Ludeman, authors of the *Corporate Mystic*: "Most business people would not mess up half as much if they just took a few minutes to think." I always remember my friend Anese Cavanaugh trying to coach one of her good clients through a rather reactive moment. Fortunately, he called her to go over the draft of an angry note he was about to send to some coworkers. Her immediate reaction before even getting into the content was a crystal clear: "Step away from the computer. Do not send that email!" We all need a little angelic Anese in our heads to help avoid the embarrassment, pain, and chaos we can cause when we act out of anger.

3. START WITH SELF-RESPECT

It took me a long time to actually get this one. I had a hard time believing that what was going on inside my mind could be making such a difference on the outside. I refused to acknowledge that my internal self-criticism could possibly be "heard" by others. But now that I get the concept, it's as logical and clear as can be; learning to adjust the way that I speak to myself was one of the most effective things I've ever undertaken in an effort to improve my leadership work. If we don't respect ourselves, we'll consistently, if unintentionally, convey disrespect for others. No matter how hard we try to hide it, the feeling we carry inside us will be felt far more strongly than whatever words we use. *When it comes down to it, the tone we take when we talk to ourselves is directly tied to what others will take away from our interaction, regardless of what we actually say.*

The consequences of negative self-talk are significant. As Robert Greenleaf wrote about Servant Leadership, "Criticism has its place, but as a total preoccupation is sterile." That's certainly true for the way we treat others, and it's equally true of the way we treat ourselves. I'm not sure what it was that made me finally realize the veracity of this point. I probably heard it from a host of smart people but never really believed it to be true. I do, however, remember realizing one day that if I were to speak to the people on our staff with the same sort of tone, harshness, and lack of empathy with which I was talking to myself in my mind, they'd pretty likely have quit on the spot. They would surely never have tolerated my tone, let alone my lack of patience. I know that I wouldn't have wanted to work anywhere that treated me so harshly, with so little positive reinforcement. Even if I'd have stuck around, I'd have certainly ended up with a cynical, angry attitude. Which is, not surprisingly, what people were taking from conversations with me, even though that was far from what I was trying to convey.

To demonstrate the point, on the left are a few of the phrases that I used to frequently say, silently, to myself. For the sake of propriety, I'll leave out the expletives, but if you want a more accurate sense of my old internal dialogue, insert a fair few into each statement on the left side of the chart. On the right is what I now actively work to replace them with. The impact of this seemingly small shift has been huge. My energy is better, I feel better, and I'm better able to manage others from a more positive place. It makes sense. If I don't treat myself with respect, who will? And how can I truly treat others with genuine respect if I'm failing to do the same for myself?

What I used to say to myself	What I say to myself now
"That is so stupid! How could you have done that?"	"Wow, that didn't work out that well. You did do your best though. It's gonna be ok."
"Man, what an idiot. Why did you shoot your mouth off like that?"	"Man, that wasn't a very productive thing to say. Get centered and see if you can't get back on course. It takes time to master the way you manage yourself."
"You're such a jerk!"	"You weren't really thinking very clearly on that that one. Be patient, you can't change a lifetime of behavior in a few weeks."
"I can't believe you did it again. You're never gonna get it, are you?"	"Well, I didn't get it right this time. Take a couple deep breaths. You're gonna be fine. You're gonna figure this out."

This realization helped me finally understand why in our early years in business so many more people in the organization wanted to share their struggles by talking to Paul rather than to me. In hindsight, I can see that Paul was just much more at peace with himself than I was. I, on the other hand, was putting out energy reflecting the same critical voice that was active in my head. I judged myself harshly and gave myself little slack when I screwed up. It's not that my words to others were harsh—the issue was rarely anything I actually said. It was the below the surface, slightly angry, not very positive energy people picked up when talking to me. If you're stressed out and want to get centered, you prefer to go to someone one who is calm and sure of themselves. And to make matters worse, I often got angry with people for not wanting to talk to me. How's that for an unhealthy cycle? What really needed to change was all about me—my challenge was to bring the same courteous, constructive, appreciative energy I was trying to teach to others into play when I talked to myself.

Let me restate this point for emphasis, because I think it's an amazingly big deal. If you allow low self-esteem to bog you down, you will bog your staff down in that same sort of critical mindset that dominates your own mind. I have no doubt that making peace with ourselves is the foundation of a positive life. The Dalai Lama believes we need to actively teach others how to become peaceful individuals. "That eventually will create a peaceful family, a peaceful community, and through that, a peaceful world." As he rightly points out, "We can never obtain peace in the outer world until we make peace with ourselves."

Even when our self-talk isn't notorious for its negativity, there's still a lot of nuance to take note of in our ongoing internal dialogue. There are key phrases that most of us have learned growing up, and that we use all the time in normal everyday conversation, that I have come to realize are very serious trouble signs that impede self-management success. I've outlined them all in Secret #32 on Free Choice, so I'll just say one final thing here.

To wit, there are certain words to watch out for in our internal talk, as well as in our exchanges with others. When we think, and/or say, things like "I have to," "I should," and "I can't," I'm convinced we're surrendering our freedom, acting as if someone else was forcing us to behave a certain way. They're like aggressive bullies, pushing our intuition and instincts around in the playground of our minds. Someone else, definitely not us, is calling the shots; we just go along, grudgingly at best. Few people who use these stock phrases all day long (as I did) realize the implications of what they're saying. But eliminate them from your internal dialogue and you'll be taking a big step towards the freedom we all want. It took me nearly three years of mindful effort to excise them from daily conversation, but it was well worth the work. Truly, it was one of the most liberating things I've ever done.

Sketching Self-image

If you haven't seen the much-circulated Dove Real Beauty Sketches film clip, it's worth a look. In it, a set of women are asked by a professional sketch artist to describe themselves. He draws them as he would for a police sketch, without ever seeing them. Then he draws a sketch of the same woman based on descriptions offered by others who've met her. The sketches of the women based on others' views are more beautiful than the ones done from the women's descriptions of themselves. I'm not at all surprised by the results—many of us, and many women in particular, have low self-esteem. But the sketches are a fantastic way to demonstrate the difference between our subpar self-image and others' much more positive perceptions.

4. LIVE YOUR VALUES

Burnout and exhaustion are clearly a couple of the major challenges of the modern work world. There are countless constructs about how to avoid them—ways to reduce how much we work, techniques we can use to avoid bringing our problems home with us, suggestions for how to build boundaries between our time at work and what we do when we leave, etc. Working a lot of hours takes the rap for many things. In some settings, it can, of course, cause problems. But I believe that burnout occurs far more frequently because people are working in organizational settings that don't share their values.

The tension that comes out in that situation is significant. When we have to behave in ways that aren't true to who we are for forty, fifty, or more hours a week, work is emotionally exhausting. Selling products we don't love, serving customers we don't respect, making commitments we know we aren't going to keep, and then making up stories to cover for our slip-ups will sap the energy of even the strongest among us. By contrast, when we live—and work—in ways that are congruent with our values, things just feel better. When we go to work, we can be our full selves. It's far more fun and significantly less stressful. Even when we fail, at least we've fallen short while striving for what we hold dear.

Part of what's made my life so rewarding is that our values at Zingerman's are so closely aligned with my own. It doesn't hurt, to state the obvious, that I was part of creating the organization. I know that not everyone has that chance. But we do have the chance to move ever closer towards aligning what we believe in with what we do every day. Everything in this book, really, is about getting clear on who we are, and working more effectively to make peace with the inevitable struggles en route. All of that, I guarantee, will go better when we're living our values. At times, that means making painful choices about staying, or not staying, in certain relationships; about changing, or not changing, jobs; about taking on, or rejecting, subpar projects or products. Those decisions are often difficult to make, but the outcomes, I've learned the hard way, will always be better when we stay true to our ethical indicators. Living in a way that's not true to ourselves—i.e., turning away from our dreams to settle for something we "should be fine with"—will always erode our energy. As Julia Cameron writes, "If we ignore our inner commitment, the cost readily becomes apparent in the outer world. A certain lackluster tone, a rote inevitability, evicts creative excitement from our lives and, eventually, our finances." (For more on creating and living guiding principles—both professionally and personally—see Secret #11 in *Part 1*.)

5. SKILLFULLY SCHEDULE TIME AND RESOURCES

Natural Law #10 (see page 254) states that our strengths lead directly to our weaknesses—so it only makes sense that as a high achiever you likely find yourself lamenting how little time there is to do all the things you want to do. Having internalized Natural Law #9 ("Success means you get better problems"), I've mostly made peace with that reality—I have so many great things on my to-do list I'll never get them all done. But I prefer to have that problem than one of not knowing what to do or not liking what I'm doing.

How and where I spend my time is important, more so, to me, than money. Wherever I choose to (remember, I never *have* to) spend whatever time I have is a mindful decision, one that's based on what gets me the best bang for my chronological buck. Got ten minutes? Make an investment in something that matters, something you care about (call your kid, email a customer, read a few pages of a good book)—anything you believe will bring you, and others around you, a good return. Generosity is an excellent fallback—when in doubt, it's pretty much a given that doing good things for others will help them and you at the same time, and that's always a good investment!

The issue of time is so important that I've written an entire essay on the subject—you'll find it at Secret #37. But since we're here in self-management, I'll save you some time and get your mind going in the right direction with a few quick tips. If these interest you, you'll find far more of them on page 288.

Do a Lot of Self-Learning. If you accept that learning is a critical component of self-growth, one that contributes significantly to building energy, new ideas, creative flow, and increased fun and fascination with the world, then it only makes sense to mindfully schedule time to do it. When you have a good staff member, you take the time to train them properly, don't you? So why not do the same for yourself? The key is to keep learning. Without it, there's increasingly less fuel to power the intellectual and emotional energy we need to get to greatness.

If we take our Training Compact (page 454) seriously—and I do—then those at the top of the org chart are just as responsible for the effectiveness of our own training as any new staff member would be. It is all about helping ourselves to grow to ever greater heights of self-awareness and self-actualization. To quote one of the people whose ideas have informed many of my own, early 20th century Michigan anarchist Voltairine de Cleyre, anarchism "means the development of the individual, as well as the assertion of the individual. It means self-responsibility, and not leader-worship." And I am definitely down with that!

In our teaching about Servant Leadership (see *Part 2*), we ask everyone who's in a formal leadership role here at Zingerman's to do an average of two hours of formal learning per week. "Formal" for us, in case you're wondering, means going to a class, reading books or articles, attending training seminars, listening to audio books, etc. But since this piece is all about self-management, whatever that learning might be in your case is, of course, up to you.

Mind the In/On/Self Structure. When I do my regular reflection, I try to keep the mental lens focused on how my time breaks up between what I spend on myself, the work I do that's *on* the business, and when I'm actually back operating *in* the business. It works similarly to the way in which my financial advisor is always finagling my savings into the right structures—inevitably it's time to move some money from real estate into bonds, from bonds to stocks, or from blue chips to overseas growth funds. In both instances, there's really no perfect path, and there are certainly times where it makes good sense to overinvest in one area for a while. Generally, though, the most sustainable, long-term successes are going to come from a fairly balanced (and regularly rebalanced) portfolio. If I feel like I'm getting too far out of whack in any one direction, I just tack back to be more in synch. See the bit on beekeeping in *Part 2* for more on this one.

Mindfully Work at Multiple Levels. Since time is limited, I try to make the most of every moment, to be mindful of where I might make even a small positive impact, everywhere I go and in everything I do. It's all about maximizing my time investment. If I'm standing near a staffer, I ask how they're doing, compliment their work, inquire about what they've learned of late, or see if they'll share thoughts about a situation I'm struggling with myself. If I'm talking to a customer, it's a chance to learn about their lives, about what they do for a living, and about how we can serve them more effectively. If I find myself in front of the cheese counter and it's not busy at that moment, I'll sample eight or ten cheeses. It takes about two minutes to taste through them, but I learn a lot, and I get to engage in dialogue with a frontline staff person I might not normally spend time with. We can share thoughts about the sweetness of well-aged farmhouse gouda; the earthy sensuality of a raw milk Stilton; or the delicate deliciousness of a super fresh goat cheese from our Creamery.

The same stuff, by the way, works at home as well. And please don't read any of this to suggest that I'm saying not to take time off—by all means, go. Get away! Relax and have fun! Making peace with the way we manage our time, including taking occasional breaks from our work, is an essential element of effective self-management. My point throughout is mindfulness—the more we're aware of what we're doing, when and why we do it, the more likely we are to make our lives as fulfilling as we want them to be.

Teach Self-Management to Others. At Zingerman's, we work with the belief that there are four levels of learning. The first and most basic level is *listening* (or reading.) The second level up is *reflecting:* taking a minute or two, or twenty, to process what one heard or read, and to think about how it fits into what we already know and are currently doing. The third level is what we call *assimilating and acting:* taking what we heard and reflected on, and then putting our learning into action. My hope with this book is that you'll get at least to that third level, that you'll take

The Four Levels of Learning

1. Listening or Reading
2. Reflecting, Alone or with Others
3. Assimilating and Acting
4. Teaching or Writing

some tips from what you read here and make some positive changes in your work and your life.

The fourth, and highest, level of learning for us is *teaching*. It's at the top, quite simply, because in order to teach a subject with any modicum of skill, we have to really learn it at a much deeper level. In the context of this book, the corollary would be writing—writing is, in essence, teaching on paper. If you want to really manage yourself to greatness (or help anyone you work with do the same), setting out to teach others is one of the surest ways I know to make that happen. Whether you do the work in writing or in person, if you commit to teaching on any subject, I guarantee that you will do the first three levels far better than if you don't. When we know we're going to teach something, we listen (or read) with greater attention to detail. We reflect more intently to make sure we've got things in context. It's also far more likely that we'll act on what we're talking about—who would teach a subject that they aren't at least coming close to living and modeling effectively. Teaching is the highest level because it has us doing all the other levels and then some. Which is why I guarantee that if you teach a course on self-management, your own self-management skills will be much better than they've ever been.

Self-Management in Action:
Allie and the $10,000 Turnaround

Allie Lyttle has worked with us for about 18 months now. She's doing great work, both in the business and on herself. She's become far more in touch with who she is and what she wants. And she's ever-more mindful of how her old habits and longstanding emotional swings can get in the way of what she's now, in this new setting, working so hard to achieve. What follows is a true story—it's not one I'm proud of, but it can happen in the high-volume, high-pressure world of food service. As this story demonstrates, better self-management doesn't make all our problems go away, but it sure can keep them from blowing up into even bigger ones. Clearly, we didn't handle things on our end as leaders very well, but my point is to show how much Allie's self-awareness has made such a huge difference.

After working a really long week, Allie was pretty much physically and emotionally maxed out. It's not great, but it's not uncommon in a very busy kitchen. Always wanting to contribute, she had agreed, despite how tired she was, to use her first day off for the week to help out by coming in to cover someone else's sick call. When Allie came in the next morning (after closing the night before), the manager realized she'd been given inaccurate information. "Can you go home now and come back tonight?" she was asked. Realizing that she was so exhausted from her already long week that she wouldn't be able to honor the request, Allie said no.

Not at all an unreasonable response. Unfortunately, the response Allie got was less than Servant Leadership–focused. You could, I suppose, say that the manager was snippy. I'm not trying to put blame on them—I'm sure that they themselves were also stressed, and for all I know, two other people had just called in sick, or a couple of customers had complained, or any number of other things had happened of the sort to throw us off course, and the manager didn't do a great job of managing their own stress. Instead, they slipped, and Allie caught the brunt of it.

Already prone to let her temper take over, she was pissed. She felt like she'd been taking hits for the team all week but was being treated like a self-centered loser. "What would have happened in your old job?" I asked her. "Oh, I'd have told the manager to get screwed and quit," she said. "But this time you didn't?" "Nope. I wanted to. But I've learned how to get a hold of myself, so I just kept my mouth shut and went home." Allie didn't work the shift, which was smart—she was just too tired and she wasn't obligated to help out on her day off. Later, after she'd gotten some sleep, she was able to get things in perspective. There were definitely problems to work on, but removed from her emotionally exhausted state, the issues were far less intense than they'd seemed at the time. Discussions were had, tensions dissolved.

But here's how it would have gone without all of her work at self-management. In a kind of understandable fit of anger she would have quit. We'd have lost a very good staff member on the spot. I can only imagine the drama that would have gone down for days on end, taking time and energy away from careful quality control and good teamwork. More tangibly, Allie's shifts would have to have been covered immediately, leading to at least forty hours of overtime for others—that alone would have cost us $300 or $400. Since it would have taken weeks to hire someone else as skilled, that situation would have continued, probably for at least a month.

The colleagues who picked up Allie's hours would have then themselves been more stressed, meaning they'd be more accident prone and more likely to make mistakes. The mistakes would likely have led to more comps for unhappy customers—it's not hard to imagine five or ten orders going awry over the course of a week as a result. That cost? Let's say $500 to $1000. Add to that the added cost of the bad word of mouth going out in the community. We figure one good customer here in Ann Arbor brings us about $1000 a year. Let's say these bad scenarios cost us a couple—that's another $2000 to our stress tab.

But wait, there's more! Add to that the cost of interviewing and hiring for Allie's replacement—training someone new, we figure, costs us on average about $2000. Of course not that many people can come in and contribute at her level very quickly—it's not an easy job—which means the $2000 could have quickly become $4000 if the first person we hired couldn't cut it. And, of course, the whole thing could have become even worse if one of her colleagues who'd already been thinking of moving on decided in the moment to make the move too. Which would mean we'd be even more short-staffed, more reliant on overtime, more stressed out, more likely to give out comps, and more mired in unexpected costs. Happily, none of this came to be. All because, in the eighteen months she's been with us, Allie's learned so much about how to better manage herself.

Bottom line? The work of teaching our staff member self-management skills, helping her learn to harness her temper and not act in anger, easily saved our organization somewhere around $10,000. I'd say we paid back our entire annual investment in training with that one small crisis averted.

6. WRITE A VISION

There's an entire Secret in this book on Personal Vision, which will address this subject at length, so consider these few paragraphs a mental placeholder. We'll come to the real work soon enough (or if you don't want to wait, flip ahead now to page 191). All I want to do for now is get you thinking about it. The vision questions here are surprisingly simple: "What will it look like and feel like when we're doing a great job as leaders?" "What will it be like when we're living the life we want to lead?" If you want to get to greatness, you're going to be much more likely to succeed if you set aside a half an hour or so to draft up a vision of what that greatness actually looks like to you. As always, there are no "right" or "wrong" visions—it's your future, your feelings, your finances, your friendships, your whatever else matters to you. Visioning, as we view it, is all about going after our dreams, living our values, pursuing our passions, and in the process designing a job that we love to do every day! It's about intentionally going after what we call *good work*—work that's meaningful and that makes a positive difference in the world, work that's as much fun as it is fulfilling.

To cut to the creative chase, visioning works. My experience is that when we come clean with ourselves and when we have the courage to write those thoughts out on paper, when it's inspiring and strategically sound, when we believe in it and share it with others, it will be as Paulo Coelho describes in *The Alchemist:* "When you want something, all the universe conspires in helping you to achieve it." In Coehlo's vision, "People are capable, at any time in their lives, of doing what they dream of."

7. GET IN TOUCH WITH YOUR GUT

This is one of those pieces of advice that's entirely easier to give than it is to actually do. I spent so many years listening to other people's perspectives, worrying all along about making *them* happy instead of doing what my friend Anese Cavanaugh would call "holding my space," that I got to a point where my gut feelings were barely noticeable amid all the noise in my head. It's no surprise really—if you don't exercise a muscle regularly, it atrophies. If you tune out your gut feelings, if you stop believing (in) them, and bury them away, they become harder and harder to find. As Robert Greenleaf says, "Unless one trusts intuitive insights, one doesn't get them." I had to read that line two or three times before I got it. To clarify, Greenleaf adds, "Unless insights are *acted on,* they don't speak with assurance."

The emphasis is mine, but the point is his, and it's spot on at that. We have to take chances to test out our intuition and make sure we're truly in touch. Mind you, I don't mean that we should immediately order others to adhere to every intuitive insight we have. But ignoring or wasting those instincts is usually a big mistake. Though not every intuitive feeling I have is correct, a lot of them have paid off well for us. There are hundreds of examples, but looking at the last few years, I'll point to a feeling I had that pushed me to implement what we learned about energy from Anese Cavanaugh. We turned her teachings into an organizational recipe for energy management (see 454), which we now use actively across our entire organization. While I couldn't give data to demonstrate its value, it was clear to me in about two minutes that what

Anese had explained to me about energy would be a huge plus for our business. Although not everyone (of course) bought in at the beginning, effective energy management has brought our organization a far greater understanding of the presence each of us brings to work and to every interaction we have. The quality of our service and our internal interactions is far better for it. Similarly, our decision (Amy's, Frank's, Paul's, and mine) to pursue our passion for Hungarian cuisine at the Bakehouse is already creating a great bit of buzz, internal excitement, and sales. Or I look back to our decision to increase training during the recession rather than cut it down as most have—our staff raised their work standards even higher than they'd already been, and in good part because of our training focus, we came through the recession in pretty good shape.

Conversely, I'll say that almost every big decision that I regret having made involved, in hindsight, a situation in which I went against my gut feeling. I'm not saying my intuition is impeccable, but I do know that when my gut is going in a certain direction, I need to take note, and at least honor the feeling with a conversation with a close friend or trusted colleague. When we're not tuned in to intuition, we're increasingly adrift in a world awash with data, deluged with dozens of well-argued positions on every point. When we're totally out of touch with our gut, we'll surely struggle, bounced between the conflicting advice we get from others like an organizational pinball. Regardless of how good everyone else's input might be—and as you know already, I'm a big believer in asking for help—insights won't rise right from within when we're missing the leaven that intuition naturally adds to the mix.

So how can you know exactly what your gut feelings are? Gut feelings can come in the form of an emotional response (often, indeed, in your stomach, or gut), a voice in your head, a flow of positive energy, a buzz, the onset of unspoken anxiety and/or a strong belief that something really special is happening. On the down side, they can come in the form of queasiness, a feeling that we know what to do but we don't quite have it together to do it. When the voices kick in, they can be positive, as in, "Man, I just *know* this is the right thing to do." Other times they're about avoidance: "I just don't feel right about this." My gut feeling is that they're the things that feel *more true* for us than almost anything else. They're the dreams or desires that stay with us even when we're told we shouldn't want them. They're the fears that, unlike the fear of leaving home I described earlier, have proven themselves to be well-founded.

Being able to sort out healthy gut feelings from other, unhelpful, voices isn't easy. The only way I know to sort out which is which is to track them.

Journaling has been a hugely helpful tool for me in this regard—it allows me to say (to myself) what I'm excited about or what I'm worried about. And then, as I act or don't act on those feelings, I can continue to catalogue the signals, voices, or feelings that are healthy indicators of intuition to follow through on, and which are the ones to set aside. The drive to honor intuition is, I believe, imperative. Without it, we are, literally, lost to ourselves.

Why Effective Vision Writing Will Get You to Your Gut

When it comes to vision writing, many people procrastinate and make excuses. Others begin the work but won't finish. A significant number know that writing a vision is the right thing to do, but they're a bit afraid of what might come out when they put their future down on paper. They know *their* right answer, but they also know that the consequences of actually living it are large. So instead of writing, they worry.

One morning a friend of mine came by to chat about a project she'd been dreaming about for many years. I'd given her a copy of *Part 1* and suggested she first read the recipe for vision writing and then go ahead and draft one before our meeting. She arrived as scheduled, but sans vision. "Did you write one?" I asked. "No," she said, looking down. "I suppose I should. But it's a bit scary." I shared my experience of the effectiveness of the vision writing process. She acknowledged it but still didn't seem ready. And then, about an hour into our conversation, while I stepped away to respond to a customer query, she took out some paper and a pen and started to write. I came back but kept my mouth shut and let her keep going. After about twenty minutes, she paused to ask me how long she'd been at it. I told her, she nodded, and then went back to work. Fifteen minutes later she looked up and smiled. "Well, that was interesting," she said. Without even having read what she wrote, I knew it was good. I could see it in her face—her energy was about eighteen times lighter than it was when she arrived. Her intuition, I'm sure, had been honored and her gut feelings had, finally, come to the fore.

8. MANAGE YOUR ENERGY

Energy management is not on the topic list for most corporate training sessions (yet!), but one day I'm sure it will be. As I said above, it's one that just felt right to me from the first time I heard Anese Cavanaugh explain the concept. Quite simply, the better we manage ourselves, the better our energy is going to be; the better we manage our energy, the more effectively we'll be able to do the right things for ourselves and those around us, and the less likely we are to slip and do something stupid. The more we do all of it, the more effective our leadership, and our lives, are sure to be. It's a very virtuous and very sustainable cycle.[4]

If we're not managing our own energy, who will? If our energy is swinging rapidly from positive to negative, soaring, swooping, and then sinking within a matter of moments, we—and everyone around us—are sure to suffer. In that setting it's all reactive—we become like a rudderless ship floating free at sea. We still have a fair bit of power and can cause a lot of damage, firing guns (even well-aimed ones) off the decks, but the boat and everyone aboard it will continue to drift, or even careen, dangerously and aimlessly about.

While none of us has total control over our energy, we do have a high likelihood of managing it well if we put our minds to it. And the energy we bring to anything is, by definition, going to set the tone for everyone else on the team. If we want positive, enjoyable energy in the business—and we certainly do here—then it's incumbent on us to initiate it. If we want positive energy in our own existence, it's up to us to manage it for ourselves. If we don't, who will? As Paul says beautifully, "Positive energy has a heliotropic effect—people are attracted to it." A very good thing if you're looking to lead.

Energy management, I would argue, is the unspoken essence of our success. If you stay positive in the face of adversity; if you have fun with friends, family, and coworkers; if the energy you emanate out into the world is enjoyable, calm, and confident, then good things are almost sure to happen. Check out this idea from author Shawn Achor: "Only 25% of your job successes," Achor says, "are predicted based upon intelligence and technical skills, though we spend most of our education and most companies hire based upon this category. The 'silent 75%' of long-term job success is based upon your ability to positively adapt to the world: optimism, social support creation, and viewing stress as a challenge instead of as a threat."

If you like to work from data rather than intuition, I'd say try out the two extremes for a couple of weeks. First, spend seven days trying to stay as grim as you can get, not completely horrible but clearly not happy. Forget fun, just stay serious, focused, more negative than not. No letting up. I want to see frowns and scowls aplenty. Then, switch gears. For the second week work things the other way around; this time, I'd ask you to be as positive and upbeat as you can. Smile often, laugh a lot (even on difficult days), share liberally, appreciate others, and be as supportive and sensitive as you can be. You don't have to have a PhD in positive psychology to forecast how each week is going to go.

Here at Zingerman's we have adapted Anese's teachings to include three "types" of energy that we work to manage:

Physical: We manage this well when we get a goodly amount of sleep, when we eat well, and we exercise regularly.

Mental or Emotional: Everyone will, of course, respond to energy inputs differently. Most any sort of spiritual activity—organized or otherwise—will make a big difference. Meditation, prayer, and focusing on the positive are all good ways to improve it. And for me, learning takes it all up quite a bit.

Vibrational: This is the one that really got my attention. It refers to the energy that others pick up from us, basically, the feeling that others take away from the interaction. Things that greatly impact vibrational energy include smiling (I'd say more than half of the world doesn't), good posture, and deep breathing. A spirit of generosity, compassion, empathy, and a sincere belief in what we're doing will also jumpstart our vibrational energy.

For our four-step recipe for energy management, see page 454. For much more on energy and what we learned from Anese, see Secrets #19–21 in *Part 2* of the *Guide to Good Leading*.

The Three and Out Rule

This is a little self-management mechanism I made up a few years back. I wrote about in *Part 1* (it's on page 214 if you want to see it in the original). It's such an elegantly simple and eminently effective tool for self-management that I couldn't stand to leave it out of this piece just because I'd already put it in print earlier on.

It goes like this. When I feel my energy sliding into the negative realm, I find someone around me—whether in person, on the phone, or via email, and I thank them. Sincerely. For something that they've done that I honestly do appreciate. I always get back positive energy. Then I immediately find someone else and do it *again*. Bingo. I get back more positive energy.

Within a matter of minutes, I repeat my act of appreciation *a third time.* Voilà! More positive energy comes my way.

In the face of all that positivity, I simply cannot stay in a bad mood. The smiles, the warmth, and the wealth of good feeling that others give me for having unexpectedly appreciated them *always* turns my day around. And if my mood gets better, consider the impact on the rest of our organization. Talk about time as an investment—what better use of ten minutes can you imagine than doing the Three and Out Rule? Try it out. It is great stuff!

9. Ask for Help

While I've got you thinking about your vision of success as a leader, you might want to consider how frequently and how effectively you seek support and advice from others. While many look askance at people asking for help, here we see it the other way around. At Zingerman's, the most successful leaders are those who seek assistance with great regularity.

We all need help—not one of us, no matter how insightful, is going to consistently get it all right without support and input from others. While this concept is simple, for most of us the idea of asking for help runs completely counter to the way we were raised and the way the rest of society works. "Successful business people" in the US are said to stand alone. Those who never seem to need help are considered "strong" and "independent." So to gather input and assistance, to collaborate, to go to therapy, to admit weakness, and to ask directly for help is counterintuitive for most of us.

Getting help can come in many forms—asking peers, employees, bosses, customers, coworkers. It can come in the form of reading or seeking out seminars and study programs. It can come in the form of regular counseling or spiritual support. The point is that the more we gather insightful and helpful input from others, and then balance that with our own views and intuitive insights, the more effective we're going to be. Musician and artist Amanda Palmer (who, by the way, starts one of her songs, "I am an anarchist") has eloquently advocated for the art of asking. "Through the very act of asking people," she says, she's made a myriad of supportive connections. "And when you connect with them, people want to help you. It's kind of counterintuitive for a lot of artists—they don't want to ask for things. It's not easy to ask.

Asking makes you vulnerable." And yet, to Amanda's point, caringly communicating our vulnerability helps make us real, improves our energy, and increases the odds of getting ourselves and our group to greatness.

Putting the Therapeutic Process to Work

It's been nearly twenty-five years now since I started going to therapy. I went originally out of need—I was struggling in parts of my personal life. I agonized for about a year before I finally took a deep breath and called to make an appointment. Although it went against what I'd learned growing up ("you shouldn't need to go to therapy unless you're really messed up"), it finally dawned on me that what had worked for me at work would likely be effective outside of work as well. If tapping outside expertise, studying in depth, and then working to implement what I'd learned had helped me a lot in business, it only made sense that the same approach would also be effective in my personal life. My intuition was accurate—it helped then and it still helps now.

The sense of urgency has long since ended, but I still to go therapy regularly to help me keep in good (emotional) shape, to help me stay centered week in and week out. It just made sense to me that if therapy was helping, there was no point in stopping. We don't work out only when we're overweight. I don't wait until I feel terrible and have gained twenty pounds to start running. Rather, it's the opposite—I run every day so that I feel good and never gain the twenty pounds to begin with. The way I see it, my weekly therapy session is like a gym visit for my mind. It doesn't fix all my problems, but it sure does help keep me balanced, both personally and professionally. I often talk about work issues as much as I do about anything else in my life. It's proven an excellent investment in making my life what I want it to be. In *Train Your Mind, Change Your Brain*, Sharon Begley quotes Buddhist monk Matthieu Ricard, who says, "Mind training is the process of becoming a better human being for your own sake and for the sake of others."

In the context of self-management, a good therapist serves pretty much the same role for me as an experienced mentor or professional advisor would with organizational issues. Seeking out mentors and job coaches has become a well-accepted way to learn, stay on track, seek solace and support when we're struggling, and tap wisdom from someone who knows more than we do about work. The therapist serves the same role for self-management. They know more than we do about the workings of the mind, they've studied and seen the way the thought process unfolds, the way the emotions swing, the struggle we all go through to find ourselves and our way in the world.

The right therapist, like the right mentor, is aligned with our values and supports us in finding our vision. Abraham Maslow, I learned only recently, advocated for this approach. "What [leaders] need is not so much personal therapy of the psychiatric sort, which implies psychiatric sickness, but rather personal development or *psychogogy* [his term for positive psychology] or self-actualization training or something of the sort." Maslow wondered aloud, "Why do I not see ... more stress on personal therapy for would-be leaders? Certainly, I would recommend it very strongly."

10. GET AROUND THE RIGHT PEOPLE (DON'T STAY DOWN WITH THE JONESES)

One good way to get help is to get around good people, people who share your values and who have already traversed the same path to success on which you've more recently embarked. Just their calm and experienced presence can increase the odds of you succeeding, avoiding impulsive decisions, and effectively staying the course. Their focus is on helping you become the person you want to be, never on judging you. They may offer insight but never harsh criticism or cut you down for going after your dreams. If you don't have a fair few of those people in your life, now is a great time to start looking for them. Thinking back to #6, above, if you write into your personal vision that two years from now you have ten of them and then start sharing that vision and working towards it, the odds are high that you'll have at least that many.

To that end, young teams bound for the playoffs almost always bring in a veteran or two to help them win a championship. It's not that the more experienced players are necessarily going to contribute all that much on the court, but rather that they can offer advice, insight, good grounding, and effective energy management for younger, less-experienced teammates. The same goes for groups of all sorts. If you're doing new things, you'll more than likely benefit from a new-to-you, "been-there-done-that" set of advisors and mentors. It can be people in the organization or outside it or, best of all, a bit of both. It can be people you know, or people you know only through their writing—reading Emma Goldman, Brenda Ueland, Robert Greenleaf, Murray Bookchin, and others has had a hugely positive influence on my work and my life. Remember—if you're up for reading and learning (and so many studies show that successful people almost always are), you have access to the most amazing minds and consummate creativity the world has to offer you any time you want. The stories we glean from what we read can resonate as powerfully as what we might hear in person. As Gary Snyder says so beautifully, "Books are our grandparents."

One reason it's so important to get around greatness is to find solace and support for the inevitable struggles that go with trying to be great. While on the one hand, "moving up," getting promoted, studying harder, etc. are often applauded, they can also meet with negativity from one's former peer group, if those individuals haven't chosen the same path. When one person starts to go for more responsibility, it's unfortunately not at all uncommon that their colleagues might get mad at them for moving forward. There's often a percep- tion that, if someone follows their own ambitions, they're selling out their old peer group (unless the whole group is going "up" together). While many people will offer verbal support, they may not come through when it's time for action. Which is why, in my experience, it takes courage to rise through the ranks, to leave behind what's worked okay to go after grander dreams.

It's been a long time since I faced that situation myself. But in trying to help others adjust to the realities of their new roles, I usually share what I heard a long time ago from my friend Lex Alexander. I've learned many things from Lex over the years, and this is one of the best. Although everyone *says* that they're "trying to keep up with the Joneses," Lex pointed out to me that most people are actually afraid to move *up*. Because of this fear of advance- ment, they unconsciously hold themselves back. So Lex turned the old adage around: *"Don't stay down with the Joneses!"* This still resonates for me, and for most folks I've shared it with. Peace activist and author Marianne Williamson says it well: "Our deepest fear is that we are powerful beyond measure. . . . We ask ourselves, who am I to be brilliant, gorgeous, talented, and fabulous?" She continues, "There is nothing enlightened about shrinking so that other people will not feel insecure around you."

That others might be less than enthusiastic about a friend's decision to move past the place where everyone else has been comfortably residing is neither surprising nor unnatural. To quote from Hugh MacLeod, in *Ignore*

Everybody: "Good ideas alter the power balance in relationships. That is why good ideas are always initially resisted. Plus, a big idea will change you. Your friends may love you but they may not want you to change. If you change, then their dynamic with you also changes. They might prefer things the way they are, that's how they love you—the way you are, not the way you may become." In Ireland, they call it "cutting the tall poppies." On the East Coast, I've heard it called "crabs in a barrel"—the other crabs will always pull down the one that's starting to crawl too high up the sides.

Please understand, I'm not saying that you need to abandon old friends and colleagues when you make a big move in your life, and I'm not saying that none of them will support you as you go. The key is to find people who get you and get what you're doing—to my taste, that's a diverse group, with each member bringing their own uniqueness to contribute to the world. The most self-aware, the most mindful, and the most grounded within themselves will almost certainly stay true and support you as you go after what's good for you. You want to surround yourself with people who are inspiring, who have valuable insights to offer, and who've made the same sorts of changes that you have. In *Where Good Ideas Come From* Steven Johnson notes, "A good idea is a network. Good ideas are not conjured out of thin air. The connections [we make] are the key to wisdom." Who we hang with will have a significant impact on how innovative and creative our existence becomes.

11. BE WILLING TO WORK HARDER THAN YOU HAVE TO JUST TO GET BY

Excelling at anything—leading, loving, or learning—is always a lot of work. I've yet to meet anyone who's great at what they do that doesn't work their butts off. I don't mean that they don't do other things, take vacation days, or have great family lives. I just mean that, in whatever way they figure out how to divide their time, they work really, really hard at whatever it is they want to do well.

This last bit is really just Natural Law #7 in action (see page 247). I have lodged in my mind the story that Mac McCaughan shared with me four or five years ago. Although I met him as the man who's married to my friend Andrea Reusing (the James Beard award-winning chef and owner of Lantern in Chapel Hill), Mac is better known in the world as a member of the band Superchunk and the guy who cofounded Merge Records. He once toured with the band Yo La Tengo. Most bands he'd worked with took travel time on the bus between towns to sleep, read, drink, or whatever. But in Yo La Tengo's case, as soon as the bus headed out from their hotel, they immediately started reviewing the previous night's performance, practicing subtle changes to the way they played the songs, and working on the next night's set. Mac said at first he was a bit miffed, but he pretty quickly came to realize that that little extra bit of work was a big part of what kept Yo La Tengo at the top of their game, highly esteemed in the indie music world for over two decades—no small feat in an industry that "shoots" stars faster than the Milky Way.

You can turn to a hundred others to get pretty much the same message. Malcolm Gladwell's *Outliers* references Anders Ericsson's 10,000 hours theory—that people who are super successful in anything turn out to have mindfully worked at whatever it is they do for 10,000 hours at least. Gladwell makes a good argument for the theory, and cites Bill Gates and the Beatles among his examples. The number of hours one works is clearly just one way to monitor effort—they have to be productive, focused on achieving something special, and not just mindless days devoted to a repetitive and time-consuming task. But you get the point.

The benefits of working harder aren't just about skill development; they're essential to the goals of effective self-management, emotional engagement, and mindfulness. Whatever I've learned on this subject has come from twenty or thirty years of study, and thousands of hours of mindful self-monitoring. So many recent studies are showing strongly that we all possess the ability to rewire ourselves. Learning to manage our emotions more effectively, to listen better, and to breathe more evenly all require much more work than just passively putting up with the status quo. But the sense of success, the improvement in energy, the positive approach to work on oneself that replaces unproductive worry are really positive stepping stones en route to a successful and rewarding life.

Everything We Do Sets an Example

The reality of every workplace is that, whether we want them to or not, the staff is tracking the leader's behaviors very closely. They watch how we deal with customers, how we handle money, how well we meet our commitments. They look at little things and big things alike. They see it all. They hear it all. And through our vibrational energy, they actually feel it all too. What that means is that we need to mindfully manage our own behavior in order to set the tone we desire on all fronts. Certainly, just leading by example won't ensure that our organizations are successful, but it always improves the odds. And there is absolutely no down side to modeling the values and work style you want your staff to pick up on.

In *The Corporate Mystic,* authors Kate Ludemens and Gay Hendrickson argue that the culture of our organization begins with our own behaviors. "When you are the source, you take full responsibility for bringing into being the corporate culture you want." If we want a high-integrity organization, it will by definition be driven first and foremost by what we ourselves do every day. The good news is that one of the most effective ways we can improve the performance of our organization and change its culture for the better is to alter our own behavior, which, by now, having done all of the above, we'll be much better at self-managing. Given that everything we choose to do is basically an investment in something we believe in, here are some of the more significant areas of operation in which changing our own behavior will influence our organization:

a. What we pay attention to, measure, and actively manage. When we opt to measure something we're taking a step towards improving it, so what we choose is sure to have a meaningful impact on the rest of the organization. If we focus first on individual performance, we'll get a group of individual performers; by contrast, move to measuring group achievement, and the team will steadily pull together.

b. The ways we define success. This is in essence about vision, about where we've dedicated ourselves to going and the ethical nature of the path we choose. What goes into the vision (and what's left out of it) will send strong messages about what we value, what we think about others in our lives, and how we see the world around us.

c. The way we react to critical incidents and crises. This is especially important when there are ethical issues at hand, which happens, of course, in many small ways, pretty much every day. The quickest way to undermine our principles is to abandon them under pressure.

d. The criteria we use in allocating rewards and promotions. When we reward those who model desired behaviors, who have come through on commitments, who are creative, principled, etc., we send a clear message to the organization that these are the things we value. On the other hand, if we promote someone who is clearly not living our guiding principles, we send a message that our values aren't really very important.

e. The small acts of care and kindness we commit. The little things we do really do matter. To quote my partner Paul, "Small kindnesses, small considerations, and small courtesies, habitually practiced, will give a wonderful charm to your personality and make people want to be around you and listen to you. No one owes you their attention; you need to earn it." These small, unexpected extra miles are a sure way to steadily but effectively change both your own energy and your organizational culture for the better.

f. Who we trust. Paul is a master on matters of trust, and I've learned a lot from him on the subject. His advice? "Start out by trusting others. I think that this is essential. It is so easy for us to believe that we are personally trustworthy, but to doubt the motives of others. We are not authentic, sincere, or worthy of trust if we don't begin with mutual trust."

g. What we teach. As we improve our leadership, we find ourselves teaching more and more often. Whether in formal or informal ways, what we teach to our staff will have a significant impact on the way they learn and the way they view their workplace.

12. BE WILLING TO EMBRACE THE UNCOMFORTABLE

In his book *Wherever You Go, There You Are,* Jon Kabat-Zinn writes, "If you are truly strong, there is little need to emphasize it to yourself or to others. Best to take another tack entirely and direct your attention where you fear most to look." Effective self-management often means going where we're reluctant to go; it's about learning to discern the difference between the places we resist going because they're dangerous and destructive, and those we shy away from out of discomfort, but from which we'd actually gain enormously if we have the courage to go. Often that means embracing uncertainty, moving towards tension creatively and constructively rather than trying to keep it away at all costs. When we do that well, we're most likely to be actively learning.

Please don't wait until you're "ready" to move forward on all of the tips and insights listed above. If you're waiting for the day to come when you feel completely comfortable, well, that day might never come. Honestly, it's never really come for me. I just started doing the work anyway. As someone much smarter than me (I can't remember who) said a long time ago, "Often, the action must precede the emotion." We need to move forward *before* we start feeling solid about what we're doing. You start working on this stuff, and then only much later can you get comfortable.

What you'll likely find if you do fight through the discomfort to do some of the work I've written about is that as you practice it, you'll gradually need to devote less mental energy to conscious, cautious, careful self-management. Which means there's more time and energy freed up to deal with other things. The more effectively you manage yourself, the more successes and the fewer shortfalls you'll have, and the more resources you'll have for "investment" in the results you seek for yourself and your organization. Fun goes up, and frustration, while not eliminated, is at least reduced.

Emotional Resilience

It's become ever clearer to me that one of the keys to making it through the maze of life successfully is to develop emotional resilience. People who don't have it will usually give up long before they have a good shot at success. When things go wrong, they blame themselves or others around them; they feel defeated, deflated, and demoralized. And when those things happen, more often than not they give up. People who are emotionally resilient may experience some of those same feelings, but before the feelings take over, they can right their emotional ship; where others stop, they keep going. The ability to work through those difficult emotional days, to look away from defeat and move toward a meaningful future, is a huge piece of success for most people I've met.

Five options that can help get you back on track when things seem to be turning down:

Breathe. Usually when we're starting to slide, we're not breathing. Deep breathing helps us get centered.

Do the Three Good Things exercise (see page 287). The simple act of calling up three positive things can help turn the tide back in the right direction.

Reread your long-term vision. Reminding ourselves of the positive future that we've already actively committed to can help us pull through tough times.

Do a reality check. When you're starting to make up extreme stories about "who intentionally messed you up" or how "things are never going to work out," you're probably doing what psychologists call "catastrophizing." In other words, we're allowing what might really be a relatively small problem turn into a major disaster, painting our peers to be devious plotters out to take us down, or demeaning ourselves through severe self-deprecation. In any of those cases, we've probably overstated what's really happening. The resulting stress makes it almost impossible to assess anything realistically. By simply asking ourselves, "Is this really the most likely scenario?," we can help back off from the extremes and return to a more manageable, and significantly more likely, middle-of-the-road scenario.

Do the Three and Out. Find three people, one after another, and give them a sincere, heartfelt compliment and appreciation. The positive energy you get back is sure to significantly impact your own!

If you want to make your management—both of yourself and of others—more effective, then the stuff on this list will surely help. Implementing any of these tips will get you at least moderately good results. Even a modest effort will make a meaningful difference. These tips are what work for me; the odds are high that you too will have tips of your own—after all, it's unlikely that anyone will know your inner workings better than you do. If there are things that work well for you and you're up for sharing, send 'em on—I'd love to learn about what you do to help make your life more rewarding.

Success, to sum up, always starts with a positive commitment to ourselves, to difficult self-reflective work, and to mindful self-management. If it feels uncomfortable, keep pushing onward. As David Bayles and Ted Orland write in *Art and Fear*, "What separates artists from ex-artists is that those who challenge their fears, continue; those who don't, quit."

I hope you enjoy the ride—I know I have.

Open Book *Self*-Management

Looking over the list of self-management tips above, draft a half dozen or so new habits that you'd like to cultivate to move you further into the future you desire. You might want to read more, spend more time with supportive friends, commit to a regular period of solitude, or set a target for how many small acts of kindness you want to perform each week. Obviously, the choice is yours.

Once you've settled on the list, you can apply the basic principles of open book management to help you mindfully move forward by creating a personal score board. To start, simply set up a grid on a piece of paper or a spreadsheet. On the left side, list each of the new habits. For each week you've committed to working at it, you'll need three columns—Plan, Forecast, and Actual. The first column to the right of your new habit list is your Plan (P)—how many times per week do you intend to follow the new habit? Write the number into that column. The Plan number should get filled for each week all the way across your chart. This is what you're hoping to do. The next column will be your Forecast (F)—each week, as you go, knowing more about what's happening in your life at that moment, fill in what you're shooting for. (If, for example, you're extremely busy with the holidays one week, you might not have time for solitude.) The third column indicates your Actual (A) performance. When the week is over, fill in what you actually did.

At the far right, you'll add two more columns. One is the cumulative Plan number for the entire time you're tracking this work. If it's twelve weeks, for example, you'll add up all twelve Plan columns to get this total. Next to that, mark a column for Actual + Forecast. Knowing what you've already achieved, you'll adjust that number anew each week—hopefully the new Actual + Forecast figure will be at least as good as, if not better than, the number in your Plan.

Personal Scoreboard	Week 1			Week 2			Full Time Span	
	P	F	A	P	F	A	P	A+F
Days Journaling	3	3	2	3	4		6	6
Habit								
Habit								

Each week, preferably at the same time, spend a few minutes to fill in last week's actual performance and the coming week's forecast. Take a few minutes to reflect on what worked, what went wrong, and what you're going to do differently in the coming week. While you may fall short one week, remember you can make up the difference by raising your forecast—and your results—

for the week to come. Some people are helped by making time to review the numbers each week with a colleague or coach. Once you know what you've committed to doing, it may help you to actually schedule the time to do what you've forecasted into your planner—the more you account for the time needed to take action, the more likely it is you'll get to your goals successfully.

To really get yourself moving, you'll want to track your new habits for at least twelve weeks, and ideally even more. To really make the habit a solid part of your week, I'd recommend you track it for a year. That may feel like a long time, but new life habits aren't forged in a few days. If you do well with this structure, there's really no reason to ever stop the tracking. If one habit becomes so much a part of who you are that it's no longer necessary to have it on the chart, you might add another one to the list in its stead. If you're like most people I know, the simple act of setting a Plan, mindfully Forecasting what you're going to do, and then writing down what you Actually did will almost always lead you to successfully building new habits and, in the process, a life that's ever closer to the one you want to live.

Mark Johnson, Retail Staffer, Zingerman's Delicatessen

The first thing that attracted me to Zingerman's was the personal development opportunities afforded to me throughout the Community of Businesses. Zingerman's runs on the philosophy that the company is only as strong as the people who work here. One way we help improve and retain employees is through classes. It's the backbone of the effort to improve our workforce. It really helps that these classes are developed and maintained by a fantastic group of people called "the training engineers." They are helped by, and in some cases work for, ZingTrain, the training company created by Zingerman's.

The sheer amount of classes we offer on a monthly basis is one way in which we help to get employees on the path to improvement. In any given month, more than 40 classes are offered. There are a number of teachers for each class, which allows different perspectives, thus becoming more effective for real-world training. Using real experiences and situations allows us to more effectively train people for their job. There is a lot of corporate knowledge in there as well, but put into easily manageable chunks to allow for easier digestion and retention.

The biggest thing we offer as a company is the chance to develop your skills with responsibility. Placing an emphasis on complete 100 percent commitment on both sides puts you in charge of your own training and in essence gives you the tools to do your job well and with confidence. Giving you the skills and freedom to make Zingerman's run smoothly within the culture that has been established over the last 31 years is a testament to the learning culture created here. It is by far the most complete and thorough training culture that I have seen in any company, let alone one that I have worked for, and I am thankful for the opportunity to be here and continue to learn.

justin dennis preparing to take down a donut sundae at the roadhouse

SECRET #32

It's All About Free Choice

Or, How I Spent Three Years Learning That I Didn't Actually **Have To** *Do a Darned Thing*

Free choice is clearly a central political principle of American life. But what follows is, as per the rest of this book, about what goes on inside us, not what happens in the halls of Congress or on the bench of the Supreme Court. My focus—learned the hard way, through personal struggle and self-study—is on how important it is for each of us to embrace free choice from the inside out.

—

It was about a year or so after I first started going to therapy (over two decades ago) when my counselor started to call me out on how often I acted as if I had little or no say in what I was doing every day. My language, he pointed out, was sending him clear signals that I was acting like a victim, feeling compelled to comply with the demands of others, real and/or imagined, rather than freely opting into, or out of, what I truly desired to do. Of course, when he called me on it, I was clueless. In fact, I argued with him for a good while before the truth of what he was telling me finally sank in. He was right on. My language was the tip off—it was laced with words (see the exercise on page 107) that shone a spotlight on my struggle. I might have been running an $8,000,000 a year organization but when it came to free will I was acting more like an unempowered eight-year-old.

While it may seem simple, getting myself to own my own choices took a long, long time. Like all significant changes, I made small bits of headway, then almost immediately slid back. Fortunately, I'm fairly determined. I was intent on taking back my freedom to choose. Finally, about three years later, I was at least acting of my own volition much more often than not. It was worth the work—understanding how much power I had over my life and my way in the world changed everything for me. Choosing choice improved my energy and my enjoyment and made it infinitely easier for me to give more effectively and more freely to others. It's like Jimi Hendrix wrote in his song "Freedom," some forty years ago.

Freedom, give it to me
That's what I want now
Freedom, that's what I need now
Freedom to live
Freedom, so I can give

In hindsight, my move to mindful free choice was all about what my friend Daphne called, from her deathbed, "owning my life." Being mindful of what I was opting (or not opting) to do, and recognizing that I was making my own choices and that other people were free to make theirs (even when I didn't like what they were deciding) changed the way I relate to almost everyone, and everything, around me. It shifted my energy enormously. As the late Illinois-born anarchist David Thoreau Wieck said, "When we say, people can become free only by will, only by acts of freedom, we are not juggling words. We mean that freedom is not merely the absence of restrictions—it is responsibility, choice, and the free assumption of social obligations."

Who, you wonder, would argue against "responsibility, choice, and free assumption of responsibility?" The answer is hardly anyone. But like many others, for the first thirty or so years of my life, though I would freely advocate for choice, I regularly failed to make my own choices. I couldn't grasp what it meant to truly, internally, spiritually, and intellectually *own* the decisions I was making. I'm not talking about big strategic issues—I was fine with those. This was about the small stuff—going to meetings, attending social events, saying no to an invitation I didn't want to accept, claiming time for solitude when social strictures push me in the other direction. It was about learning to stop letting social norms and group pressures dominate my life rather than freely choosing to go my own way and do what was right for me. And when I did do what others asked, understanding that they weren't "making me," but rather that I was making a free choice to honor their request.

I'm pretty sure that a whole lot of men and women I've met were living in much the same way I was. We would never say, nor even believe, that we weren't living freely. After all, on the surface, we have the luxury of living in a free country where we get the chance to vote, to voice our concerns, and to try to make the life we want for ourselves.

Choosing choice is not about waiting for something others will offer us. In fact, no one else even has to do a thing to make what I'm advocating for a reality. While social and psychological pressures abound, the final choice is still all ours, and only ours, to make. It's about opting, internally, quietly, almost covertly, *to own our choices.* While almost no one around you may notice the shift, it may be one of the biggest moves you ever make. If you make it, as Robert Greenleaf, who wrote *Servant Leadership*, says, "You will have a better chance of helping maintain a society in which external freedom is a right if you feel free—on the inside. The search will make you free."

This internal freedom may seem elusive, but I think it's essential. To wit, I've chosen to stay up late a lot while working on this essay. Although I was tired and could happily have gone to bed before it was "done," I made my own call to keep typing. I owned the choice, I owned the consequences. The achievement, the excitement, *and* the exhaustion that went with it were all mine. I work hard to apply that same mindset (about choice, not necessarily about staying up late) to everything I do. Believe me, it wasn't always that way. I used to feel like I was being forced to do, well, whatever it was I was doing. Those days are over. Today, whatever it is I do, I do because I decided to do it. Knowing that *I* made all those decisions has made my spirit lighter, lifted my energy higher, and made my life more fun. Choosing choice has changed my life.

Embracing the Challenge—Three Years on the Freedom Trail

Free choice, mind you, does not mean choice free from influence; there is always some sense of outside pressure to perform. But I've realized that, although others want me to do certain things, at the end of the day, no one can force me into anything. Others give me choices or ask things of me, as they are always free to do. What happens from there is up to me. Sure there's pressure, even intimidation or anger at times, but the choices I make remain my own. When I'm feeling tired or frustrated, for example, when I'm trying to finish an essay, I remind myself quickly that I don't have to do any of this. I could leave the book unfinished, I could ignore the promise I've made about getting it to print; heck, I could blow off the whole thing and go hang out at the beach. Consequences, of course, abound, but the choices are still all mine to make.

Given how much the mindset of freedom lies at the foundation of our society, it's amazing to me how foreign free choice can feel in the contemporary American workplace. Anarchist author and poet Paul Goodman suggests, "Perhaps the neglect of occupational liberty has been inevitable." I'm not sure that it was inevitable, but I do love the term, and I believe Goodman is correct—"occupational liberty" is not a part of everyday American existence (or, for that matter, of existence anywhere). Goodman's phrase makes me think about each of us, our spirits, or souls, or whatever you want to call them, as "occupied" territory. Although we were "there" first, we've turned much of our daily lives over to an "occupying power" that seems to tell us all day what we can and cannot, or "should not," do.

This essay is about gently removing that occupier from our heads and getting back to owning our own lives. I'm not talking about politics, the Bill of Rights, or revolution in the Middle East—I'm focusing inward, on the way we think, the way we process whatever it is we do with our days and our decisions. *The choice issue that I'm interested in here is all internal*—things that happen quietly, behind the closed doors of our minds.

As I've said, this is all stuff I've personally experienced, struggled with mightily, and, eventually, benefited from in big ways over the last twenty years. It's not, of course, as if anyone was threatening violent action if I failed to do things I was begrudgingly doing. I wasn't afraid for my life, but I was clearly letting others lead me where I didn't want to go, and then being mad at them for "making me go there." I was dragging my mental feet on a goodly portion of what I was doing. Sure, I showed up where I was "supposed to" show up, but mostly I did it because I was "supposed to." Which meant that a majority of my emotional, and probably intellectual, energy as well was left lagging, probably somewhere back in the suburbs. As 19th century English anarchist Edward Carpenter wrote so powerfully, "To pass through one's mortal days . . . like a slave under continual compulsion from others, is not to live; it is only to exist."

Real Change Takes Time

I will come back to this theme more than once as we move through the book. Because it's so important, it can't hurt to repeat the point. When I say it took three years to change the way I handled free choice, I'm not exaggerating the timeline. My effort to own my choices was made very mindfully, but it was painful, and it seemed absurdly hard to make it happen. With focus and practice and stubborn persistence (all internal ventures—no one but me even really knew I was working on it), I did get there. While it may seem a long time to make a seemingly simple change, knowing what I know now, I'd argue that to make any kind of meaningful personal change, a change that really sticks and has a significant impact in our lives, generally takes two to three years. For more on the subject, see Secret #36.

Freer Choice + More Fun = Better Everything

Being clear that everything I do is my own choice has radically increased my energy, significantly lowered my stress, and greatly raised my fun level. And I'm confident that my change has, in turn, helped take our organization to a higher level of effectiveness as well. Add to that the fact that we're teaching this mindful choice approach to everyone here, and you can start to see how big the impact of this activity—invisible to the casual observer— actually is. If you're up for some inexpensive but highly effective improvement activities, this is an excellent place to start. There are no additional budgets to balance, no tax credits you have to count on, no forms you have to fill out, no others to cajole into cooperating—it's all internal and it's all free for the choosing.

Learning to Choose Choice

Though people often mouth the words, it's my belief that "free choice" is not as present as many might think. I'll posit further that if we were to make it so, the workplace, the country, and most everyone in it would likely live better and far more peaceably. You don't need to be anarchistic in your outlook to make the move to free choice and to make that move count. The reality is that the lack of choice is endemic and universal—there's no political position that's prone to it, nor is it related to age, background, ethnicity, or any other category that I can suss out.

This ever-present, if generally unacknowledged, sense of compulsion manifests itself in most of our everyday language, but it's so subtle, so much the norm, that I think hardly anyone even notices it. Take ten minutes at the next meeting you go to and count how many times someone sitting at the table says "I have to," "I can't," or "I should." On occasion I've heard very successful people say things like, "I'm a slave to my schedule." There's a lot of power floating around those conversations, but when we're using language like that, I can tell you from personal experience, the power is noticeably not inside of us. As Emma Goldman writes, "No formulaic change in social conditions [is] a guarantee against subjugation to one's inner tyrants."

Though it may seem like it ought to be a no-brainer, the free choice mindset is oddly alien to the way most of us are raised and certainly to the way most workplaces work. Making the approach of anarcho-capitalism—or really, any interaction in life—successful requires something of a bloodless coup inside our brains. Although so much political rhetoric asserts the value of freedom, strangely, most of the (corporate) world is used to operating as if free will is a concept that is somehow left at home when one heads into work. In essence, we want to "take back the right" to make—and own—our own decisions, which we somehow seem to have handed off to others. In USDA grading, "prime" and "choice" are two different, mutually exclusive categories of meat quality. But in organizational behavior, they're very much intertwined—we're going to have a hard time producing the former without first opting into the latter. Greatness will rarely emerge without freedom. As Julia Cameron writes in her excellent work on creativity, "Art requires us to empower ourselves with choice."

Freely Choosing to Collaborate

None of this focus on free choice precludes collaboration, cooperation, or a high level of interactivity. Collaboration, to my sense of it, is anything but compliance. It must, to work well, be freely chosen. As anarchist George Barrett wrote, "To get the full meaning out of life we must co-operate, and to co-operate we must make agreements with our fellowmen. But to suppose that such agreements mean a limitation of freedom is surely an absurdity; on the contrary, they are the exercise of our freedom." If you want a freethinking organization, you have to think freely. When leaders or followers act as if they're being forced into doing what they do, the organization will always suffer. In essence, we are the organization we work in. In the words of Buenaventura Durutti, "I believe, as I always have, in freedom. The freedom which rests on the sense of responsibility. I consider discipline indispensable, but it must be inner discipline, motivated by a common purpose and a strong feeling of comradeship."

Revolution in My Mind

While all this is really quite radical, I'm not talking about overturning the existing social order or turning the cheese counter into a re-creation of the American Revolution. But it is a big change, especially in the workplace. Bosses generally operate with the belief that they can order employees around; while we advocate free choice for the voting booth and for their own free time, at work people are expected to basically do what they've been told. I don't want to get too political about this—that's not my point. Whom we choose to vote for, to me, seems completely unrelated to whether we choose to respect the reality that everything works better when we encourage others around us to take ownership of their own conscious and considered decisions. As Gustav Landauer wrote a hundred years or so ago, "There can be only one monarch: the inner being of each individual. If our situation is to improve, it is this monarch who must claim his rule and point us in the right direction."

That doesn't mean everyone should do whatever they might want, whenever they want to. I'm not talking about chaos—just considered and conscious choice. Free choice definitely doesn't mean some sort of mass freak-out; we have lots of systems here at Zingerman's, and plenty of processes that we've all *chosen* to be accountable to, and that we can all work to start changing, *if we so choose.* With that bit of clarification in hand, I'll say straightforwardly that, in our world at least, our work is almost never (crises excepted) about giving orders. The idea is to lay out expectations in advance, explain "why" they exist, be clear about consequences before they come due, engage in dialogue before decisions are made, and teach everyone how to initiate changes they believe are for the better.

We, of course, still want our work to get done well, and leaders here do lead; it's just that we understand that those who follow do so by choice, not because they're forced, and the truth is that most anyone can step up to lead when they need or want to. Is it easy? No, but great things rarely are. Speaking of which, please take note that free choice is definitely a two-way street. While few frontliners anywhere like being lorded over, most will still sit back and wait for those in charge to give orders before they take action anyway. The average American employee—this is my opinion only—acts as if they are being compelled to do everything, from going to work, to going home, to living the Golden Rule, to giving good service. The worst thing is that few folks even realize it.

This isn't just a personal problem. People who feel (and act as if) they're being compelled (even if they're not) create huge problems in an organization —more often than not, they come at things from a place of anger, feeling like helpless victims in a setting in which they have no say. This mindset of being "made to do things" is a subtle but significant poison that steadily weakens any organization's effectiveness. Every modern business book you buy will tell you the same thing. So too did most of the anarchists. Here's Alexander Berkman: "And as you are invaded and violated, so you subconsciously revenge yourself by invading and violating others over whom you have authority or can exercise compulsion, physical or moral. In this way all life has become a crazy quilt of authority, domination and submission, of command and obedience of coercion and subjection, of rulers and ruled, of violence and force in a thousand and one forms." Berkman's book came out a hundred or so years ago, but it sure sounds like a sad portrait of 21st century corporate life to me.

Opt In, or Move Out

The good news is that it doesn't have to be that way. Our approach here asks that we all make and encourage mindful decisions all day long. Which is why:

a. **On an internal level**, most humans will feel freer and more fulfilled if they actively decide to decide, to own that all day long, we're each *actively*—if not always mindfully—making lots of choices. We decide whether we're going to move quickly or slowly, to be in a good mood or a bad one, to smile or be sullen, to stop and pick up trash on the street or simply walk past it as we've done two thousand times before. A huge part of our training work here at Zingerman's is then, in essence, to help everyone who comes to work with us clue in to this level of consciousness. When we're all making mindful decisions about our state of being, tensions tend to drop, energy increases, and everything just works better. Speaking personally, life became a whole lot more rewarding and far less stressful after I set myself free and realized everything I did started with a decision I had made freely.

b. **On an external level**, we need to encourage others—especially those who aren't accustomed to working this way—to choose choice as well, to help them make conscious decisions about what they're doing or not doing. In part, this means we need to respect that others will make choices we won't particularly like, encourage people to be themselves, and tell them to speak up for what they believe. Clearly, this is far easier said than done. Being a hard-ass is a hard habit to break; the traditional work world is all based on the belief that we're paying these people, so of course they're going to do what we tell them to. The idea of letting staff say no in a constructive manner—and not be immediately stomped on for doing it—is not, I know, the way it works in most businesses. But we'd be better off to make it the norm—while performance may be poor, discussions may be difficult, and employment may ultimately end anyway, dialogue, respect, and fair treatment are essential, even if someone opts not to do what we would have liked them to.[5] After a lifetime of being the "boss," this approach is always easier to adopt intellectually than it is to implement. I know from experience. Wait until the first employee politely tells you to take a hike. But I believe that it's imperative, from the bottom of my very hard-working heart, if we're going to grow to become the kind of caring, creative company we aspire to build.

When each of us owns our choices for ourselves, there's not much room left for victims to populate the team picture. If someone opts not to pursue positive outcomes—even after being regularly encouraged, respected, and rewarded for going after what they believe to be right—it's clear that they've made their own choices. Pretty much everyone in the organization gets that, and, honestly, the group here won't put up with a "victim" mentality for long. If anyone regularly chooses a negative approach, it's usually only a matter of time before they end up leaving, more often than not by their own (free) choice.

In my ideal, we all own our actions, energy, and emotions. Which means that if we choose to go along with something we don't really like because it's awkward to address it, then we need to remember that it was *our choice*, not someone else's directive, to stay silent. It will likely always be awkward to raise awkward issues, no matter what anyone does to make it easy—that's why they're called "awkward." We just have to take a deep breath and raise them regardless. If anyone's waiting for the bosses to fix things or make them feel better, it's gonna be a long wait. The organization's obligation is to make it reasonably safe for everyone to speak up. Whether they do or not is up to them.

Partying Down and Opting Out!

To illustrate how much mindful free choice matters, I'll share a personal story that helped me shift my own energy significantly. I'm an introvert and I'm shy. People who don't know me well have a hard time believing it, but I really don't enjoy group social activities. (If I've declined an offer you've made, now you know why.) One-on-one conversations are great, but faced with a socially active room full of people, I usually move quickly to the kitchen where I can talk to whoever's cooking or catering the event, and then I count the hours—minutes, actually—until I can leave.

Still, before I came to realize how much I needed to free my mind from the feeling of being forced, I'd usually, grudgingly, go along. I felt like I "should" be there and it was hard for me to say no even when that's what I really wanted to say. Giving in over and over again is exhausting. In hindsight, Julia Cameron's statement, "Afraid to appear selfish, we lose our self," hits close to home. If someone asked what I was doing for the evening of the event, my answer was always something like, "I have to go to so-and-so's house." Once I arrived, I stayed quietly, but stubbornly, frustrated that I'd basically been "forced" to go. After the gathering was over, I'd continue to ruminate on how much time I'd wasted and how annoying it had been. You can imagine how much fun all that was.

All this changed after my, shall we say, internal revolution. First, I pretty much just stopped going to parties. I realized that there was really no reason I needed to go to 90 percent of them, and that I would just deal with whatever fallout I might face from others—personally or professionally—for not going. Talk about a better use of time! I would spend the extra three hours or so doing things I was excited to do. Having learned to exercise my already existing, but previously underused, ability to say no to social activities, during the other 10 percent of the time when I'd freed myself up to make the mindful decision to attend, I stopped saying "I have to go," and switched to the simple, but far more affirmative, "I'm going." Because my mindset now is one of having made a conscious choice to go, I make the most of every minute that I'm there. If I start sliding back down into depression about having wasted time or feeling forced to go, I remind myself, respectfully, that the decision to attend was all mine and was freely made. Within minutes, I'm right back to feeling calm and centered again.

To move this conversation closer to home, most of the work world could effectively plug in "meetings" where I've written "parties." Ever gone to one grudgingly? I know I did. Then, in the years after my little mental emancipation, I simply started to mindfully decide that I was going to show up—physically, intellectually, and emotionally—at every meeting that I went to. If I decide not to go, then I don't go. But I almost always opt to attend—the difference is that I now actively decide to be there. And rather than just wait for the session to end without incident, I now make the most out of the meeting that I freely chose to be a part of.

This simple shift of mental emphasis has made a significant difference in pretty much *everything* I do. The implications are enormous. Consider how many times you or others in your organization make the statement, "I have to go to work now." And then think about what it means when people's internal energy about their job involves feeling obligated to do it, rather than freely choosing to engage in it. I will guarantee you—it makes a difference when people are opting to be at work (or in class or at the family dinner table), not just showing up so that they can stay out of trouble. Do the math—multiply how many meetings you have a month by how many men and women work in your business (subtracting a couple who might have already chosen choice), and you can calculate the negative cost the feeling of being forced has on the organization. I don't know about you, but for me at least, freedom is a far happier inner landscape to live in and a much more productive one at that.

Owning Up to Freely Chosen Consequences

"Free choice," as I've said earlier, doesn't in the least mean "choice free from influence" or "free of consequence." Both are fine fantasies, but unless you live alone on an otherwise uninhabited island, there's just no such thing. Every decision we make will have ramifications, and there are always reasons why others won't like what we do. In the context of building a great organization, this means that we need to find effective, positive, and uplifting ways to work together, even when we don't agree with each other. Living and leading with free choice means that we all need to learn to communicate using a positive, adult-to-adult approach, through which we encourage mindful choice-making, openness, collaboration, and conscious commitment. It's an approach that teaches everyone in the organization to negotiate as peers, *not* like the stereotypical settings in which "superiors" manage "subordinates," or "subordinates" succumb to CEOs. (For more on this, see Secret #24 on the subject of Stewardship in *Part 2*.) It's a construct in which no one can really compel anyone else to do anything, while building a culture at the core of which are free will and creative freethinking.

It's not an overnight achievement, but the more we work at it, the better we'll get. Emma Goldman put down the following thoughts about women gaining freedom in the early part of the 20th century, but I think they apply to each of us as individuals, regardless of gender or the era in which we exist: "True emancipation begins neither at the polls nor in courts. It begins in a woman's soul. History tells us that every oppressed class gained true liberation from its masters through its own efforts. It is necessary that woman learn that lesson, that she realize that her freedom will reach as far as her power to achieve her freedom reaches. It is, therefore, far more important for her to begin with her inner regeneration." Anarchist George Benello said "Freedom, to be understood, must be lived." Or, as Mohammed Bamyeh, a modern day anarchist professor from Pittsburgh, put it: "Freedom is the exercise of freedom."

This last seemingly small statement has big implications. A while back I was listening to a friend who was frustrated with his colleagues. He felt pressured to follow their lead but wanted, understandably, to go his own way. (Who doesn't?) "I just want the ability to make my own choices," he announced angrily to half a dozen of us to whom he was telling the story. People in the group started to react to various parts of what he'd said, but I focused on this last statement of his. I'm sure my eyebrows were arching, as they're wont to do when I've heard a thing I can't quite believe. "Wait. Did you say that you want the ability to make your own choices?'" I asked. "Exactly!" he answered effusively, as if happy that someone had heard his frustrations. His sense of relief lasted only a few seconds. "But you know you already have that ability, right?" I said slowly. I felt bad for pointing out the obvious, but what he was saying was so far off our base that it seemed pretty imperative. I didn't want to embarrass him; I just hoped to help. He looked at me like I was a little crazy, but I decided to push the point. "You were born with the ability to make your own choices. We all are." He seemed a bit bothered, but I continued apace. "Other people may not respond well or agree with whatever it is you do. But they can never take away your ability to decide."

A Little Bit of Language Goes a Long Way

The words we choose every day say a lot about how we're thinking and viewing the world. Check out the work of world-famous linguist Edward Sapir, who wrote early in the 20th century, "The interdependence of thought and speech makes it clear that languages are not so much a means of expressing truth that has already been established, as a means of discovering truth that was previously unknown. Their diversity is a diversity not of sounds and signs but of ways of looking at the world."

The chart on the next page illustrates Sapir's point. The phrases on the left are, I believe, so embedded in everyday language and mindset that hardly anyone even notices they're using them. Apply Dr. Sapir's insight, and it's clear that they are the language of the unempowered. Using them, things might get done but only grudgingly. Energy is low, guilt is high. The right-hand phrases seem similar, but to follow Dr. Sapir, they represent a radically different "way of looking at the world." They're all about free choice, free will, and conscious commitment. Though the phrases might be easily interchanged in everyday conversation, they represent two totally different ways of living. The seemingly inconsequential, easily overlooked words in the left-hand column took me a good three years to essentially eliminate from my language, both what I hear in my head and what comes out of my mouth. Never underestimate the power of language or of the people who use it.

Try out the words in the right-hand column for a day and see what it feels like—there's not much to lose by opting in on this one. See how long you can go without using any of the phrases on the left.

The words I used to say	What I say now
"I have to"	"I'm going to," "I will"
"I should"	"I'm going to," "I'm thinking about . . ."
"I can't"	"I'm not going to," "I hear you that this is important, but given my other obligations right now I'm going to turn down the offer"
"I need to"	"I want to," "I'm going to"

notes from the back dock

Leo Chen, Line Cook, Zingerman's Roadhouse

I started my culinary journey with Zingerman's Roadhouse four months ago. For the past eight years I had been working in the medical field. During those years I was constantly searching for my purpose, but was never satisfied. I joined countless hospital committees, applied to nursing programs and *even* took pre-med classes. At the end of each day I was certain about one thing, I loved to cook. I would spend my days off reading cookbooks, learning about ingredients and preparing delicious dinners to enjoy with my wife. I started a recipe and restaurant review blog too.

My wife is a major proponent of this career change. Her enthusiasm and support gave me the push I needed. I am faith-based and felt led to the culinary industry. My vision is to work towards becoming a head chef and eventually opening my own restaurant. Taking a look back on the past three months, I couldn't have found a better place to start my culinary career. My involvement in the kitchen committee challenges me to take ownership of my work. I am given the privilege to share my thoughts and ideas on how to improve our work. I am currently working on a collaborative project with the chefs on lowering food cost expenses. This project, like all the other opportunities within Zingerman's, is available to anyone. The only requirement is commitment and then you can expect to get as much support as you need from Ari, Paul, and anyone else that works in the ZCoB!

maia and eLi having fun at the deLi

Mindfulness Matters

Staying In Balance Is Better Business

Self-management, it turns out, sometimes starts in strange places. This is the story of how a serious pain in the ass helped me gain a radically better perspective on my life. Mindfulness, like everything else in this book, has helped me enormously to make both my life and my management richer and more rewarding. Practicing it is, of course, a piece of effective self-management. But I've found it to be such an important one that I decided to devote an entire Secret to sharing my sense of it.

Best I can tell from a quick look, there is no formal, widely accepted, American definition of mindfulness. The term seems to be the English translation of the ancient word *sati*, which, in the Pali language of North India implies awareness, attention, and remembering. As I understand it, it refers to what goes on in the brain before we actually explain anything to ourselves or to others in conscious form. Or, you might say, it's a barely noticeable moment where we take in what we've just absorbed in order to then communicate it to others.

I feel more than a little awkward writing about all this. To put my creative cards on the table, I've never done a day of formal study of anything even remotely related to this work—no Buddhism, no meditation, no yoga, no travel to Tibet. But, in reflecting, it struck me that that might actually be a good thing. Granted, I have no credentials, no accreditation, nor any certificate to cite on my resume. But at the same time, there's a positive piece to my lack of formal training. I figure if I—a Midwestern male who makes a living running a moderately sized specialty food business—can benefit from making the effort to become significantly more mindful, so too can anyone else who's interested in improving their leadership and/or life skills.

In his book *Mindfulness in Plain English*, Bhante Gunaratana writes, "Mindfulness could be described in completely different terms than will be used here and each description could still be correct." This strikes me as a perfect anarchist concept: imagine an approach to life that matters greatly to all who embrace it, but where each of us can form our own essentially unique definition. Mindfulness, after all, is not a government-mandated mindset, just a way of moving sustainably and effectively through the world. Sharon Begley explains in her book *Train Your Mind, Change Your Brain*, "Mindfulness, or mindful awareness, is the practice of observing one's inner experiences in a way that is fully aware but non-judgmental. You stand outside your own mind, observing the spontaneous thoughts and feelings that the brain throws up, observing all this as if it were happening to someone else."

Jon Kabat-Zinn says in *Mindfulness for Beginners*, "Mindfulness is awareness, cultivated by paying attention in a sustained and particular way: on purpose, in the present moment, and non-judgmentally." To me, mindfulness is
a way to make vocation—the "falling in love and it works out" approach that
Paul Goodman wrote about—a reality. As Kabat-Zinn observes, "Ultimately I
see mindfulness as a love affair—with life, with reality and imagination, with
the beauty of your own being, with your heart and body and mind, and with
the world. If that sounds like a lot to take in, it is." Having worked at it, ever
imperfectly, for many years now, I'd say it's well worth the effort.

A Moment of Mindfulness

I doubt the way I do it here is how they teach it when you study mindfulness in
more professional settings, but this down-to-earth, in-the-moment approach
works pretty well for me. Practice doesn't really make perfect, but it does help
me make progress. With mindfulness, as with most everything else in life, the
more one a) works at it and b) is committed to getting to greatness, the better one is likely to get. Like so much else in this book, making the effort costs
nothing—the only investment needed is a few minutes of your time, a good
bit of emotional energy, and intellectual awareness. Mindfulness matters. To
quote Robert Greenleaf again: "Awareness has its risks, but it makes life more
interesting; certainly it strengthens one's effectiveness as a leader."

Rather than racing ahead full speed though, I'd like to take a more, well,
mindful approach to the subject. I usually start with a deep breath. Or two or
three. This helps me disengage my mind from everything else that's distracting
me from what's really going on. Often I do this bit of practice while journaling,
but today I'm doing it live, mid-"Secret," writing down right now how I feel,
what I hear, what I think, what I smell, and what I see, all the while working
on this essay. I track my emotions and listen to what's going on in my mind. I
make note of the feelings in my body: my face, fingertips, feet, etc. I'm not as
perfectly disciplined about it as a fighter pilot would be while running through
his before-takeoff checklist, but even a modicum of attentiveness will likely
put you far ahead of most people and give you a good sense of what's possible.

When I'm at work, mindfulness might mean paying close to attention to
all that surrounds me. It could be a kid who's playing near the table where I
sit in the back corner of the Deli's dining room. Today it's Eli, a two-year-old
(actually two-and-a-half, his six-year-old sister Maia reminded me) who's basically grown up coming to Zingerman's. It makes me smile that when he sees
me from the other side of the store, he smiles big and exclaims loudly, lisping

slightly, as he runs through the Deli shouting, "Awwee's heah!" I try to take in as much as I can. His smile and the wide-eyed way he walks towards me. The way he pauses when he gets near me to take in what I'm doing. His fascination with the old-school phone receiver (it plugs into my cell phone) I have in my shoulder bag, which makes me realize that, if you're a kid of Eli's era, a phone is a flat, rectangular piece of plastic and metal, not a long, handle-like thing with rounded knobs on either end.

"What's in it?" he asks me. A great question, one that only a kid would ask. It's an excellent example of what a Zen Buddhist would call "beginner's mind." In Eli's case, it's real—he knows nothing of late 20th century telephones. For me, it takes more work. It's the first time, I realize, that anyone's ever asked what's "in" a phone before. "Voices" is what comes to mind, so that's what I say. He seems satisfied, so I am too. I start to go back to work but keep watching him eat his breakfast. I take in his long eyelashes and ruddy cheeks, the smile on his face as he savors his toasted bagel and handmade cream cheese. The way Maia plays with him and makes him laugh while she hugs him. The way he keeps saying "I don't know" to whatever anyone asks. And the way I start to laugh silently with my eyes every time he says it.

I listen closely to customer conversations, the tone in their voices, the words they use, the content of their talk. I watch the relish (or lack thereof) with which they eat. I note which foods go first, which go fast, which they finish, and which are left uneaten. I listen to staff members—what they're talking about, the energy behind it, what they're wearing, how they interact with each other and with customers. I note what they notice and what they walk right by as if it weren't there. I watch their pace—not to get them in trouble or give them grief but because that's what mindfulness is about. Tuning into the tiny details.

I look inward as well. I test my tiredness, take in the touch of the computer keys on my fingers and the feel of the sun through the window on a wonderfully warm spring day. I monitor my mood and my mind to see where I'm at, how I'm feeling, what's fun and what's frustrating. In the moment, I'm a little anxious about a new staffer, about whom I've just gotten some less-than-glowing reports. I'm also thinking ahead to some out-of-town training I'll be leading soon. I'm excited about a long-awaited, newly arrived Sicilian olive oil, and tired from staying up later than I probably should have in order to catch up on some emails. I sit with some sadness, too, because I just found out yesterday that in six weeks or so Maia and Eli, after a lifetime at Zingerman's, plan to move (with their parents) to Seattle.[6]

Because food is so much a part of my existence, I pay special attention to it all day long. In meetings, when I'm sitting still and when I'm walking around, I'm constantly tasting and tracking my taste buds. The act of tasting professionally for so many years might have given me some help when it came to learning to be mindful. Awareness of detail is what it's really all about. Writing so regularly over the years has also, I'm sure, helped me to be more mindful—describing what I experience with food and drink has given me a great deal of practice. In fact, I have a whole essay on the subject of "Mindful Eating" in *Zingerman's Guide to Good Eating.*

Today I pay attention to the delicious Darjeeling tea I'm drinking—I love its green-leaning, beautifully amberish, tannic, intentionally out-of-balance flavor. And the dark, almost bittersweet, crust of the well-baked loaf of Roadhouse bread (my favorite) that I've got on the table. And, by contrast, the light flakiness of the dough on our apricot-cheese—I almost said "strudel," but then I mindfully caught myself. We're calling it "retes" ("ray-tesh"), the Hungarian word (since ours is from the Hungarian tradition—see page 369 for more on what's happening with Hungarian baked goods here at Zingerman's). As I eat it, I mark the contrasts, the crisp flaky crust wrapped around the soft, subtle, sumptuous blend of cream cheese and jam inside. The sweet floral notes of the apricot and the lovely milkiness of the handmade cream cheese from the Creamery, the same one that Eli was eating on his bagel. Then there's a bit of that really beautiful, peppery olive oil that just arrived from Sicily. And the well-balanced, sensual, cinnamony swirl of the dark chocolate we just brought over from Ben Tre province in Vietnam, the gorgeous green of the paper label it's wrapped in, the way its flavor sits superbly on my tongue for ten or fifteen minutes after I taste.[7]

None of this nuance may, in itself, be particularly notable. Experiencing life in this way, sort of in slow motion, may seem a waste of time when there's "real" work to be done. But that, I suppose, is a big part of the point—to take in the tiny things that are otherwise off the radar, things that most people miss, things that then enrich my life, that make up the vast majority of my existence. I will argue that the willingness to work at taking note of it all—both the internal and the external activity—is a big part of what makes a great leader effective. The quality of our decisions, after all, is decidedly driven by the quality of the information we have at hand. We aren't likely to make good choices when we're basing them on inaccurate or radically incomplete information. The more mindful I am, the more richly textured the material I have to work with, the more likely I am to make better decisions.

Which is why what might easily be dismissed by most people as a dull day of "having" to work on a weekend was for me filled with joyous little jewels—Eli's exclamation, his enthusiastic mispronunciation of my name, Maia's laugh, the tea, the olive oil, the sadness, the sun through the window. While the big events like James Beard awards, the good press, nice sales numbers, etc. are satisfying, it's the little things that make my day. I've realized over the years that those little things are pretty much all there is. When it comes down to it, despite the heft of the headlines that lead us to believe otherwise, the vast majority of what goes on around us is just that—small, seemingly insignificant, primarily peripheral stuff. Add it all up, along with a big event here and there, and you have your life. You now have a few minutes of mine on this slowish Sunday morning.

Moving Mindfully Through the Day

Whether we're mindful about it or not, life does go on apace. Like almost everyone else, I have work to do. The world doesn't stop while I sit at the back corner table and take careful notes all day like a culinarily and culturally focused court reporter. Luckily, the world and my work to take note of it can now pretty easily coexist. It wasn't always that way, though. My early efforts at mindfulness were awkward, a minor if definite disruption in my day—I really had to stop everything then to notice what was happening. The trick I've learned over time, I think, is to track as much as I can while continuing to do everything else I do at the same time. Taking a few minutes every morning for active mindfulness practice is essential, as it would be in developing any other skill. In this case, practice will never make perfect—none of us ever comes close to truly mastering mindfulness. But if we go after it with a consistent, focused practice, it's highly likely that over a long period of time we can get pretty good at it. You don't, after all, have to be born a Maharishi or achieve Zen master status for mindfulness to make a positive difference. Anyone who aspires to can learn it and grow with it.

Which is a good thing because I don't think that mindfulness is a skill we get much help developing when we're young, at least not where I grew up. While everyone is born creative, my gut feeling is that mindfulness is something different; by definition, we have to mindfully work at! To use a bit of (Zingerman's) training talk, I don't think you can be "unconsciously competent" about mindfulness. We can learn it and practice and get good at it, but I don't think it comes naturally, nor can we ever do it totally on autopilot. To the contrary, if we're not mindfully working at it, we lose it. Before we know it, customers, chaos, kids, cramming for exams, or watching ESPN rush in to fill the mental space.

But developing attentiveness to internal and external details is worth the work it takes. As Daniel Goleman says, "Emotional life is richer for those who notice more." This increase in effort actually helps me stay centered and slow myself down; more mental work, in this case, serves to reduce my stress level and makes for a greater general sense of calm. It's pleasantly paradoxical—the more effort we put into paying attention, the less effort we expend unnecessarily missing things, making hasty and unsound decisions, and doing all the work to make up for our shortfalls.

It would make sense that, as Emma Goldman argues, "*Methods and means cannot be separated from the ultimate aim.* The means employed become, through individual habit and social practice, part and parcel of the final purpose; they influence it, modify it, and presently the aims and means become identical." Her angle was an anarchist one, but the essence of it is all Eastern philosophy. Whichever world you approach it from, the message is much the same: if we want to move to a high level of mindfulness, the only way we can do it is to very mindfully work at getting there. And if we want a centered, mindful, attentive organization, *we* have to lead the way.

Mindfulness, I would say, is the multiplier on everything else in this book. The more self-aware we are, the more we're able to maximize the benefits of free choice, vision, creativity, and all the other "Secrets" I've shared in the *Guides to Good Leading.* Isn't it more interesting to take in all the wonderful details during our relatively too short time on the planet? Staying closed off to the world while living our lives is like getting a free trip to the Grand Canyon and then staying in the hotel room watching TV with the window shades shut—the beauty, fascination, fresh air, fun, and blessed nature of the world are all around us, but we're choosing to keep them at a distance. As Sam Keen says in *Inward Bound,* "Pay attention to what is happening. Learn to concentrate. Become a gentle observer, a fair witness, of your inner life and of the world around you. This simple, and yet difficult, prescription will lead you on a journey through the self in which your old limits will be stretched until you can live fully in the wide world of wonder rather than in the claustrophobic prison of the ego."

With all that said, here then is my own definition, relying once again on the inspirational Viktor Frankl. In his book *Man's Search for Meaning,* he writes, "Between stimulus and response, there is a space. In that space lies our freedom and power to choose our response. In our response lies our growth and freedom." To me, mindfulness is about actively moving into and spending as much time as possible—living, breathing, feeling, thinking, and sensing—in that space. *Choosing mindfulness is a conscious move towards self-growth and freedom, better leadership, and a better life.*

How a Pain in the Ass Got Me Paying Attention

Like so much that's good in our lives, the importance of this work became clear to me through an experience of pain. My move to mindfulness started, literally, as a pain in my butt. To be more specific, the problem was my piriformis, a muscle that's deep in what my grandmother used to call my *tuchas*. Although I'd never even heard of it until mine went wacky, I became intimately familiar with the pain and disruption it can cause when I ended up with a bad case of what physical therapists refer to as "piriformis syndrome." It's akin to very intense back spasms, but in this case, they're in your butt. I'm sure my piriformis had informally acted out at some earlier time; over all the years I've been running, I've experienced an array of muscle strains, aches, and low-level pains. But what happened this time was much more serious; one day I got out of the shower and I discovered the pain had gotten so bad I could barely walk, let alone run.

I take my running pretty seriously, though not in a competitive, race-running, record-setting way. I'm the opposite of the people who win marathons. I'm an anarchist, an introvert, an afternoon runner, and my pace is pretty slow. I run on my own, 99.8 percent of the time, usually in midafternoon. It's a great way to break up my day and clear my brain. I particularly like running in the sun, all the more so when it's really hot out—it helps me sweat out all the CEO stress I take on all day. Running, for me, is the opposite of an organized or competitive activity; it's free form, mostly about resetting my energy and keeping my blood and my brain flowing. I put on running shoes, leave the house, move my legs for thirty to sixty minutes, and then come back calmer and emotionally refreshed.

Running has been a near-daily event for me for well over twenty years now. I rarely miss more than a few days a year. I run when I'm traveling, I run in the snow, I run in the heat, I run when I'm tired. Running for me is a relief. When I heard that my mother had died, back in May of 2008, I was out in Albuquerque doing ZingTrain work. I got the call on the sidewalk in front of my hotel, as I was stretching to take off for a run. Stunned, scared, uncertain, standing alone in a city in which I knew no one, I decided to go ahead and run in the sun for an hour. Even though it didn't quell the pain of her loss, and it didn't keep me from crying—my tears must have looked a lot like sweat while I was running—it did give me time to get grounded before I had to go back and face the world.

My piriformis problems started up about six months or so after that strange, somber, soul-strengthening run in New Mexico. Hoping that it would go away with a bit of stretching and some patience, as other muscle strains had, I just kept running. In the past, that had always taken care of things for me; this time, though, it didn't work at all. The pain got worse, not better. One day I didn't think I'd be able to walk the ten yards from my post-run shower to the bedroom. Needless to say, I didn't run the next day, or the next, nor any day after that for nearly six weeks. Lots of good physical therapy finally turned the trick; my muscles (clearly as stubborn as I am), finally relented, and I started to run again. I was happy. At least for the ten days or so that I could do it. Because no sooner had I gotten going than the same problem popped up on the other side—the body, like an organization, often works by redistributing stress; what started on my right side was now wretchedly cramping up my left. The result? No running for *another* four weeks. As you can imagine, I was starting to go out of my mind from the inactivity.

The interesting thing, though, is that as much as I've long known that I liked to run, it was only the *absence* of running that drove home to me just how much I count on its calming influence to maintain my emotional balance. Staying stationary was more than just an inconvenience. If you look at it from a straight and narrow time management standpoint, it should have helped—it freed up an hour or two every day! But in fact, my piriformis problem made me *less* productive, not more. It threw me completely out of whack. I was definitely not myself, or at least not myself in the way I'd come to know myself over the two decades or so that I'd been running so regularly. I felt perpetually out of balance, off kilter, seriously uncentered. For the first time in my life, I was cold all the time. Even in midwinter I usually wear t-shirts every day, but the year the piriformis put me out of commission, I was pulling old sweaters out of storage and layering up to keep myself from shivering. My everyday energy level, both physical and emotional, dropped drastically. The pain was coming from my butt, but it was manifesting itself in my brain.

All of this is a long way to say that I was unwittingly, unwillingly, and unpleasantly jolted into a newer, noticeably heightened sense of awareness while sitting around wishing I could go out and get my legs moving. It became a big struggle just to catch my mental breath. It wasn't that I really decided to work that hard at mindfulness; it just emerged out of my efforts to deal with loss, in this case, the loss of a routine that I didn't fully appreciate until I couldn't do it. Shaken from the stability of my regular grounding routine, I started to pay a lot more attention to what was going on inside and around me. Absence made my heart—and my head—grow ever more mindful.

Serendipitous Stretching

It's funny what you find when you start looking. As I began to consider writing about what I was learning, mindfulness began to appear in my life at every turn. I was sitting on the couch one day that winter (probably wishing I was out jogging), flipping through a newly arrived issue of the Drucker Foundation's magazine *Leader to Leader*. About halfway through the journal, I stumbled on an article by a guy I'd never heard of, Deepak Sethi, called "Mindful Leadership." It started to raise my awareness about something I'd previously been only peripherally conscious of. And then, less than a week later, I was sitting at that back corner table in the Deli when a long-time customer came by and greeted me with a calm, quiet, smiling hello. All I really knew about the guest was that he liked our sandwiches, he was a nice guy with exceptionally graceful energy about him, and that he appeared to be of Asian origin. It turned out, though, that he wasn't just "any" customer. His name, I learned later, is Gelek Rimpoche. I'll save you the trouble of looking him up by telling you that he's an internationally known Buddhist teacher whose students have included poet Allen Ginsberg and composer Philip Glass. This particular Sunday he'd brought thirty of his disciples to the Deli for lunch to celebrate the successful completion of the annual ten-day retreat he runs here in Ann Arbor on the subject of—you guessed it—mindfulness.

This all speaks to one of the most helpful tips I've taken away from my work with mindfulness—when you start paying attention, you never know what seemingly disparate dots might turn out to be connected. These cool coincidences can act as serendipitous calls to creative action. (This same theme comes up again, in depth, in Secret #39 on Creativity.) In this case, it was piriformis syndrome, immense frustration with not being able to run, an article in an obscure business magazine, and an internationally known Buddhist teacher deciding to come to the Deli for lunch that coalesced into my newly heightened appreciation for just how deeply mindfulness matters. I couldn't run, but I could read the signs. Clearly, I would do well to listen to what the world was telling me.

Making the Move to Mindfulness

Mindfulness, for me then, is about being tuned *in:* to myself, my moods, my mania, my mindset, my surroundings, all five of my senses—and really the sixth supernatural and intuitive one, as well. It's about being aware of as many of the easily missed things around me as I can be. It's about appreciating every small interaction, breathing in and basking in the beauty of the world; it's acknowledging to myself and to others how many great things are going on in our organizations, even if we're working all the while to make everything much better than it already is. I may be at work, but there's still beauty to be found.

While all this may sound fabulous, pulling it off every day is pretty freaking hard to do. It's tough enough to lead well when my mind is where I *want* it to be. But what about when things are going totally awry? In her insightful book *Confidence,* Rosabeth Moss Kanter quotes Connecticut women's basketball coach Geno Auriemma on the subject of leading through those sorts of super stressful situations: "You feel like you're in a car wash," Auriemma says. "Everything's happening around you and you have no idea where to get a handle." I've never coached a basketball game in my life, but I know the feeling he's talking about all too well.

The car wash analogy is just as accurate in business as it is in basketball. It's one thing to say we're going to stay calm under pressure. But it's another to actually pull it off. What happens when the financials don't come in where we forecasted they'd finish? When major customers suddenly send a note to say that they're switching to a new supplier? When a long-time staff member angrily and unexpectedly gives eight days notice that they're leaving? When someone we're close to comes down with a serious illness? Or when we ourselves aren't feeling good in the first place? Any one of those can send you spinning; two or three together can take you down hard. All of them in the same week could turn even the best of us into a wreck.

I know—it's happened to me. Whether in basketball or business, the craziness is coming at you so fast that no matter how much you know you shouldn't, you start to slip. You're reeling and reactive rather than steady and centered. You want to escape, but there's no way out except to move forward *through* the madness. Instead of the cool, professional, thoughtful poise you know you *should* be displaying, panic starts to set in. When it happens, you can feel the fear start up in your body. You can taste the anxiety in your mouth. Despite your best intentions, you start freaking out, forgetting everything you've been taught, taking action when you really need a time out.

If we're not careful, we're completely caught up in the emotional cacophony; before we know what's happened, we've sent the rest of our organization spinning right along with us. If you're playing basketball, and you start to lose your sense of the game, you get faked out of your shoes, you speed up the game when you're supposed to slow it down, you start taking shots way too quickly when it would have been better to pass the ball to a teammate. On the postgame show, it's easy to point out how bad a player's judgment was, but in the moment, heck, he's lucky he hasn't lost hold of his head altogether, or just fled for the locker room when he thought no one was looking. In business, the corollaries are equally unappealing. I shoot my mouth off when I should have kept it shut, make a bad decision under duress when I'd have been smarter to do nothing, send an angry email to an employee when it would have been better to exit the building instead. None of those scenarios is a good one. Add two or three together and I'm headed for big trouble.

Ready or not, the carwash craziness can come at us any time. In the course of writing this essay, I've had weeks in which I was dealing with the death of one of my closest friends; having difficult conversations with a business partner; learning about how hard the worst drought in two decades has been for local farmers; and trying to comfort a dear friend whose father was diagnosed with cancer. It's always something. Being mindful while waiting to see what will happen is better than being obtuse, but it's only half the equation. The minute we let our mindfulness guards down, trouble looms. But that's the point—we're all imperfect. Even the most mindful of managers is still moving back and forth across the border between blindness and reaction on the one side, and balance and positive awareness on the other.

My goal is just to spend a lot more time on the latter side of the line. Mindfulness, for me, is really a means, not an end. What follows is a set of techniques that, diligently practiced, have helped me make mindfulness a part of my everyday existence, all in the interest of living a more rewarding life and being a better leader at the same time. You will, of course, have your own list. I'm pretty sure these practices are a lot less painful than piriformis syndrome. I hope they're helpful in getting you going on a mindful path of your own.

1. BEING MINDFUL OF MYSELF

To the untrained eye, mindfulness may seem like leadership magic. In truth, it's a very hard—if exceptionally rewarding—way to invest our energies, one that gives us more information, a better sense of the world, and a chance to make more creative connections and demonstrate caring and appreciation. Deepak Sethi says, "Self-awareness is perhaps the most critical leadership competency." It's a theme I'm repeating regularly throughout this book: *self-reflection is the base upon which all other leadership work is built.* The leader who's not in touch with themselves is doomed to disaster. Even if our strategies and tactics might be terrifically innovative, our energy, enjoyment of life, and ability to inspire others will surely suffer.

But mindfulness, for me, is not just a 9 to 5 job. I try (ever imperfectly) to gently monitor my moods, reactions, feelings, breathing, energy level, and everything else that's going on inside me pretty much around the clock. The key is that if I do well in that struggle and successfully claim—and then calm—my own unconscious, my leadership in particular and my life in general will both be better. As with so much of what I've written about, mindfulness is a very natural and self-sustaining cycle. The more I monitor, the more effectively I manage myself, the more effectively everything else goes. And, in turn, the more we teach mindfulness to others in the organization, the better they do as well, the better the business does overall, the lower my own stress will be, the better I do, and on and on, happily, we go.

Interestingly, this emphasis on inner consciousness is all over the work of the anarchists. Emma Goldman writes, "Anarchism is the only philosophy which brings to man the consciousness of himself." In Gustav Landauer's words, "This freedom can only come to life in ourselves and must be nurtured in ourselves before it can appear as an external actuality." He writes further, "You could only call those people anarchists who possess the aforementioned ambition naturally; people who have worked so hard on their own transformation that, once they find enough like-minded spirits, they are instantly able to establish an anarchist society. "

Mindfulness allows me the chance to modify what I'm doing and how I'm doing it, to maximize my own effectiveness and that of the organization. If I find myself sliding into negativity, being mindful helps me catch myself before I create a big organizational mess. If my energy and enthusiasm levels are low,

I remind myself how much everyone else here is looking to—and at—me for energetic leadership. It helps me take tough stuff with a grain of salt, slows me down just enough to avoid doing too many dumb things (at least not all on the same day). While the headlines usually go to the big strategic successes (or failures), I'd argue that the behind-the-scenes internal work of self-awareness is frequently a bigger factor in business success.

2. BEING *IN* THE MOMENT

Please don't misread the subheading. I don't mean, "Live only for the moment, past and future be damned." I'm a former history major *and* I also teach and write a lot about creating positive visions of the future. But no matter what I'm doing, I try to connect my awareness of myself with awareness of the people, places, process, and priorities that are all around me at any given moment. Ultimately, that's really all we have. As Annie Dillard writes, "How we spend our days is, of course, how we spend our lives."

Worrying was a way of life in my family growing up. It's a hard habit to break, but worry, I've realized, only adds to my stress level, which, in turn, adds to the stress level of everyone around me. Energy expended on worrying, guilt, second-guessing, or regret really help no one. Staying in the present—not getting caught up in what could have been or what could be—is, quite simply, a significantly more rewarding way to live. Compared with all the worrying I was raised with, mindfulness is downright relaxing. The energy and emotional space I used to use for society's "shoulds" and "coulds" and holding grudges or fears about the future was freed up for thinking and feeling more positive things and, better still, for *taking action* to do something to make what I wanted a reality.

Of course, just because I advise you (and myself) not to sink into stress over things that you can't impact doesn't mean that we won't ever worry. It's a lot easier to *know* that worrying is unproductive than it is to significantly reduce its role in our lives. Over the years, I've started to realize that my worries are almost always independent entities unto themselves, floating freely through my emotional universe. Worries, when it comes down to it, are just worries, and that's about it. Only rarely are they fully accurate reflections of reality. While there are likely some elements of what's keeping us up at night that are really real, more often than not I've found that all I'm doing by agonizing over them is fanning my anxiety further, blowing things even more out of proportion than they were when I first realized I was worried. As long as I can keep that perspective, I'm fine. The problem is that anxieties can act a lot like sirens, calling out to vulnerable souls, seducing us into taking action when what we probably need is to take a long walk.

Even if we minimize it, though, worry will still work its wily way into our world when troubled times trip us up. The old way is to obsess over the stress, and then either beat ourselves up by internalizing it or act out by dumping our discomfort on everyone around us. Neither is very helpful to ourselves, to others, or to our organizations. But there may actually be an opportunity to build positive connections out of the pain. The key, I've found, is to productively engage the assistance of caring and compassionate folks who can help through empathy, listening, and understanding—and thus make an enormous difference in calming our emotional state.

Being in the moment for me is about not fighting what comes but rather just noticing it all as it unfolds in front of and around me. I can work on fixing it later. Ludeman and Hendricks sum it up well in *The Corporate Mystic*: "Every minute you spend thinking about the way it used to be or the way it ought to be is a minute you haven't been thinking about the way I could make it be." Really living in the moment is about noticing, appreciating, listening, and learning in the here and now. Anese Cavanaugh, who coaches corporate leaders all over the country, writes, "When we are fully present, we experience life. We can see more clearly what has to happen. We can see the truth about the moment. We can see the truth about our impact. We can fully feel our feelings: joy, anger, sadness, excitement, etc.—we are present."

When it comes down to it, being in the moment is just a lot more real—both in the positive and in the painful senses of the word—than obsessing on past or future events that aren't impacted by our worrying. In fact, what's happening in the moment is the *only* thing that's real. Being open to appreciating the good things even in trying times can help a lot. Experiencing the less overtly desirable emotions—sadness, hurt, anger, etc.—can be hard, but they too are important elements of being effectively mindful (and mindfully effective). Pretending that I don't have them, I can tell you from experience, only means that they'll reemerge later on—the longer we block them, the bigger the blowup will be later when they finally do come out in the open.

Although it's hard to remember while we're working through tough times, positive things often emerge when one least expects them. My piriformis problem certainly sent me for a loop, but it also ended up leading me to a very interesting—and ongoing—dialogue about business and leadership with

Patrick Hoban, who owns and runs Probility, the progressive physical therapy clinic I went to. He gave me great service and good treatment, and the situation ended up giving me—despite the pain and frustration of the moment—a good learning experience with a new friend; new connections; and helpful understandings about health, business, and life in general.

I'll leave this point with a bit of paradoxical, yet profound, wisdom from the Indian mystic Osho, who says, "I live my life based on two principles. One, I live as if today was my last day on earth. Two, I live today as if I am going to live forever."

Compassion Counts

In many ways, this snippet of a sidebar underlies *all* of the tips I'm covering in this essay. Whatever situation I'm working in, I try to remember to run through in my mind what it must be like for those around me, and to tune into what they might be experiencing, fearing, and anticipating. Empathy improves the energy in the room as well as the outcomes of the conversation, and provides some comfort to those who are having a hard time. Putting ourselves in others' shoes; listening with an open heart; not judging, even when we want to, and especially not when we think we know the answer; and working to feel the feelings others around us might be experiencing will help us maintain mindfulness and increase our effectiveness and enjoyment in most every area of our lives.

Neglecting these qualities of empathy and compassion can mean that anger and rage take over. The assumption that others are out to get us, that something bad happened because of others' ill will or malice, rarely makes for anything productive. Learning to breathe deeply, get grounded, and be sensitive to others' suffering can help get us back to a more productive place. To cite Paul's pearl of wisdom once again, "When furious, get curious." And in the words of an equally wise innovator, Ben Franklin, "Anger is never without a reason, but seldom a good one."

Effective self-management may mean actively increasing our ability to be compassionate. In *Train Your Mind, Change Your Brain*, Sharon Begley references the work of Dr. Phillip Shaver. "In study after study," Begley reports, "he was finding that whether a person acts with compassion or not reflects the person's sense of emotional security. People who feel emotionally secure, who feel that there is someone to whom they can turn in times of need, are more sensitive to the suffering of others." Like any other skill, we can become significantly more compassionate by mindfully working at it. Over time, our minds will begin to work differently, to shift more naturally to a compassionate place.

(For an exceptional story of how a compassionate extra mile can make a difference, see Julie Parrish's story in Notes from the Front Porch on page 432.)

3. PAYING ATTENTION TO THE POSITIVE DETAILS

For high achievers like me, it's so easy to sink into frustration and anger over what's not being done right. But I believe that negative way of being in the world is out of whack. What I've learned over the years is that *the more I can focus myself on the good things, the more they seem to happen.* The more I compliment others (sincerely), the more they see the positives, too. And the more they see the good things and talk about them, the more other great stuff starts to happen. It's an amazing cycle to engage in. The people I praise feel better, their energy improves, the people around them then feel better, customers get better service, and quality goes up, which in turn contributes positively to the organization and to my mood.

Being mindful of others' achievements and efforts means that they, not I, need to be at the center of my daily leadership universe. Easier said than done, but the work of mindful management is to be attentive to those around me: to treat coworkers like customers; to remember people's names and acknowledge their needs; to know what they like, what they do outside of work, and what worries them. None of us, least of all me, gets it all right all the time. But each small piece of effective sensitivity, each additional iota of awareness, and each small bit of encouragement to help others excel adds up to make a markedly positive difference. To quote the man behind Servant Leadership, Robert Greenleaf, "The effort is always to be aware, always to know that something important is going on all of the time."

This focus on positive attentiveness is an example of how mindfulness can be used, proactively, to make good things happen. In his "Leader to Leader" article, Deepak Sethi writes, "Focus is power. Cognitive scientists have known for a couple of decades that the brain is capable of significant internal changes, a dramatic finding when it was first made. We now also know that the brain changes as a function of where an individual puts his or her attention. The power is in the attention because it continually reshapes the patterns of the brain." I'm living proof of the effectiveness of this process. While I was raised to focus on faults, there are usually way more good things going on than there are problems. My life and our organization are both clearly better for my shift to focus on the positives.

In the interest of self-improvement, I actively practice enhancing my positive attitude. *If I'm feeling down, I take a few minutes while I'm journaling to start listing all the positive things that I have around me.* When I feel my energy flagging, I immediately take two or three minutes and write down a free form list of good things to be found in my life. It may be how much a particular staff member has improved, how beautifully someone on the counter handled a customer complaint, the great energy that a new staff member exhibits, the deliciousness of a sliver of Spanish cheese, or the beauty of one of the heirloom tomatoes coming in from our farm. Because it's about writing rather than interacting directly with another person whose positive energy builds my own as in the "Three and Out" practice, this exercise is probably more like "Ten and Out." It's hard to stay in a bad mood once I've done it.

Speaking of farm-fresh produce, here's a fine quote from food writer Angelo Pellegrini, noted in his wonderful book *The Unprejudiced Palate*: "We are living in an age when man is rapidly losing his identity. There is everywhere a pervasive feeling of insignificance . . . My home and the surrounding plot of ground reflect an attitude and a way of life; and the achievement of this harmony between myself and my dwelling has given my life a personal significance it would not otherwise possess. *I have sought and found the significance latent in little things.*" The words are Pellegrini's, but the emphasis at the end is mine. The things that catch my interest are rarely the ones that get great attention in the world at large, but they're the ones that get me motivated to improve and to push through challenging times.

Chris Peterson and the Study of Positive Psychology

Positive psychology is a relatively recent area of study, which happens to be a strong area of focus here at the University of Michigan. Chris

Peterson was one of the positive psychology pioneers: a U of M professor, a longtime Zingerman's customer, and an all-around great and insightful guy whose primary message in life was "other people matter." Sadly, Chris died suddenly in the fall of 2012, at the relatively young age of 62.

I asked Walter Sowden, one of Chris's graduate students, how Professor Peterson had viewed this work around mindfulness. "The human tendency to focus our attention on the 'bad' vs. the 'good' actually has a name," Walter said. "It's called the 'selective attention to the negative' and it has to do with the evolutionary properties of our consciousness. Chris believed, and had evidence to support his theory, that optimistic people habitually explained negative events or experiences by attributing their cause to external, transient, or specific factors such as prevailing circumstances, whereas pessimists explain negative events or experiences by attributing their cause to internal, stable, global factors such as personal failure. Applying this to organizational psychology [the study of how the organizational context influences our thinking, feeling, and behavior], you could see that optimistic leaders are more inclined to look at problems as challenges that are caused by contextual factors (less stable, or more fixable) where a pessimistic leader may look at the same situation and blame it on the more permanent aspects of the organization (the people, strategy, capabilities, etc.)."

The impact of these findings on our lives and our organizations is pretty enormous. "Chris would also tell you," Walter went on, "that there are some real demonstrable benefits to being an optimist. Optimism has been linked to positive mood and good morale; to perseverance and effective problem solving; to success in a variety of domains; to popularity; to good health; and longevity and freedom from trauma. Pessimism, in contrast, foreshadows depression, passivity, failure, social estrangement, morbidity, and mortality. The link between optimism and positive affect is particularly interesting in the context of organizations. Optimism leads to more positive affect, and more positive affect allows people to thrive in the workplace by broadening their cognitive ability (e.g., learning capacity and memory) and building personal resources (e.g., resilience and intelligence)."

4. ACTIVELY SEEKING BALANCE

While the highs and lows of life are what make it into the movies, the magic of mindfulness is mostly found in the middle. It is a Natural Law (#10) that our strengths will lead directly to our weaknesses. Which is why one of the almost inevitable downsides of taking mindfulness to an extreme is what we call the "burden of awareness"—the more aware we are of what's going on around us, the more little things we notice, the more stressful things can get and the harder it can be to stay centered. At any given moment, a thousand things are either undone or done incorrectly. If we're not mindful about our self-management, any eight of them are enough to send us over the edge in an instant. The other end of the emotional spectrum, one I for sure don't want to be at, is what's known as blocking or tuning out. Of course, there can be, I admit, a certain calm in not knowing what's going on, *à la* the old saying "Ignorance is bliss." Personally, though, I prefer the burden to the bliss.

Staying in the middle, owning the pain and the positives at the same time, isn't easy, but I think it's the most effective way to live life. Mindfulness of this sort is all about maintaining some modicum of balance without blocking out the ups and downs that accompany any healthy daily existence. While our feelings and/or others' perceptions, may swing significantly—often in a matter of minutes—reality stays what it is.

I was explaining this approach one day to Gauri Thergaonkar, a longtime member of our organization, who said, "Oh, you mean *moksha.*" Apparently, I did—*moksha*, like Gauri, is of (East) Indian origin. It's a term that beautifully illustrates the approach to mindfully staying "in the middle." Gauri describes it as a "freedom from the tyranny of your emotions without losing track of them." Staying true to the mindset of moksha can be difficult at times.

Social media, of course, is a complicating factor. As soon as anyone says something good about your business on line, it's almost a given that someone else will try to discredit whatever compliment was just given. If you read all the responses in a row, you're setting yourself up for a kind of spiritual whiplash. When criticism comes in on the fly, I can't take a week off to get myself centered again—customer complaints need to be answered, unhappy staff members heard, replacements or repairs brought in for broken equipment. But, by staying centered, remembering that my emotional state usually swings about sixty or seventy times faster than reality, I have a far better shot at dealing with it all more effectively. When I start to feel myself soaring or sliding after some strongly biased bit of input, I try to breathe my way back to the middle.

It's not that I don't appreciate the positives, nor respond seriously to the negatives. I just keep in mind that my emotional response will almost always make what's happened seems far more extreme than reality really is. If I'm cut down by an angry customer, my heart sinks and I feel horrible. But rather than plunge into depression (as I used to do years ago), I try to remind myself that while there might be truth to the criticism I've heard, so too is there truth in all the positive things I was excited about up until the minute before I opened the negative email, or whatever. If we've just won an award, I smile and enjoy the experience, but only for a moment. The truth is we're really not any better than we were the day before our newfound fame. It's the same mindset you'll get from any great athlete after their team wins a big game: "It's a great win, but what we're really focused on is winning the championship. Tomorrow we've got another game to play." It's about staying centered, not letting ourselves be either artificially inflated or sadly let down.[8]

Being aware of the emotional swings can be a huge help in anything we undertake. A practitioner of mindfulness actively works with our fluctuating states of mind in order to abide peacefully in the midst of whatever may happen. While the Western world likes to focus on facts, graphs, grids, strategic plans, and financial statements, the reality is that each of those is a constant swirl of confusing, often conflicting, data. A single statistic may be made up of millions of interactions that have been condensed, for corporate conversation's sake, into one very "big" number. Yet behind that number are real people whose actions and feelings rarely fall as neatly into the columns of a report as those writing it might like. Much to the frustration of financial analysts and others who operate in the fact-based world, emotions are rarely properly aligned with strategic plans, nor are they in synch with tactical initiatives. They come at odd times, in odd ways, and often appear to undermine what it is we actually want. Mindfully watching and appreciating the little things that make up that complex reality—the people, our products, the planet—helps me to avoid the emotional roller coaster and stay steady in my approach to the world. Which, in turn, means less stress for the rest of the organization, fewer problems I create for myself and for others, and more time and energy that I can expend on enhancing all of the already positive things we have going.

Taking Off—or Putting On—the Glasses

There are times when a mindful manager will do well to actively reduce their level of awareness in order to get through in-the-moment stress. That may sound a bit off base after everything I've just explained above, but when a crisis is brewing, a major illness is at hand, or people on shift are starting to lose it, it can actually be helpful to mindfully block out other bad news in order to fully focus on the higher priority that's at hand.

To wit, Bee Mayhew Roll, the boisterous and witty woman who owns and runs Beezy's Café in neighboring Ypsilanti, was relating to me a few years back how she became conscious of the fact that she was getting very stressed about some of the cleaning details (i.e., small stuff not cleaned to her appropriately high standards) in her then newly opened restaurant. Realizing she couldn't conquer every issue at once, and realizing too that she was starting to make herself and everyone around her a bit crazy, she decided to stop wearing her glasses for a while. By choosing not to see the small things, she used her intentionally bad vision to help her let go of her stress for a few weeks. After other, more important issues had been resolved, she decided it was time to put the glasses back on and get back in touch with, and on top of, the details. Not surprisingly, within a couple days, the cleaning was back up to snuff.

5. Breathing Deeply

The importance of deep, steady, mindful breathing comes up in so many contexts that it would be easy to dismiss it as clichéd. But simple as it may sound, deep breathing makes a remarkable difference. Faced with fear, pain, or frustration, we often unconsciously hold our breath or, conversely, start to hyperventilate. Breathing deeply and evenly—as we do while working out, singing, or meditating—restores oxygen, energy, and balance. By simply taking a series of deep, even breaths—long in, slow out—I can help myself get centered in most any situation. It doesn't solve the problem, but it certainly helps me stay calm enough to make better decisions and avoid doing really stupid stuff that gets me into trouble.

If you haven't actively taken up breathing in this way, I'll just say that there's nothing to lose by trying, and pretty much everyone I know swears by it, too. By taking a dozen deep breaths, almost anyone can re-center themselves and improve their energy. Bad breathing is one of the most common causes of negative vibrational energy (see Secret #21 on page 80)—the dissonant energy that any of us may inadvertently put out into the world when we're not coming from a calm and grounded place. A bit of mindful deep breathing will work wonders in about two minutes. As Julia Cameron suggests, when you make time to breathe mindfully, take a moment and "ask yourself how *you* are feeling. Listen to your answer. Respond kindly."

6. EXERCISING

Regular workouts, by definition, mean regular bouts of deep breathing. Exercising also clears our minds, alters the flow of our day, and contributes to creativity. Everyone who does regular exercise will have their own routine. Whatever it is that we do, the point is the same—it's a conscious break from what we're doing all day at work and at home. Running, for me, is like a little daily vacation, a bit of time off to clear my head, let my thoughts wander, and get myself re-grounded. I always run outside, which means that I get a direct daily dose of fresh air. I count on my running so much that I'm afraid to stop; having worked through that piriformis syndrome stuff, I now know why. As I've said, not running regularly threw me totally off my game.

But to back up a bit, I started running because I was having a rough go of it in my life, and someone I liked suggested I try it. At that point, I was pretty open to trying almost anything that might help me. Running seemed low risk. I didn't know this when I started doing it, but Sam Keen writes in *Inward Bound*, "When middle-aged men begin a program of jogging, they become more emotionally stable, calm, self-sufficient, and imaginative." It's certainly worked that way for me. By the time I'm done running each day, I've often come up with two or three insights or ideas (some small, some large) in the process. It offers time to ponder, to reflect, and to make mental connections that might otherwise be missed. All of which can quickly pay tangible dividends in almost every part of our lives and affect the positive impact we make on the world.

How do you work out? It's up to you whether you walk, run, lift, swim, spin, sweat, dance, whatever. There's the obvious physical benefit—staying in shape helps you feel better and reduces your risk of heart disease, obesity, and all that other stuff we're all trying to steer clear of. But I think it's of equal benefit mentally; running, for me, is really the equivalent of meditating. I have 30 to 60 minutes with no other mental inputs, no distractions, no one talking to me, no phone, no computer, no colleagues, no need to smile or say anything. I just run. My mind goes where it wants to go. My legs keep moving, my breathing stays pretty steady. The act of running forces me to breathe deeply and regularly, which expands the chest and helps to quell unconscious fear as well as increase both calmness and creativity. When it's over, I just plain feel better at pretty much every level.

Running is also good practice for my leadership work. While I frequently *want* to stop partway through a run, I just keep going. I have this little rule for myself, which I've only broken on rare and extreme occasions, that I will keep running until I get back to where I started (or to my destination, if the two aren't the same). I realized after many years of taking this approach that my "get to the finish line no matter what" mindset is very much in synch with success in business or life in general. Wanting to stop is one thing; doing it (or actually, not doing it) is another. While we all fall short on occasion, making effective completion the norm instead of the exception can only help in all areas of our lives.

Although I don't do it much, walking might be even better still. It's pretty likely, if I live long enough, that I'll end up there. My knees, I know, may not last forever. And as anarchist poet Gary Snyder says in his essay "The Etiquette of Freedom": "Walking is a great adventure, the first meditation, a practice of heartiness and soul primary to humankind. Walking is the exact balance of spirit and humility."

7. APPRECIATING SOLITUDE

While solitude comes naturally to me, I know that's not the case for others—for many people, time alone is awkward and uncomfortable. If you're a strong extrovert (and many of my best friends are), you're familiar with the challenge. Without a structure, solitude gets lost in the daily shuffle. Arranging for a regular dose of it requires discipline, rigor, and some sort of scheduled regimen. As Julia Cameron recommends in her classic *The Artist's Way*: "More than anything else, experiment with solitude. You will need to make a commitment to quiet time."

While much of this essay is about taking information in and making the most out of every mental minute, solitude is a way to intentionally unwind our spiritual springs. Rather than focusing on outside stimuli, in solitude we sit with ourselves, moving out of the social spotlight and into a mode where we can pay close attention to our internal energy and insights. It's a time when our main focus is on getting centered and in synch with ourselves, not in keeping up with the chaos of the world. When I fail to set time aside for it, I start to stress out. I can relate to writer Henry David Thoreau, whom Emma Goldman called "the greatest American anarchist," when he says, "I have an immense appetite for solitude, like an infant for sleep, and if I don't get enough for this year, I shall cry all the next." Solitude is so much the norm for me that, rather unmindfully, I almost forgot to include it in this essay as a practice to maintain. And as Thoreau asserted, "I have never found a companion that was so companionable as solitude."

Mindfully reviewing my routines for the purposes of this piece, I realized that jogging—the absence of which sparked my own active efforts at mindfulness—provides me with both a heart-healthy workout *and* a healthy dose of solitude. I've come to see that solo activities like swimming, biking, and running do double duty in a way that team sports like football, basketball, soccer, etc. don't. While the latter work well for staying in shape, reducing stress, and building camaraderie and collaborative team skills, they deliver a very different emotional experience of exercise. That's not a criticism—team sports are a terrific thing. But they require much the same split-second attention to others, intensive communication, and all-out group effort that so many of us put out in our other mindfully engaged activities all day. While that sort of full-on focus has its benefits, it's a very different emotional experience from the one I get while I'm out running or doing some other solo workout.

Take note that solitude is not the same as loneliness. The latter involves a lack of connection, a longing to be with others; it's something we flee from, not something we seek. Solitude is the opposite—it's about being at peace in one's own skin, connecting with ourselves and our surroundings, and learning new things that may help those around us. There will always be some creative tension between time spent alone and time spent engaging with the other people in your life. Many people would like some time alone but give it up quickly to meet the demands of work or families. While it's hard to find that middle ground, disrespecting our own needs ultimately helps no one. One way or another we need to do both to stay in balance. It's an elegant dance that, as Sam Keen explains, "entails a continuous alternation between retreating into oneself and going out into the world: it's an inward-outward journey. There is a solitary part to it, but that solitude helps us to develop richer and more in-depth relationships with our friends, our children, our community, and the political world. It's always a back-and-forth." Getting comfortable with being alone can be a big help in making peace with ourselves and our role in the world.

Whether it comes to you naturally or not, I would agree with existentialist anarchist author Albert Camus, who argued, "In order to understand the world, one has to turn away from it on occasion." And as his colleague Jean-Paul Sartre says, "If you're lonely when you're alone, you're in bad company."

8. JOURNALING

Even if it's only for fifteen or twenty minutes, I journal almost every morning. I'm adamant about making it happen, as adamant as I am about running. Like with the running, my methods are free-form. I rarely use journaling if I'm writing for a book or an article for publication. It's more about the routine of regularly letting whatever emerges emerge, clearing my mind and getting myself centered, than it is about actually achieving anything. My method is hardly high end. I just sit down and write whatever comes to my mind. I use a black roller point pen on a fine-lined yellow legal pad with detachable paper. There's no order or requirements to what I write—the only thing that's not random about the way I do it is that I do it every day. Once I start writing, it's really just about whatever comes to mind. What I write might be coherent or confusing, compassionate or callous, significant or stupid, focused or freaked out. On occasion, I'll reflect back on what I've written, but usually, I leave it completely alone and ignore it. The key is that it comes out. As with group brainstorming, quality is less important here than quantity.

Although I wasn't at all ready to hear it at first, I now resonate fully with what Ram Dass suggests: "There's a way of surfing the silence, the outside silence . . . So why don't you join me, and surf right into the deepest space within you, which is silent awareness." I write down everything, from new ideas, to complaints I would never voice aloud about customers or coworkers (no, not about you!), to descriptions of the antique salt and pepper shakers that are on display at the Roadhouse or the great service work of someone new working the counter at the Bakehouse. Other times it's about the weather, the way the wind is blowing, or the music that's playing. It might be memories of my mother, frustrations over perceived failures, or high hopes for a positive future. Sometimes its just a long string of swear words. When I don't know what to write, sometimes I just run my mind through the exercise of noticing all the subtleties around me and inside my mind.

The point of it all is to see how I'm feeling before I enter the fray that we leaders live in most of the time. Journaling can help reverse the negative flow—it's good for me to get the stress out of my head and into the world where I can work with it much more effectively. The process helps me keep any crabbiness that might have crept into my mind away from customers and coworkers where it can cause serious damage in a matter of seconds. To keep the momentum going in the right direction, I regularly push myself to find the positives when I write. I use journaling to challenge myself to think about things I haven't appreciated of late—people, products, purveyors, even posters and artwork. Two or three minutes of musing on the good things all around me is pretty much guaranteed to get me in a better mood!

Fortunately, I've never had to go long stretches without journaling the way I did with the running when I had the piriformis syndrome. But I know reflective writing works, because on the odd day that I miss it, my mind is notably off kilter. It's so helpful to me that I will generally get up at an even earlier than early hour to do it if I know that time will be tight. Journaling each morning gives me a good runway to effectively take off for the day's work. If I'm feeling frustrated, it's good to know that beforehand so that I don't get overly reactive. If I'm feeling low energy, I have time to figure out how to rev myself up before I get too far into the day. It does pretty much the same thing for my management performance as stretching before I run does for my muscles—loosens me up, reduces the tension, brings a bit more resilience, improves performance, and reduces end-of-the-day pain.

Training Our Minds; Putting LB/NT to Work in Journaling

LB/NT is a training technique that Maggie Bayless from ZingTrain taught us many years ago. The initials stand for "Liked Best/Next Time." Probably because it's both practical and elegantly simple, it's long been a staple of the hands-on, on-shift training that's so important here at Zingerman's.

When a shift is finished, the trainer and the trainee debrief. The trainer asks the trainee what they liked best on the just-finished shift. Then the trainer tells the trainee what they liked best. The trainer then asks the trainee, "What do you plan to do differently on your next training shift?" The trainer also shares what they hope will happen on the next shift. The whole thing can be done in a matter of minutes. But if you use it systemically, great things can come of it. You almost ensure that some positive feedback will be shared, the dialogue is balanced, there's clarity about expectation, and the conversation about success and next steps becomes routine.

It dawned on me the other day while I was out running that we could use that same LB/NT technique to help us with mindful self-management in our journaling. For anyone who seeks just a bit more structure in order to stay on course, this technique is a top-notch way to move forward. If you devote just ten or so minutes to it each morning or evening, you'll be building your self-esteem while also pushing yourself to go for improvement each day.

To those who don't do it, journaling may seem inefficient, an exercise in immodesty, or a waste of time and energy. A cynic might make the argument that it's the equivalent of a half hour of intellectual doodling, time that could be far better used to do something productive. Hear this, though: it's exactly the opposite. Journaling is, without question, one of the most productive things I do. By getting grounded, clearing my mind, centering my spirit, and making sure I'm emotionally ready to go into whatever it is I'm about to do, I significantly increase the odds of my day going well and of making a positive impact on those around me. It's also, I've come to realize, a rather anarchistic act—it has some structure, but within the general framework, really anything goes. And from that seemingly unstructured stuff, seriously good things emerge.

Not only does the journaling help me avoid "accidents" in the form of reactive decision making, maintain my perspective, and keep calm, it also does double duty as a source of innovation and creative new ideas. Robert Greenleaf suggests that "all who would be strong [should] become journal writers. As the questions are asked and allowed to sink into the mental apparatus, write. Write what comes to mind. Ask the questions, reflect on them, and write something every day. Occasionally, reread what you have written and extend it. Cultivate spontaneity. Let the pen capture fleeting insight." As per Greenleaf's point, *journaling is made for mindfulness.*[9]

Although I only learned of her work this year, writer Julia Cameron is a strong advocate for journaling. "Morning pages" is what she calls it, charging each of us to write three pages of the same sort of random thoughts I've described above, at the start of every day. Interestingly, she gives the morning pages credit for all of the same positive attributes I've experienced. "They are," she says, "a pathway to a strong and clear sense of self." Journaling has been a huge help for me in understanding my emotional swings. "Working with the morning pages," Cameron writes, "we begin to sort through the differences between our *real* feelings, which are often secret, and our *official* feelings, those on the record for public display." The work is fully conducive to effective self-management. "Anyone who faithfully writes morning pages," she says, "will be led to a connection with a source of wisdom within."

I hardly had any of that in mind when I began my journaling work, but I clearly gained all of those benefits. For the cost of a pad of paper and a pen, it's perhaps the best investment I've ever made. To quote Robert Hass, former poet laureate of the United States, "Take the time to write. You can do your life's work in half an hour a day."

A Vote for Visual Journaling

There are, of course, many ways to reflect and gather one's thoughts. I write, Martin Piszczalski draws. Martin is a business writer and consultant who now lives in Boulder. Back in the early '90s, Martin helped us with process management when we wrote our mission statement. He had studied with Ron Lippitt—the man from whom we learned a lot of what we now call visioning.

Martin's process, though visual rather than written, is much the same as mine. Each morning, he gets out his pad and draws whatever comes to his mind. When he first sits down, he doesn't know what he's going to do, he just starts to sketch. The drawing work helps him to get his struggles, emotions, and uncertainties out of his head and onto paper where they're less difficult to deal with. Like me he saves all his pads, and like me he has about twenty years of them stacked up somewhere. He rarely goes back through what he's journaled, though. And like me, he's adamant that it's an enormously positive process to go through.

9. DEBRIEFING WITH FRIENDS

Just as journaling has helped me to regularly unload, and eventually lighten, my internal conversation, consulting and conversing with friends helps me stay centered. I feel better for having shared my thoughts and bared my soul. Because good friends (for me at least) are able to listen without judging and without offering immediate solutions for my struggles, there's a great deal of therapeutic benefit to being with them. It calms me and helps me feel clearer about what I've missed, while at the same time freeing me to be more myself. When I can, I like to fill the same role for others; being a good listener is a skill I've worked hard at and continue to try to practice regularly. In the right setting, either role can energize; in a good, well-balanced relationship, both parties leave the conversation feeling cared for.

I love what early 20th century film critic, anarchist, and writer Siegfried Kracauer said on the subject: "Friendship civilizes." Having good people to get reality checks from when I'm starting to slide into the craziness of leadership life is a huge help. I can't stress enough how much easier it is to get through tough times when I have a set of competent and caring peers I can talk to—in person, on the phone, or through email—who help me keep a grip on things when the "carwash brushes" of life are beating the heck out of me. While I would include colleagues on this list, of equal import has been finding friends that I *don't* work with—the latter are able to listen and share thoughts without all the emotional ebbs and flows that inevitably come up when we stay within the mental walls of our own company. Julia Cameron calls these people "believing mirrors." "Put simply," she says, "a believing mirror is a friend to your creativity—someone who believes in you and your creativity."

I'm not talking about people we know that we casually complain to or coworkers that go to the bar with us after work. As one of our long-time staff members once said, "I find myself surrounded by people almost all of the time, but I have difficulty feeling that I am connecting to people on an intimate level that resonates in a way that makes me feel satisfied." Acquaintances are great, but good friends are something different altogether.

It was only around the time that I turned 30 that I realized how important it was to have close friends. People who I will really open up with, who care deeply about me, and I about them, in very personal and private ways. Friends whom I support through their struggles, encourage to pursue their passions, and am patient with when they procrastinate—and they do the same for me. Martin Seligman sums it up well: "The most important thing in life is the cultivation of quality relationships. Everything is about relationships. Success in business, work, intimacy, friendship, family and even the self . . . is determined by the quality of your relationships."

Lex's Lament

Lex Alexander has been a good friend of mine for over twenty years now. Back in 1981, he and his wife, Ann, founded Wellspring Grocery in Durham, NC. We met in the late '80s when Lex came to Ann Arbor and stopped by the Deli to visit. The two of us have traded ideas about business and life ever since. Two years ago, Lex suffered a severe stroke in the middle of the night. He's worked hard at recovery with a great deal of success. But strokes of this sort are no small thing—while he's doing well, the stroke has significantly changed his life. Lex shared this touching bit of prose about his struggle. I thought it was a great example of mindfulness done under duress. Lex's story of living life to the fullest sets a great example for the rest of us.

> I had a stroke. It came out of nowhere. I've had a traumatic brain injury. I do not know what the road ahead looks like regarding work, sex, and health. With this uncertainty, I cannot control it by worrying about it. But I do know that . . . I have a great family. I have many friends. I have things I am interested in. I still have creative thoughts . . . I am working at recovery as best I can. I don't have to be perfect. I cannot control everything.
>
> People often ask how I'm doing. My standard answer is, "Pretty good. Some days better than others." . . . What I've learned in these last few weeks, and this was confirmed by a therapist a few days ago, is that I shouldn't expect, and it's impossible in fact, for people to really understand, so maybe it's not such a good idea to go into detail. Here's what the therapist told me: "All people can do is go to their library of life experience to try to stand in your shoes. And fortunately, not many people have had a traumatic brain injury." When people ask, "How are you doing?" And I respond with, "I'm feeling terribly anxious today," people often ask, "What are you anxious about?" Or even worse, "You've got nothing to be anxious about. All you have to do is enjoy the fresh air today." But if I knew how to not be anxious, I promise you I wouldn't be because it's not fun.
>
> Here's the thing: I usually do not know why I'm anxious. That's the

nature of the free-floating anxiety. It's different than situational anxiety where you can usually pinpoint the cause of the feeling and maybe do something about it. I just feel that fight or flight uneasiness in my belly, but there's no tiger! I'm practicing all kinds of techniques to try to deal with the anxiety or lessen it. But sometimes there's just brain chemistry that produces free-floating anxiety and there's nothing I can do except just keep breathing. And there's nothing anybody can do to take it away. Sometimes people's concern and caring for me drives them to want to "fix me," but there's nothing they can do about it either. The best response, and I get this sometimes is, "Is there anything I can do?" And I assure them that there is not.

10. COOKING AND CALMING

You could plug in gardening, crocheting, playing polo, or praying. The point is that it's productive and positive to have a few regularly repeated, much-loved rituals that help bring you back, literally, to your senses.

I feel fortunate that the thing I do for a living is also something that helps me stay centered; not everyone gets that kind of continuity and congruity in their life. One of the cornerstones of my day and of my ability to stay in balance is the custom of cooking a really delicious meal at home almost every evening. People often look at me with incredulity when I tell them, but I really do go home each evening and cook dinner. "Why don't you just eat at work?" they ask. It's a reasonable question—customers come very long distances and spend significant sums to enjoy our food. But the truth is that a) I *like* cooking; that's why I first got into the food business, and b) there's something peaceful and peacemaking with the world that I gain by preparing a good meal. So I do it and do it happily—cooking and then eating what I've made helps bring me back to a calm and considered, full-flavored place at the end of each and every day.

If you don't work with food for a living, good cooking might be worth doing too. It really is an exercise in sensory awareness. Smells, colors, cooking sounds, physical feel, and flavors are what it's all about. Mindfully handling each great ingredient, appreciating aromas as you move things around the counter, marveling at the way each vegetable looks when you cut it, letting the flavor of each morsel settle in your mouth, smelling the mint leaves as they're torn, checking the spicing for balance. The smell of bacon frying, the perfume of a just-cut summer melon, the compelling aroma of toasted cumin. And the sounds—the plunk of polenta simmering for hours on the stove, the sizzle of that aromatic bacon, the light click of the knife on the wood cutting board. Each, for me, is almost meditative. In fact, even describing it is helping reground me. Better still, at the end of all that, you have a marvelous meal to eat!

11. KNOWING YOUR HISTORY AND VISION

While I work hard to live in the present, it's also very true that having a good sense of where we've come from and a clear, documented, agreed-upon vision of the future make it infinitely easier for me to do that. To have neither history nor vision at hand is, to me, akin to sailing in the open ocean without a compass or wandering in the woods having lost track of where we entered. If we know where we've come from, and we're clear on where we're going, it's a heck of a lot easier to keep moving constructively forward no matter what happens in the moment. When things feel like they're falling apart—as they so often do—it's far easier when I can ground myself effectively in both the past and in a positive future.

Having a clear sense of our history is all about sinking intellectual and emotional roots. Our history and our self-knowledge might be personal, familial, cultural, social, ethnic, or organizational—there's no limit. We all have complex, well-integrated, and highly interesting identities. Embracing all the elements of those identities is, I believe, a big and positive piece of accepting and knowing ourselves. From an organizational perspective, I'm adamant about the importance of founders and leaders of organizations taking time to share history with new arrivals. The more new staff members know about where we've come from and why, and how we got to where we are, the more they can be a positive part of our future. (See Secret #8, Vision Back, in *Part 1* of the series for more on that subject.)

On a personal level, history has much the same benefit, but the responsibility for the research in this case resides only with each of us. We all have much to learn about who we are, where we've come from, and how we got here—parsing our past with a higher level of mindfulness will almost always reveal new insights and new understandings. Our stories are always complex, often conflicting, and rarely totally clear. As with all history, there is never a fully objective truth to be told. No matter where we choose to fit in and contribute, we each have a unique past, present, and future. In his excellent book *In the Name of Identity,* Amin Maalouf explains, "I haven't got several identities: I've got just one, [but it's] made up of many components in a mixture that is unique to me, just as other people's identity is unique to them as individuals. Identity isn't given once and for all: it is built up, and changes throughout a person's lifetime."

Having an agreed-upon vision of greatness for the future can be very calming. (If you don't have a vision of the future documented for your organization and/or yourself, let me again take this opportunity to recommend it—it works.) No matter what happens in the moment, I don't need to expend energy agonizing over where I'm going. We've already decided what our long-term organizational future is going to look like. (For example, Zingerman's 2020 Vision outlines what success might look like for us in the year 2020.) The same applies on a personal level. As per Secret #35, I've already written and shared my personal vision with the world. Unless something shocking drops from the sky, it is the future towards which I'm steadily, mindfully, making my way. Knowing what that future looks like makes it far easier to stay focused when new problems and opportunities present themselves—as they generally do—every few hours. It's not so much about what you "could do" but rather what you really wanted and dreamed about doing during the mindful moments that make up the visioning process.

Mind you, I'm not saying that I'm going to blindly pursue that future *just* because I've already decided on it. At times, I certainly check on the vision to make sure it's still strategically sound and inspiring. There are many days where I feel like I'm careening through the chaos of the world. There are others where I doubt myself and the direction of our organization. But I *really* need to remember that those crazy-making moments are the *worst* possible time to rethink a long-term vision. And that since our vision was the product of a *lot* of good work by a *lot* of very smart, experienced, and insightful people, I need to breathe through the doubts and stay true to the future we drew up. I've learned over and over again that if I just keep moving towards it, I'm likely to get through the uncertainty in good shape. By contrast, if I lose track and forget where we've committed to going, I start sliding around in a mental panic, burning energy and making no progress, like a man who gets lost in the woods and walks frantically in circles until he dies, still as confused as he was when he first realized he was lost.

12. Always Remembering the Vase

The paragraphs that follow were written a week or so after I went on that run in Albuquerque immediately after I'd learned of my mother's death. They're a part of what I said at her funeral, but they also fit fully with everything else I've written here about mindful management, balance, beauty, and the benefits of deep breathing. Rather than reframe those ideas, I've decided to leave the remarks as they were, a raw but told-from-the-heart effort to make peace, stay centered, and remain appreciative in the face of extreme sadness. My mother died while travelling in Israel, somewhere around 9:00 a.m. mountain daylight time on the morning of May 16, 2008, at the age of 78. What follows was written a few days later.

Although I've never studied Zen, there's a Buddhist thing I read about once that's always stuck with me. It's about a beautiful vase on the wall—the admonition, our charge, is to look at the vase and fully appreciate it for what it is, but then at the same time to imagine it's already broken as well. Because when we do that, we're able to appreciate the chance to see it and its beauty every day while it's there, but if and when it should break we won't be awash in regret for having failed to appreciate it. We'll be saddened that it's gone, we'll miss it deeply, but we'll have known that we paid attention to it at deep and meaningful levels for all the time we were near it.

I've tried to live for many years now with the mindset of appreciating the beauty of the "vases" in my life, and, at the same time, with the understanding that neither I, nor any of them—in this case my mom— are guaranteed to be here the next day. Which means that if there's something to say, I try to say it and not wait for some future better time. To appreciate things as they are, not get stuck in how they should have been. I feel like both my mom and I spent most of the last ten years or so doing that with each other. In that context, while her death was surprising, I don't think it really shocked me. She was like that vase on the wall, and I think we both knew the vase would eventually break. In truth, my mom and I had this little unspoken ritual going for years— every time one of us went out of town (which happened a lot) we'd call to say something like "Have a good trip." It was always said, I'm pretty sure, with the knowledge that one of us might not come back.

As sad as I am to summon up those memories, it's important to remember to visualize "the vase" in the vagaries of my everyday existence. To appreciate my partners, the business, my dog, my friends, the sky, the sun, and my sense of taste and smell (without which I'd be hard pressed to do my job). Almost every day when I go running, I remind myself that it could be my last day, and I try hard to take in the feeling and the fun of it as if it were also the best.

Some Things I Don't Do but That Definitely Work for a Lot of People I Like

Meditation. Although I suppose my work with journaling approximates the approach, I've never done any sort of formal, mindful meditation. It's worth considering. Deepak Sethi (and I'm sure many others as well) recommends that leaders start each day by meditating, aka concentrating or sitting practice, for twenty minutes. Longtime Zingerman's customer and world-renowned Buddhist teacher Gelek Rimpoche "meditates for a living." He's written extensively about the value of focusing on breathing and, in the process, disengaging from all the other things around you to clear the mind.

Yoga. So many people I respect swear by this that I'm surprised I haven't done it yet. But maybe soon!

Long Drinking Binges. Just kidding—thought I'd see if you were paying attention.

Time Off. Taking time off means different things to different people. I do it daily with my morning journaling, running, and cooking. I get out of my everyday element by traveling all the time too. Others like to take two or three or four weeks to walk in the woods, or lie on the beach, or parasail off the Pacific Coast. It's essential to take time to reflect and recharge, and to do it in whatever way works for you.

Getting Out into Nature. This is only relevant if you're an urban dweller or work inside a structured setting. One of the beauties of my work, with our businesses spread all over town, is that I'm rarely inside for more than a few hours at a time. On top of which I run outside every day, even on 18° winter days in Michigan. Getting fresh air and, even better still, getting to walk in the woods or commune quietly with the sea can work wonders for one's energy.

Mindful Endings

I remember the very first time I went running: how hard it was to make it even ten blocks, how sore I was afterward, and how much I never wanted to go again. The first two parts of that—the pain and the soreness—were replicated when my piriformis problem started up a few years ago. It hurt like hell, my rhythm was wretched, my breathing patterns were bad. The difference is that twenty years ago, when I'd only just begun, when pain or exhaustion set in, I really considered quitting; I had no allegiance to running, no commitment to sustaining it, and little understanding of how much it might really help me. Today, having had a long and generous taste of its benefits—physical health, fresh air, emotional stability, and solitude—pain or low energy just make me more determined to get myself back in synch. I know now, more so than ever, that I want to and will continue to run regularly as long as I'm able.

The same is true for all the other tips I've shared here. I've got a long ways to go in doing all of them more effectively, and on any given day I can find myself losing focus or coming up with (very good, mind you) reasons not to do them. But I know that they work and that when I use them I do better, and so does the organization and everyone around me. As Julia Cameron writes, "The quality of life is in proportion, always, to the capacity for delight. The capacity for delight is the gift of paying attention."

In "Mindfulness; What Is It? And Where Did it Come From?," Ronald Siegel, Christopher Germer, and Andrew Olendzki write, "through mindfulness we develop street smarts to manage the mind." They go on to explain: "Mindfulness is not new. It's part of what makes us human—the capacity to be fully conscious and aware. Unfortunately, we are usually only in this state for brief periods of time, and are soon reabsorbed into familiar daydreams and personal narratives. The capacity for sustained moment-to-moment awareness, especially in the midst of emotional turmoil, is a special skill. Fortunately, it is a skill that can be learned." My personal goal is to expand these mindful periods of time; every little bit helps make my life more rewarding and allows me to more effectively help those around me.

The returns on that investment of time and energy have been, for me, very real—less stress, a healthier life, a more vital organization, better relationships in every direction, and more effective decision making. The latter is at the core of it all—staying mindful and centered allows us an extra bit of time and mental space in which to make better choices, to move more fluidly through the world. It's not always easy to do, but there's little to lose and much to gain, and you have to start somewhere. To quote from Hendricks and Ludeman in *The Corporate Mystic*: "Learning the information in this book is useful, but mastery becomes possible only when you practice it in key situations."

Ultimately, mindfulness is about living my life, collaboratively and relatively calmly, allowing me to be myself while still being respectful of everyone else around me. It is a very anarchistic way of working in the world. As Jon Kabat-Zinn writes in *Mindfulness for Beginners*, "the real challenge of mindfulness [is] the challenge to be yourself. The irony, of course, is that you already are."

Mindfulness Practice for Beginners

This is a simple but effective way to bring awareness up and take tension down. When I do this practice, I actually write down the answers on paper, combining it with my commitment to daily journaling. It's based on the five senses, with the addition of a sixth element, that of awareness—what's going on in my head. I rely on this regimen any time I'm feeling tense, starting to slide into reactivity, or feeling disengaged from what's going on. In essence, it's me putting on my "writer's hat," only in this case I'm writing about my own state of mind and the reality that's unfolding in the moment, right in front of or inside of me.

What do you see? Give details, i.e., it's more than just "a wall." What's on the wall, what color is it, what's its texture, etc.

What sounds do you hear? Describe them. Are they high, low, calming, anxiety provoking . . . ?

What do you feel in your hands? On your skin? The sun? The humidity? A gentle breeze blowing?

What do you smell? Put some adjectives on what you notice. Close your eyes, breathe deep and do it again. What's out there around you?

What about taste? What flavors are in your mouth?

What's in your mind? What emotions are you feeling? What reactions are starting to come up? What can you do in your mind to manage them better before you act?

Jon Kabat-Zinn's books (see the reading list on page 445) are full of excellent ways to practice mindfulness and meditation.

notes from the back dock

**Lionel Bryant, Receiving Supervisor, Zingerman's Mail Order;
now Deliveries and Distribution Assistant Manager,
Zingerman's Bakehouse**

The consistent positive responses around the community are what drew me to Zingerman's. Two of my high school classmates and people around the Ypsilanti and Ann Arbor community told me the same thing: "It's a great place to work."

Once I was presented with an opportunity to work for Zingerman's Mail Order, I took it. I have been a part of the Zingerman's family for 4 years and 5 holidays. As an employee, I can sincerely say, "This is a great place to work."

It begins with the leadership caring about the staff as people, and not as labor or a number. I have personally witnessed the passion of Zingerman's living in the hearts of our founders Ari and Paul. This energy flows through the managing partners, leadership, and from there to the employees. The common thread is "to live what you say, and do what you believe." This is done by applying our 3 Steps to Great Service to the employees as well as the customer. I enjoy working here because I enjoy being a part of something great.

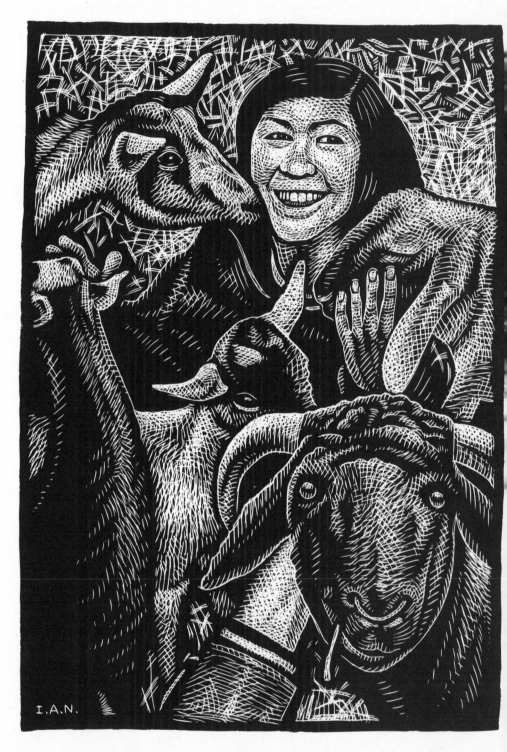

kelly young and our newly arrived herd of goats at cornman farms

Schein On, You Crazy Diamond

A Tribute to Edgar Schein's Essay on
"Leadership and Organizational Culture"

The essay that follows isn't, per se, about self-management. It's an in-depth look at the style of leadership that's needed and appropriate for various levels of organizational development. Which, in turn, is fully in synch with the idea of effective self-management—it's hard to manage ourselves well without a good sense of how what we want to do fits with what's likely best for our business. So, with that in mind, I've placed this piece in the book before we get into personal visioning. My hope is that it gets you thinking about how your personal style, drive, and dreams mesh with what it will likely take to bring your organization to the success you've so mindfully chosen. The more you understand where you are and where you need to be, the higher the odds of getting to greatness and having fun en route.

While this piece appears under my byline, the real credit for it goes to Edgar Schein. It is, I suppose, the compositional corollary of a musician doing a cover of a song he respects and admires. What follows is a tribute to the original writer, but with my cover artist's respectful take overlaying it. My hope is that, as in the best cover songs, I can pay appropriate homage to Dr. Schein, bring my own insights and experiences into the mix, and add my voice to the insightful intellectual foundation that Schein so generously built back in the early '90s.

While only a handful of people reading this piece will likely have heard of the man, I think that Edgar Schein is one of the most insightful writers on leadership and organizational culture that I've ever come across. A graduate of Harvard, Stanford, and the University of Chicago, and a longtime professor at MIT, he must have a wall full of well-framed diplomas and awards. He's an expert extraordinaire on organizational behavior, change, leadership, and, most especially, corporate culture. In fact, Schein is generally said to be the one who invented the term "corporate culture" back in the mid '60s. I could go on at great length, but you can look up his long list of accolades online as well as I can. Suffice it to say that the man is kind of brilliant and well beyond distinguished. What follows is just a small slice of his studies. I highly recommend all of his works, but this is the piece that's resonated most with me, that helped me through some hard times in my career, and that continues to provide insight and assistance twenty years after I first read it.

The article in question, "Leadership and Culture," came out in the mid '90s. We now teach it routinely at ZingTrain seminars, but my first reading of it was an amazing and unexpected experience. You know, one of those epiphanies where you suddenly see your struggles in a new way, and what had long seemed inexplicable, impenetrable, suddenly emerges as clear as can be. If I were to put together a book of all-time greatest management articles, this one would surely be in it. While I can't say that "Leadership and Culture" magically made me into a new person, what it did do was give me an almost immediate increase in my perspective and understanding of effective leadership and what it takes to make that happen. Thinking ahead to the Secret (see page 309) on thinking, it reminds me that we have the power within ourselves—if we set our vision sights straight and then work our butts (I mean, our brains) off—to really change the way our minds operate.

Clarity on the Questions

I've come to believe with ever-greater certitude that an effective leader's responsibility is not, as in the old model, to always be the authority figure with an answer at the ready. Rather, our work is to ask the right questions (and then also require timely responses and completion of the commitments then made in response). Schein's essay pushed me to explore the right questions, and it's been helping me keep those questions clear for close to twenty years now. To my sense of things, Schein took the same pitch others had been scuffling around with for years and hit an intellectual home run.

He starts by getting square with the subject. "One reason so many different theories of leadership exist," he explains, "is that different researchers focus on different elements. At one level all of these theories are correct, because they all identify one central component of the complex human situation that is leadership, analyze that component in detail, and ignore others. At another level," he added, "*all of these theories lack a concern with organizational dynamics, particularly the fact that organizations have different needs and problems at different stages in their evolution.* We tend," he went on, "to treat the topic of leadership in a vacuum instead of specifying what the leader's relationship to the organization is at any given time." The emphasis is mine, but the point is purely Schein's. The insight I took from the article is essentially this: Everyone argues about what the "right style" of leadership is, which style each expert supposes to be the best and which ones are considered outmoded or wrongheaded. Of course, the experts never agree, and the arguments on the subject seem to go on forever. What I got from Dr. Schein was a loud and clear wake-up call to end the otherwise endless squabbling about styles. It made me want to get hold of everyone I'd ever heard argue about this and set them straight. "Hello!!" I would call out. "You're all asking the wrong &*&@@$ question!"

The right question, according to Schein, is "what style is best suited to the level of organizational development your business is at?" Now that, to me, makes much more sense. Otherwise, it's akin to arguing about parenting styles without knowing the age and ability of the kid in question. Clearly, what works for a four-year-old would be outdated at eight, a near-certain failure at fourteen, and a total disaster at twenty-four. Sure, some themes—love, respect, patience, support—are universal. But the close supervision and frequent over-rides that are right on for a four-year-old would be beyond absurd for an adult. The same, Schein shows us, is true in organizations as well. The right style of leadership at one level of organizational development will pretty surely fail if you try to use it at the wrong point in a company's development. Which is why, quite simply, I felt so strongly about getting this essay into a book on self-management. How can you write a strategically sound vision of yourself as a leader if you don't understand the style of leadership that's right for where your business is, and where it will be? If you're unwittingly living and leading in ways that are incompatible with what your organization needs, it's unlikely that you're going to be leading a very fulfilling life. Nor are the odds very high that the business will be doing well either.

The thing I loved, too, about Schein's article is that it helped me understand why what had worked so well for us at one point in our organization's existence had long since ceased to be effective later. Doing what was optimal in those get-up-and-go, early years of opening the Deli become a big liability later. Schein's stuff made so much sense, and it made me realize almost immediately why I—and others I knew—were having so much trouble. What had for so long seemed confusing and counterintuitive was turned inside out into an insight I've used and built on ever since. Dr. Schein showed me with great clarity that the same skill and same strength, applied in a different stage of organizational development, will likely lead to a totally opposite outcome. *Much of what works in the beginning becomes gradually more ineffective as you grow; and conversely, what would have sunk you as a start-up becomes essential at a later stage of an organization's development.*

Clarity couldn't have come at a better time for me. I wasn't—Schein's work made clear—completely crazy; I wasn't going through the looking glass. I just needed to get my act together and take my talents to the next level—of leadership, that is. The implications of this point are pretty huge; many of the skills that brought us as a business, and me as a manager, success early on are the same ones that were screwing us up (both as an organization and as individuals) as we gained greater success. I'll write more on this in a minute, but just to prime your intellectual pump, here's one example: in a startup, the leader needs to be able to make quick-in-the-moment decisions, often turning on a dime when the business demands it. But five years later, let's say the business has grown a great deal, managers have been hired and systems set up. At that point, an owner who's changing direction every two days will wreak havoc and create chaos within their organization.

Without awareness of this reality—that leadership styles need to change as we grow—we're basically fighting with the world, acting unwittingly to undo what we've worked so hard to effectively create. That sad state of affairs is, unfortunately, often the norm. The rest of this essay is all about how that happens—what it looks like, how it feels, and how to fix it.

Schein's Four Stages and the Styles That Love Them

Dr. Schein looks at organizational development in four stages. Of course, the progression through the levels isn't as linear as I'm going to lay it out here. Organizations frequently have a foot in one level while the other has already crossed over the dotted line of life that might separate it from another. Having worked with them, and actually through them, all, I know for a fact that you can have leadership and business success at each of the four stages. The key, throughout, is to look at what strengths and skills we as leaders need to have to help our organizations succeed at the level that we're at.

That insight alone is helpful. But Schein's essay gets even more intriguing for me when he shows that what was personal strength at one stage will, if we're not careful, become our downfall as we develop. As strange as that might sound, it's actually a Natural Law of Business. Take a look at #10 (on page 254), which says that one's strengths lead inevitably to one's weaknesses; in that context, what Schein says is actually quite predictable. The leadership challenges implied may be inevitable, but this is hardly about being helpless. To the contrary, it's about helping ourselves in order to help our organizations and everyone in and around them. The more mindful we are of what we need to do and what it will take to lead our organization to the next level, the more effectively we can manage ourselves to the sort of success we seek.

I'm adamant in my belief that almost anyone who is willing to do the internal work can succeed in any or all of the four stages. The key is knowing which one(s) you're naturally good at it, where you are now in your development, and what you need to do for the organization—and you in it—to succeed. No need to do a lot of mining; Schein's already given us the gemstone. The rest of this piece, my cover of the old Pink Floyd song slightly adjusted for the subject, could be titled "Schein On, You Crazy Diamond," is to take this diamond of an intellectual construct that the good doctor is kind enough to lay out for us, and make each facet clear so that everyone interested has the chance to learn and benefit from it.

To be clear here—you never *have* to move forward, and, most certainly, no one can ever make you. This will work best, of course, when it's framed, as per Secret #32, in free choice. But if your vision (or if you don't have a vision, let's say your desire) is to grow, go forward, be fruitful, and multiply (I'm talking sales, not sons and daughters), then these are good signs that it's time to go, or perhaps "let go," as the case may be.

I should point out too that the stage that your organization is at overall may be different than the stage that one particular part of your business might be at the same time. For instance, if a large company has just started a new side venture, the organization overall could be operating "in prime," while the side business might be "creating." In the same way, different departments or units within a single business may "Schein" at different stages at the same time. A cheese department that opened a few years ago might be in the "building" stage, while the store as a whole is in the process of "changing." Here at Zingerman's we generally have exactly that situation: different aspects of our Community of Businesses at different stages of development, making for an excitingly diverse organizational portfolio.

Stage I—Creating: The Leader as Animator
LEADING IN THE STARTUP STAGE

"At the early stages of organizational creation a unique leadership function is to supply the energy needed to get the organization off the ground." That's what Schein says to start out the discussion of this first stage. It's a very polite and considered way to put it, but he's right on. The first stage—that crazy, chaotic, high energy, totally focused, necessarily stubborn, almost shockingly resilient, daredevilish way of working—is what those of us who've done it lovingly call a startup! If you've been part of one, you know what running it is like and what strengths a leader needs for the job. So many folks will have been through this that I'm hesitant to even go through the scenarios, but assuming that at least some readers haven't, I think it's best to start there, at the place where businesses begin.

Leading effectively in the startup stage is a lot about learning to love organized chaos. Like doing a shot of adrenaline every couple hours in order to keep going. Like taking speed while already being on steroids. Like playing a whole season of football with only a two-minute offense. Like being at a party for a year straight, where you clean up the mess quickly each morning but only just enough to get started on another day. And those are only the good startups. Alternatively, there are the super stressful, super slow startups, where it's like being at a party you spent six years preparing for, but almost no one comes other than a few of your closest friends. That, as you and I know, is *not* a good feeling, especially when the bills start coming in and your savings account is getting smaller by the day.

If you've been through one, you probably already know that the startup stage isn't for everyone—the chaos, the kookiness, the uncertainty, the pressure. I guess if you enjoy performing improv, taking the last shot in a big basketball game, or cramming for exams, you might actually like it. Leading in a startup business is sort of like eating Nashville Hot Fried Chicken (go to Prince's in Nashville to experience the original, or come by the Roadhouse on Tuesday nights for our take on it).[10] While ours isn't nuclear (the original at Prince's can be if you order it HOT), it is definitely very hot. I tell people that if they're asking me how hot it is, they probably would be better off ordering something else. The same, I'd say, holds true with a startup—if you don't know by now whether or not you're excited about effectively leading one (either before today or after reading the little bit of what I've said here), then I'm guessing this first stage is not for you.

To be good at making a startup successful, the leader's got to be ready to live with all kinds of craziness. Everyone can create their own list, but here's a lot of what I think it takes:

Huge amounts of positive energy. The startup leader, whether they like it or not, is the star of the show; if you don't do well with stardom, then more often than not the startup doesn't do well either. Someone has to have the appeal, the positive energy, the charisma, the star power to successfully draw people—customers, staff, suppliers, the press—into the fold and get them to rally behind this new cause. As Dr. Schein says, "[I am] always struck by the fact that the leaders have so much energy and manage to transmit that energy to their subordinates."

Very high stamina. To lead successfully through a startup almost always requires high doses of both physical and emotional resilience. The importance of this is generally underappreciated by those who've never been through the experience! The physical piece is more readily realized—you have to be able to work long hours and most everyone knows that. But it's the emotional element that I think is more often than not the unexpected brain-breaker; the psychological strain has done in more than a few very smart and well-meaning new business people.

The ups and downs of a day in a hectic startup can be *hard*—advice comes at you from every angle, all the time. One customer tells you they love you, the next hisses at you like an angry serpent in a bad B movie; one staffer totally loves working with you, and another who promised you a decade of dutiful work walks out in the middle of the busiest day of the week. Your best supplier decides to retire and close her business after you've spent your first six months making her product the cornerstone of your menu, and another supplier decides to alter their offerings—in the process, eliminating three ingredients you totally depend on. Six bloggers believe you're the best thing to happen to the town in ten years, but the mainstream press pans you on the same day. On Yelp, you find one writer pronouncing it the best meal they've ever had, and the next one saying it sucked. All of this is sure to conflict with the advice you'd already gotten earlier in the day. Sound exhausting? It is. As Schein sums it up, "Much is said about the vision of entrepreneurs, but not enough is said about the incredible energy they display as they try one approach after another, facing repeated failures, in their efforts to start an enterprise."

A willingness to shoulder a huge share of work and stress. While many of us have tried right from the get-go to put systems and a culture of shared responsibility in place, the reality is that at the startup stage the leader is still the one to take on the brunt of the business stress, the one who willfully keeps it all going, signs on the loans, takes the lead on most every important issue, and stands out front with the customers and the crew every day of the business week. Leading at this stage of the game, even for the more organized among us, works a lot by example. (See Natural Laws #7 and #11 for more on this.) When you're there all the time, everyone sees how you do things, and generally they either get with the game or they get gone.

An ability to make good intuitive decisions. While I'm all for gathering good data, intuition remains an integral part of everything that's effective in a startup. A leader with a strong intuitive sense of the marketplace, the customers, and the products is essential—there just isn't time to dally while we collect large amounts of information.[11] When life is uncertain, and bank loans are solely secured by your personal finances, you need to have a pretty good gut read on what's going to work and what won't. A leader at this stage needs to be able to sort through all the distractions to decide what to stick with even when everyone else is telling you it's ridiculous. And at the same time, you need to be able to give up on a product or service you've long loved because it's clearly not working, and it's costing you money you don't really have.

We Called It Macaroni

The example that comes to mind for me in the moment is the Roadhouse's macaroni and cheese, although in this case, the issue was more the name than the recipe. When we first opened back in the fall of 2003, we were taking lots of flak for having a $12 macaroni and cheese on the menu. As in, "Who the heck do you think you are to charge $12 for something that should be more like $4?" I would explain that we were using amazing ingredients like Martelli pasta from Tuscany (see *Zingerman's Guide to Good Eating* for more on Martelli's macaroni), raw milk Vermont cheddar, and a homemade cream sauce. And when we looked at other menus around town, many restaurants offered pasta dishes made with ingredients I knew were not as good as what we were using, and they were charging $15 to $20 a plate, but no one seemed bothered. "Experts" all advised that we should put the problem to rest by changing the name of the product. "Just start calling it 'pasta' the way the others do," I kept hearing. "Once you just change the name, no one will complain."

I did it give it some consideration—we don't want ever want to dismiss customer feedback too quickly. But I kept coming back to the reality that "macaroni and cheese" is a great American dish, dating back to the work of Jefferson (the greatest culinary president, he's generally given credit for bringing macaroni to North America), and that the cost of the high-quality ingredients we were using meant we had to charge what we were charging. On top of which no one was complaining about how it tasted—in fact, people loved it. So after a good bit of discussion, we decided to ignore the input and stay the course: we kept the name "Roadhouse Macaroni and Cheese" on the menu. This turned out to be a good move. It's been one of our signature dishes for a nearly decade now, we sell loads of it, and a few years back Alton Brown billed it "the best comfort food in America" on his TV Food Network show.

At the startup stage, the owner(s) are pretty much *the* personality of the organization. There's a culture for sure, but about 89 percent of it is pulled from that of the founders. Regardless of organizational size, it's still the leader's personality that snaps, crackles, and pops so powerfully over everyone else's. As Schein notes, if the leader has unmanaged internal conflicts and neuroses, those behaviors and worldviews are likely to be firmly embedded into the organization's culture. Almost inevitably the organization will start to take on the leader's list of strengths and weaknesses; the things we do well tend to also become things the organization does well, too. And what we're not so good at the organization will probably be weak at as well. Ideally, we bring in others to help us with these things, but more often than not, we simply try to overcome our skill gaps through stamina and sheer stubbornness.

Good partnerships can help with this problem. Paul and I are so different that we bring different strengths and weaknesses to the mix. We each have our neuroses, but for the most part, mine aren't the same as his, so together we brought a more resilient form of psychological strangeness to our organizational mix than either of us would be able to imagine on our own. I kind of say this as a joke, but it's also true. Diversity can help a lot, even in (lovable) dysfunction. While either of us might engage in an extreme behavior, or have weak points that we miss, together we bring a more balanced and effective leadership to the business.

 Signs That It's Time to Shift to Stage 2

While there aren't any hard and fast rules, here are six scenarios that I've seen and experienced fairly frequently over the years.

a. You're still in business a year or so later! Most startups fail, as you probably know, and fairly quickly at that. The stats are especially severe in our industry—restaurant mortality rates are murderously high.

b. You take time to breathe. Anyone who's been through this first stage knows what I mean. While you're in the middle of the madness, you don't realize how little time you've had to catch your breath, either literally or figuratively.

c. You realize just how incredibly drained you are. This feeling, in my experience, follows immediately after you take time to breathe. Anyone with high stamina will likely be familiar with this fall from one's own emotional grace. You can maintain a high pace for a remarkably long time. But as soon as you stop, you're exhausted; after going nonstop for ages, it's hard to find the energy to even get up in the morning, let alone make big, new, bold decisions. Letting up is hard to do; if I take time to get away and go to the beach, it actually takes me about three days afterward to stop falling asleep every few hours.

d. Everyone's actually getting paid. You included. If you've not been part of a startup, you might not realize it but a lot of owners simply don't get a paycheck in the early years. Or, if they do, it's for far less than they'd command if they did comparable work in some big corporation. Sales in startups may seem high, but cash flow is still usually very tight, and in order to keep things going, it's pretty common for the founder to take little or no salary. Often the owner's (or owners') friends and family help out for free, too. When you reach the point when everyone's actually getting paid, that tells me that you're entering, or have entered, the second stage.

e. You start to think about what might come next. As soon as you have even a bit of business success, it's likely that people are going to start throwing opportunities your way. All the people who didn't help you when you were trying to get off the ground now want to be your best friend. Even though you're still barely holding things together, almost everyone, you'll discover, has an idea about what you ought to do for an encore. All of a sudden, someone offers you a second location, you think about expanding your office, or you want to work on a new way to leverage your website. In the startup stage, you don't have the time, the money, or the emotional energy to do any of these things. But when the dust starts to settle, when you allow yourself time to actually breathe and have a salary, and maybe start to hire a few more good people, those offers start to resonate more meaningfully. The fact that you're even giving them serious consideration tells me that you're likely entering that second of Schein's stages.

f. You're more and more frustrated with everyone around you for not seeing what's so incredibly obvious to you. This is one that pretty much everyone can relate to, and my personal favorite. For those who get startups successfully off the ground, this experience can be very painful. Having worked with a fair number of leaders of these sorts of businesses, and having been one myself (though I've never played one on TV), I will vouch for the difficulty of this problem. Imagine that you're on a team where you started out as the superstar, surrounded by competent players to help fill out the rest of your lineup. Then, over the course of the next few years, you go to the gym regularly to work out (in business terms, this might be called "intellectual development") so that now you're stronger and more able than ever. Since your stamina was already higher than most everyone else's in the first place, the longer the startup goes, and the more you work and study, the more the rest of the "normal" people may just want to go back to "normal" life, while you want to push the envelope and take things to the next level. Which means that what was initially a generally acceptable gap in passion, intention, and ability starts to become almost unmanageably large—tensions and frustrations grow and fun levels fall.

Vision Check

As you've likely heard from me about twenty-nine times elsewhere, I highly recommend that you have an inspiring, strategically sound, well-written, and well-communicated vision in place before you open any business or undertake a new addition to what you're already doing. If you don't have one in advance, let me strongly suggest that you take time out now to draft one. My anarchist orientation, of course, leads me to restate the obvious—you certainly don't *have* to have one. But if you want to get to greatness, it's a lot more likely to happen if you've articulated to yourself and others what success really means to you.

Assuming then, for the moment, that you have a written vision of the future you desire, it's important to regularly compare your present reality against what you wrote down. It's particularly critical if you're growing more and more confused, if you've lost your drive and energy. If you've been in business for a while, it is not at all an uncommon occurrence that your original vision has been fulfilled without you even realizing it. This is what happened to Paul and me back in the early '90s. (See page 305 in *Part 1* for more on this story.) Thankfully, Paul had the instinctive insight to realize something was wrong—he intuitively knew that we needed to shift stages. He sat me down, rather suddenly, on the Deli bench to ask where I wanted to be ten years into the future.

A year later we were done writing our vision for Zingerman's 2009, at which point we essentially entered into Stage 4, changing some of our strategies in order to start afresh. I won't say it was easy—it wasn't—but, clearly, it's worked out pretty well. And the vision we wrote over the course of that year successfully sustained us for nearly 15 years! The next long-term vision after that—Zingerman's 2020—was written in 2006. It was done with Schein's stages and the power of visioning clearly in mind— we were actually able to write the 2020 vision while operating successfully in "prime"—the third of the stages. The year we put it on paper was one of the best we've ever had—we wrote the vision not because our star was falling but because we were getting too close to fulfilling the 2009 vision. If all goes according to plan, we'll be penciling in time to work on the next one in, oh, about 2017 or so.

Because we'd put a date on our 2009 vision, it was clear from chronology alone that it was time for us to write the next one. But more often than not, the only place an entrepreneur's vision resides is in their mind. Without a dated document, it's far harder to determine when you're "done." That's one of the reasons why it's so important to write it down. But also, if you know the signs it's pretty clear when the time has come to reestablish one's long-term direction and definition of success. The signs that one's vision has been surpassed (as ours had back when we sat on that bench) are the same at every stage.

- You're having a hard time (either on your own or with your partners or colleagues) deciding what to do next. Opportunities crop up regularly, but you're often seriously conflicted about how to respond.

- The passion that got you started has waned. I don't mean that you're tired and you need time off. I mean that the cathedral you set out to build, the dream you were driving so hard to make real, has more than likely been realized, and nothing new has taken its inspirational place.

- Something in you or your life has changed in a way that makes your vision a poor fit with who you want to be or what you want to be doing.

When this sort of stuff starts to happen with increasing regularity, the answer is surprisingly simple, I've found—just sit down and draft your next vision. Put a date on it, preferably one that's five, eight, ten, or twenty years out. Though others may insist otherwise, it's actually amazingly easy to do. The in-depth essay on vision writing appears in the middle of *Zingerman's Guide to Good Leading, Part 1,* and my views on personal visioning are in Secret #35.

The story that follows came from Nzingha Asantewa, who wrote me from Atlanta after reading an excerpt of the visioning essay from *Part 1,* which ran in *Inc.* magazine in February of 2011. Her comments speak straightforwardly to how much easier and more fun it is to work with a vision rather than to follow the old model in which everything starts with a strategic plan.

> *I'd been struggling for weeks to complete a business plan, which is a must-have for the SBA business development program. Well, yesterday afternoon I discovered I had a flat tire. While sitting in the lobby of the car dealership as they replaced my tire, I had a chance to read my first mail-order subscription of Inc. magazine. Lo and behold, page 84 was the answer to the very thing that I knew was wrong with my business planning: I was attempting to MapQuest the business route with no destination. Imagine that!*

> *Reading your article immediately put me on the right track. It was, as Oprah says, my Aha! Moment. I've struggled with the writing of the business plan for going on three months. I've been wrestling with the plan and even the design of my website, etc., etc., . . . all because I simply didn't know where I wanted my business to go. I knew something was wrong from a planning standpoint. I just couldn't figure it out.*

> *I started putting your suggestions into practice last night. Truly, your wisdom and your work is making a difference in my life (and I'm just getting started).*

Nearly two years later, Nzingha reached out to let me know the work was still working. Since she's been using the visioning process well for a while now, and has never worked at Zingerman's, I figured it would be great to have Nzingha share her experience. What advice, I asked her, would you give others about the visioning process? She wrote, "Seeing is believing . . . even through the mind's eye. Taking time to visualize what your business will look like in the future, and then writing it down, is like being cast in the leading role of a George Lucas film. Your visualization techniques are a powerful tool when put into action. The exercise helps to crystallize your vision. . . . Visualization actually helps provide many of the answers necessary to arrive at your ultimate desired state!"

Stage 2—Building: The Leader as a Creator of Culture

HIRING AND DELEGATING OUR WAY INTO THE NEXT LEVEL

I think that few leaders actually know that they or their organizations are shifting from Stage 1 to 2; more often than not they just make the transition naturally, almost unconsciously, because it's just what you do when you've survived Stage 1. Heck, it's not like some red light illuminates on your cell phone to indicate you've moved on to Stage 2. Nor will you get a new form to fill out from the government or a certificate of Stage 1 completion from the local Chamber of Commerce. All you get is a shot at leading successfully in Stage 2.

Most folks are tired when they get to this point; they're clear, though, that they want more—more clarity, more sales, more success, more profit, more peace of mind, more effective operations. Most are ready to bring in new people to work with so that when an opportunity presents itself they'll be ready to take it. Not to mention that it's nice to take some time off now and again and having skilled coworkers and a bit more structure makes that possible. In the Creating stage, as a startup, it's mostly about just "doing it." Certainly, there's some training, accounting, marketing, and managing involved, but mostly you're in there pulling a great amount of weight to make it happen every day. The leader in Stage 1 is kind of it—most of the rest of the team is there because someone has to fill the other positions on the court. (Even LeBron James has to bring four other guys with him to play basketball.)

But at Stage 2, the leader's role shifts. We spend a bit less time doing and much more time developing people. Instead of being almost all about the leader, at Stage 2 it starts to be more about the team. The leader begins to hire with a better understanding of what potential team members can contribute, how they fit into the leader's style of work, and what tasks need doing that were previously falling by the wayside. Usually, a few folks in the organization will start to step up and take more responsibility. While you're still a long way from having the entire workplace defined and mindfully designed, a consistent effort is being made to gain clarity and stability.

Leaders at this stage start to delegate with ever more effectiveness—it's imperative if you aren't going to be on site every second. After all, no one can do everything on their own, and most folks want to be able to go home; take a vacation; have a kid or see the ones they already have; or take on additional ideas, projects, or products. Leaders who do well at this second stage generally start doing more sharing of thoughts and thought processes. There's more time to think things through and then explain what we're thinking and why we're doing what we're doing. While there may not be a ton of formal training or procedures in place, this sharing of how one thinks becomes ever more mean-ingful—it helps those you've hired have a good shot at making decisions as you would. In truth, I think it's a prerequisite for effective delegation.

The ability to hire like-minded folks is also essential at this stage. As others start to make more of the decisions, it only makes sense that an effective leader at Stage 2 would want to bring in "good people," of the sort who can stick to the original storyline and help move things along. Generally, they're "good people" because they're comfortable fitting in around the stardom of the leader. They bring their own skills to the game, of course, but people who really want to take charge, to take the last-second shot, or go after that really tough client generally don't sign up for these roles. They either go out and do it on their own, or they go to work in bigger settings where there's room for them to create their own area of significant influence.

This second stage, to me, is sort of an in-between state of organizational being. People rarely shift to the second stage thinking that's as far as they want to go. If you use the analogy of moving from childhood to adulthood, let's say, Stage 2 means you're about 18. You're out of the house. Maybe you're going away to college. There's a chance to build a new life, though it still depends a lot on how you grew up. You're still the same person you were at six and sixteen. But you're trying to calm down a bit, to settle in some, while still being a bit footloose and fancy free.

Please note that it's perfectly ok to stop your growth at Stage 2. The great artisan workshops of the past were probably comfortably settled at this stage, and there's a lot to be said for staying in it and choosing not to grow bigger. The key is that the decision be a mindful one. If your vision is to have a single shop, a smallish craft studio, a very personal fifty-seat restaurant, or a modestly sized medical practice, you don't really need to move beyond this level. If you're happy here, I'm all for it. Growth for growth's sake rarely gets one anyplace but into trouble—going where you don't really want to go just because you "should" or because "it's too good to pass up" is likely to become a very bad scene.

 ## Signs That It's Time to Shift to Stage 3

You're arguing about having too many meetings. This may seem comical, but it's proven to be true in too many cases to ignore it. If you're spending way too much time and energy disagreeing about whether you should have more meetings, you're having an argument over organizational tactics that tells me it's time to move to the next stage. By dint of who they are, the people who've been happy being on a Stage 1 and/or 2 team are going to chafe at the seeming "confinement" that comes when you start shifting to Stage 3. They can stretch a bit to go from the adrenaline rush and freelance style that dominates Stage 1 into the somewhat more manageable hands-on, more organized work habits of Stage 2. But structure is not likely to be their favorite word, and sitting in meetings will never make them happy.

Most Stage 1 and 2 leaders want to go out and "work hard and have fun," not sit in meetings making abstract decisions about issues that "really don't even matter." They may also lack the expertise to handle skill areas at this third level. To state the nearly obvious, doing HR for 500 is a lot more complicated than it was for 50. For most of those folks, Stage 2 is something of a stretch, but Stage 3 often just plain sucks. By the way, I don't blame them for resisting —they are, I believe, living the elegant simplicity of Schein's supposition: the right style of leadership at one stage becomes more and more ineffective as you move into the next.

b. It's getting harder and harder to make major decisions. Important things are ever more frequently bottled up in the owner's head and hands. When the leader's not there, no one really wants to make decisions, which means that they're likely calling, emailing, texting, or whatever other techno-technique has been invented since I wrote this article about things that they really ought to be able to deal with on their own.

c. It's all piling up on the boss's back. Although you may well have hired a manager (or a group of managers), it still feels like things are falling more and more back on you.

d. You cycle through flavor-of-the-day management. In an effort to improve, you try a bunch of seemingly good systems, but nothing seems to stick. You're always fishing for better philosophies in an effort to do the right thing, but they all seem to go wrong. New programs are flying around like cards at a poker table. If someone doesn't like today's topic, they hope that the folks at the top will slowly forget about it and quickly come back with a "better" way to work. Intentions are good, but the reality is really anything but. The leader is kind of caught between stages; things are past the point where they can just get something done by force of personality, but they're not process focused enough to get things rolling really effectively.

e. Effort is high but results fall short. Leaders can no longer score enough points on their own for the team to win consistently, but neither do they have the highly skilled performers around them who can carry the day. The boss's frustration grows daily, and so does that of the rest of the team. The more projects you take on, the bigger the gap gets between what your Stage 2 managers can do and what needs to be done, the more they unwittingly resist the changes, the more frustration grows and energy flags. The business has neither the infrastructure nor the organizational ability to put more advanced approaches in place in a way that really sticks. It's a rough paradox to power through.

f. You're increasingly annoyed with others' inability to see what's so obvious to you. As a result, the fun factor is probably falling fast.

Fun Falling Index?

This last bit, the fun falling off, is applicable to the need to shift tactics at each of the four stages of organizational growth. As Paul Hawken writes in *Growing a Business,* "Laughter and good humor are the canaries in the mine of commerce. If employees, customers and vendors don't laugh and have a good time at your company, something is wrong." He's right on. When the fun is falling faster than whatever else it is you pay attention to that falls, the odds are you need to move mindfully to the next stage and adjust your leadership style accordingly. It might well be time to refer back to the old *Rolling Stones* cover of Mississippi Fred McDowell. As the song says, "You got to move!"

Stage 3—Maturing: The Leader as Sustainer of Culture

Operating in Prime

Schein calls this stage "maturity," but I'm going to go with a different name. While he and I are in synch on the details of leading in this stage, I shy away from using this term because it carries negative connotations. Perhaps I'm still struggling with my own rebellious tendencies, but I think many creative entrepreneurs hear "maturity" and immediately translate it to "over the hill." I prefer the terminology of author Ichak Adizes, whose book *Corporate Lifecycles* I loved. Adizes calls his comparable level of development "operating in prime." That just sounds better to my ears. Whatever you call it, though, the point is that things at this stage are well organized, vibrant, innovative, and very well run. Most everyone in a Stage 3 company knows what's going on and knows the role they can play in bringing success to the organization. If Stage 1 is about "doing it," and Stage 2 is more about "developing people and culture," Stage 3 is about effectively building an organization. Systems development and effective and consistent processes become critical.

Prime doesn't mean perfect, mind you, but it does mean that things are running well and mindfully so. The business at this stage is no longer dependent on in-the-moment leadership heroics, and the organization itself becomes the focus far more than the founder(s). At the third stage, there are systems and structures in place and they actually work. As per Natural Law #4 (see page 236), people are doing great work because they're part of a great organization that has been created—and is being regularly improved upon—by the great people who are part of it. Problems probably pop up with much the same frequency as they do at every other stage, but what's different is the way the organization responds to them.

As Adizes explains, "Prime organizations know what they're doing, where they're going and how to get there. . . . A Prime can tell you why they are going to make money. And they do . . ." It's not that things are in control—to the contrary, nothing is. But when economies dip, key people take ill, competitors open nearby, or whatever other of the fifteen million things that can go wrong do, an organization that's running in prime will "know" what to do and, generally, if imperfectly, can do it. The obvious analogy for me is the experienced, championship caliber basketball team that finds itself down a dozen points going into the fourth quarter, but somehow manages to win by ten, all the while working together; taking charge of the game's tempo; staying calm, cool, and confident throughout. Businesses that are operating in prime can, I would posit, stay that way for a very long time—there's no expiration date on organizational excellence.

Leading successfully at Stage 3 is no small achievement. Since most entrepreneurs enter business at Stage 1, and are comfortable with the chaos and the adrenaline rushes that go with it, leading well at Stage 3 is more often than not a major internal challenge. Most folks who succeeded at Stage 1 sort of naturally "grew" and matured their way through Stage 2—a reasonable rate of learning and a modicum of willingness to delegate and let go can help make that move successful. But for someone who started in Stage 1, to shift successfully to leading well at Stage 3 takes a *lot* of *internal* effort, of the sort that's outlined in this book.

Like it or not, we can't just will the organization to move successfully into Stage 3. To the contrary, as per Schein's solid supposition, if we're not careful, the very things that made us successful at Stage 1 will become our undoing at Stage 3. Keep in mind that to become great at anything is not an overnight activity. (You can take a look at Natural Law #11 on page 255 for more on this subject.) It takes many years of mindful practice and a lot of hard work to make one's way towards a high level of skill and success. That means that to become *strong at systems development and organizational structure* when you've mostly excelled with high energy and acting on intuition, to move away from a hands-on approach to mindful, big picture management, is probably a four- or five-year project. You, of course, don't have to be outstanding overnight; just know that it will be a lot of work and that you will pass through a good bit of frustration en route. Having done it, I'd happily recommend making the effort. It took a long time to get there, but I'm far more effective, calmer, and more able to attain what I want for having learned how to do it.

At Stage 3, a leader's also got to have the *willingness to bring in significant technical expertise* that they didn't need, and couldn't afford, as a smaller organization. At Stage 1, most of the nonfinancial capital—the ideas, the intuition, the personality, the stamina, the energy, the stick-to-itiveness, the job skill and expertise—likely comes from the leader or leaders. At Stage 2, you can still succeed by getting some smart, supportive, like-minded souls around you and delegating effectively. But to operate a larger organization in prime, leaders need to have the insight and the wherewithal to go out and bring in expertise in areas they're used to figuring out for themselves. Stage 3 is a lot about hiring people with formal training who, in theory at least, know a lot more about their subject matter than we do. And we probably have to pay a lot for their expertise—which might mean salaries as high as, or even more than, whatever it is we're making. All of which can mean unseating or eroding the power of longtime managers in the organization.

This work—bringing in high-end outside experts—was for me the toughest change to make. Promoting from within feels easier, but it's hard to do in a way that brings real growth and success to the organization; the people who were fine at Stage 2 often don't have the drive or interest to work well at this level. Even if they like the idea of it, they rarely have the expertise and often (not always!) aren't ready to really go out and study aggressively in order to learn. They were fine with the leader being the one that always takes the big shot. Stage 3, though, calls for others to be able to step up and really lead, broadly, effectively, and innovatively, on a regular basis. Being ready and then able to find, hire, trust, pay, and stick with those people—whom we usually haven't known for all that long—while they get oriented and actually start to contribute a lot is no small thing. It's like sticking me, with my low-level claustrophobia, in a spot where I have to go through a long narrow opening to get into a much more open space. It's scary. Getting through to the other side requires steady breathing to stay calm when you want to panic; you need to work your way through the seeming insanity and feeling of impending doom that inevitably inserts itself into the transition.

Of course, it's easier to *talk* about finding the right people than it is to *do it*. Unlike other spots in our organization, where we have anywhere from a couple to a couple dozen of the same job slots to fill (bakers, bussers, sandwich makers, cheese sellers, etc.), we'd usually only bring in one finance expert (or HR or IT or whatever) at a time. And like it or not (I don't), it takes a good six months, or probably more like twelve, to really tell how they're going to do. The whole thing is hard. It's tough to get others in the organization to accept the newcomers and their new ways of working. It's tough to stay out of their way when they start to do things we don't like. And it's tough to know when to intervene or even to end things—just because these folks have expertise doesn't mean they're guaranteed to excel. We took three shots at an upper-end HR person before finding an excellent match. In the end, we got a highly skilled service provider, but the process was really anything but pleasant.

One side note—it remains imperative that we intervene if and when these newly hired experts start doing things that are in direct opposition to our organizational values. If you're stepping up and making the move mindfully into this third of Schein's stages, it's pretty likely that, sooner or later, this is going to happen. To quote Hugh MacLeod, from his masterful book *Ignore Everybody*: "Your idea finally seems to be working, seems to be getting all sorts of traction, and all of a sudden you've got all these swarms of people trying to join the team, trying to get a piece of the action." Sounds familiar. I've been there. MacLeod goes on, "As soon as they get a foothold inside the inner circle, you soon realize they never really understood your idea in the first place, they just want to be on the winning team. And the weirdest part is, they don't seem to mind sabotaging your original idea that got them interested in the first place, in order to maintain their newfound social status. It's probably the most bizarre bit of human behavior I've ever witnessed firsthand in business, and it's amazingly common."

I've lived through this, and I know it's true, and it still kills me just to read about it. Here's the same story from the very sad saga of John Peterman, owner and founder of the once very successful J. Peterman catalog. His essay gave me great perspective at the time it appeared in the *Harvard Business Review*, and it still does today. It also makes me very anxious. J. Peterman was a very special catalog that failed, after years of success. While we all know that failures happen in spite of everyone's best efforts, it's not easy to be reminded of that unfortunate reality. As I've known and said about sixteen thousand times over the years, no one can guarantee our continued existence as a business.

With that in mind, here's Peterman's take on the process of bringing in experts as part of this third stage of organizational development:

> *Doing what we did, the way we did it, caused problems on several levels. For one, our existing staff felt slighted. The people we brought in were in many cases making higher salaries for no good reason except that to hire them we had to meet what they were already making. And the spotlight was on the new folks. When decisions needed to be made, we paid more attention to the new staff than to the old-timers.*
>
> *For another, the culture started to fray. We didn't have a hard time recruiting. It was well-known that our culture was one of creativity and respect for people; there was no shortage of people who wanted to join that culture. But when you hire people from a culture that isn't respectful or from a culture that is very controlling, it's like bringing an abused dog into a friendly home. It takes time and a lot of patience and positive reinforcement for the dog to trust you—to know that every time you walk by you're not going to whack it.*
>
> *When you don't have the time to offer continual positive reinforcement, the natural tendency is for the new people to slip back into old cultural habits. After all, that's what they know best. In the absence of constant reminders that they now have the authority to do this, and that the organization is structured so that they should feel free to do that, they'll re-create their old culture and set up boundaries between people, levels, and departments where none previously existed.*

That's the scary scenario. How can you avoid it? It's not easy. Having your values, vision and mission in writing—and actively in use—before you hire these new experts definitely helps. Having a solid of set of outside advisors, leadership soul mates, that you trust to get a reality check when you're struggling to stay on course can help as well. Clear written performance expectations that are reviewed before the person takes the position are also very beneficial. Still, there are no guarantees of success. Which I guess leads me to one other tip—early in the new expert's employment, while things are still pretty sure to be going well, ask them this question: "In case things don't go as well as we both hope, how would you like me to tell you about my concerns?" You will at least then have some clue as to how to best communicate concerns if tensions get high. It won't solve the problem, but it will at least make it easier to work on it.

Fortunately, bringing in high-level expertise can also succeed. We've had—and still have —some great people who've come to work with us in this way. Ron Maurer, who manages our entire admin team, has been a near-perfect match, and we feel fortunate to have found him!

Of course, once you hire your experts, it's important to manage them effectively. It's necessary at Stage 3 *to move away from mere delegating.* At Stage 2, we delegate a task; at Stage 3, we hire people to head up entire areas of responsibility. In the process, things shift so that we are now helping them, rather than them helping us. Stage 2 is paying someone to do your e-news and someone else to make some signs. *At Stage 3, you shift to putting a single person fully in charge of all marketing activity*—everything to do with marketing will fall onto their job description.

Another area of great importance is a new *emphasis on systems.* Stage 2 leaders generally fight this—to impose structures makes them feel like they're being strangled. But when you're in the prime stage, you need to think about well-balanced systems, designed in ways that promote personality and individuality. In fact, the creativity of good people and well-designed systems should actually support each other. I think that's what we've worked so hard to do with anarcho-capitalism here at Zingerman's. The systems are set up to bring out individuality, creativity, and intelligence, which in turn helps make the systems better, which in turn attracts better people to the organization and makes new arrivals more effective more quickly, and on and on, in—hopefully—a never ending cycle of steady improvement. To Rosabeth Moss Kanter's point, it's "not the players and it's not the system. It's the players in the system."

Given all of what I've said—bringing in new expertise, assigning entire areas of responsibility to others, and successfully implementing new systems—it's not hard to figure out that changes will need to happen more slowly at Stage 3 than they would have at Stage 1 or 2. Natural Law #10 says that strengths lead to weaknesses—at this third level, you have far more stability than you did as a startup, which is great. But the flip side of the cultural coin is that it takes, commensurately, considerably longer to make meaningful change happen. For a new HR person to put processes properly and respectfully in place is probably a yearlong project, often even longer, and it can take two or three years for that work to be well woven into the fabric of your culture. This is tough for folks who like immediate gratification. Even the thought of it will make most of us who love the fast pace of Stage 1 start to twitch.

I understand that most entrepreneurs reading through this probably see the word "bureaucracy" wedged tightly between the lines of what I've written above. But done well, Stage 3 is about anything but bureaucracy. To the contrary, it's about starting to see system design and organizational development as creative arts in themselves. It's a willingness to see beauty and grace in setting up, and sticking to, due process. It's about designing systems that are as creative and compelling as a new dish in the kitchen would be to a cook or an exciting new social media campaign might be to launch. A successful leader at this level can experience the development of key people as one of the highest creative acts to undertake, not a task to be turned over to HR.

In Kanter's context of successful teams, the winning organization is the one that builds on tradition, that is confident but not cocky, that triumphs regularly but takes little or nothing for granted. *Its key strengths,* she says, *are accountability, collaboration, and initiative.* People get used to winning and they like it. "In a Prime organization," Adizes adds, "there is a climate of repetitive success. Failure is unusual and it gets attention." When you're in prime, if things go bad—and clearly they still can—the crew can usually pull together, fall back on existing systems, muster up some emotional resilience, reread the vision and the values, converse with customers, collaborate with each other, and make something good happen to turn the situation around. Of course, the work is never done—we never really reach mastery; we just try to get ever closer. (See Daniel Pink's book *Drive,* or the epilogue in *Zingerman's Guide to Good Leading, Part 1,* or both). As Adizes emphasizes, "Prime does not mean that you have arrived, but that you are still growing. It is a process, not a destination." And when you get into the process, if you're good, you can stay there for a very long time.

 **Signs That It's Time to Move to Stage 4**

Unlike the moves from Stage 1 to 2, or 2 to 3, I don't think anyone really relishes shifting from Stage 3 to 4. Many of us want to improve, but hardly any of us are actively after the kind of drastic change that Stage 4 is all about. Unless you're a turnaround expert, it's probably not going to be your favorite phase. All the work one can do around building self-awareness; getting the right people involved; learning to stay centered and grounded; going with your gut and not with what others, more invested in the status quo, will say comes into play here. Having the courage to carry on and lead the way as your business reinvents itself (and, perhaps, you personally as well) is very hard to do to. It requires a great deal of acceptance and self-reflection to own the idea that was once cutting edge and high energy but is now headed towards being irrelevant and out of date. It's admitting to ourselves that what worked so well for so long isn't helping us anymore. Here are some of the signs that it's time to change.

a. Sales are still up, but profits are steadily going down. I used to think this was just what had happened to us at Zingerman's, but I've heard it from so many others that I'm pretty sure it's a universal sign of trouble. I'm not talking about a year or two where you consciously configured your budget to invest in expansion or something purposeful like that. Rather, it's when everyone's working harder than ever, and sales are successfully increasing, but despite everyone's best efforts, there's less and less left at the bottom line. If you haven't been there, it's not as odd as it might sound. As the business grows, as people get paid their "fair" share more and more, as everyone becomes (understandably) less interested in scraping along the bottom without spending, as people become somewhat less hungry and less worried about failure, costs go up. And at the same time, your once-unique product, service, signature, and destination item is ever more widely copied in the marketplace. That means it's harder and harder to get the margins that made your business sustainable in the first place.

b. There's no longer an inspiring, strategically sound vision that shows the business becoming something truly special. In many cases—as it was for us in the early '90s—the original vision of the organization has been pretty much completed. But without a clear vision of the future, it becomes harder and harder for anyone to make big, bold decisions. The rumor mill is buzzing. And because people aren't clear on where the company is headed, it's hard for staff to grow and pursue their passions within the existing framework of the organization. Everything starts to feel too risky. No one wants to take a chance, and everyone wants more data before they decide. Some people can see the need to change, but it's impossible to prove the benefits of any initiative beyond the shadow of a financial doubt. Staying with the status quo just seems safer.

To be clear, don't assume that lack of vision implies a lack of action—at this stage, there's usually no shortage of tactical activity, plenty of arguing over near-term strategic decisions, introduction of line extensions, etc. But the drive to build a clearly described and widely agreed upon, hard to get to but compelling "cathedral"—that inspiring vision of the future that we're always driving towards far out in the future—is no longer there. Following the metaphor, it becomes more and more about redecorating the rooms of the already existing structure, adding a bit more space here or there, or doing a study on what sort of bushes are best to put out front. But the sorts of innovations, the major departures from the past that probably marked the organization's initial success, aren't happening.

c. The Twelve Natural Laws of Business, which at one point (knowingly or not) formed the foundation of the organization's existence, fall further and further from the forefront. The entrepreneurial energy that made you so successful is harder and harder to find. Intuition has been done in by institutionalized intransigence. Holding onto one's territory becomes more important than taking chances to try out new things.

d. Systems subvert creativity instead of supporting it. Although staff may still work hard and diligently punch the clock, more and more people take their passions elsewhere. This, by the way, is the bad bureaucracy all entrepreneurs have nightmares about, and for good reason—it's a recipe for a disengaged and disinterested work force. (For more on this situation, see the "Energy Crisis in the American Workplace" section in *Zingerman's Guide to Good Leading, Part 2*.) More and more, it feels like you're on a once-good team, still fairly strong but playing not to lose rather than taking the risks that really get you to greatness.

The Not-So-Great Diversion

Feeling constrained and lacking a clear next vision for the organization, many founders will pursue some big opportunity and strike out for freedom that allows them to steer clear of structure. I've found that this is rarely a productive long-term solution to the problem of growth. It's a way to put off dealing with the issues, but it never makes them just disappear. It's akin to a middle-aged guy going out and buying an antique Corvette convertible when his family is falling apart. Nothing inherently evil about it. But it can start to feel a bit incongruous if other things aren't in synch.

Stage 4— Changing: The Leader as Change Agent

TAKING THE ORGANIZATION INTO A NEW ERA

Stage 4, I think, is probably the most challenging one in which to lead. It's the point in an organization's life cycle where the time has come to make major change—to leave behind many of the things that might have made us what we are and begin to drive towards a new, innovative, and inspiring future. Pulling off successful Stage 4 leadership requires us to simultaneously employ all of the skills needed in the first three stages. A leader at this level has to be bold, willing to act on intuition, and to have the emotional stamina to stick with things when almost no one else is ready to make the changes that need to be made. The leader needs to be able to see a future; develop an inspiring, strategically sound, long-term vision; put it in writing; and communicate it effectively to the organization. But unlike in the other three stages, where the majority of men and women in the organization are into what they're doing, at Stage 4, hardly anyone other than the boss is likely to be excited about the changes the leader wants to make. Which means that while the leader needs the stamina and energy activity they had in the startup stage, they also need to possess the ability to effectively assign entire areas of responsibility and bring other leaders on board.

Getting going in a startup situation takes guts. But having the courage to change an organization with a long track record of success and take apart what's worked well for many years is, I think, far harder. Hardly anyone on staff will still have a "take one for the team" mindset. Impatience is high, interest in taking on more work is low. Most long-time customers and staff will still be loyal to the way things have been and not be excited to embark on a big new path. Many others will have grown disenchanted and have long since checked out. Everyone has high expectations but little hope. But it can be done. You can do Stage 4 and succeed! I know because we've done it.

Another Look at the Four Stages

I've never played organized sports and I rarely even watch them anymore. But because I grew up paying a great deal of attention to them, I still have sports metaphors embedded deep in my brain. It strikes me that Stage 1 (creating) is like getting a pickup team together to play a few games of basketball. The leader is the star. If the team does well, the other players are generally happy to be in supporting roles. Nobody minds that it's all very informal. In fact, they kind of like it that way; it's fun, it's free-form, it's funky, and it works! If the leader sits out, gets hurt, or gives up, the game's probably over.

Stage 2 is more like getting your little pickup team into an intramural league. There's a schedule, and the leader gets some better players around them who can support the style they like to play and who are more talented than the folks that originally signed up. People have positions that they line up in, and you even draw up a few plays to run and people will learn them. Mostly, though, it's still the leader who's calling the shots, setting the tempo, making most of the big plays. When the leader sits out or get hurts, the team can keep going for a while, but more often than not they start to founder fairly quickly when they're on their own.

Stage 3, I think, is akin to turning your little team into a full-on professional franchise. You now need a VP of admin to run ticket sales, someone to make sure the players you've drafted get vetted and trained. You need a trainer, a coach with assistants, a community relations expert, a PR person, a stadium to play in, someone to negotiate the lease and manage the building, etc. Getting the idea?

At Stage 1, you're the star player. At Stage 2, you become more of a player-coach. At Stage 3, you're the owner of an entire team, while still probably coaching as well and, on occasion, acting as the star player. At Stage 3, it's as much about running a business as it is about basketball. If you look at the history of sports or business to see how many individuals have been able to succeed on all three levels, I'm guessing the list won't have a lot of names on it. Many try, most fail. Why? *Because, again, the same skills that lead to success at one stage lead to failure at the others.* If we don't adjust our approaches and learn new ways to lead, the likelihood of being good at all three is next to nil.

To finish my metaphorical cycle, though, Stage 4 is the point at which you realize that the entire way you've been playing the game (whatever game it is you're playing) is getting old, outdated, and ever more ineffective. What was once cutting edge is now barely cutting it. To return to a business framework, it doesn't mean you're on the verge of closing down—the early indicators that it's time to change often come while the company still appears, to a casual outsider, to be booming. It's not an overnight event; the increasing irrelevance of the organization and the commensurate decline in energy are generally gradual things. But in its inexorable way, it is happening; with each passing day, the business becomes just a bit more uninspiring. Customers who like to be market leaders are shifting their loyalties to more innovative competitors. Without an intervention from the leaders of the organization, the business is bound to become ever more moribund.

That's not, I know, an assessment that's easy to accept. It requires a lot of letting go, grieving what had been so great, accepting that things as they once were will never be again. Change like this is terrifically tough to go through. As Schein says, "Unlearning is an entirely different process, involving anxiety, defensiveness, and resistance to change." I've been through it and I didn't enjoy it. But the harsh reality is that it's way better than the alternative, which is to eventually go out of business. The organizational reset that takes place at this fourth stage can be done. If the leader is strong enough of heart and vision to venture into this zone, great things can eventually come of it. Our ability to work hard to learn how to lead in each of the four stages is a significant, if little understood, element of our success here at Zingerman's.

Stage 4, "Changing," is what we went through during the period of 1994–95 when we rolled out our Zingerman's 2009 vision. We were, in essence, on the down side of Stage 3. Things had been going well and we were, by all surface level standards, a success. But we weren't rich and we weren't ready to retire. And because we'd fulfilled our original 1982 vision, there was little inspiration ahead other than a lot of work and a lot of discussion about what we might want to do next. It's not like things were bad or that we were bereft. But all those signs I've suggested happen when it's time to move from Stage 3 into 4 were happening. (How did you think I knew what the signs were, anyway?) This is where many previously great organizations get stuck. Without either the intuitive sense of things that Paul had when he asked me in 1993 where I wanted to be in ten years, or the awareness one can have after studying and accepting Schein's stages, most previously successful leaders really struggle. It's hard to let go of what was. But without the clear vision of greatness, the innovative edge in the marketplace, and the fun and passion of earlier eras, burnout begins to set in.

A Staged History of Zingerman's, à la Schein

I thought it might be helpful to give you a sense of what we've been through here. All of the dates below, as in much of recorded history, are estimates. I could, of course, create a similar chart for each of the Zingerman's businesses on its own, but here I've done it only for the organization overall.

1982–84   **Creating:** The Deli goes successfully through its first few years

1984–88   **Building:** We get bigger, we expand, we hire our first managers

1988–91   **Operating in prime:** A good management team, good results, continued growth

1991–93   **Time to change:** Our original vision had been fulfilled. Things were still good in many ways, but less and less inspiring. Our future wasn't in doubt, but no one knew what it was. It was Paul's intuition that saved us really when, in the summer of '93, he asked me where I wanted us to be in ten years. The Bakehouse opened in 1991, in hindsight, a piece of the work of beginning to change

1994–95   **Changing:** This is the period in which we wrote out our 2009 vision and started all of the work to turn what we were doing at the Deli into the Zingerman's Community of Businesses.

1995–96   **Creating:** The early years of the Zingerman's Community were filled with fun, but also the frustrating and emotionally exhausting sort of events that are the hallmark of any startup. But we were moving, steadily if at times shakily, towards our new future.

1996–2005   **Building:** Gradually figuring out how all this was going to work, starting to grow by opening other businesses. Things settled down some, and we corrected some of our early tactical errors and gained some traction.

2005–Present   **Operating in prime:** While we're far from perfect, a lot of good pieces—and good processes—have been put in place. Open book finance, better annual planning, Net Promoter scores, a big increase in the range of our training work, etc. Bringing in expertise a few years before this period helped a lot—Ron Maurer joined us in December of 2000 as our vice president of operations. It probably took him three or four years to help bring more structure and stability to our financial and other infrastructure. We brought in others with expertise as well into HR, Marketing, IT, etc.

Where Each Zingerman's Business Is as I Write

The chart to the left is my sense of where our organization overall fits into Schein's stages. Below is my best shot at where each of the businesses *within* the Zingerman's Community currently stands.

Business	Founded	Stage
Deli	1982	**Changing:** We've just finished a seven-year expansion project and are in the process of emerging from that work and coming out the other side.
Bakehouse	1992	**Operating in prime**
Mail Order	1996	**Operating in prime**
ZingTrain	1994	**Building,** moving towards operating in prime
Creamery	2000	**Building**
Roadhouse	2003	**Building,** moving towards operating in prime
Coffee	2003	**Building**
Candy	2009	**Creating**

Many leaders at this point let go and sell the business; others fight hard but fail. A few have the insight, courage, or good fortune to go forward and turn what was once great into something new and often even more interesting and exciting than the original. With all due humility, I have to think that's what we pulled off with the Zingerman's Community of Businesses. In essence, we took apart much of what we'd so carefully constructed, and then reconfigured it into a new, challenging, and inspiring long-term vision. Hardly anyone other than Paul and I and a few friends were exceedingly excited about the new future we'd set our sights on. Most people thought we were crazy. The vision we wrote was completely different from what anyone else we knew, or knew of, was doing, so there were no comparable models to benchmark against. Breaking new ground sounds great after you've succeeded, but it's anything but easy while you're doing it.

The good news, as you know, is that we made it successfully through that changing stage and have since worked our way back up, through creating and building, into now operating again in prime. This year, as I write, we'll do about $46,000,000 in sales and have six hundred or so people on our payroll. I hope that we can stay in prime for a long time to come. Not all change efforts work out so well, but ours, I believe, has radically altered our business ecosystem for the better (see page 397 in Secret #39 on Creativity for more on that subject). Having the heart and mind to let go of what got you to where you are is no small thing.

How do you know it's time to change? There are hundreds of examples, mostly obvious only after the fact. The music world's move from vinyl to tapes to CDs to downloads is one example. The end of newspapers as the dominant news source has clearly happened in the last decade. In basketball, what comes to mind is the demise of the set shot. Few people now know it, but sixty or seventy years ago, the jump shot at the core of today's game was basically nonexistent. The shot that everyone was trained for on a professional level was called the set shot. You took it with both feet flat on the ground, facing the basket, with the ball held in both hands, one on either side of the ball at about chest level, and then released—with proper form of course—at the basket. In those days, to quote sportswriter Lew Freedman, "coaches commonly issued reprimands if they saw daylight beneath a player's feet."

Today, of course, the set shot seems silly. Most people have never even heard of it and *no one* uses it. It was replaced by the "invention" of what we now know as the jump shot. (Even if you don't pay much attention to basketball, I'm sure you've seen a jump shot—a player bounces up off the ground, hands overhead, holding the ball in one hand and guiding with the other. At the height of the jump, the ball is released towards the basket.) Freedman posits that the inventor was one Kenny Sailors, who worked out the jump shot while playing for the University of Wyoming back in the '40s. Other writers give credit elsewhere, but the backstory is basically the same: shorter players like Sailors started to ignore their coaches' instructions. They jumped, their feet left the floor, and they lifted the ball over their heads to shoot over top of taller players. Their rule breaking broke down the old order; they were pioneers.

Sailors was probably smiling; he successfully beat the system. But imagine that you were on the other side. Let's say that in the first years of jump shooting, you were running a basketball team whose coaches and players had long been considered the best set shot shooters in the business. They'd learned it, studied it, practiced it, and come as close as one could to perfecting it. They'd relied on their prowess to power them to a series of championships. They'd won acclaim and felt good about their acumen. The set shot was, not surprisingly, woven into everything the team did, from training camp all the way through to the poses taken for team photos. And then one day this strange short guy starts doing an unprofessional thing we now know as a jump shot. Would you have the courage to drop what had made you successful and switch everything and everyone over to this new-fangled way of playing the game? Statistics show that unless you were one of a very small segment of innovators, you would have pooh-poohed it. And your organization would have paid the price.

The subsequent slide for your team probably wouldn't lead to overnight collapse. Over time, the team would realize that they ought to learn to defend against the new approach. But mostly they still shoot set shots. The team's record starts to slide, but you're still okay. You proceed apace. You start to dip deeper and deeper in the standings, which sucks, but it's not an easy fix—most everyone on your team is tied to, trained in, and excels at set shots. It's what earned you your success. Can they learn to shoot the jump shot? Maybe. But the skill set is different. Plus, you might wonder, do they even want to learn the jump shot? I mean, who wants to go from being great at what they've been doing for decades to being an awkward novice in an approach someone else invented without asking you if it was ok? Next to no one! But at some point, if you don't adjust and get with the new program, you'll become a dinosaur. The organization may have the money banked up to keep going for a while, but the sense of being the leader, the winners, feeling good about what you're doing, will evaporate.

Somewhere in that cycle—preferably earlier rather than later—a Stage 4 leader has to have the insight to understand what's going on and to make the needed changes to bring the group back to greatness. It's certainly possible that some within the organization may be able to make that move along with the leader, but more often than not they don't. We lost pretty much our entire management team at the Deli in the years following our decision to pursue the 2009 vision. They were good people, they cared a lot, they'd contributed quite a bit to getting us to where we were, but they just weren't well suited to the new direction we were taking. Their departure was painful and it took a long time, but the good news is we're still on good terms with all of them. Looking back on it all 20 years later, I can say with certainty that it might have been easier if we'd made the move more quickly, but of course that's easier said than done.

In Stage 4, the hardest of all the stages, you need to go for broke the way you do in a start-up, but you have to do it with people who are used to things already going well, with staff who've known success and assume stability is the norm, and with a significant segment of your customer base (shrinking though it might be) who don't like the new way you're going to do things. As Schein says, Stage 4 leaders "have to have the emotional strength to be supportive of the organization while it deals with the anxieties attendant upon unlearning processes that were previously successful, that is, the ability to create for the organization a sense of 'psychological safety.' And second, they need a true understanding of cultural dynamics and the properties of their own organizational culture."

Concluding Thoughts

As you already know, I didn't invent this outlook on organizational growth, the four stages, or the jump shot. All I've got is some experience of having led, with varying degrees of success, through all four of Schein's stages and a bit of insight gathered from studying and teaching others about them. Most people, I've found, are more comfortable with one stage or another, or they like one of the four far more than the rest. I honestly don't think I'm particularly comfortable in any of them. Start-ups scare me, but so do big organizations, and the prospect of being confined in strict, well-structured systems; I don't like standing pat, but change makes me nervous. And yet I've actually gone through—and had success—at all four levels. If I can figure this stuff out, so can you.

Looking at this from my own experience and projecting outward, I see three keys for leaders who want to succeed at any level.

a. Acceptance. Whether we like them or not, Schein's stages are the reality of what all organizations, and the leaders within them, experience. When our business is at a level that we as leaders personally prefer, everything seems as it should be. "This is what business is all about," is a common refrain from a leader who's well matched with their organization's level of operation. But when the business passes into a stage that we're not comfortable with, frustration will surely set in. The most common outcomes are anger, antipathy, burnout, and head banging. My hope is that Schein's construct will give you the understanding and insight to make better decisions about the style of leadership you're pursuing. With this knowledge in hand, acceptance is of the essence if we want to get to a better place. We can't fix what we don't believe is broken, and we can't learn to manage in the style best suited to the level our organization is at when we don't even know that there are different styles for different stages.

b. Vision. Without a clear vision of the future, it's hard to get to greatness in any context. The longer we've been in business, the longer we've been leading, the more the lack of a vision can cause confusion. I'm actually talking about *two* visions—one for yourself as a leader at whatever stage you're now consciously choosing to go after, and then an agreed-upon vision for the overall organization.

c. Commitment to Learning New Skills. Having a vision of success that's in synch with your Schein stage is a great start. But the decision to adapt our leadership style is only the first step—then we need to begin the long, slow, steady work to get good at the skills that are needed at the level of development your organization is at. Be prepared for that process to take a long time (see Natural Law #11 on page 255).

Anyone who's up for all three things—accepting the stage you're in, writing a vision of greatness, and making a commitment to learning new skills—will, I'm pretty confident, succeed. If you want to be good at this stuff and are willing to work hard at it over a long period of time, you can do it.

To close, I'll again turn to the prescient, 20-plus-year-old words of Dr. Schein. I first read his excellent essay in a compilation put together by the Drucker Foundation, called *The Leader of the Future*. Hence, Schein's closing remarks address that subject: What will leaders of the future need to do to succeed? Speaking about the four levels, the good doctor forecasted:

> *Perhaps the most salient aspect of future leadership will be that these characteristics will not be present in a few people all the time but will be present in many people some of the time, as circumstances change and as different people develop the insight to move into leadership roles. Leadership will then increasingly be an emergent function rather than a property of people appointed to formal roles. Whereas today the process of appointing leaders is a critical function of boards of directors, electorates, government agencies, and so on, we can imagine that, in the future, appointed leaders will not play the key leadership roles but will be perpetual diagnosticians who will be able to empower different people at different times and to let emergent leadership flourish. They will not assume that all groups need leadership, they will not assume that leadership means hierarchy and control of others, and they will not assume that accountability must always be individual. Instead, the leader of the future will be a person with the characteristics mentioned above who*

*can lead and follow, be central and marginal, be hierarchically above
and below, be individualistic and a team player, and, above all, be a
perpetual learner. If the world is to learn to manage itself better, many
more people in organizations will have to be leaders and the leadership
functions described above will have to be much more widely shared.*

This description of the leader of the future sounds a heck of a lot like what
I've written about us doing here at Zingerman's—the forecast seems fully in
synch with what I've come to call anarcho-capitalism (see *Part 2,* page 259)
and why I believe everyone in a sustainable organization needs to take responsibility for effective leadership (see *Part 2,* Secret #22, We're All Leaders).

As I write this, Dr. Schein is 83 years old and still going strong. I hope he
keeps shining his intellectual light on the rest of us for many years to come.
This particular essay and his hundreds of others, are, to me, like marvelous,
well-polished diamonds in a very messy mine of business literature. His insight
has helped me get to where I am, and I'm eternally grateful for his help. I
hope this cover version of his work will help many others to do well too. Many
thanks to Dr. Schein for showing me how to grow as a leader in ways I'd never
even have imagined. I don't think I'd be where I am without his insight.

Postscript: Levels of Leading and Circles of Trust

Part of why I love teaching is that I learn something new every time I do it.
At a ZingTrain session not long ago, I was sharing the lessons I'd gleaned
from Schein's essay with a group of business people from around the country. Among the various folks in the audience was Ricki Carroll. Ricki started
her business—New England Cheesemaking Supply—back in 1978. For many
years, it was just her, operating on her own out of her Massachusetts home,
selling and shipping supplies to small creameries and home cheesemakers
around the country. I've known Ricki for over 25 years; where she's at right
now epitomizes the idea of mindful, centered, positive energy.

As we discussed the Schein levels that day, it seemed pretty clear that
Ricki's little mail-order operation had steadily moved forward, going from
probably twenty-something good years in the "creating" stage into the "building" stage. The business, which moved out of her house only last year, now has
a staff of nine and is being ably run by her daughter Sarah. After we'd spoken

about the various skills leaders need to have at each level, Ricki raised her hand. "It seems like at the first level the leader needs to trust themselves. And at the second level, where they start delegating, then they need to learn to trust others." As she so often is, Ricki was right on.

As I reflected more on the wisdom of what she'd said, I realized I could take Ricki's insight even further. At the third level, I started to see that the leader needs to "trust the process"—business at that stage isn't only about people, but about putting effective systems and structures in place to make good people's performances even better. To succeed as a change leader at the fourth level, we need to trust in all three directions at the same time. We need to trust ourselves, because it's really only from our own intuition that we can decide to take the organization in a new direction. We need to trust others, because the business has likely gotten way too big to pull off a change all by ourselves, the way we could when we had a small startup. And we also need to trust the process, because when all the upheaval of the change gets underway, we have to believe that the systems, structures, and long-term vision of greatness that we're putting in place are going to work, even though it'll look pretty scary partway through the change.

At Which Stage Do You Shine?

Having now had an in-depth look at Dr. Schein's four stages, take a few minutes to think about your own work. Can you chart your organization's history as I've done above with ours? In which stage do you think your organization is? Or is it in a transitional stage, moving from one level to the next?

Then think about yourself and your leadership skills. In which level are you most comfortable leading? How does that compare with what's needed from a leader at the stage of development in which your organization currently exists? What skills would you need to master to excel at leading at that level? Are you ready to really work at learning them? Or would you feel better finding a place to work that's more aligned with what you're already good at?

notes from the back dock

Maggie Bayless, Managing Partner, ZingTrain

When I started ZingTrain in 1994, I had a two-year-old son and another baby on the way. I'd read Ari and Paul's Zingerman's 2009 vision of creating a Community of Businesses and was thrilled by the opportunity to help make that vision a reality. My vision for ZingTrain was to create a business that would be the "keeper of the corporate knowledge" and support the growth of existing and yet-to-come Zingerman's businesses. I believed that if we were successful in building our businesses—and creating the positive culture of service that was central to the Zingerman's 2009 vision—then other organizations would be interested in learning about how we'd done that. For myself, I envisioned meaningful, challenging work that would allow me the flexibility to take family vacations and spend time with my kids as they were growing up. When I thought of my own childhood, the memories that stood out the strongest were of family vacations and travel—the benefit of a father who was a college professor and had the opportunity to take sabbaticals and longer than average summer vacations and a mother who loved to plan trips.

As this book gets ready to go to press I've realized that my initial long-term vision—both for ZingTrain and for my life—has come to pass. This summer we dropped my younger son off at college at The New School in NYC. His older brother is a senior at Clark University in Worcester, MA. Most of the summer was spent preparing to be "empty nesters" and I was more focused on what was happening at home than with my vision for ZingTrain. But as I look back over the past 19 years, I realize that my initial vision for the business has, indeed, been realized. ZingTrain is a thriving business that could exist without me—and, I hope, some day will.

One aspect of being an older woman who owns a business is that

I'm often asked for advice by young women who are early in their careers and wondering what their life is going to be like and how they'll balance everything they want to do—in particular, having kids and being in business. They often say something like "how did you do it? " Or "you've been so successful—it's very inspiring." Or (my favorite) "you make it look easy." And while for a long time I would protest that I was a) not especially successful and that b) it wasn't easy, I've now changed my answer to c) Yes, I've been successful. And it hasn't always been easy.

In fact, at any given time—on any particular day—it more often than not felt out of control and completely out of balance. But with age I've gained the ability to have perspective—pulling back from time to time to look at my life over the past 19 years—and I'm realizing, taken as a whole, these years have been completely successful—based on my personal vision of success.

ZingTrain is a thriving, profitable enterprise that is providing meaningful employment to a number of people. The work we've done within the Zingerman's Community of Businesses has definitely improved the quality of the training ZCoB employees receive. We've hosted hundreds of companies in our public seminars and done one-on-one work with hundreds more—and most of those organizations have implemented some aspect of what they learned here to improve their organization's effectiveness and strengthen their service culture.

On the personal side of the equation, I've traveled around the country to visit clients and have made lasting friendships with many of them. Every summer until my sons were 17 and 20 (and had full-time summer jobs of their own) we took a family vacation of usually 2, and once 5, weeks. I've spent every Christmas with my extended family and my in-laws. My husband and I have had trips alone together and I regularly get together with my college best friends. With my sons now both in college, I'm excited to put my attention on what's next: getting plans in place to take ZingTrain beyond 2020—when my vision is that I'll be stepping back from full-time, day-to-day management responsibility.

kieron hales standing out front of the roadhouse on a sunday morning

The Power of Personal Visioning

*Applying Natural Law #1
to the Business of Living*

The idea of a set of Natural Laws of Business originally came to me from Paul. He used to talk about his belief that these laws applied to all organizations, everywhere. And that like the law of gravity, they held true regardless of how we felt about them. Over the years, I built on Paul's concept and ended up with an essay—"The Twelve Natural Laws of Business" is Secret #1 in Zingerman's Guide to Good Leading, Part 1. *In the years since they appeared, the Natural Laws have proven themselves ever more solid. They now serve as the basis for ZingTrain's Zingerman's Experience Seminar and I've taught them to hundreds of organizations around the country. The basic concept remains clear. All successful organizations—for-profit, not-for-profit, large and small—basically live in harmony with the Natural Laws. So too, it turns out, do successful individuals.*

Because personal visioning is such a big part of sustainable self-management, I've devoted this entire essay to Natural Law #1: An inspiring, strategically sound vision leads the way to greatness (especially if you write it down!). Secret #36, which comes next, addresses the other eleven Natural Laws. They all come together to make some very positive things happen. It is my ever-firmer belief that in the right settings, most of us have a pretty good shot at living them, and in the process creating meaningful and positive lives and successful organizations. I want to acknowledge, as always, that there are millions of people in poverty or living on the edges of society who have little chance to embrace this stuff the way most others of us do. My hope is that, if the rest of us work at it hard, contributing positively to our communities to assist those who have less, we can help those in need to have a better shot at success as well.

It only took me a few years to figure it out, but I'm glad it's come clear now. Reflecting on the "Twelve Natural Laws of Business" essay that we put into *Part 1* of this series, I realized that the same set of guidelines that organically frame the way any successful organization works apply—with equal elegance and comparable effectiveness—as a format for successfully living our lives. I've adjusted the wording slightly to make them more applicable to individuals rather than organizations, but the concepts are the same. In fact, now that I've opened my mind to the message, it's amazingly obvious. The Natural Laws, after all, are *natural;* they stay the same whether we invoke them intelligently or ignore them out of hand. And since we know that congruency counts in creating a graceful, sustainable existence, it only makes sense that living in synch with the way we want our businesses to work would work well, or even work wonders, for us as individuals too.

Since I've gone on at length about mindfulness, I guess I should share the story of how I arrived at this insight about the Natural Laws and their role in everyday living. The story starts with an introduction.

Over the years, I've been introduced in a wide range of ways; people bestow different monikers on me in different settings. "The Zingerman's guy" is probably used the most often, but depending on where someone's heard of me or seen my name, there are a host of other descriptors that come up. Frequently, it's just "Ari from Zingerman's." In the food world, I'm often smilingly welcomed as "the bacon guy." (When you write a book about something, you quickly become the "guy" or the "gal" for that product or subject.) People who eat at the Roadhouse like to call me "the water boy" (Secret #25 on Managing by Pouring Water in *Part 2* of the *Guide to Good Leading*). In the business world, I'm most frequently presented as "one of the founders of Zingerman's." Sometimes it's all slimmed down to the factually inaccurate but spiritually correct, "Mr. Zingerman."

Even after having heard all of these and more a number of times, I'm still occasionally caught unprepared by what people say, which is what happened last fall when a customer introduced me to her friend. "Ari's basically, well, he's like a life coach," she said. That one threw me for a bit of a loop. It wasn't a bad thing, but it was definitely a surprise. "Leader," "line cook," "entrepreneur," or even "author" all sound ok. But "life coach"? What in the world, I wondered, would qualify me, a history major, who has never even attended a colloquium on career development, hasn't had formal training in much of anything other than anarchism, Russian history, and elementary algebra, and knows way more about corned beef than coaching, to be a life coach?

Later though, having had a little time to reflect, I realized that, awkward as it felt, there was something to what she was saying. While what I write about and what we teach in our internal classes and through ZingTrain seminars is most directly about our way of doing business, it's also, in practice, all about how to live a better, more rewarding life. If it is—as I strongly believe— *all one life,* then it only makes sense that the work that would lead to sound, sustainable, and successful organizational development would do pretty much the same for any of us as individuals. Why hadn't I seen the connection more quickly? No good reason really—it just takes time for intellectual connections to turn into an epiphany (see the Secret on Creativity on page 349 for more on this). It had long been clear to me that what works in professional life can be effectively applied outside of work. But I'd never translated that into a lens with which to view my teaching and writing work.

Vision and Vocation Speak Volumes

Whatever I've achieved in my life over the years is largely a testament to the power of visioning, and to living the other eleven Natural Laws as well. (If you aren't familiar with the list, see the sidebar on page 197.) We've spent thirty-plus years envisioning a place that we want to go to work in every day and, for the most part, it's played out as we wrote it. The life that I live every day, imperfect though it is and will always be, is very much the one that I've envisioned—in writing—for myself. Life for me is as Lao Tzu, the founder of Taoism, described in the 6th century BC: "The master of the art of living makes little distinction between his work and his play, his labor and his leisure, his mind and his body, his education and his recreation, his love and his religion. He simply pursues his vision of excellence in whatever he does, leaving others to decide whether he is working or playing. To him, he is always doing both."

Work and play, organizational and personal development, really do all come together quite beautifully. The more everyone in our group is growing and learning, the better the business is going to be. The more we teach everyone to go after their dreams, the more fulfilling their lives will be. The more fulfilled they feel, the better the quality of their work, and the better the organization will operate. In the process, everyone involved is going to benefit. Even if pursuing their dreams means that some members of the organization opt to leave, I would still call that a win—staying here when they dream of being elsewhere isn't helping them or the organization.

This is all in synch with what the anarchists advocated a century ago. To quote Emma Goldman, "Anarchism is [a] philosophy which brings to man the consciousness of himself." And as Emma and her colleague Max Baginsky said at the International Anarchist Congress in Amsterdam in 1907, "the true function of organization is to aid the development and growth of [the individual's] personality." When businesses are living the Natural Laws, they're bringing out the best in the people who are part of them, which in turns makes for a better organization. All of which creates a virtuous, positive, self-sustaining cycle. In a natural, organic setting, what's good for one element of the ecosystem—each of us as individuals—will also usually benefit the ecosystem overall, which in our case is the organization.

Looking at things from the other end of the spectrum, I realized that if organizations that don't live the Natural Laws suffer from an energy crisis in the workplace (see Secret #19 in *Part 2*), it only makes sense that individuals who don't live the Natural Laws are likely to be equally exhausted and similarly uninspired. At worst, they're angry and frustrated. You can try survey-ing people you meet as an experiment and see what the data dictates about the various dispositions and attitudes you'll encounter. I'd bet that most of the people you like to be around, people who are inspired and inspiring, are mostly living in synch with the Natural Laws, and that the Negative Nellies, Vic the Victims, and Arthur the Autocrats of the world are not. People who feel good about themselves and who are making a positive difference in the world almost always have a vision of where they're trying to go. They believe in what they're doing, have a service orientation, understand that they can't be all things to all people, are more appreciative, and have far more fun than the world's fuddy-duddies ever will.

It is, after all, a Natural Law. When you write a vision and get others around you on board with it, it's far more likely that you'll achieve the results you want. When it comes to the work of living a rewarding life, we would do best to begin by writing an inspiring, strategically sound personal vision of the future. I'll emphasize the "inspiring" part—it's *your* life, so dream big.

Rudolf Rocker was a German anarchist who moved to England and learned Yiddish in order to lead the Jewish anarchists of the East End. Known as the "Anarchist Rabbi," he was a great thinker, writer, and leader. He wasn't afraid to think big. In 1905 he wrote, "People may shake their heads wisely today over us and call us dreamers, and say that we had no sense of the real-ity of history. They fail to see that dreams are also a part of the reality of life, that life without dreams would be unbearable . . . no change in our way of life would be possible without dreams." And, as Emma Goldman emphasized, "When we can't dream any longer, we die." I'd rather dream big and live well than cut my hopes by half.

Natural Law #1 An inspiring, strategically sound vision leads the way to greatness (especially if you write it down!).

There's a scene in *Alice's Adventures in Wonderland* that sums up the key sup-position on which this "Secret" of visioning is based. It goes like this: "One day Alice came to a fork in the road and saw a Cheshire cat in a tree. 'Which road do I take?' she asked. 'Where do you want to go?' was his response. 'I don't know,' Alice answered. 'Then,' said the cat, 'it doesn't matter.'" In line with an anarchistic approach to life, I want to make it clear up front that I'm *not* saying where you're headed has to "matter" to you. If it matters not, make haste, and study something else in this book that does. To me, it matters a lot. To quote

Sam Keen, writing in *Inward Bound*, "To ask the simple question, 'What do I really want?' is not merely risky, it is revolutionary."

I think that going after a vision of greatness that we ourselves have authored is simply a more rewarding way to live. So much of the world revolves around reacting, following other people's leads, living lives that society or your sister-in-law or whoever laid out for you. We all worry that we're doing the wrong thing: too much of this, not enough of that. Or we let life go on too long without really living it the way we wish it would be. Only rarely do people truly sit and come clean with themselves about their dreams and desires, and then literally write out the story of the future to which they aspire. I'd rather go after what I want than wait and hope for others to hand it to me. To me, that's what the vision work is all about. As Larry Lippitt (son of Ron Lippitt, who led the way in developing the visioning process half a century ago) wrote, "Freedom . . . means being able to actively and consciously participate in the creation of your own future. If your future is decided by others you really are not free . . . there is a relationship between freedom and our willingness to determine what our future will be."

Having worked with our approach to visioning for nearly twenty years now, and having taught it extensively and intensively for the last ten, I will say with total certainty that it's one of the single most powerful processes I've ever been a part of. I know it's had a massively positive impact on our organization, and I'm confident it's done the same for hundreds of other organizations around the country who've put it to use as well. From delis to designers, academic institutions to IT companies, legal firms to luaus, nonprofits to pancake houses, I've witnessed it being used powerfully and well in almost every walk of organizational life.

Anne Good, who's been working at the Bakehouse for about ten years now, wrote me a while back, "I can't say enough good things about visioning." Companies and individuals with a clear—and better still, clearly written—vision of where they're going are just far more likely to get to greatness. How can they not? Whether it's in a personal or professional context, how can you not have higher odds of arriving at a place you're pleased to be if you're clear up front on what that place is? While very few folks will ever argue the logic of this question, I've found that when it comes time to write down a vision, most people will find a wealth of "good" reasons to resist, or in extreme cases forget about it altogether. While most people won't argue with the idea outright, they find more restrained ways not to write one—somehow they never seem to have time, or if they did once begin working on a vision, they never managed to "finish."

The Twelve Natural Laws of Business. And Life.

1. An inspiring, strategically sound vision leads the way to greatness (especially if you write it down!).

2. Successful people engage in compelling activities.

3. Without good finance, you fail.

4. People do their best work when they're part of a really great organization.

5. If you want to be successful, start with a service mindset.

6. Be clear about expectations and give yourself the tools to help yourself meet them.

7. Successful people do the things that others know they should . . . but generally don't.

8. To get to greatness, you've got to keep getting better, all the time!

9. Success means you get better problems.

10. Whatever your strengths are, they will likely lead straight to your weaknesses.

11. It generally takes a lot longer to make something great happen than people think.

12. Successful people are appreciative, laugh more, and have more fun.

I can relate to their struggles, and I certainly understand how those holdups can happen. Visioning for most is unfamiliar, and for many it is—consciously or not—downright frightening. When you're stuck in survival mode, focused mostly on getting by and avoiding what you don't want, it's hard to see that there's a lot more out there to be had if you're willing to vision big. It's so much easier to just lose ourselves in the day-to-day. For most folks, it's much more comfortable to succumb to the status quo of everyday life, even the stresses of success, and get stuck on the treadmills of today, running hard just to stay stuck, than it is to come clear with ourselves about what we really want.

It was completely counterintuitive to me, and years ago I argued against the value of visioning rather adamantly. I doubt I would ever have started doing it if I hadn't been pushed by Paul, Stas', and others.

Here's what anarchist great Peter Kropotkin wrote over a century ago in his 1899 book, *Memoirs of a Revolutionist*: "It often happens that men pull in a certain political, social, or familiar harness simply because they never have time to ask themselves whether the position they stand in and the work they accomplish are right; whether their occupations really suit their inner desires and capacities, and give them the satisfaction which everyone has the right to expect from his work. Active men are especially liable to find themselves in such a position. Every day brings with it a fresh batch of work, and a man throws himself into his bed late at night without having completed what he had expected to do; then in the morning he hurries to the unfinished task of the previous day. Life goes, and there is no time left to think, no time to consider the direction that one's life is taking. So it was," Kropotkin concluded, "with me."

While few of us will argue with the logic of Kropotkin's insight, the paradox is that, when we're in it, that downward spiral is, sadly, the exact time that we're *least* able to see how badly we need to get out. Vision is one of the best ways to break that energy-sapping cycle. My natural resistance to visioning was not uncommon, but it was entirely unhelpful. While good things can certainly still happen to folks who haven't come clear on their desired future, the odds of living a life we fall in love with have to be higher when we document our dreams and then share those dreams and desires with others around us.

A vision, as we define it here, is a richly detailed, emotionally engaging picture of what success means to us at a particular point in time in the future. The work we do with vision at an organizational level is described in detail in *Zingerman's Guide to Good Leading, Part 1.* A vision for us is not a mission statement. We like those too, but they're far too brief to really paint the sort of descriptive portrait that we want in our visions. While the length of a vision will vary from one to the next, just for context I can tell you that our 2020 vision for Zingerman's is about seven pages long. Nor is a vision a strategic plan. Both are important, but for us they're two different things. The vision is where we're headed; the strategic plan is how we get there.

Visioning, the way we teach it—actually writing down our desires, setting it at a particular point in the future, and including enough detail so we'll know if we've arrived (or at least how close we've gotten)—is hardly the norm in North America. But that said, I do think that if you survey successful people,

people with positive energy, people who you want to emulate, most of them have a pretty clear picture, if only in their minds, of what they want—or wanted—to achieve. Some, like me, may have stumbled into some elements of early success, then over time clarified what's compelling and where they're going with it. But even if they, or I, couldn't have detailed every element of their preferred futures, the main themes and key goals were all pretty clear in their minds long before they really happened.

Most of those folks are what Maggie Bayless from ZingTrain, and others of the world's training experts, would call "unconsciously competent" when it comes to visioning—they're so good at it and it seems so natural to them that they can't really even imagine not doing it. They don't spend a lot of time worrying about it and they're definitely not using someone else's preordained process. Visioning isn't something they've ever expended much time contemplating—they just do it. Successful people of that sort just seem to have some special skill others missed out on. Outsiders, the uninitiated, those to whom visioning doesn't come naturally (like me), on the other hand, look at those who've "arrived" in this way and worry that "we're not like them." I would—in fact, I will—argue the opposite: as anarchist Gustav Landauer said a century ago, "No one lacks the ability, the disposition, the potential."

But while no one lacks the ability to vision, what we all too often do lack is direction on *how* to do it. Most people need some structure, framework, and guidance. Sadly, most of the advice out there focuses, mistakenly, on the details of what should be *in* the content of one's vision: "What," most of us wonder—or even worse, worry—"are we really supposed to be doing?" "What do all those successful, seemingly happy people I see around me have that I'm failing to figure out?" The secret is that there is *no* majestic, magic answer, no brilliantly sage advice that's going to give you that "perfect" life plan so many people are looking for. Fortunately—or unfortunately for those who want an easy, externalized answer—the important information is all, already, inside us. All we have to do is get at it.

There are certainly times in life when gathering data and opinions is of value, but with visioning, I believe the process needs to work in reverse. Visioning is not about having the other people in your life play the part of career planning professionals imparting insightful advice. It's not about an outside expert explaining the most strategically appealing alternative or giving you detailed demographic data. While the rest of the world is quick to advise us all on what success *should* be, the only thing you need to get going towards greatness as *you* define it is an understanding of the process I'm about to explain—and the dreams and desires and passions already in your head and in your heart. While there's no such thing as choice free from outside influence, while people in our lives will be impacted by what we do, and while many of them will not like what we choose, the choice of what vision we'll pursue is ultimately our own to make.

The Process *Is* the Point

The advice, the insight, the input that I believe is twenty-nine times more helpful than telling someone *what* they should have *in* their vision is to *focus instead on how to effectively write one*—the prize is not only inside, it's also in the process. *The writing, I'm adamant, is the key.* Putting the dreams, the glimmers, the secret desires we all have down on paper is the thing that makes the process we use here so particularly powerful. While worrying about finding the "right answer" for what your life *should* look like might last you a lifetime (without ever, I should add, helping you make your dreams come true), the visioning process will almost always work. In a shockingly short period of time—twenty to thirty minutes—most everyone who uses the process will come out of it with a picture of a positive and inspiring future, one they feel good about and are excited, if anxious in a good way, to go after. When you write a vision the way we teach it, the wisdom will most certainly come.

What emerges when we write our vision is almost always stuff that we've actually known about—at some conscious or unconscious level—for a long time. We knew it, but never let ourselves really own that we wanted it, or believe we could make it real. Visioning work brings those (sort of) secret passions to the fore, gets our creative juices flowing, and helps to remind us that we really can make much of what we want a reality in our daily lives. If you're willing to try it and to trust it, the visioning process will almost always successfully bring out a positive picture of the future. And, as per Landauer's point, with practice, *anyone who wants to can master the process.*

Visioning, Zingerman's style, takes ideas and thoughts and turns them into a concrete tool, a guiding light to keep us on course, a constructive and engaging entrée into a future we're excited about living. Daydreaming can be delicious but it rarely changes reality. The vision writing, on the other hand, brings our dreams alive. It keeps us on course and increases the odds of our dreams all coming to fruition. To quote 19th century English poet, writer, designer, and architect William Morris, "If others can see it as I have it, then it may be called a vision rather than a dream."

Commonly Asked Questions about Personal Visioning

The process of writing your personal vision is remarkably simple and straightforward—much simpler than the in-depth discussions that it provokes. Let me try to make it more accessible still by answering a few:

Does a vision make it more likely we'll succeed? Quite simply, the answer is yes. As Paulo Coehlo wrote, "And, when you want something, all the universe conspires in helping you to achieve it." Acknowledging what we really want, and being clear on where we want to go, can only help us to manage our energy, make better decisions, and effectively find our way through the world to a place that we want to end up in. Actively and creatively participating in designing one's own future has to feel at least five hundred times better than waiting for someone else to determine it for us. Because it involves greater self-knowledge and it's rooted in free choice. Because it helps keep us on course when seventy-five other things start to blow us off. Because once others around us know where we're headed, it's much more likely that they too can (and will) contribute to our cause. I've seen it so many times now that it's almost, but not quite yet, unremarkable when it happens. The reality is, quite simply, that there are often strange and inexplicable things that start to happen once you set the vision down on paper. Or, in Rich Sheridan's case, on an iPad.

A few years ago, Rich, the founder of Menlo Innovation here in Ann Arbor, realized he'd reached a point with his company where they had very successfully fulfilled their original vision of the business. (In the context of Schein's stages, he'd realized it was time to move into Stage 4, changing.) One morning over coffee at the back table at the Deli, where I often set up shop early in the morning, he asked me what I thought his next steps should be. "You know what I'm going to tell you," I smiled. "Yeah, I know," he laughed, "write my vision."

Three or four weeks later, we found ourselves on a plane together, headed to Dallas for an *Inc.* magazine conference. While we waited to board, Rich related how he'd gotten going on his vision, and how he was excited about what was in it. Happy to hear his positive experience, but not at all surprised—*I know this stuff works*—I asked if he'd be ok if I called on him to share what he'd learned when I was presenting on visioning at the conference the following morning. He was amenable, so about halfway through my talk, I mentioned that Rich Sheridan from Menlo Innovation was in the audience, that he was actively engaged in writing a new vision for himself and his company, and that he was willing to share thoughts about what he'd learned.

When Rich stood up in the center of the room—at 6'6" he's easy to see—all I expected him to do was talk a bit about his experience of writing a vision. Instead, he opened his iPad and said, "Let me read you my draft. It's not done yet but you'll get the idea." He cleared his throat and began to read in his big booming voice. Here's how his vision started: "It's May 1st, 2018, and Rich is putting together his talk for *Inc.* magazine's Top Small Workplaces Conference." How strangely serendipitous that the vision Rich had just drafted positioned him doing the thing he was at this moment doing: presenting his thoughts at an *Inc.* conference. When we write out our visions, the universe comes together and does effective work in strange ways.

Does having a vision of greatness limit your options in life? Contrary to the beliefs of those who—like me—are naturally wired to worry about "being boxed in" by putting a vision on paper, the answer to this question is, quite simply, "No!" Writing and sharing a personal vision is *not* about locking oneself into a mind-numbing, nothing-left-to-the-imagination, paint-by-numbers map of your life. Visioning isn't about locking down—it's about opening up and letting out the dreams, hopes, and desires—whatever they may be—that we have held deep inside us but have been too wary to let out.

The point here is that a personal vision need only detail what *you want it to*. You don't have to say specifically what city (or town or village) you'll be living in five years from now—if you don't have one in mind, just describe some of the key characteristics of the community you'd like to be part of. Say how you feel about it, how you know it's a good place for you to be. If you feel like you want to move every two years but aren't sure where it is you want to move to, just write your vision to say that you're living in your third city in six years. You get the idea, I'm sure. The beauty of the visioning work is that there are no right, and no required, answers other than ones that are deep inside us.

Similarly, your vision draft doesn't have to say exactly what you do for a living if you don't want it to. Instead it can just describe how you feel about your work, or how you feel when you head home every day. Feelings may not be facts on financial statements, but they're just as serious as salary level when it comes to telling the story of your life. And remember, it is YOUR life. If you know in your heart that you'd be happier in a warm climate, write the warmth into your vision. If having a lot of close friends is critical, add something in about what that feels like. If you know you like to learn a lot, put that in there, too. If you want to contribute to the quality of others' existence, help repair the environment, eat well, enjoy work, or whatever else, write that in as well. Relationships, food, money, time off, time out, time for TV watching—whatever it is, just write it right in there. It's *your* life, *your* voice, *your* vision.

Does writing your vision of greatness guarantee that everything will happen exactly as you write it? Of course not. What the vision *does* do is radically increase the odds of getting you where you want to go, making it more likely that you'll be living a life very close to the one you'd like to live. Although we often make it difficult to get ourselves to do it, and though it can be daunting for those who haven't ever done it, a vision of greatness is rarely very hard to write. Visioning might well be the emotional equivalent of rocket science—but it's much easier. Using visioning, either personally or organizationally, can be akin to going to another, far more positive, significantly more fun planet. It can tap the natural energy we have inside us and power us to a place where meaningful success and great happiness happen regularly.

Here's an unsolicited testimonial from artist and improv actress Alex Carbone: "I've been experimenting with visioning, and it is pretty amazing how it makes the pieces fall into place. I'm the proud owner of a biodiesel-capable car right now. I don't think I would have it if I hadn't put it in my vision. And my daughter just got into a free Montessori school. It was also in the vision for the kids to be in awesome charter schools. I think the key is it forces you to examine your priorities and values so the choices you make align yourself with them. The extra work to find the school and the car I really wanted was minimal, but it would've been easy to let it slip by the wayside and end up with an easy second choice. What motivated me to do the few extra Google searches, etc., was the vision."

What if you just love the randomness of life? Flying by the seat of your pants is not out of synch with writing a vision. Just write in the "randomness"—say in your vision that surprises sit at the center of your life, and very successfully so at that. The process is just about getting clear with ourselves—and where relevant, with others around us—how we envision our life will be. It's your vision—if chaos is compelling or randomness is what resonates, go for it!

If you're really stubborn about it, can you still show that visioning is a silly waste of time? Yes, of course. I'm sure if you're incredibly obstinate and super cynical, you can successfully show that visioning won't ever work. But just to be clear, in the process, you'll actually be inadvertently proving my point. If your vision is to demonstrate that visioning is dumb and you succeed—well, you can do the math on that one. Visioning will successfully outscore cynicism every time.

If you don't feel like writing a vision can you just skip the whole exercise? Really, if you don't feel like writing a vision, then by all means don't write one. Remember, there's nothing about visioning that requires you to write, or do, anything you don't want to. It's about free choice, after all. I know I never would have dreamed of doing anything like visioning thirty years ago. Of course, with the benefit of hindsight, I can say that by not getting clear on my vision, I made my life—and the lives of those around me—a lot harder than it needed to be. Continuing to *not* let myself get clear about what I wanted only made things worse, and often just left me mad at myself and at the world.

Worse still, I frequently, if unwittingly, backed my way into almost all of the worst-case personal scenarios I was worried about. The more my vision was only to avoid them, the more they seemed to happen anyway. It's uncanny how these internal, even unspoken worries can work our lives over if we let them. To quote Gustav Landauer, living this way shows us "how something dead to our [conscious] spirit can exercise living power over our body."

Does it have to be a vision of *greatness*? Can you write a vision of so-so? Over the years, I've clearly come to favor the idea of working towards the exceptional, setting my sights on doing something special. It is, of course, your call, and you can write any vision you want. There are many reasons people prefer to back off on going for greatness. If you've been let down badly by others; if you doubt yourself; if others you cared about have uncaringly told you you can't do it; if everyone around you asks, "how are you going to get there?" when all you're working on is the "what," you'll have more than enough legitimate reasons to shy away from anything very significant. All I'll say is that, if you're going to go after something that means a lot to you, why not go for great? It's far more fulfilling and way more fun than settling for the safer but uninspiring path of mediocrity.

Psychologist Abraham Maslow shared the story of asking his students to tell him what they were going to do once they graduated to be great at their work. Most were uncomfortable with the question and sloughed it off. Maslow persisted, though. "You must have wanted to be a first-class psychologist, meaning the best, the very best you are capable of becoming," he told them. "If you deliberately plan to be less than you are capable of being, then I warn you that you'll be deeply unhappy for the rest of your life. You will be evading your capacities, your own possibilities."

Clearly, how far you take things in the final version of your vision is up to you. Personally, though, I've learned to push myself further with my first drafts and then see how it feels later on. In general, the refining and reviewing process over time is prone to buffing the sharp edges of one's work. Nothing really wrong with that—it can keep us from being too extreme. But with that in mind, I find it more effective to embellish early on and let the process and time work on my draft as the days and weeks go by.

Over the years, I've become ever more convinced that the people who are having more fun, feeling more rewarded by what they do, and gaining energy from the engagement with their own freely chosen focus are the ones who are going for greatness. Staying in the center may feel more secure, but it's rarely more rewarding. I agree with the scholars at the Center for Organizational Study at our local educational institution (that's the University of Michigan), who wrote that "excellence is a function of uniqueness."

I also try to heed the advice of my friend Anese Cavanaugh, one of the world's leading advocates for positive energy, who pushes her clients to "turn up the want dial." As Anese explains, most of us are trained by society to hold back, to "be reasonable," to not be too full of ourselves. While there's much to be said for modesty and moderation, the greatness that gets us going, the uniqueness that leads to excellence, the creativity that feels so fun almost always comes from pushing the envelope. Just for the fun of it, try Anese's advice and "turn up that want dial."

Imagine the volume knob on an old-style stereo system and think about cranking it up high as you redraft and recraft your vision. The stuff I self-edited out in my first draft I try now to include. I know I'm not obligated to leave it in when I/we decide to really run with the vision. But at least we know what we desire in our dreams. The best stuff, the things we deeply desire and have secretly dreamed of for ages, will usually emerge when we turn up the want dial. And our energy almost always increases in the process. You know how, when you really love a song and you turn the volume up high, you start dancing around the room, rocking out even if you're alone in your car? You might have done it this week. I know I have.

What if you leave the "volume on low"? More often than not, I've found (through my experience and that of my friends) that we give up what we really want and run with what others want for us. It's hard, I know, to go against everyone else who "knows better," "has more experience," or is an "expert in their area" and stick to our own crazy dreams. As Julia Cameron writes, "Each of us has an inner dream that we can unfold if we will just have the courage to admit what it is." She adds, "To kill your dreams because they are irresponsible is to be irresponsible to yourself." This is where, I say, it's time to turn to your inner anarchist, to the Emma Goldman in your soul who will encourage you to turn that want dial way up, to dream big and go for what you believe in, not what others believe you should want.

If you want another opinion and a bit of firsthand experience other than mine, here's what writer Debbie Millman has to say in her beautifully crafted book, *Look Both Ways*. I share her strongly held belief that many of us hold ourselves back out of fear, worry, insecurity, overthinking, and the critical voices of others. "These common, self imposed restrictions are rather insidious, though they start out simple enough," she writes. "We begin by worrying we aren't good enough, smart enough or talented enough to get what we want, then we voluntarily live in this paralyzing mental framework, rather than confront our own role in this paralysis. Just the possibility of failing turns into a dutiful self-fulfilling prophecy. We begin to believe that these personal restrictions are in fact, the fixed limitations of the world. We go on to live our lives, all the while wondering what we can change and when we will be ready to do the things we want to do. And we dream. If only. If only."

Writing about the first half of her career, Millman reveals, "I know deep in my heart that I settled. I chose financial and creative stability over artistic freedom and I can't help but wonder what life would be like if I had made a different decision. If you imagine less, less will be what you undoubtedly deserve. Do what you love, and don't stop until you get what you love. Work as hard as you can, imagine immensities, don't compromise, and don't waste time. Start now. Not *20 years from now*, not two weeks from now. Now." Writing a vision makes it easier to make the right choice—when your dream is staring back at you, smiling and beckoning from the future, it's a lot easier to say no to the theoretically safe (since nothing is really safe) but rather boring alternative others might recommend for you.

What if you're afraid of what comes out when you start writing? This is pretty common, actually. I've heard a lot of people that are doing visioning work start to sink into self-doubt. They feel the critical voices that they'd set aside long enough to get going—a half an hour or so is all you need—start to creep in again and question. "Who are you to want all that? Get serious. Who do you think you are? Where did you get the idea that *you* could do all that?" As Maslow wrote, "We fear our highest possibilities (as well as our lowest ones). We are generally afraid to become that which we can glimpse in our most perfect moments. We enjoy and even thrill to the godlike possibilities we see in ourselves. And yet we simultaneously shiver with weakness, awe, and fear, before these very same possibilities. The trick, I believe, is to pursue it all anyway."

The vision work the way we do it is a way to access the area of our soul where, pardon the borrowed image, the wild things live. By writing without editing en route, we overcome our tendency to overthink almost everything important in our lives. Visions are very much about dreams and desires, not data. Even those who were anxious about how big their vision drafts felt are, nevertheless, almost always excited about what's in them after they've taken some time to let things settle and then sit down and read them anew.

Will having a written vision of greatness guarantee that we won't screw up? Of course not. The vision is a great start, but it's only the beginning. A written vision is not a guarantee from the universe that nothing will ever go wrong. And having a vision is not a free pass to go on vacation—you still have to do the work, you still need to bring some talent to the table, and you still need to catch a few breaks here and there. But when we've come clear with ourselves, and the world, on where we're going, good things start happening. And when problems do pop up, it's far easier to deal with them. If you want a more down-to-earth, ass-kickingly modern, poetic-anarchist approach, here's Patti Smith, who made the irreverently inappropriate statement on stage and then again on a record, "I don't fuck much with the past but I fuck plenty with the future."

Will writing a vision fix all your problems overnight? No. This isn't magic—a vision should be aspirational, but it also has to be strategically sound. If it's only the former, we call it a "fantasy." Mind you, as long as we're clear about what they are, fantasies can be fun. I have a lot of them. Like many people, I'd love to be a world-class athlete or a masterful musician, but it's safe to say I don't think I ever had even the slightest shot at making either a reality. I just don't have the talent. At fifteen, it was still fun to daydream. At fifty, I think acceptance is a more effective way to go.

The trouble comes if we're not clear on the difference between being "strategically sound" and being silly. Nineteenth century Russian writer Alexander Herzen was good friends with the most famous anarchist of his era, Mikhail Bakunin. The son of a Russian nobleman, Herzen was a leading figure for social change, a big believer in freedom and helping people develop their human potential. Having nothing, per se, to do with any of that, but everything to do with the importance of having a reasonable shot at hitting your vision, Herzen wrote, "A goal which is infinitely remote is not a goal at all, it is a deception." Here at Zingerman's we say much the same thing; when something we wish for is "infinitely remote," or impossible to make happen, we simply call it a fantasy.

All that said, writing a vision that's inspiring and strategically sound absolutely can, and almost always will, help make things better. A vision that says five years from now you're going to be very good at what you do, that details the way you love the people you live with, that lays out your efforts towards contributing positively to your community, that describes how you learn something new every day, and that indicates you appreciate all that goes on around you can be hugely powerful and very effective.

For people who grew up in less than great settings, a lack of hope—whether learned from parents, school, friends, or all of the above—can be a severe disadvantage. Writing a vision can be a small but sometimes significant way to help bring hope back into their view of the world. One friend of mine, a teacher in the inner city, decided to have her high school students practice visioning. Lest you doubt the power of the process, take a look at her note to me about the experience:

> *I thought it would be a great idea for the students to write personal vision statements and used your essay as the foundation for instruction. Well, the assignment was powerful. Writing in the present tense made their dreams seem possible, concrete. I asked them what the effect of writing a vision statement was. Here are a few responses: Now, I feel I have control over my goals; helped to focus goals; realize the need to earn excellent grades; helped to realize what I really want to do in life; excited to graduate so I can start my future; written visions make them more concrete and real; thought school was a game, attended to get away from home, now I realize it's a place to learn and have fun; it changed the way I looked at school; all the people I care about are gone, but I felt their presence while writing the vision and realized all my hard work was worth it; it encouraged me to complete my goals and strive for excellence.*

Are you ever worried that you wrote the wrong vision? Or that it might not happen? At best, worrying is distracting; at worst, it's downright destructive. Mindfulness and effective self-management have taught me that worrying gets me nowhere. In fact, worrying will often bring on the very thing I was worried about. Worrying, I believe, is like driving our energy in reverse—it takes all of what we *could* put into attaining positive things and drives us down into dissonance instead. It drains energy away from more positive and appreciative activities and turns my focus towards the negative.

I used to worry to a fault, but after a lot of unproductive years of that, I finally realized how insidious it was and grasped the reality: worrying never works. Worrying about the rest of the day is like walking down the street, dropping dollar bills out of a big stack in your hand, and then later, when you arrive at your destination, being suddenly shocked that you have no cash. The agonizing effort it takes to attempt to figure out the "right" answer is exhausting and unproductive. Worrying about things I can't control, though a habit that's often hard to break, doesn't help either. It drains energy away from more positive and appreciative activities and turns my focus towards the negative. If much of this book is the story of vocation, as Paul Goodman described, "like falling in love and it works out," then its flip side is the story of overcoming worry to be present in the world. Worry will almost always undercut love and passion. As poet, anarchist, and eroticist Anaïs Nin wrote, "Anxiety is love's greatest killer."

Imagine holding a beautiful and intricately folded piece of paper in your hands. Inside the folds, something wonderful—your vision—has been written. Worrying about your future, crumpling up the paper in frustration, or throwing it out rather than opening it up and reading it, you can't realize what wonderful words await inside. Trusting in your vision is one of the best ways I know to bring it out and, in turn, to then make it a reality. If you insist on worrying, I'd rather you worry about not having taken twenty-five minutes to write a vision than that the one you wrote will end up being all wrong.

What if you're really stumped and nothing comes out? I've never seen anyone sit and write the way we ask them to, straight through for thirty or so minutes (no editing allowed), and not come up with something special. The vision process always yields a positive result. If your fingers keep moving, good things will make their way out of your mind and onto the page.

But let's just say you're totally blocked, that you sit down to write and your pen's all out of emotional ink and you stare sullenly at the page and your hand just won't move. In that extreme instance, you can probably still succeed by practicing what I've come to call "Pruski's Law." I named this little process after Scott Pruski, founder of a financial services firm in Grand Rapids, Michigan. During a ZingTrain visioning seminar, he found himself feeling completely and totally blocked. Rather than sit there staring at the paper, Scott started listing all the things he knew he *didn't* want. Within a matter of minutes, he had drafted the basis of the vision he'd been looking for—all he had to do was flip the list and write the *opposite* of what he *didn't* want into his vision. By listing all his "don't-do's" like that, he was able to spark the sort of positive vision of the future that we're aiming for.

Poet David Whyte, writing in *The Heart Aroused*, recommends a similar approach. "The *via negativa* [the negative road] is the discipline of saying no when we have as yet no clarity about those things to which we can say yes. We

209

take the *via negativa* when there is not yet any sign of the *via positiva*." Going negative isn't the first option I'd recommend, but when all else seems to fail, give it a try. As Whyte writes in a poetic restatement of Pruski's law, "in the continuous utterance of the no is a profound faith that the yes will appear."

Looking back on my own life, the main reason I chose to stay in Ann Arbor after graduating from U of M had to do with what Whyte calls the *via negativa*. I was adamant about not sliding back into a life in the suburbs, and staying in Ann Arbor was one way I knew I could avoid that. As a starting point, it probably wasn't the best way to move forward—a positive vision would surely have been more powerful—but it did at least position me to have all the good things that came out of the decision to stay here happen as they did.

Do you *have* to have a vision to succeed? No! I'm an anarchist. You don't *have* to do anything. To state the obvious, most people in the world don't, and won't, ever write one. That said, I would still argue that if you aspire to get to greatness—whatever that means to you—writing a vision is a very good way to increase the odds that you'll get there. Given that it takes only about twenty or thirty minutes to put the bulk of yours down on paper, what's the risk?

But if you're insistent about not writing one, you might want to consider what Anaïs Nin once noted: "Societies in decline have no use for visionaries." Since I've already made the leap from business to life and back again, I'll take Nin's approach and apply it to both businesses and personal lives: organizations and individuals in decline have no use for visions. As is so often the case in life, those who stand to benefit most from crafting a vision statement are often the most reluctant to try something new.

How Vision Makes a Difference Every Day

A while back, I was presenting on our history and vision to a group of very smart, very creative, and socially conscious business people. In other words, I was in my element. One woman raised her hand to ask a question. "It must be hard," she said, "to turn down the offers you get all the time to open in other cities. There are so many opportunities outside Ann Arbor. Why don't you take any of them?" I smiled. The question, in most corporate settings, would call for a six-month strategic analysis, data gathering, pro and con lists, and a great deal of study and soul searching. For me, it took about six seconds. Our vision and our values—driven by personal passion, not politics or a ten-point plan for market domination—are clear. The question was challenging but the answer was easy. "Cuz I don't wanna," I said with a smile. The woman looked at me as if I'd just dispensed some deeply held dharmic secret. "I love that!" she said. "Cuz he doesn't want to! I love that!"

Is it really that important that I sit and write it, quickly, the way you recommend? While, of course, you can do this in any way you want, I'm going to give a very loud answer in the affirmative. *YES! The process is absolutely essential. Writing quickly, without pausing to ponder and edit and excise your existential insights, is what makes it all work.* Please take my word for it. You will get five hundred times further in well under an hour if you stop trying to "figure out" what you want and just sit down, follow the recipe, and write.

Here at Zingerman's we always ask people to "*write a vision.*" But what most people hear, I suddenly realized one day, is that they need to "*figure things out.*" That's too bad, because the two processes are actually opposites. This insight is a relatively new one for me. As I've said, teaching others also continues to inspire my own learning. To wit, I've taught this visioning stuff about two thousand times, but it only just dawned on me while at a ZingTrain session in Atlanta that the way we talk about the act of writing the vision is absolutely *essential* to understanding, and effectively doing, the work.

Figuring something out implies an act of analysis, from which we think insight and clarity will somehow emerge. The mistaken belief is that the harder we think, the more creative and on course we'll be. In that well-intended but inherently flawed spirit, we assess our situation. We examine opportunities, we do stuff like SWOT analyses (Strengths, Weaknesses, Opportunities, and Threats), and we ask for advice from outside experts. "Figuring out the future" implies an intense amount of thought and complex calculation, and the implication that if we're good at it, we'll come up with some brilliant strategic approach. It's as if there's some "right answer" out in the universe, and we just have to study hard enough to—well—figure it all out.

While that's very much the way I was raised, I don't think that old-school approach works very well. "Figuring out" one's vision is like playing chess against yourself. If you're as good at overthinking things as I am, that means your intellect will almost always force your soul into submission; checkmate in chess is reason to celebrate, but when our mind does it to our spirit, over the long haul all we get is suffering.

Writing our vision is another thing altogether. It isn't magic but it is pretty marvelous. A good friend of mine wrote this note that she slipped into a package she sent me. "Let your mind start a journey through the world. Leave all thoughts you knew before. Let your soul take you where you long to be." The writing, not the result, is the point of the process. The *act of going through the writing* is what helps us get clear on what we really want, to see what we're most inspired by, and to get a good sense of where we'd really like to be. To quote Beat poet and Buddhist anarchist Gary Snyder, "There are more things in the mind, in the imagination than 'you' can keep track of—thoughts, memories, images, angers, delights, rise unbidden. The depths of the mind, the unconscious, are our inner wilderness areas, and that is where a bobcat is *right now.*"

I love the image of the bobcat. Putting our vision out there releases the wildness that, whether we want to own it or not, is in all of us. By writing, rather than analyzing, we push through what I've realized is essentially "the thought barrier"—the walls that our conscious mind constructs to keep the bobcat boxed in. As Snyder says, "The conscious agenda-planning ego occupies a very tiny territory, a little cubicle somewhere near the gate, keeping track of some of what goes in and out." It's the creativity behind the "cubicle" that the vision process puts us in touch with. If you're willing to tell all those gatekeeping, cubicle-dwelling, critical voices to keep away for thirty minutes, you can push past it too. We can all, as Jim Morrison wrote, "Break on Through to the Other Side," to bust the bobcat out into freedom.

Can anyone write one? Absolutely. Anyone who's willing to just follow the recipe (see page 222). Not long ago, I got this email from Heather Kendrick. Heather is all of nineteen years old and has been working at the Deli for the last few years while attending the University of Michigan's School of Music. She's a violinist, and she's also recently enrolled in the Organizational Studies program. I was preparing to teach our two-day ZingTrain seminar on visioning when this note from Heather showed up in my inbox:

> *I've been at this institute for musicianship and public service at an arts org in Providence these past few days, and I am SO incredibly thankful for how prepared I am to talk to professional musicians and nonprofit sector people because of my experiences with you and at Zing. I was by far the youngest person at the seminar, but felt totally comfortable participating and offering my thoughts because I understand community, visioning, and the rest of our guiding principles (these were things we were talking about a lot). It was so cool to be drawing these*

parallels between what we do at Zingerman's and what community music programs are doing. I can't wait to talk to you more about it later this week, but I had to send a quick shout-out of a thank you.

When we talked later, she shared how the people in the program—all industry professionals with very impressive resumes—had struggled with the concept of vision, talking about how hard it was to do one and how unsure they were of their futures. "Finally, I just decided I'd say something," she told me. "So I said, 'You guys, it's really not that hard. Where I work, we do visions all the time. You just sit down and write it.'" Heather now sees visioning as a normal and productive part of living a good life, not much harder than making coffee in the morning.

Heather's hardly the only one who feels that way. Kelsey Johnson is a 21-year-old who was attending a ZingTrain seminar courtesy of her boss, Jerry Zubay (who was also in the seminar), from ZZest Market in Minnesota. My presentation on vision went very much as it usually does. The concept caught people's attention. When I put them to work to practice writing a vision for the first time, most everyone did just fine. As is generally the case, a lot of people love it but one or two have a hard time.

When we got to the Q and A, one of the folks who'd struggled shared how she really had a hard time pushing herself to write. Kelsey, the youngest person in the group of thirty people, raised her hand to help. "It's really not that hard. You just write whatever comes to your mind. You'll see. It'll be fine." I was sort of surprised to hear such sound advice coming out of the mouth of someone so young. She, however, seemed totally at ease. "When you're writing a vision statement," she continued, "people spend all this time thinking about what they should do. But what you need to do is just sit down and write. The things you value most will come through. If you write from scratch four or five times you'll see that the things that are important to you will come up each time. It's really clear and direct. It's bringing your dreams from your head and your heart out on the paper."

Her explanation was concise and clear, and she presented it calmly and matter-of-factly. I've seen CEOs of multimillion dollar companies struggle for days to get their minds around what Kelsey had casually communicated off the cuff in a couple of minutes. "That was fantastic!" I said. "Where did you learn that?"

"Oh, my mother used to have us do it," Kelsey said. "She'd have us make vision boards and always taught us to keep in touch with our dreams and hearts. I guess I've basically been doing visioning my whole life. I know I have a much better intuition because of it." Our ability to write a vision of greatness isn't due to genetics but comes from the culture in which we live. For most Americans, visioning is an alien concept. For Kelsey or Heather, far younger and with almost no business experience to speak of, it's not much harder than riding a bike.

Why does the visioning process work so well? In his insightful book *Imagine: How Creativity Works,* Jonah Lehrer explains why certain circumstances lead to certain kinds of thinking. "When our minds are at ease, we're more likely to direct the spotlight of attention *inward,* towards that stream of remote associations emanating from the right (big picture focused) hemisphere of the brain. In contrast when we are diligently focused, our attention tends to be directed *outward,* towards the details of the problems we're trying to solve. While this pattern of attention is necessary when solving problems analytically, it actually prevents us from detecting the connections that lead to insights."

What we learn from Lehrer, as well as from Ron Lippitt, the man who developed the visioning process in the first place, is that the old "problem solving" method—where people sit and focus hard on fixing what's wrong—turns out to physiologically shut down big-picture creativity. *By contrast, focusing on the positive and relaxing the mind, as we do in the visioning process, generally leads directly to intuitive insights.* As Lehrer explains, it's when those positive feelings are at the fore and we're not forcing ourselves into near-term problem solving that "we're finally able to hear the quiet voices in the back of our heads, telling us about the insight. The answers have been there all along—we just weren't listening."

This last insight is one of the most frequently repeated reflections we hear from people after they spend half an hour or so writing out the first draft of their vision. The trick isn't just to relax and let free association emerge. It's essentially to daydream in a waking state where your mind can go where it wants to go, but you're taking notes as it meanders. Lehrer quotes psychologist Jonathan Schooler on the subject: "Letting your mind drift off is the easy part. The hard part is maintaining enough awareness so that even when you start to daydream you can interrupt yourself and notice a creative thought." As Schooler says, we need "to be more disciplined in [our] mind-wandering." Focused, documented daydreaming that helps each of us access what's long been inside us can result in inspiring, creative, caring, and darned cool visions of greatness for the future. The more common experience—in which people put down a goal that they haven't really emotionally engaged with—may mean that some short-term action steps get taken, but it rarely results in deep, meaningful, lasting personal change. Those sorts of changes come only, it seems, after we've really sunk our emotional roots into the soil of the future.

Why It's Worth Doing a Personal Vision

Visioning accesses what's already deep inside us anyway. Imagine you have this seed of an idea in your subconscious. The usual things that happen when we try to "figure out" our visions—stressing, analyzing, obsessing, and advice getting—are almost all about obstruction. While career advice is usually well intended, in practice, it often serves to pile the emotional equivalent of rocks and debris atop the healthy, unique, and irreplicable creative seed of one's soul. Get enough stuff stacked on top of that seed and it will never grow. But clear away the debris, give the seed some air, water, and sun, and it's got a way better shot at success. As Anne Kellogg-Reed, who works at Zingerman's, said when she worked through writing her life vision, "What came out is less like an 'aha' and more like 'aah,' a sense of calm and relief."

Sitting down to physically write the vision allows the seeds of ideas and dreams inside us to emerge into the light of daily life. It lets the seeds blossom into beautiful flowers. It starts us down the path towards the future *we* want instead of the one others want us to have or the one the fates forced upon us. Visioning is not about politics, but it is all about empowering ourselves to pursue a life we're passionate about, to take charge of the road we're on, to live in a way that's inspiring, exciting, and rewarding. Twentieth century British anarchist Colin Ward wrote, "Anarchism in all its guises is an assertion of human dignity and responsibility. It is not a programme for political change but an act of social self-determination." The same should be said about visioning. It, too, is an assertion of human dignity and responsibility. Because it's positive and proactive rather than restrictive and reactive, visioning may be, paraphrasing Ward, the ultimate act of social self-determination.

Having a clear vision of greatness also helps us to make more effective decisions. If we've gotten clear on where we're going, it's about eighty times easier to make the most of the decisions we're going to make every day. Once we've determined what our long-term future is going to look like, most of the decisions we'll need to make are merely tactical milestones en route to the future we've decided to head for. For me at least, that saves stress and makes it so much easier to move forward. As Sam Keen urges in *Inward Bound*, "Dare to do something definite." Once we're truly clear on where we're headed, it's just so much easier en route—most every decision can be framed in terms of whether or not it helps move us closer to our vision.

A vision helps us stay the course. Opportunities and diversions abound, but having settled within ourselves (and written about) our vision of success, it's infinitely easier to stay focused and stay the course. When my mind starts doubting, challenging, worrying, wondering about all the "what ifs" it can muster, having a vision that I've already decided upon and shared increases the likelihood that I won't lose my way. When others' objections, advice, and obsequiousness start to overwhelm me and make me think that I might be doing the wrong thing, the vision helps me stay focused.

Having been through this work many times now, I know that in the beginning, when I start to go after what I believe in and really want, it's fairly common that others will advise me to abandon it. It's especially true when the path I've taken is out of the mainstream, too far north (or south) of the stuff everyone else is doing. The resistance isn't really that shocking. Actually, it's all too predictable. But afterward, quite often, everyone ends up loving what we've done.

It's what happened to Hugh MacLeod—he's now famous for the cartoons he draws on the back of business cards. But early on he took plenty of flak for his "foolishness." It's also what's happened here at Zingerman's. As science fiction writer Arthur C. Clarke says, "Every revolutionary idea seems to evoke three stages of reaction. They may be summed up by the phrases: 1) It's completely impossible. 2) It's possible, but it's not worth doing. 3) I said it was a good idea all along." Of course you probably aren't a genius. I know I'm not. But that's kind of the point—visions of greatness aren't limited to some Mensa-level minority. Anyone who wants to devote a modicum of time to write one can do it.

And writing down a vision could be the highest honor we can pay to our consciousness. It is, in essence, the elevation of our true dreams and desires to documented status. It's often a lonely path: "The pioneer, the creator, explorer," Abraham Maslow explains, "is generally a single, lonely person rather than a group, struggling all alone with his inner conflicts, fears, defenses and arrogance, and pride, even against paranoia. He has to be a courageous man, not afraid to stick his neck out, not afraid even to make mistakes, well aware that he is . . . a kind of gambler who comes to tentative conclusions in the absence of facts and then spends some years trying to find out if his hunch was correct."

You'll feel better and live longer. These are not phony statements I stuck in just for fun. A lot of data out there shows that people who are driving towards a meaningful future of their own choosing do better in pretty much every way you can imagine. Following an inspiring, strategically sound vision that we really believe in correlates with greater life success, higher skill levels, better physical health, and a far greater sense of fulfillment. Martin Seligman, generally acknowledged as the father of positive psychology, in a speech at his fiftieth high school reunion, said, "There are two things we can do to maximize the chances that we will attend our seventieth reunion. The first is to be future oriented: to be drawn towards the future, as opposed to dwelling in the past. Work not just for your personal future but the future of your family, this school, your nation, and your dearest ideals." And the second thing? "Exercise," Seligman said. My suggestion is to write into your vision that you're working out regularly, enjoying it, and feeling better for it—and you'll make the best of both his wise points in one very effective vision of greatness.

Moving from academia to East Africa, here's an inspiring anecdote from chocolate maker Shawn Askinosie. Shawn's chocolate is exceptional and so is his commitment to making a positive difference in the world. Having learned how to do visioning here at Zingerman's, he's put it to work in pretty much every part of his life, including with some of the farmers who grow cacao for him in Tanzania. As Shawn told me: "We had an afternoon session on a ten-year vision for the Mababu Cocoa Farmer Cooperative. I posed the following question to them: 'When I come back here ten years from now, what will I see?' They started with an enthusiastic discussion right away. After much discussion they listed the following areas of visioned improvement: electricity, housing, transportation, motorbikes, trucks to help transport beans, learning about the world thru TV and media. Interestingly, it is not their goal to grow in size but they would like to diversify into other businesses." Already an inspiring story, but the capstone on the conversation was the closing comment from one of the farmers, Mr. Livingston. "I'm an old man," he said, "but this discussion makes me feel young again."

Why Bullet Points Are Not Enough

Many people who aren't comfortable with writing will, understandably, resist the act of putting their vision down in prose form. When we do the writing exercise in our ZingTrain seminar, there are often a few folks out of fifteen who will make a plea to skip out on full sentences because they're "not good at writing." They want to just put down bullet points instead. I resist their resistance, because I think limiting your mental flow to bullet points is a big mistake. Headlines are helpful, but they're not the same as the story. In fact, in journalism, it is generally accepted that the story and the headline are written by two different people. I have a feeling that the same thing occurs in the body and the brain. The headlines usually come from the head. The vision, the emotional engagement, the feeling, and the fun come from the soul.

If you look at bullet points on their own, they look clear and concise; they're certainly more helpful than a blank page or a blank stare. Don't get me wrong—I love a good list. But with bullets alone there's a flatness, a one-dimensionality, a dulling of the depth, density, and complexity of life, which is actually the very stuff that, when we write it out, gets us excited and energized. A vision without details is probably better than no vision at all, but it misses the point. The idea isn't to synopsize, it's to tell a story—to spill the emotional beans, to tap excitement, and dream big. If you compare a list of bullets to a beautifully written, straight from the heart, Zingerman's-style, prose vision, you'll notice the difference immediately. If you're used to working with bullet points, they may well be a good place to start your work. But I'd still stubbornly suggest you use the bullet points as a beginning, *not* as a be-all and end-all vision. The bullet points are just the headlines. They never tell you the whole story.[12]

"Bulls Win Title!" is a great one (especially if you're a Bulls fan like me). "Two-Year-Old Killed in Car Accident" announces something terrifically tragic. While each headline tells us exactly what the key fact is, both are absent the story, the detail, the drama, and the people behind it. We have no idea how it happened, how anyone felt before or afterward, how the family expressed their sadness or how the players celebrated. We lack the luster, the love, the layer upon layer of detail that add meaning to our lives. "The devil is in the details," the catchphrase goes, but in our case the details aren't the devil; they're the delight and deliciousness of the vision. The details are where the depth, spirit, soul, energy, connection, caring, and excitement are—and they're ultimately what make a vision come alive.

If, after all that, you think life can be summed up with bullet points, let me show you what my next long-term vision (for 2017) would look like:

- Go running with dog
- Zingerman's profit at 5.1 percent
- Improved quality
- Help others

- Learn
- Feel good
- Write two books
- Learn about other cultures
- Study hard
- Feel fortunate

If that's all you want to know about my dreams and what I'd like my life to look like four years from now, then there you go. But most of you, I'd guess, would be more compelled by a richer picture. So for my full personal vision, flip to the endnotes.[13] There's even more detail about what we'll be doing down the road in our Zingerman's 2020 Vision—see *Part 1* or visit www.zingtrain.com for the full vision.

Getting Ready to Write

In preparing to write your vision, you might take this advice from Brenda Ueland, the woman who taught me more about writing than anyone else: "So remember these two things: you are talented and you are original. Be sure of that. I say this because self-trust is one of the very most important things in writing . . . The creative power and imagination is in everyone, and so is the need to express it, i.e. to share it with others. But what happens to it?" For more on creativity, see Secret #39, but for the moment, I'll run with what Brenda wrote. The creative spirit, she says, "is very tender and sensitive, and it is usually drummed out of people early in life by criticism (so-called 'helpful criticism' is often the worst kind), by teasing, jeering, rules, prissy teachers, critics, and all those unloving people who forget that the letter killeth and the spirit giveth life. Sometimes I think of life as a process where everybody is discouraging and taking everybody else down a peg or two."

Writing the vision, the way we do it at Zingerman's, involves the implicit understanding and agreement that we often *don't know* (at least not consciously) what will emerge on the paper (or computer screen) when we start to draft. We just sit down, start writing, and keep at it for twenty or thirty minutes. It's just a draft so it doesn't matter whether what you've written seems "right." Don't let the fact that the story hasn't actually happened yet slow you down. It's a good story, and you already carry the seeds of it inside you.

Starting the Process

The details will emerge as you write. Please don't try to figure out the "answers" in advance. *Just write it.* Here's some advice from novelist Bobbie Ann Mason: "I've always found it difficult to start with a definite idea, but if I start with a pond that's being drained because of a diesel fuel leak and a cow named Hortense and some blackbirds flying over and a woman in the distance waving, then I might get somewhere." Historian Lynn Hunt, in her essay "How Writing Leads to Thinking," says much the same thing, albeit from a slightly more academic angle: "Something ineffable happens when you write down a thought. You think something you did not know you could or would think and it leads you to another thought almost unbidden."

What I've learned over the years is that I frequently don't realize how much of what I want I already know until I sit down and force myself to write. Sure, I have some idea of what I'm going to say when I start. But what I also know is that somewhere in the process some snippet of a thought, some significant—if seemingly small at the time—something-or-other will almost always emerge while I'm writing. Having done this work for many years now, I'm more able to identify what those things are in advance, but even so, stuff will get said when I sit down to write that I didn't realize was in there. What I get in those moments is almost always good, pure, particularly special, and personally significant.

Vision Delivers the Drama

If you doubt the depth and dramatic effect of a personal vision of greatness, I will tell you that when I read one aloud to a group—sometimes mine, sometimes someone else's—attention almost immediately goes up. People listen intently, as if I was about to open an envelope at the Oscars or reveal the winning numbers on the Daily Lotto. Most of the time, the audience doesn't even know the person whose vision I'm reading. And yet they sit up straighter, they start to smile, they get very serious, their eyes light up. Some start to tear up too. I understand why—a well-written vision is the ultimate in meaningful vulnerability and life altering authenticity.

The vision tells a story in emotionally rich detail, a story that hasn't actually happened yet. Personal vision is powerful drama, more engaging and more moving than most feature films. While cinema can be entertaining, all but the most important movies stay only on the screen; they're fun to watch, but in real life nothing really changes. Personal visioning work, by contrast, is compelling because it's personal, and we know that if people attempt to act on it, their dreams will start to become reality.

One of the questions I get asked most often about visioning is "Where do you find the time?" As I've said, it only takes twenty or twenty-five minutes to get a great first draft of a personal vision of greatness. (You can give yourself twice that much time if you really have a lot to say.) In the time it takes to go to a movie, a family of four could sit down together and each one could draft a personal vision, then share them with each other, gather feedback, and make appropriate adjustments. They could put their drafts down to rest for a bit, dine together, and refine the documents after dinner. It's just a minor reallocation of a day, but it could change their lives.

Writer Joel Arthur Barker observes, "Action without vision just passes the time; Vision with action can change the world." To Barker's point, hardly anyone will write a personal vision, actively share it, read it over regularly, and then completely ignore it. Writing it is the beginning. Regular rereading keeps it at the front of the mind and helps us to internalize and assimilate what we've written. Summing up, I'll just say, quite simply but very strongly, *visioning works*. It ain't always easy to make what we write real, but it's way more rewarding to be working on what we want than it is to just meander through life, hoping nothing bad happens. I'm down with what Henry David Thoreau wrote in his conclusion of *Walden:* "If one advances confidently in the direction of his dreams, and endeavors to live the life which he has imagined, he will meet with success unexpected in common hours."

Postscript: Martin Seligman and the Science of Well-Being

Martin Seligman makes a very good case for why using the Gross National Product as our universal standard of success is misdirected. He suggests instead that we ought to focus on the way people feel as much as do on their finances.

Dr. Seligman details five elements that make up well-being: *positive emotion, engagement with the world, good relationships, meaning,* and *achievement.* He uses the acronym PERMA to pull them together. This reminds me of "permaculture" a well-known term in the world of sustainable agriculture, defined as "an ecological design system for sustainability in all aspects of human endeavor." Sounds good. I'd argue that Seligman's PERMA index is a design system for quality of life.

If you want to see how your vision might increase your odds of living a rewarding life, of attaining well-being, you can use PERMA as a checklist. If your vision draft touches on each of the five elements, you're in good shape. If you've missed one (which is not uncommon), you still have time to add to the draft and get it included.

Positive Emotion (P): feeling good and having good feelings.

Engagement (E): connecting with colleagues, with ourselves, with the community, with the world.

Relationships (R): experiencing rewarding and resilient relationships.

Meaning (M): finding meaning through learning, connecting, caring, and helping others.

Achievement (A): making significant things happen in our lives and/or for those around us, i.e., developing a new product, raising a child, becoming a masterful massage therapist, etc.

Visions that touch on all five of these areas are likely to be well-rounded and genuinely fulfilling.

Follow The Recipe for Writing a Vision of Greatness

For a much more detailed description of how to write a vision, see Secret #8 in *Part 1* of the *Guide to Good Leading*. Here's a synopsis of the eight-step recipe.

INGREDIENTS FOR EFFECTIVE VISIONING

- Belief in the Process
- Your Gut
- Some Time
- Willingness to Make Yourself Vulnerable
- Readiness to Do Something Great
- You've Gotta Wanna
- The Willingness to Stick with the Process

PROCEDURE

Step 1: Pick Your Topic. In this case, it's your life!

Step 2: Pick Your Time Frame. I'd recommend going at least three, or probably five to ten years out.

Step 3: Put Together a List of "Prouds." These are things that will help you get into a positive mode to write. They may be both *facts* (things you've achieved in your life already that will help you get to greatness in the future) and/or *feelings* (how you felt when you experienced success in the past). This small step helps to get us thinking positively, which helps in turn to open the creative door to more effective visioning.

Step 4: Write the First Draft of the Vision. The first time through is only a DRAFT! Write what you like—you can edit it later many times! The key of getting going is to write, and write, and write straight through until it's time to stop. Analysis and critical thinking, at this stage, are anything but helpful. Just sit down, get ready, and write with the following in mind.

- Go for Something Great. Don't hold back. It's the only life you're likely to get, so make it a great one!

- Write from the Heart. Put the passion, the feeling, the dreams, and emotion into it!

- Get in the Future. We always write our visions as if they've already happened. So if you were writing today (in 2013), you might start by saying, "It's December 31, 2017, and I'm heading home from work. I'm more excited than ever about . . ." and then move on from there. Keep remembering to write it as if it's already happened. I can't explain why, but it makes a huge difference!

- Go Quickly. On the first draft, don't edit at all. Just write what comes to mind. If you hate what you wrote later, you can always throw it out. But I'll say that hardly anyone ever does.

- Use the "Hot Pen" Technique. Once you start writing, just keep writing. Whatever it is that comes out of your head will be helpful. The key is to keep the computer keys or the pen moving! In under 30 minutes of "hot pen," continuous writing, I guarantee you will have a very good start on a personal vision of greatness that will impress even you!

- Get Personal. Add adjectives, names, places, tastes, smells, etc. that mean something to you.

For personal visioning, I've taken to recommending that people consider starting with a line I took from the personal vision of Stephanie Randall, who works at our Creamery. You can alter the details to fit your desire. Here's how Stephanie started hers: "It is February 14th, 2015. I am 25 years old. *My life has become exactly what I want it to be.*" Having shared her vision with any number of groups over the years, I know that every time I read it aloud, I come close to crying. And so do many people in the audience. Try it. "It's —, 20—. I am — years old. *My life has become exactly what it I want it to be.*"

Step 5: Re-View and Re-Draft. Set the vision aside for a few days and then take it back out and re-read. Feel free to adjust.

(Optional) Steps 6-A, 6-B, and 6-C: More Re-Drafts. Repeat as in Step 5 a few times so you can continue to refine your draft.

Step 7: Get Input from People You Respect. Share your vision and listen to what others say, what questions they have, etc. Incorporate or ignore their input as you like. I'd recommend going to people who believe in you, folks with caring, open minds, not the ones who are going to chop you down and tell you how unattainable your vision is. After you've gathered ideas from others you trust, then adjust and make changes. At some point—usually much sooner than anyone with perfectionist tendencies will want to admit—you're done! You have a personal vision!

Step 8: Let's Go—Start Living the Vision. Sharing it with others makes it real. I guarantee that your vision will be good, that you'll feel better for having done it, and that it will help you with decision making, improve your energy, and guide you towards creating the life of your dreams!

Life is short—have fun!

Val Neff-Rasmussen, Service Center Supervisor, Zingerman's Mail Order

I wrote this vision in June of 2012. At the time, it felt incredibly ambitious. The job I describe is pretty different from the role I was in at that time: at Zingerman's Mail Order we call it "service star," but the world at large might call it "customer service representative." The role I envisioned was one that didn't exist at all when I wrote about it. It doesn't fully exist now, either, but it's a lot closer to being a reality—and to being my reality.

While it was exciting to write my vision of the future I wanted to create, it wasn't easy for me to share it. When I say I'm going to do something, I mean it, and it was really scary for me to put all of these things out there that I wanted, but that I wasn't sure I could achieve. Almost as soon as I shared the vision with my managers in August 2012, amazing things started to happen. I had hoped to go to Italy for work a couple of years down the road; I had the opportunity to go to Italy in September 2012, and again in April 2013. I had hoped I might be able to scout out one or two new products good enough to be offered in our catalog; as I write these words in the fall of 2013, we're selling a half dozen products I brought back from those Italy trips. There are still pieces of the vision that are in progress—after all, I wrote it to take place in fall of 2014—but it has been incredible to see pieces of the vision come together in ways I never even imagined.

Focus on what you want. What excites you. Not on the reasons why it may not work.

DRAFT DRAFT DRAFT DRAFT DRAFT

Fall 2014.

I am about to enter my fifth holiday season at ZMO (!). When I first came on as a holiday service star back in 2010, I don't think I could have imagined I would be where I am now. I feel luckier than ever to be a part of such a special organization.

I spend 30–40 hours in the office weekly, plus another 5–15 hours working at home each week. It's a schedule that has worked well since I switched to a salaried position. Here's some of what I do during that time:

I learn. I came to Zingerman's to learn about food. In the last four years (can it really be four years?!), I have found the experience to be so much more than that. And while I have learned a ton about food, I also recognize how much I don't yet know. My passion to learn more is as strong today—in fact, probably stronger—as it was when we tasted sourcream coffeecake on my first day of training.

These days, I learn in many ways. I read regularly—I'm usually reading three or four books at once, in addition to numerous articles and other shorter pieces. I attend classes, both in the ZCoB and elsewhere. I taste all the time—both new foods and ones we've carried for years. I'm regularly on the phone chatting with producers and vendors. I've also had the chance to visit some of them, to see what they do first-hand. On a few occasions, I've even gotten my hands a little dirty with them!

I travel. Speaking of visiting producers, that brings me to my second point. I travel within the US frequently—at least 3–5 times annually on my own time, and at least 1–2 times annually for work. Even when I travel on my own, I often seek out one of our producers or new food finds for a quick visit. My travels have also introduced us to at least a couple foods that we now sell.

I've also spent some time traveling internationally. I spend 3–4 weeks abroad every two years. First there was the trip I took in spring 2013 in Europe. Though it was mostly a trip I planned and paid for myself, I also took advantage of the opportunity to meet some of the folks that we work with and see more of our food at its source. My trip also helped to spark the discussion of how the ZMO travel bonus, as laid out in the ZMO 2014 vision, could work.

Up next on the travel agenda is the Staff Scholarship that I won. In a few weeks, I'll be headed back across the Atlantic to see the olive harvest and press. One of my goals for this trip is to work on setting up some kind of staff exchange program, as mentioned in the 2020 vision. I don't want to give too much away on where I'm headed, but I will tell you that I'm grateful that I started learning some Italian back in 2012!

I write. The main reason that I want to learn and to travel is so that I can share some of that knowledge and that experience with others. I spend a fair amount of time writing. In a given week, I may write posts for our Facebook page (though rarely more than 80 characters at a time!), blog posts for the Zingerman's community blog, new or updated copy for our products, or the occasional longer article.

Something I've written has been published by at least one entity outside of ZMO, too. Currently, I'm considering whether it's time to start working on a book.

I teach. Back in March 2009, when I attended my first tasting at the Deli (British cheeses), I was blown away by how much the instructors knew. I remember thinking to myself, "Wow. I want to know this much about food. I want to be able to do *this.*"

They say to be careful what you wish for, and they're right. Luckily, this time I made the right wish.

I feel so lucky to have the opportunity to learn so much, and I love having the opportunity to share what I've learned with those around me. On a small scale, I lead tastings at ZMO at least once a week. During the holidays, I lead multiple tastings weekly, and I teach the ZMO Intro to Great Food class that gives holiday service stars a great introduction into what makes our foods so special. At the end of the 2013 holiday season, a handful of service stars told me it was one of their favorite parts of the whole holiday experience, and with the tweaks I've made for this year I'm expecting it to be better than ever.

Around the ZCoB, I teach three internal classes, which results in me teaching a class roughly once or twice per month.

I teach food classes through Zingerman's that are open to the public at least three times each year. The ZXI scores I've gotten for these classes consistently come in at a solid 90. At least one of the attendees of one of my classes was inspired to learn more about food like I was back in 2009.

I also share the learning with our guests through fun, informal tastings sessions at ZMO. About once a month, we've invited a small group of guests to come in for an intimate tasting session focused entirely on their personal tastes and preferences. Our guests love the opportunity to come in and taste some of our products, and I love being able to share some of my knowledge and enthusiasm while we literally break bread. And all of us at ZMO love that after tasting, our guests are inclined to make sizeable purchases.

There are so many moments that stand out for me related to teaching, but one that I'm especially proud of was the first time that I consulted for a ZingTrain client.

The more I teach, the more I learn—and so the cycle begins again.

kristin wagle, westside farmers' market manager,
showing off some of the market wares

Making the Most of Our Lives

A Look at the Other Eleven Natural Laws

Of the Natural Laws of Life, the first—about the importance of vision—is one of the least recognized in the wider business world, but it's probably the most powerful of the twelve. It's also the most expansive and inclusive—writing a personal vision gives you a chance to weave any or all of the other eleven into your desired future. With that in mind, here's my take on why each of the Natural Laws contributes meaningfully to being successful and leading a rewarding, creative, and connected life.

I doubt that many—or even any—successful people you know will reference the Natural Laws when they talk about what's made their life what it is. The construct is one I created. But the reality of these principles and their impact is universal. Try a little experiment. Ask those whose lives you respect how they got to where they are and why they like the way they're living. Ask what they recommend you keep in mind as you move forward with your life. And then cross-check what they tell you against the list of Natural Laws. I'll bet you'll find they touch on most, or even all, of them.

As Russian anarchist Mikhail Bakunin wrote well over a century ago, "The liberty of man consists solely in this: that he obeys natural laws because he has himself recognized them as such, and not because they have been externally imposed upon him by any extrinsic will whatever, divine or human, collective or individual." Starting to live the Natural Laws won't guarantee that you'll attain world-class success in a week, but I'm confident that over time they'll contribute positively and progressively to the quality of your life.

The open book finance model we work with is based on several beliefs: a) most of the people playing the game of business, i.e., the frontline staff, don't know the rules of the game; b) they rarely know the "score" and have hardly any understanding of how their "team" is doing; and c) even if their team wins, they have little idea what they might have personally done to make that happen. I think the same situation actually exists—and is endemic—in life. Most people don't know the rules of how it's played. Like frontline employees with business finance, they often make up their own stories to explain what they see happening, but sadly, those explanations are often wrong. Nor do many folks keep score very creatively—nearly every way we're taught to measure "success" (money, power, prestige, etc.) comes from standards set by outsiders, not by us. And while some people do share in some success—unfortunately, much of the time, they've gone after standards of success that were not their own.

Our approach to open book finance is about reversing that flow—we teach everyone the rules of business; we keep score regularly and in the open; and if the business does well, everyone in the organization does well too. Of late I've come to believe that teaching visioning, and the other eleven Natural Laws that follow, does for people's lives what open book management does for frontline staff members' relationship to finance. The Natural Laws are the rules of living a sustainable life. Number 1, writing a vision of greatness, is where each of us can describe and design the future of our own choosing—and once we have that, it's far easier to track our progress en route. As with open book finance, visioning and the other Laws that go along with it help everyone to understand how life works, and give them the tools, the rules, and the confidence to deal with it actively, mindfully, and constructively. And because they all come together to help us live the life of our dreams, they most certainly add up to a meaningful share of the success.

Here they are then—Natural Laws #2–12.

2. Successful People Engage in Compelling Activities

What strikes me as I reread the title of the second of the Natural Laws is that the word "compelling" is itself very compelling. At least it feels that way to me. As soon as I hear it used to describe a book or a business, a loaf of bread or a beautiful piece of art, my curiosity goes up! Why is it so compelling? And to whom? Successful people, quite simply, do stuff that others are drawn to, that excites both them and those around them. As the man sitting next to me in the café this morning just announced with great passion to the little girl he's breakfasting with, "Life is a delight! I have great dreams. Life is a delight."

Dreams and delight take me directly, delightfully, back to the power and poetry of an inspiring and strategically sound personal vision. A vision of greatness—one that we wrote for ourselves or at least actively participated in creating—is a marvelous (self-) motivator. People who are pursuing a path of their own creation, a life they freely chose to lead, doing work they believe in, living in synch with their values and vision, are the kind of people I want to be around. Though I don't always succeed, it's also the kind of person I want to be. As Julia Cameron writes, "as we are creative beings, our lives become our work of art."

By contrast, when we follow a path prescribed by others, a life that's been painted strictly by numbers, we're rarely fired up; regardless of the practicality of it, the persuasive powers of our peers or our parents, or the social pressure to con-, and per-, form, pursuing a future that originates outside our souls is never compelling. There may be dozens of data points behind this decision—a large salary, a dependable career path, pleased parents—but if it's not in synch with one's own spirit, something is missing. Having ventured down both roads, I can say from experience that there's a freedom, a lightness of being, and a compelling energy that comes with doing things we believe in and going after the life we want to live in a grounded, generous, and just way.

I think that energy, the compelling, attractive, and inspiring nature of what we do, is translated (when we do it well, of course) into every element of our lives. It doesn't guarantee that all our work will be successful, but it certainly increases the odds. University of Michigan student Seth Samuels struck a chord when he shared this thought about Zingerman's one day when we were having coffee at the Deli. During our conversation about what makes for a great business, Seth said, "I don't think a thing is really great until people start talking about it." Which is, he noted, exactly what happens at the Deli every time he comes in. Even before people start on their sandwiches, they'll remark on the staff, the service, the signage, or the samples. They'll mention how different this environment is from what they're accustomed to. "And, once the food arrives," Seth added, "they really get going!"

The power of this kind of buzz is clearly important for businesses. I would argue that it holds true for us as individuals as well. People spontaneously say good things about people with compelling personalities, folks that bring positive energy into the world and pursue interesting paths. Quite simply, *successful people do compelling things*. They engage in out-of-the-ordinary activities. Their lives are devoted to doing things they believe in, things that make them feel more themselves. When what you do is different and interesting, interesting people want to be around it; they want to meet you, they want to buy what you're selling, they want to engage, learn more, and benefit from your example.

Successful people, as I experience them, are always inspired by what they're doing. They believe in it, they believe it makes a difference, they believe it matters to the world, they believe it's contributing to others around them. Whether their work is child rearing, poetry writing, playing Ultimate Frisbee, or teaching philosophy, they're drawn to what they do. Even when they're frustrated, they're still fascinated. Whether it's being a parent, a professional athlete, or a pizza maker, they're passionate about their profession; they find what they do compelling, creative, fulfilling, and fun. They could study it for life and still not have enough time to do all they want. What they do helps them be more themselves. And the more they become themselves, the better they feel and the more successful (as I define the term, which would be that they're living true to their vision and values) they're likely to be.

In essence, in writer Wendell Berry's worldview, *they do good work*. While doing work you love to do doesn't guarantee that you'll have great energy every single day, you're surely a lot more likely to come across as positive, compelling, and attractive when you believe deeply in what you're doing. Whether it's being a brain surgeon, a baker, or a banker, the point is the same—the people we all want to be around lead interesting, engaged lives. And they have a grounded, calming energy that others want to emulate.[14]

By contrast, people who are mostly just passing time, getting by, doing bad or even neutral and unobtrusive work, rarely have that good glow, that bright buzz about them. While they themselves may well be brilliant, their energy tends to be flat and is rarely rewarding to be around. The same goes for organizations. Ineffective businesses usually take the approach that people "should" want to buy their products and services. They act like they have something coming to them. They view the world from a victim's vantage point. Their energy is all about entitlement. It's true, too, for each of us as individuals. People who act like they have something coming to them are rarely those I want to hang around. And while they may boast of financial gain or social status, they rarely do well, over time, in the positive ways in which I'd define success. (They, of course, get to define what success means to them.) Others around them may deliver what they demand, but it's almost always done from a shaky foundation or a position of fear, not from admiration, respect, or a sincere desire to assist.

The people (and organizations) that get my attention in a positive way are the ones who go out and try to earn it over and over again, people who take nothing for granted and who enter each day determined to do good things for themselves and those around them. They regularly set out to re-earn the trust, care, and respect of everyone in their lives. They give others good reasons to want to continue to connect, to care, to communicate, and to share community. They take the initiative to start relationships on the road towards mutual success. They are, on their own terms, almost always successful, and they're almost always interesting to be around. Others want to contribute to their cause. As Simon Sinek says in *Start with Why,* "When you compete against others, no one wants to help you. But when you compete against yourself, everyone wants to help you."

That's the crux of Natural Law #2: attractive, engaging energy. People who go calmly and determinedly after greatness are far more fun to be around than those who are angry at the world because it hasn't already gifted them what they thought they had coming. To quote my good friend Daphne Zepos, those in the former group "own their lives." Joseph Ishill, Romanian anarchist and publisher and printer of some of the most beautiful books I've ever seen, said that in the pursuit of success, "It is first necessary to possess one's own self, to revolve around one's own axis which must radiate ideals and not mechanical reproductions of a pattern designed for millions of duplicates."

If you want a simpler, more lyrical approach to all this, here's a little something from anarchist hobo poet Utah Phillips:

Sing your song
Dance your dance
Tell your story
I will listen and remember

Values Imperative

People who are clear about their values and then live them consistently are far more likely to feel good about the way their lives are going. Values are woven all through the Twelve Natural Laws, but I wanted to call them out specifically here because in my experience, they play a huge part in creating quality of life. Knowing who we are, what's important to us, what turns us on and off, what makes us feel right with the universe and what doesn't—the more we know all that inside and out, the more likely we are to be able to live it. Having a clear sense of your values and weaving them into everything you do isn't news. But it is important.

When we're not clear on our values, we're essentially adrift in a sea of others' opinions and arbitrary advice. Knowing how we expect ourselves to behave in any ethically oriented situation helps lead us to greater success. Even the struggle to figure out what to do and how to do it will be more productive when it's done within the framework that clearly elucidated ethics will offer. Coming at things from a place of passion, belief, and ethical orientation will always lead to better energy and almost as often to better results. Even when we fail in the moment, it's easier to assimilate the situation if we've gone at things from a grounded and values-oriented angle.

3. Without Good Finance, You Fail

Without trying to oversimplify things, "good finance" is about having as much money as you want to have and living accordingly, and effectively, within those means. How much money that translates into is very variable: "enough" is one of the most subjective words in our vocabulary. Money has never been the main driver for me in anything I've done. It's a helpful tool, but it's never been the height of my sense of achievement. Nevertheless, money remains an important piece of our existence; if we have too little of it, we're going to have a hard time getting by.

Two points to make up front, neither of which will be shocking, but they're worth stating rather than assuming my way into trouble.

a. While money definitely does *not* buy happiness, it does buy some of the stuff that forms a foundation of solidity and safety, without which a mindful life is difficult to construct. (For more on this subject, track down any article on Maslow's hierarchy of needs.)

b. Success is a personal thing. Whether it's about money or almost anything else in life, there really isn't any objective standard. For better and for worse (actually, it's all for the better), there's no national board that bestows a Certificate of Life Success on anyone. *It's up to each of us to determine what our own dreams and desires are.* One person's "more than sufficient" is another's "severe shortage." Take four different people and you'll have four different definitions of what "good finance" means.

There's so much value judgment in the world about money. Some people blame it for all the world's evils, and others see it as the solution to all our problems. Personally, I think money's fine, if not, in and of itself, particularly fulfilling. I like having enough to pay bills, live securely, enjoy a positive, food-filled environment, give gifts to people I care about, contribute to the community, and set aside some savings so I have more security for my future. I know my life is less stressful for not having had to live paycheck to paycheck for a long time now. I know I'm in a position of security that most people in the world won't attain. I know too that although I started from a comparatively privileged position, it's not like it all just fell into my lap either. I came from a middle-class home—my parents were educators, not entrepreneurs.

To be clear, there are loads of people who have way more money than I do now, or ever will. And there are many times more people than that who have far less; for whom the money to make this month's rent payment, to buy food to feed their family for the next few days, or even to buy this book would be a big deal. I feel extremely fortunate for my lot. I hope that by building a sustainable business, by creating good work, and by giving regularly to the community, we make a small but still meaningful dent in that difficult situation.

Natural Law #3 is all about getting some clarity on what financial success means to you, and then going after it. I'd suggest including something about finance in your personal vision, or drafting a separate vision for your personal finance. Either approach will work. The key is that you have a plan of some sort and that you're working actively to make it a reality. While I'm happy to spend money for things I value, at my core, I'm a saver. The way I see it, it's about living sustainably, paying bills on time, having savings, and giving to the community and to others I care about. It's about managing money well enough that I'm not freaking out about cash flow every Friday morning. More than anything, I think it's about having a positive personal relationship with money. Personally, I'm going for a healthy mutual respect, an abundance mentality, and—through my work—a chance to contribute positively to the cash standing of those around me. You, of course, can be anything you want: savage spender, super safe saver, day trader, dishwasher. The question is, are you clear in your personal vision about what financial health will mean for you? If not, there's no time like the present. It's your future, your finances, your life.

4. People Do Their Best Work When They're Part of a Really Great Organization

While I like to think of my introverted anarchist self as a freestanding, free-thinking, free from influence, independently operating entity, the reality is that I always have been, and always will be, greatly influenced by my surroundings. None of us—even those who, like me, would probably prefer it so—is an island. Like it or not, we're all impacted by the environment in which we work. As Steven Johnson says in *Where Good Ideas Come From*, "Our thought shapes the spaces we inhabit, and our spaces return the favor."

Unless we're living in the wilderness in a cabin without anyone else in sight, we're never fully on our own; our colleagues, the community, and the organization around us influence what we do and how we feel enormously. Everyone who takes a leadership role in their own lives will find themselves walking a road (or two or three or four) less traveled en route to wherever they're going. We're on our own, and yet, at the same time, we're almost always connected to others. What we know is that the better the people we surround ourselves with, the better we ourselves are likely to do.

With that in mind, I'm fortunate to be part of a healthy, creative, caring organization that's aligned with my values and whose vision is well in synch with my own. It helps, of course, that I was involved in starting it thirty years ago (though, of course, that alone would be no guarantee of getting to greatness or even of being in business this far down the road). Clearly, I've contributed to making the Zingerman's Community of Businesses what it is; but just as clearly, that Community has contributed greatly to bringing out so much that's good in me. As Gary Snyder writes, "To know the spirit of a place is to realize that you are a part of a part and that the whole is made of parts, each of which is whole. You start with the part you are whole in."

This doesn't mean that those who are in less constructive work communities are helpless. When we're *not* part of a great organization, it's up to us to either improve the place as best we're able and/or get ourselves, if we can, into a more constructive setting. The simple, down-to-earth, easier-to-say-than-it-may-be-to-do-it directive, then, is if you want to lead a good life, get yourself into a business in which the people who are part of it are living good lives as well. Join an organization that's already good at the things you want to be good at, that lives the values you want to live, whose vision is compatible with yours, and the odds are you'll be doing better yourself. If you can't find one, and if you happen to have both the courage and the cash, then start your own.

Please understand too that this Natural Law does *not* mean everyone does their best work while actively IN a group setting. Some folks may, others (like me) may not. What the Natural Law lays out is only that we do better work when the group we're a part of is a positive and productive one. The reality of the world is that most of us will gravitate towards the direction in which others around us are already going. I'm sure there must be some name for this. Some social version of "the law of supply and demand," only in this case it might be "the law of organizational optimization." Much as we might try to fight it, it's hard not to go with the flow. When we're around others who are at peace with mediocrity, most of us will move towards the middle of the road as well. When we're surrounded by cynicism, eye rolls become an everyday activity. But when we're with a high-achieving group that's going for greatness, well, you guessed it, we're pretty likely to start going for greatness too.

Work, of course, is not the only important organization of which people are a part. Families, not-for-profits, religious groups, scout troops, marching bands, booster clubs, and weekly poker games all function in much the same way. The quality of our community in every case is the key. As Maslow said, the more effectively we get ourselves into settings where we're around other good people, the easier it is to be good at whatever it is we're doing. And the more we live as active members of a culture that encourages us to dream big, the more likely it is that we can make those big dreams a daily reality. This organizational support system often comes into play on an informal cultural level as well. An organization that makes asking for help a strength is likely to help everyone in it grow stronger. And an organization that values quality, creativity, caring, and positive energy will bring out the best of those traits in most everyone involved as well.

Cultural context counts for a lot; being around people with positive energy is almost sure to get us to raise the bar on our own energy as well. It's hard to be dissonant and negative in the face of so much positive presence. A few weeks ago, I was speaking to a group of business visitors at the Roadhouse. When they started asking me what it was like to work in our organization, I suggested they ask the two staff members who were working their party. The first, Margaret Carollo, gave a clear, compelling, and fully accurate assessment of how the organization works and why. She talked about what motivated her, how we trained, how we hired, how we kept our energy so high all the time. While the mainstream business world would probably say that she's "only" a twenty-six-year-old server, I thought her performance was superb. If you put her in a suit, you could have convinced people she was the CEO, or at least among the folks next in line to take over the company. Seriously, she was that well-spoken.

The second staffer, Randy Norris, was a busboy who had been with us for a grand total of something like six months. "To be honest," he said, "when I got here I was pretty cynical. But everyone here is so positive that it made my energy a lot better. It's actually changed my whole attitude to work. It's changed my relationship with my girlfriend, and really, it's changed my outlook on life. My energy is way more positive now than it's ever been." Now, I'm not saying that either of those two wouldn't have achieved great things on their own; Zingerman's did not make them what and who they are. But I think the culture and systems with which they're working every day helped to bring out the insight, understanding, and confidence that might otherwise never come to the surface in a work setting. And all of that will contribute significantly to making their lives more enjoyable.

Similarly, the quality of the systems in any organization can also contribute a lot to an individual's success. Although most organizations see systems work as a way to deliver product consistency, improve efficiency, and avoid crisis, I believe they can also make a major contribution to helping bring out the best in each individual we employ, which in turn makes us a better organization. An absence of structure may sound appealing to those who are trapped in the bowels of bureaucracy, but in truth, other than for the most totally self-directed among us, a blank page is not enough. Healthy organizations use systems and structures to encourage their members to make the most of themselves and their lives. As anarchist Max Baginsky wrote at the beginning of the 20th century, "the true function of organization is to aid the development and growth of the personality."

Five Characteristics of Constructive, Sustainable Systems Design

The way I see it, organizational structure and processes in a well-designed sustainable setting ought to:

1. Assist people in becoming, and being, themselves.

2. Ensure that everyone who's supposed to be on the same page is clear on what that page looks like.

3. Constructively push each of us to be creative and think for ourselves within an agreed-upon framework of vision and values.

4. Allow the people who are doing the work to influence and help design the processes of which they're a part.

5. Encourage great results for all involved in a sustainable and supportive way.

The kinds of systems I'm thinking about here at Zingerman's might include our "recipes" for personal visioning; 3 Steps to Great Service; 5 Steps to Handling a Complaint; 4 Steps to Great Food; Bottom Line Change (our process for organizational change), etc. All bring clarity and consistency while also encouraging creativity and individual initiative. Since we encourage everyone here to think freely and to own their choices, for the most part people approach the work outlined by these systems out of positive belief and commitment, not from the more usual bureaucratic constructs of compulsion, constraint, and compliance.

One other important piece of this to point out: for an individual, a "great organization" must, by definition, be one that shares the individual's values. Joining a group whose values (as in lived values, not lip service) are in synch with your own will only help all involved. Values alignment unleashes positive energy; it's more fun, it feels good, and it makes work way more rewarding. You might say that when ethics and worldview are aligned, you're swimming with the current of the organization's "values stream." If, by contrast, you're going against the current—if there's a mismatch, disconnect, or incongruity—then instead of people doing great work, they're going to get worked over. All of which is why, when it comes to organizational life, the culturally rich generally get richer while the "organizational poor" tend to bring in people that are less driven to do great things.

Being part of an unhealthy organization like that is exhausting. The people in them are generally assigned to do what Wendell Berry calls "bad work." It's not rewarding, it's not enriching, it's not engaging, and it's not likely to lead to greatness. As anarchist Howard Ehrlich writes, "Everyday life in most organizations is stultifying. Rarely is there an opportunity to conceptualize anything better. So one does what one has to do. And by going about one's work, people reaffirm their negative self-conceptions." It's a remarkably dysfunctional way to work. When people feel bad about themselves and the place they're a part of, it's almost impossible for either the individual or the team to get to greatness. The way I see it, though, it's our work as leaders, not the ineptitude of our employees, that makes all these problems. As Canadian anarchist Colin Ward writes in *Anarchy in Action*, "The system makes its morons, then despises them for their ineptitude."

Creating good work inside a bad organization is possible but pretty unlikely. Aside from the fact that the organization fails to encourage people's self-growth, few in these settings have even experienced good work enough to know what it is. The number of people who are likely to offer up positive leadership in an otherwise unhealthy organization is very small; *they have to know what good work is before they can work to make it happen.*

Conversely, people with positive energy, people who want to do good work, are most often drawn to healthy, positive organizations. And to make the equation even more positive, anyone who joins a great organization is simply more likely to do better work because they're around good people and good structures. Which, in turn, makes the organization more effective, which, in turn, improves the quality of work, etc., etc. I would argue, as Maslow does, that "there is a kind of feedback between the Good Society and the Good Person. They need each other, they are the *sine qua non* [indispensible] to each other. I wave aside the problem of which comes first. It is quite clear that they develop simultaneously and in tandem."[15]

Bottom line? If you want to get to greatness, get yourself into a great organization!

"This Place Will Change You!"

That's what Roadhouse line cook Allie Lyttle regularly says to newcomers who ask what it's like to work here. "Coming to Zingerman's was an inoculation of positivity that I never knew could exist. After working many years in really unhappy corporate settings, I took a leap of faith and went to work at the Roadhouse full time. I don't know how else to explain it other than it fundamentally changed who I am as a person. Being in an environment where everyone cares for your well-being and your own personal growth makes you strive to be that better person every single day. I'm happier than I have ever been, and it's because of the energy surrounding the work we all do."

What Allie intuited from her own experience turns out to be supported by science. Studies of human brains and behavior show that constant framing of experiences into positive or negative will eventually change the shape of your brain and the way you think about things. Martin Seligman writes "happiness happens to be more contagious than depression," and he presents a long list of good things that happen from being surrounded by a strongly positive environment. Allie and many others here, I believe, have benefited from most everything on it.

---

5. If You Want To Be Successful, Start with a Service Mindset

There are many people in the world—probably the vast majority—to whom Servant Leadership is still essentially an alien concept. Service is a language they've heard about but have never made time to study. I suppose that some of those people succeed in parts of life despite their lack of interest in the subject. But those are *not* the successful folks that this story is about. They may attain some accolades for whatever achievements they've made, but I've rarely observed peace, joy, and positive energy to be at the center of their existence. What I would say is that the people I know who successfully weave service into their everyday existence; who work a service approach into almost everything they do; and who enjoy giving service to those around them, to their world, and to themselves are generally those I'd like to emulate and learn from.

It's synergy really. You serve, you give freely, you help those you interact with, the world around you does better, you make a difference, you feel better, your life is better for it. This is, in essence, aligned with the early work on the subject done by pioneering anthropologist Ruth Benedict. She defines synergy as "social-institutional conditions which fuse selfishness and unselfishness. I automatically help others, and when I try to be altruistic, I automatically reward and gratify myself also; i.e., when the dichotomy or polar opposition between selfishness and altruism is resolved and transcended." To my mind, it all starts with service—what we get back isn't the point of the giving, but it's certainly true that, as Benedict believed, when we give of ourselves consistently in the right setting, synergy and success is what we'll more than likely get out of it.

Starting with a service mindset does not mean that any of us have to do exactly what everyone around us is asking us for. As per Secret #32, this is all about freely chosen activity, not about being forced into some sort of service submission. Service that's forced feels phony and is ultimately doomed to failure. Service that's freely given will feel authentic and will make about eighty times more good things happen. It's the simple yet profound stuff surrounding the Golden Rule, and it's sure to contribute to a more rewarding life. Smiling, sincerely greeting others, offering caring, compassion, and kindness—you don't need me to make the list for you.

As for dealing with people's complaints, I don't always get that right, but I work hard at it all the time. When someone I'm close to complains, I try hard to respond effectively, receptively, and encouragingly. And really my response begins just as it would with a customer. I acknowledge what's being said, sincerely apologize, and then work on respectfully arriving at a mutually rewarding outcome. If I'm really on my game, I'll thank the person for complaining. Service may not lead straight to financial success, but it definitely drives us towards a rewarding and productive existence, one that makes a positive difference for ourselves and everyone around us. And as Muhammad Ali said, "Service to others is the rent you pay for your room here on earth."

Having a service mindset isn't only about what we do for others—it's just as important, I believe, that we serve ourselves as well. In the case of Natural Law #5, the service that leaders give to their staff sets the standard for the quality of the service that the frontline crew will give to customers. Personal success follows a similar model. *The courtesy and respect with which we treat ourselves and those around us is the cap on our ability to lead and succeed.* If we want to do great things in the world, if we want to have a great life, we're going to have a better shot at it if we treat ourselves with the same respect and dignity that we would deliver to others we serve. It's only when I started to treat myself with the same high standard of compassion, caring, clarity, and fun that I was seeking to project that I really succeeded in serving others as well. Internal rudeness, I've learned, will always translate out to others through vibrational energy as disrespect and dissonance. See page 66 in Managing Ourselves for more on this.

Living the Steps to Great Service with Yourself

If you want to experiment with this internally, take our 3 Steps to Great Service and practice them in the privacy of your mind.

3 Steps to Great Service	How to Apply Them on a Personal Level
Step 1. Find out what the customer wants. Engage the customer: spend as much time getting to know the guest as we can.	Write your vision. Get to know yourself well—a huge piece of self-management.
Live the 10/4 Rule: make eye contact and smile at 10 feet, then offer a greeting when we get within 4.	Smile regularly upon seeing yourself (literally or figuratively).
Read body language and tone of voice.	Engage in mindfulness practices.
Step 2. Get it for them accurately, politely, and enthusiastically. Follow through on our commitments to customers, with a high degree of accuracy and enthusiasm.	Follow through on your commitments to yourself and treat yourself with dignity.
Step 3. Go the extra mile. Do some small thing for guests that they didn't ask for but that will enhance their experience.	Find small, unexpected ways to enhance the quality of your days, treating yourself to the same small acts of generosity you would do for others.

5 Steps to Effectively Handling Complaints	How to Apply Them on a Personal Level
Step 1. Acknowledge what the customer is saying. We usually start out with a simple, "Oh," or "Wow," or "I hear you."	In handling your own complaints about yourself, accept yourself as you are; own your feelings rather than fighting them.
Step 2. Apologize. A simple heartfelt apology goes a long way. "I'm very sorry" can really help with recovering from a mistake.	Give yourself the benefit of the doubt instead of berating yourself.
Step 3. Make things right. We do whatever we need to do to make it right for the guest, while keeping the best interests of the organization in mind in the process.	Living in the moment, do what you need to do to be at peace in an ethically sound way.
Step 4. Thank them for complaining. We simply say something like, "Thank you so much for letting us know."	Accept that the problems the world presents you with come for a reason, providing opportunities to learn.
Step 5. Write down the experience. In our customer service work, we document all complaints and compliments (For more on this work, see *Zingerman's Guide to Giving Great Service*.)	If it seems helpful, do a bit of journaling to transcribe what you've learned.

My guess is that these seemingly small things can have a big impact on the positive nature of your life, both personally and at work. Using our 5 Steps to Effectively Handling Complaints with yourself can have and equally positive effect.[16]

exercise This idea of giving great service to ourselves is an interesting and important theme in helping us improve the quality of our lives and also our energy and effectiveness at work. Here are a few exercises you might try:

List ten things (not people) that you love but don't normally get to be around. It could be nice sweaters, fine paper, hand-picked peaches, etc. If you're giving yourself great service, why not give yourself one a week? Or one a month?

List ten small things you've long wanted to do. Going to the farmers' market, attending a concert, walking in the woods, etc. Why not schedule time to do one of them each month?

List five people in whose presence you feel more yourself, more positive, more energized and appreciated. Try calling or emailing or writing a real letter to one of them a week.

To sum up, I'll say that a service-oriented approach, focused on giving positively to others; cultivating humility, self-reflection, and self-respect; and figuring out how we can better contribute to others around us is likely to lead to grounded, respectful, holistic success. Leaders who are self-centered, by contrast, may gain short-term, surface-level ego gratification, and probably a big paycheck for a while too, but in terms of earning real respect and affection from those around them—well, it's doubtful. Giving generously of spirit is much more likely to make for a rewarding existence.

6. Be Clear About Expectations and Give Yourself the Tools to Help Yourself Meet Them

Going back to Natural Law #1, it's a lot easier to have clear expectations of ourselves and others when we have a documented vision towards which we're heading. Natural Law #6 says that the clearer we can be with ourselves about what we want and what we will, and won't, do to achieve it, the easier it will be for us to succeed in whatever ways we've chosen. Lack of clarity about our own expectations of ourselves will lead to lack of focus, which inevitably leads to diffusion of energy, which, in turn, brings on frustration and feelings of failure. Getting clear on what we expect from ourselves, and learning to come clean with others about what our expectations are of them, can only help to make everything we do more efficient and more effective. People may choose not to do what we've asked, and we need to honor their choices and negotiate openly and to agreement. Having lived way too long with hidden agendas and unspoken expectations, it's not like I get this right all the time, but it sure is a good framework for working to enrich pretty much any relationship, both with ourselves and with others. My life is a lot more rewarding and a lot more fun when I put things politely, courteously, and appropriately on the table. Being clear about what I want, who I am, and where I'm going just makes life way more rewarding. In the process, decisions become easier— if still not always easy—to make. Here's what Maslow says on the subject: "as people 'know' more and more consciously, their solutions, their choices become more and more easy, more and more automatic."

In the same vein, giving ourselves the resources to do what we need to do is important. We can't learn to do much of anything without some sort of study—learning by doing, attending formal classroom training, participating in electronic learning, etc. If we don't get around good people, if we don't get ourselves into a learning environment, if we don't feed our brains and our bodies and give ourselves some solitude and a simultaneous sense of community, it's hard to get to greatness. The ratios in which we each might want those items is, of course, up to us. But we all need some of each: learning, laughter, alone time, and positive social associations are clearly key contributors to the kind of success we're seeking here.

Again, drawing on Maslow, what each of us "should be pursuing is the discovery of vocation, of one's fate and destiny. Part of learning who you are, part of being able to hear your inner voices, is discovering what it is you want to do with your life." I can't stress the learning part enough. As Peter Senge says in *The Fifth Discipline*, "Through learning we re-create ourselves. Through learning we become able to do something we never were able to do. Through learning we reperceive the world and our relationship to it. Through learning we extend our capacity to create, to be part of the generative process of life"

Managing Our Energy

I've written extensively about energy management in *Part 2* of the *Guide to Good Leading* series, and again in the essay here in *Part 3* on Managing Ourselves. Since this is only a sidebar and not a full-fledged "Secret," I'll be brief. *Learning about energy and how to manage it has been one of the best things that's happened to me, and to our organization, in the last ten years.* Most everyone we've taught it to has taken it to heart as well. Other than a few cynics who probably pulled a couple of muscles doing eye rolls when I first related the concept, literally everyone we've shared it with has benefited. Dozens of employees have talked about how much being mindful of their own energy has impacted both their work quality and the quality of their relationships outside work. If you want to do well in life, then energy management and awareness are always of value.

What's energy? Quite simply, it's the buzz we bring with us wherever we go. It's the feeling that's inside us, the feeling that people pick up on when we're around them, the feeling we leave long after we've left a room. You can use your own term if you like—I've heard others call it soul, spirit, mojo, flow—any of them work. The point is that positive energy is enjoyable to be part of. It's lively, loving, and lovely to be around. While I won't tell you that having good energy will always get you good results, I will totally guarantee that it will increase the odds of getting them. When it comes to energy, effort isn't everything but there's no question that it counts for a lot.

Living the Natural Laws (of Business or of Life) is a pretty certain way to inject positive energy into our existence. When we live in harmony with nature, our energy will surely be more positive. But energy improvement isn't just an outcome—if we're mindfully managing ourselves, *we can actively manage our energy to make even more good things happen around us.* I have no doubt that the better our energy, the better we're going to do. The better we do, the more good things come to us, the more likely it is that we'll enjoy our lives, the more we increase the odds of good things happening.

For the full energy recipe see page 454. For an in-depth look into what energy is all about, where I learned about it, and how we make use of it at Zingerman's, see Secret #21 in *Part 2*.

7. Successful People Do the Things That Others Know They Should . . . but Generally Don't

If you're achieving at a high level, this law may seem like a no-brainer. Everyone who's great at anything will almost always be doing all the little, if less-than-glamorous, things that ultimately add up to greatness. Sure, the big stuff makes a big difference too. But there are so many struggling people I've met who are waiting for the "big one" to land, to win the lotto (of life, if not the state-sponsored jackpot), to get lucky, that they don't do the little things they know in their hearts they really ought to do. You can look at any field you want. The stars in sports who shoot more free throws, work out harder, and watch more game film than the others. The surgeons who study for countless hours late into the night to find things others may miss. The teachers who take the trouble to learn the names of every student on the first day and to adjust their lesson plan every semester just to keep things fresh.

The import of these little "extra" things is pretty easy to grasp intellectually—it's not hard to figure out that actively mastering the art of making cocktails will help you become a better bartender, or diligently studying for the bar will make you a better lawyer. The challenge is more a mental one. It can be difficult to maintain the internal discipline to do these little extra things. They're rarely glamorous in the moment, and there are always about eight hundred good reasons to get out of doing them on any given day. Stunning creative acts are what get the star billing, but it's the hard, often repetitive work that ultimately brings home the awards, the championship rings, or whatever sign of success gets you going.

Maslow said it well some sixty years ago: "The difference between the inspiration and the final product . . . is an awful lot of hard work, an awful lot of discipline, an awful lot of training, an awful lot of finger exercises and practices and rehearsals and throwing away first drafts and so on." This grueling work is vital. In Maslow's words, "the creativeness that results in the actual products, in the great paintings, the great novels, in the bridges, the new inventions and so on, rest as heavily upon other virtues—stubbornness and patience and hard work and so on—as they do upon the creativeness of the personality."

It's all about the things that we know in our gut are good to do but for which we have a hundred excuses handy that help us to avoid them. They are, now that I think about it, the very things that all the work on mindfulness (see page 111) is likely to help you with—the more you're mindful of the little things and the impact they have on the world, the more likely you are to do them and appreciate others around you who do the same. These little things often seem extraneous and unimportant to casual observers and low achievers, but they add up to make a very big difference.

To be specific, one of the things I get the most compliments on is my habit of regularly returning phone calls and emails, and generally doing it in a timely fashion. How hard is that? It's all about the little stuff that anyone who's willing can do but which people often neglect. I take the time to write down and learn employee names the same way most CEOs study financial statements. I'll drive across town to the Deli solely to sign a book for an out-of-town guest. I'll taste and taste and retaste a new product we're testing out. Almost every other successful person I've met likely has a comparable list of things they do. It's a Natural Law. Picking stray napkins out of the gutter won't, on its own, guarantee you success, but most every successful person I've met does some equivalent of it in their own world.[17]

To close this section out, I'll turn things over to one of my favorite writers. Hugh MacLeod, in his insightful and funny book *Ignore Everybody*, writes, "If somebody in your industry is more successful than you, it's probably because he works harder at it than you do. Sure maybe he's more inherently talented, more adept at networking, but I don't consider that an excuse. Over time, that advantage counts for less and less. Which is why the world is full of highly talented, network-savvy, failed mediocrities." Which brings us full circle—the little tasks, the unglamorous work is what this Natural Law is all about!

You Are What You Eat / It's a Lot Easier to Get to Greatness If You Eat Great Food!

It's hard to believe I could have forgotten to talk about food in a discussion of this sort, but I did. The only reason I eventually remembered to write about the role eating well plays in our personal success is that I agreed to meet on a Sunday morning with Molly Thompson, a woman from Toledo who was trying to get her new business off the ground. Molly's passion is to help organizations understand that the quality of what their people are eating has a direct and very real impact—for better or for worse—on their work performance. When people primarily eat fast food and commercially produced preservative-laden products, the quality of their work is compromised: their energy is lower, they feel worse, and their work can't help but suffer as a result. Conversely, when they eat good food—traditionally made, wholesome, fresh, flavorful, healthful products—their energy and their work quality almost always go up. While I suppose you can sometimes succeed while eating poorly, generally eating well leads to feeling well, which leads to doing well in most every other area of your life.

Molly, of course, was preaching to the converted; selling, cooking, and eating good food is what we do here at Zingerman's. But Molly's passion and pursuit of better eating, and its connection to organizational effectiveness, served as a reminder. *I'm so accustomed to having high-quality* food consumption as our organizational norm that I'd totally forgotten how much this simple practice adds to the effectiveness of our work here at Zingerman's. When it comes to providing appropriate resources for ourselves to do great work, it only makes sense that one of those resources would be good food! Part of what keeps our energy at such high levels is that what we're putting into our bodies is good stuff. The bottom line? Even if you're not selling food for a living, better eating still makes for better business and better quality of life. As Virginia Woolf writes in *A Room of One's Own*, "One cannot think well, love well, sleep well, if one has not dined well."

8. To Get to Greatness You've Got to Keep Getting Better, All the Time!

Call it continuous improvement, call it a drive for quality, call it self-improvement, or call it working hard to get better. Whether it's being a parent, a professor, a professional athlete, or even an anarchist, the best of the best, the people who go places, make positive waves, and get the world's great work done are, quite simply, always trying to get better. By dint of the fact that you're reading this book, I'm pretty sure you're already on board with the concept—people who aren't into self-improvement rarely read 400-plus page books on how to better manage themselves. But still, it's worth saying aloud—great performers, people that get to greatness, aren't only doing all the little extra things; they're also, always, working to get better at what they do.[18]

You only have to look at the artists and writers whose work continues to win acclaim year after year. They don't stand pat, because "pat" is a problem. If all one's doing is essentially just what one was doing last year or five years ago, one is falling steadily behind. Because while we're standing still, the rest of the world—organizationally or individually—is getting better. People around us are learning new things, practicing hard to improve, developing new insights—which means that if we want to achieve at a high level, in anything, we'd better be getting better too.

Stories of this in sports and business are everywhere. Whether it's a business practicing continuous improvement, an athlete who's always looking for one more little edge, or the surgeon who's studying every new idea in their field—all are pushing themselves to improve even when things are already going well. They don't wait for failure or a fusillade of harsh criticism—it's just the way they live their lives. That same commitment to ongoing learning and a constant drive to improve have been at the core of our culture here at Zingerman's since we first opened. I love this nugget from the amazingly talented John Buckland Wright (check out his woodcuts), who wrote, "In fact there is nothing I have done which I can honestly say expresses just what I want to express, however, I suppose that it's a good thing . . . satisfaction in one's work means certain death to one's artistic sensibility." Mind you, continuously moving forward with your work doesn't mean you can't be positive about your past achievements. Of his world-class art, Wright reflects, "The fact that I would have done some over again if I had the time does not mean that I dislike what I have done but merely that by the time I have done the last block I already see the first one in a different light." [19]

Moving from the creative arts to the core of capitalist thinking, perhaps the best thing I ever heard in this regard still makes me laugh today. Writer Gary Hamel and former University of Michigan professor C.K. Prahalad, in their book *Competing for the Future*, write, "Every manager must face a cold hard fact: Intellectual capital steadily depreciates. What you, dear reader, know about your industry, is worth less right now than it was when you began reading this book." The message—whether from anarchist artists, business school profs, or creative capitalists—is the same: if we're not getting better, we're getting worse. The people who get to greatness are always going the other way— their unflagging drive to improve is impressive, and they generally get the results to go with it.

4 + 8 = This Sidebar
Leaders on a Positive Path Help Develop More Effective Leaders

As I've already argued, getting around the right people is imperative to one's success—it's Natural Law #4. Going after self-improvement is equally imperative—that's Natural Law #8. If you add those two together, you get this: *The more effectively we manage ourselves and then teach others what we learn, the more likely they will be to manage themselves effectively. Which, in turn, makes an enormous difference in their lives and in all of our work.*

Murray Bookchin wrote, "Revolutionaries have the responsibility of helping others become revolutionaries, not of 'making' revolutions. And this activity only begins when the individual revolutionary undertakes to remake himself. Obviously such a task cannot be undertaken in a personal vacuum; it presupposes existential relations with others of a like kind who are loving and mutually supportive." Or go back half a century to Abraham Maslow, who wrote, "The right climate, the best climate for enhancing creativeness would be . . . a society which was specifically designed for improving the self fulfillment and psychological health of all people." Steady, focused self-improvement in an environment that's focused on community, collaboration, and creativity will very likely lead everyone involved closer to the greatness they've dreamed about. Perhaps, then, the ultimate contribution of a leader who's effective at managing themselves is to actively teach self-management skills to others.

9. Success Means You Get Better Problems

Up until about a decade or so ago, I used to think my goal was to get myself to a problem-free existence. An effective leader, I assumed, would be able to pretty much get rid of all of their issues. Then one day I realized that was absurd, unproductive, and impossible. *There are always going to be problems— the question was really just which problems I wanted to have.* It is very much as progressive business writer Paul Hawken writes in *Growing a Business*: "Good problems energize. Bad problems enervate."

If you see your problems as a pain in the ass, then that's pretty surely what they'll be; life quickly becomes a downer. No matter which way you turn, darkness, drudgery, and defeat will await. You'll find the sorrow in every situation. It's not that hard to do. Living a long life, for instance, means you get old. Personally, I'd prefer that to the alternative—the only way I know to avoid old age is to die young. Can't read everything you want to? (I have this problem big time.) You can complain about how information overload is killing you, or you can celebrate the amazing array of interesting materials you've assembled so far. The way I've come to see it is that it's all about choice. I far prefer having "too much to do" to being bored. Would you rather deliver exceptionally high quality for a decade and then have customers hold you to high standards, or stay mediocre? You know which side of that equation I'm trying to be on.

Bad Problem or Good? You Make the Call

Make a list of your achievements. Identify the bad problems each one creates, followed by the good ones. Positive psychology has shown that the more you can avoid the former and live with the latter, the more rewarding your life is going to be. I've put in a few sample problems below to give you the idea, but I'm confident you can come up with plenty of your own.

What's *your* problem?	Bad problem	Good problem
Your kids are getting older.	"I'm going to lose my babies! What am I going to do?"	"It's so great to see how my kids are maturing to become their own people."
Sales are booming.	"This is terrible. We're so short-staffed. Finding good people is almost impossible."	"This is great! We can barely keep inventory in stock!"
The local farmers' market is packed with shoppers.	"Ever since all these trendy foodies decided to love local, I can't get to the vendors I like. Plus prices have nearly doubled in the last few years."	"It's great that support for local agriculture has skyrocketed. I just go early to get to the best spots. It's wonderful that sustainable farmers are now making a living doing what they love."

Understanding that success simply meant I'd get the problems I wanted was hugely freeing. I stopped stressing about most of the challenges in my life, because I realized they were issues I'd basically picked and frequently had worked hard to create. For instance, we very mindfully wanted to have managing partners (real partners, not just long-time managers) in order to build strong leadership in the organization. The model has worked so well that today there are seventeen managing partners. The inevitable problem? They don't always agree, either with each other or with me or Paul. That, I'm sure, is a problem most people would prefer not to have—when you want to have things your way all the time, ours would be a frighteningly frustrating situation to be in. We, on the other hand, far prefer to have healthy disagreement among a set of focused, passionate leaders who bring diversity of experience and of opinion to our organizational table. It takes longer to get to agreement, but we believe the quality of the visions and decisions we get is far higher than any of us would have had on our own. Any time I start to get frustrated by this I remind myself it's the problem we chose when we wrote our vision for Zingerman's 2009.

Or try this one. I have a high appreciation of good food, which means that I also have a very low tolerance for the less-than-great fare sold in most food establishments. But, hey, I far prefer to have a well-trained palate than to be unable to taste the difference between farmstead cheese and factory fare. Knowing that the problems I have are generally ones that *I've* chosen really has helped bring an end to my worrying. Since I've actively participated in picking these problems, there's no pointing fingers, no settling of accounts I need to attend to. Looking at them through the lens of Natural Law #9, I've been able to teach myself to actively appreciate them for the successes, the big wins they really are!

10. Whatever Your Strengths Are, They Will Likely Lead Straight to Your Weaknesses

Understanding that the things I'm good at are going to lead me directly to what I'm not good at has been a huge help in reducing my stress. It doesn't mean I don't need or want to work on my weaknesses. It just means I recognize that what I do well, with its many upsides, is inevitably and inexorably linked to downsides as well. The more I embrace this reality, the more effectively I can work, constructively, on the whole cycle.

Robert Greenleaf, the man behind Servant Leadership, said it well in the late '70s. "Do I accept," he asked himself, and us as well, "that there is no virtue that, carried to the extreme, does not become a vice, no sound idea that, overworked, does not become absurd." In my case, I find that setting high standards and pushing myself to achieve them means that I can often become impatient with others when they don't deliver. It can be a big plus that I have a quick mind and can think and speak on the fly, but sometimes I respond too quickly and talk over others who aren't quite ready to hear my thoughts. The fact that I'm very passionate about what I do and what I believe leads, not surprisingly, to a tendency to overreact if others hold different views. You get the idea. It's true for all of us. It can be helpful to draw this out for yourself in chart form. You'll pretty quickly be able to see how easily your strengths and weaknesses correlate.

Poet Robert Bly writes about this in *A Little Book on the Human Shadow*. The "shadow," as he defines it, drawing on Jung and other psychologists, consists of the "unacceptable behaviors" we've put away and usually work hard to avoid. They're almost always the opposite of the characteristics that we place a high value on. For instance, if we look at what we very strongly dislike, it's usually a piece of ourselves that we're uncomfortable with, or things that we work hard and long to avoid. You can, I'm sure, trace it back to my early childhood, but I have a hard time when people don't follow through on what they say they're going to do. I'm so focused on coming through on commitments that my ire is raised—often, I'm sure, more than it needs to be—when others take a more laissez-faire approach to life. I'm not saying my way is better, only that the anxiety shines a light on an area that I'm afraid of, at times to a fault.

You can try it for yourself. Make a list of other people's behaviors that make you mad. Those are, almost always, areas that we're very self-conscious about. If "lazy people" irk you, it's highly likely that you're super (maybe overly?) diligent about your own work ethic and you might do well to cut yourself a slight bit of slack. Or maybe you obsess about how overachievers work too much? It might be that you need to pick up your own pace a bit rather than criticize them. Conversely, the behaviors we actively admire in others are usually the ones we would do well to work on more for ourselves. If you look up to people who do well at public speaking, it might behoove you to work on your own presentations. If you admire someone who's great at standing up for themselves, you might look at ways to build your self-confidence.

While understanding this Natural Law won't make one's weaknesses go away, it does make it far easier to understand how they developed and how they're often a natural outgrowth of things we're good at. This makes it easier to work at minimizing their negative impact. Ann Kim, founder and owner of Pizzeria Lola in Minneapolis and longtime ZingTrain client, wrote to say that "sometimes being a perfectionist makes it difficult for me to realize that things were never really that bad in the first place. It's all perspective I guess."

11. It Generally Takes a Lot Longer to Make Something Great Happen Than People Think

Moving from Natural Law #10 into #11, one of my obvious strengths is that

I want to get to greatness. One of my weaknesses is that I can be impatient. Which means that I have a hard time accepting what is almost always true—*it takes a lot longer to make great things happen than I think it should.* People who are committed to achieving amazing things in their lives understand that that they aren't going to get to greatness quickly. While they may be impatient, they learn to embrace that impatience and stick with their work for the long haul. Giving up may cross their minds any number of times, but they continue on in the belief that they're going to eventually get to where they've committed to going.

It's not hard to understand why most of us have a hard time making peace with this. The popular press likes to play up the moments at which stars burst successfully onto the scene, brilliantly changing the landscape of their chosen field. The reality is that this moment of glory almost always comes only after a whole lot of hard work and diligent self-improvement. Good things, whether we like it or not, usually take a very long while to develop. Even Albert Einstein, a generally acknowledged genius, embodied the import of this natural law. "It's not that I'm so smart," he said, "it's that I stay with problems longer."

In the *Guide to Good Leading, Part 1,* I wrote that I believe it typically takes two years from the time of startup to get a new business to equilibrium and four years or so to be good. At six, you might start to go for great, and at eight, you might have a shot at greatness, if you keep working really hard at it and get a few breaks here and there. I suppose there are specific aspects of a job in which one might become quite skilled far more quickly. Clearly, you don't need eight years to learn to pull a good shot of espresso. That said, though, to truly get to be great in the world of coffee could easily take eight or more years of hard work. It's not easy to stick with something for so long in a world that glorifies instant gratification. But it's important to remember that, although stories about overnight successes may dominate the headlines, it's almost always long hours of behind-the-scenes work that really make for greatness.

In his very interesting book *Outliers,* Malcolm Gladwell writes about psychologist Anders Ericsson's theory of 10,000 hours. The people who have attained great success, Ericsson's studies showed, have almost always put in about 10,000 hours of work mindfully developing their abilities. It takes a lot of serious study to get to greatness. In *Where Good Ideas Come From: The Natural History of Innovation,* Steven Johnson argues for what he calls the 10/10 Rule—it takes about ten years to really build a significantly innovative technology and another ten years to get it into wide use in the mainstream market.

My man Hugh MacLeod in *Ignore Everybody* says much the same thing with his usual wit at work. "Being good at anything is like figure skating—the definition of being good at it is being able to make it look easy. But it never is easy. Ever. That's what the stupidly wrong people conveniently forget."

Vision + Sticking with Things for a Long Time Leads to Success

Having spent quite a bit of time of late studying achievement, it's all the more clear to me that living the Natural Laws almost always adds up to success. Study after study shows, as per Anders Ericsson's work above, that doing the long diligent hours of study and practice are a prerequisite for getting to greatness. But to make those hours pay off, a person has to have a clear, well-internalized image of the greatness they're going after. In other words, what the data is demonstrating is that a vision of greatness, clearly imagined, written down, and emotionally engaged in, is what makes all those hours of practice so powerfully productive. As Daniel Coyle writes in *The Talent Code*, "when we envision ourselves doing it far into the future, we are tapping into a massive evolutionary energy source."

What this translates into is that more often than not, aside from certain physical limitations most of us can be pretty darned good at almost anything we want to be. Write a long-term vision that's inspiring and strategically sound, one you believe in and buy into today. And then, starting a week from Sunday, spend something like eighty hours a month mindfully working at getting better at it. Keep that up for five to ten years, and my own personal experience, plus all the data, predict that you'll be darned good at whatever it is you wanted to be good at. I know I sound glib here, but the point is clear: if you want to be great at something, if you're willing to do a lot of work to master the skill, all the while focused on gradually getting to greatness over an extended period of time, the odds are you will get there.

Where do you get the time? Successful people somehow figure it out. We all know the old saying, "If you want something done, ask a busy person to do it." As Sam Keen writes in *Inward Bound*, "We are seldom too tired to do what we really want to do." Why put the work in? To quote positive psychologist Martin Seligman in *Flourish*, "The real leverage you have for achievement is more effort." And he adds, "Time on task acts in two ways to increase achievement: it multiplies existing skill and knowledge, and it also directly increases skill and knowledge." The freely made choice to go for greatness tied to the willingness to do the hard repetitive practice work to get good can make amazing things happen. I have no doubt in my mind that it is the equation that supports almost everything we've achieved in our organization, and that I've done on my own as well.

12. Successful People Are Appreciative, Laugh More, and Have More Fun

In my pursuit of the positive, I find that the people I want to be around, the people I think are really great, are the ones that bring good spirit and a kind smile (or maybe it's kind spirit and a good smile) to almost everything they do. Time and again, I find that they're the folks who are living joyful lives. There's really no way around it—they laugh more, enjoy more, appreciate the depth and meaning of what goes on around them, and generally have a better time than most of the rest of the world that's waiting passively for fun to arrive at their doorstep. As the Indian mystic Osho says, the world "needs to be full of laughter. It will change everything in human life."

How then can evil-minded, ill-tempered, inconsiderate asses still succeed, as some seem to do? By surface-level standards, I suppose, it's not that hard. But to me, it seems like they're involved in a strip mining of the spirit; they forcibly extract resources, wealth, pleasure, and power from the souls of those around them, and then egotistically celebrate their own "success." In the end, though, what they're doing doesn't seem to me to be sustainable, since it's coming at the emotional and/or economic expense of good customers, coworkers, and the community. These people may find their own version of exploitative joy, but it's just that—surface-level stuff. They may get a lot of glossy press, but success gained by gross mistreatment or ghastly manipulation of others is never ultimately a good thing. Making money, collecting kudos, and toting around a lot of fancy titles isn't worth a whole lot if you're not enjoying your life and contributing to the world around you.

Life, as I'm sure you know, is short, and there are any number of great quotes about why and how we should enjoy it. All of them speak to this point: the people who are doing well in the world are those who find the joy and seek the sun rather than descend into and then live their lives in the dark and the dim. Robert "Servant Leadership" Greenleaf writes, "Purpose and laughter are the twins that must not separate. Each is empty without the other. Together they are the impregnable fortress of strength as that word is used here: the ability, in the face of the practical issues of life, to choose the right aim and to pursue that aim responsibly over a long period of time. Joy is inward, it is generated inside. It is not found outside and brought in. It is for those who accept the world as it, is part good, part bad and who identify with the good by adding a little island of serenity to it."

Optimism, it turns out, is an important element in getting to greatness. Everywhere I turn I find more evidence—both scientific and experiential—explaining why optimism is so essential to pretty much any sort of success. Martin Seligman's *Flourish* develops the point at length that optimism, in many cases, seems to make all the difference. Optimists live longer, experience less stress, learn better, and—if they're on an NBA team—win more often. Optimists are more hopeful, less anxious, and also healthier—studies show that people with an optimistic attitude have fewer heart attacks. Why does optimism have such a huge impact? It makes good sense to me. Seligman shows that optimists have healthier lifestyles, are more proactive, have more friends, more love, and less illness in their lives.

Optimists, Seligman says, "believe that the causes of setbacks in their lives are temporary, changeable, and local." They tend to view problems as things that they have a good shot at overcoming. Pessimists see things the other way, believing that bad things are likely to last forever and that there's little to be done to make them better. We all know people who fall on either end of that spectrum. But what reading Seligman made me realize is that we can promote optimism more effectively. First by considering it a criteria in hiring. At Tasty Catering in suburban Chicago, a standard interview question is now, "How many mornings a week do you wake up feeling happy?" And second by actively teaching optimism in our classes and our on-shift training. Visioning, for example, is all about belief in a better future, and clearly it has contributed to the quality of life for hundreds of people in our organization and now thousands of others around the world who are putting that positive, proactive approach to work as well.

Please note that *pretending* to be positive isn't enough. We have to really believe, not just tell others we're on board. But that said, we can—as per all of the work around brain change—train ourselves to become more optimistic over time. The keys to success? Crafting a long-term vision of the future that we believe in, one in which we see ourselves as being far more positive and optimistic than ever. And then, secondly, engaging in active work, week in week out, to view the world more positively. Rather than thinking about how hopeless things are and how the world has had its way with us, we can actively reframe things and consider how we might gain from overcoming the obstacle at hand. I'm very optimistic. If you track this regularly on your personal score-board (see page 91), I will guarantee that you will make significant improvement in six to eight weeks, and lasting change will have happened within a couple of years. And by the way, if you believe Seligman's research, you might just earn those two years back through an increased sense of well-being and the longer life span that comes with it.

In his 1931 essay "Life and Human Nature," Logan Pearsall Smith says, "There are two things to aim at in life. First, to get what you want; and, after that, to enjoy it. Only the wisest of mankind achieve the second." I'm trying to be in that group. Then there's the very famous saying attributed to Emma Goldman: "If I can't dance, I don't want to be part of your revolution."

I learned from my partner Paul many years ago that even during the dark days, we could still have a good time. We've laughed a lot together, occasionally while crying at the same time, through many a difficult day. Taking the research I did to write *Zingerman's Guide to Better Bacon*, I'll quote Maynard (like Madonna, he goes by one name), the man behind the book *Adventures of a Bacon Curer* and its sequel, *Secrets of a Bacon Curer*. Assuming that you, like 99.98 percent of Americans, haven't read Maynard's work, I'll just say here that they're full of folksy insight. He's a kind of Kahlil Gibran of pork curing, where wisdom is liberally interspersed with bacon recipes and curing techniques. "The secret of life," he shares at one point, "is seizing as much happiness when you can. If you leave it too long, and look for happiness later, it may be too late, so the secret is, when the happiness is there take it, and we did."

Last words on this one go to someone you likely haven't heard of, but I think you should so I'm putting her in here. I met Mary Beth Wood while I was teaching about the Twelve Natural Laws of Business for Anthony Wilder Design/Build, the well-known Washington, D.C. design firm whose marketing work she was then managing. In an email exchange after the event, Mary Beth closed out one note with what I thought was a particularly poignant line: "Life that has no laughter is not worth the trip." I wrote right back to ask her where she'd heard it. "I just made it up ☺," she said. I loved that, and I loved the fact that I could give *her* the credit for it. "All famous quotes have to start somewhere," I replied. "I'll add it to my file." When I asked what had inspired it, Mary Beth wrote back: "You inspire the creativity in me ☺."

This exchange drives home almost every point I want to make about the Natural Laws. Energized people have more fun and are more appreciative and, for that matter, can be insightful and innovative. Better still, put them in a creative positive setting like the one she was in at Wilder Design/Build and even more good things are likely to come of it. Mary Beth isn't famous, but she's clearly enjoying life, which, as per this Natural Law, tells you it's likely that she'll be successful. While she gave me credit for inspiring her, I'll flip it around. I give her full credit for coming up with that quote, which, in turn, inspired me. When you live the Natural Laws, creativity, laughter, and love are the natural outcomes, and a virtuous, self-sustaining cycle of success gets started.

Natural Conclusion

As you probably know by now from hanging around with me either in person or in print, I'm really not out to change the world overnight, or to force others I meet into some kind of creative anarcho-capitalist submission. People are free to pursue the lives they choose to lead; I just hope they do it in ways that are respectful of themselves, their community, and the world around them. But that said, I think the stuff we do here at Zingerman's with the Natural Laws really works, and I want to share that with others who are interested. Having spent many months writing this essay, I'm actually more convinced now than ever that living these twelve Natural Laws can lead anyone who's willing to put in the time and effort to a more gratifying life.[20]

Given my belief that *it's all one life*—work, family, food, philosophy, football, and fun—I'll close out with this. If you do want to change the world, then living in synch with your values, finding joy, and going after what you believe is a pretty good place to begin. To quote late 19th century American anarchist Voltairine de Cleyre: "The free and spontaneous inner life of the individual the Anarchists have regarded as the source of greatest pleasure and also of progress itself, or as some would prefer to say, social change." If there's a change we're looking for, we will always do best to start with ourselves, to work in small, meaningful ways towards ever-greater success and an ever-more rewarding world. In the words of modern-day anarchist Howard Ehrlich, "Who will make the anarchist revolution? *Everyone.* Every day in their daily lives."

Take a Personal Look Back at the Laws

Take a few minutes to flip back through each of the Natural Laws. Which was the most surprising? Which are you already living in harmony with? Which, now that you have them at the front of your mind, will make the most difference in your life going forward? And with the answers to those questions clearly laid out, list ten action steps you're going to take to bring your life closer to what you want it to be.

Sara Vos, Server, Zingerman's Roadhouse

Although I have only worked at Zingerman's Roadhouse for six months, it has been a life changer. When I came into my first "Welcome to Zingerman's" class, which is always taught by either Paul or Ari, I felt I was in a special place. When Ari started talking about "positive energy" and self-care outside of the workplace to enhance your life, I was flooded with feelings of gratitude and appreciation. When we discussed the Zingerman's mission statement, which includes "to show love and care in all our actions, and to enrich as many lives as we possibly can," I intuitively felt working here would become a transformative experience.

And it has. From "Personal Visioning," to the "Art of Giving Great Service," and all the other tools in place to help me be a better server, I have become a better person. It is an honor to work at a place in which everyone contributes, matters, and is encouraged to blossom into the best version of themselves. Working at this company has allowed my life to unfold into stability, especially as I experience what it is like, for nearly the first time, to work within an organization that is healthy, functional, and operating through a vision for greater and greater success and service.

This is an abundant organization, seen in the ways we contribute financially and otherwise to the entire Ann Arbor community, and I am proud of the ways learning to "Give Great Service" has transformed the ways I engage with folks outside of my hourly employed times here within the restaurant.

I look forward with joyful anticipation to the continued success of all the businesses within the Zingerman's community, as well as the continued growth and prosperity of every individual who is a part of this amazing experience. Onwards and upwards!

Tracie Wolfe, Department for People, Zingerman's Service Network

When I applied for my job at Zingerman's 5 years ago, I had no idea how much my life was about to change for the better. I feel truly blessed to be a part of Zingerman's. I can honestly say that I don't feel like I have a job, but instead a purpose. I wake up every day excited to come to "work" and my days are spent feeling like I am really making a difference. I was never able to say that before I came to Zingerman's. I know that my opinion matters and will be heard, always. I know that my leaders care about my development and growth. I know that my leaders and coworkers appreciate what I bring to the table and my work here. Our visioning, Bottom-Line Change, Servant Leadership, all our recipes, and our art of giving great service to everyone have all impacted my career and personal well-being in more ways than I can count. I am so proud to be a part of this organization and am excited about what the future holds.

emily grish decorating one of our hungarian coffeehouse tortes at the bakehouse

SECRET #37

Time Management for Lapsed Anarchists

(and Anyone Else Who's Interested)

How to Make Every Day a Holiday

I teach a dozen or so different classes for our staff here at Zingerman's—courses on leadership, service, open book finance, food, etc. While it hardly seems the most glamorous of the group, one of the most oft requested is the course I do on time management. Time is one of the key resources we can tap when we set to work to manage ourselves—and our surroundings—more successfully. Whether we realize it or not, our relationship with time is one of the most intimate we engage in—time is with us everywhere we go and it impacts every other relationship we have. Clearly, we can't live without it. While it's hard to lose any long-term relationship, if time runs out on us, it feels like—and in fact is—the end.

To be clear, nothing that follows is a lecture on why you should use your time better. It's your time and your life and I'm an anarchist—make of it what you will. If you're good with how things are for you now, then, quite simply, keep going! On the other hand, if you're up for making some modest but meaningful improvements, maybe what follows will prove helpful. I know it has been for me. There is no more time in the day than there was when I started, but I feel better about it now than I ever have.

Part I: A Historical Perspective on Time

BACK IN TIME

There are very few people I've met over the years who don't, at some point start, to lament how little time they have to get done what they want to do. But their seemingly endless laments about not having enough time are mostly misdirected. We can complain all we want, but as Jean-Louis Servan Schreiber says in *The Art of Time*, "The paradox of time is that people rarely consider they have enough when in fact all of it is available to everyone."

I would guess that most people think they know all there is to know about time. On the surface, it certainly seems straightforward: 60 seconds in a minute, 60 minutes in an hour, 24 hours in a day, 365 days a year (plus one for good luck in leap years). And yet few Americans actually know much *about* time—how it came to be what it is, how it's changed over the years, how it's seen in other cultures. As with anyone else we love, the quality of our relationship with time will benefit greatly from getting to know it—its past, its priorities, how it's changed over the years, how it works, what drives it, and what draws us towards it.

What follows may seem an incongruously long lead-in to an essay about time management. But I think it's an effective investment—while we work hard to learn everything we can about our products, people management, and marketing, we don't generally take much time to study time. And just as effective self-management starts by getting to know ourselves much better, so too is better time management best begun by getting to know more about time.

With that in mind, let me start with a bit of history. The modern concept of time, it turns out, is a rather recent one. While the sun has always come up in the east and set in the west, the way the time in between those two daily events has been measured, thought about, and managed is drastically different in the Western world in the 21st century from what it was even two hundred years ago. Time today is talked about so differently now than it was then that I honestly don't think your average man or woman from that era would even recognize it. Someone transported forward from the 19th century would likely be as confused by our tight bond with time as he would be by airplanes, cell phones, or social media.

In contemporary American society, you'll hardly ever hear anyone ask someone else what time it is anymore—our cell phones have made us always tuned in to the exact time. Everyone but the very poor, the very young, and those who opt out of this ubiquitous technology can be aware of the precise minute of the day in which they find themselves. But up until a few hundred years ago in the Western world, only a relatively small elite and those who lived near a church could have told you the time. And hardly anyone would have been interested anyway. Six o'clock in the 17th century meant little— before watches were common, the sun was what most people would watch. Back then, the passing of days was the major form of demarcation; minutes passed untracked.

The time measurement methods that did exist were rough—sundials, water clocks, etc. were all subject to heavy influence from the environment, and also to human error. By today's standards, they were woefully inaccurate. Back then, time moved mostly with nature. People had a general sense of morning and evening. Planting and harvest cycles, seasons, days growing shorter and then again longer, the waxing and waning of the moon, weather patterns. These, for most folks, were the main measures of time.

MAKING TIME

Back in the late 8th and early 9th centuries, modern clocks made meaningful appearances in the Middle East, in the kingdoms of what would now be

Iraq. In China, clock mechanisms were well in use by the 11th century, but clocks then were still powered primarily by water. Arab inventors developed a mercury-powered clock in the 13th century. Today we buy disposable Mickey Mouse watches to teach time to two-year-olds, but six or seven hundred years ago, even having a clock was a sign of social significance and wealth. Poor people probably rarely saw a clock. And what it told you may well have been wrong anyway—they remained remarkably inaccurate until the invention of the pendulum clock in the late 17th century. Minutes didn't show up until the 16th century, which is why the old English "half two" (aka 2:30) wasn't merely a figure of speech—it was just the obvious way to describe time when the clock's only hand was positioned halfway between the two and the three.

Even as recently as three hundred years ago, time in North America was understood in a very different way than it is now. In *Albion's Seed,* historian David Hackett Fischer explains "Time in seventeenth-century Virginia meant mainly the pulse of nature and the organic processes of life itself. Even among the great planters the language of time was sometimes closer to that of American Indians than to English Puritans. William Byrd reckoned the passing of time in expressions such as 'many moons together.'" The tobacco crop cycle of planting and harvesting and the days on the Christian calendar were both far more important to time keeping and cultural rhythm than clocks.

Time traditionally has been measured mostly by what was meaningful to the men and women relating to it, not, as it is today, to a universal standard set the same the world over. Harriette Arnow, writing in *Flowering of the Cumberland,* her fantastic history of the Tennessee territory at the end of the 18th century, explains that at that time, "the word 'afternoon' was still seldom used, nor were people much inclined to say 'early in the morning' or even give a specific hour. Old school contracts call for the assembling of pupils, 'an hour by sun'; others came at sunrise, the sensible procedure where life for many revolved about the sun. The day was further divided by the chores and such expressions as milking time and dinner time—noon—can still be heard. The year as in most farming communities was divided by the farm work swinging through the seasons; practically all farmers had corn-gathering time but lambing time like kraut-making time was not universal." Time, like most everything else, was a local product.[21]

Looking to the East, here's what historian James Scott says in *The Art of Not Being Governed: An Anarchist History of Upland Southeast Asia*: "If you ask a Southeast Asian peasant [today] how far it is to the next village, say, the answer will probably be in units of time, not linear distance. A peasant quite familiar with watches might answer "about half an hour," and an older farmer, less familiar with abstract time units, might reply in vernacular units, 'three rice-cookings,' or 'two cigarette smokings'—units of duration known to all, not requiring a wristwatch."

People's historical relationship with time in centuries past (and in many modern agrarian societies to this day) was, it seems, significantly more relaxed than it is for most Americans today. Even six-year-olds are now mindful of TV schedules, school start times, soccer practices, and supper at 6:00. While life was clearly more difficult in other ways in the past, research suggests there was a lot less tension around time. That more relaxed relationship remained intact in rural settings in the West well into the 20th century; the movement of the sun was significant, but the actual hour was almost irrelevant. Even today there are many American ethnic communities that proudly make claims to running on "their own" (as opposed, essentially, to the official, government-mandated, by-the-minute timeline).

On a similar note, Irish historian Peter Foynes shared this piece of anecdotal evidence with me: "I was recently speaking to a man, now in his seventies, who grew up in the Irish countryside. He said that the only events for which one needed to know the time, as in the sense of time by the clock, was for Mass on Sunday and school during the week." Foynes added, in good Irish tongue-in-cheek form, "And the latter was not necessarily of great importance."

Butter and Time in Ireland

Beginning in the middle of the 18th century, butter became one of the biggest exports Ireland had. Made in the countryside but shipped abroad from the port at Cork on the south coast, a series of roads—referred to as the Butter Roads—were built across the southern half of the country to get barrels of Irish butter from the farms to the British-controlled customs houses in the port. Of course, as we know from our own work here at Zingerman's, all changes bring unintended outcomes. One of the most interesting to our present subject was that butter carriers, having sold their butter in the city, brought back time along with their cash—in the city, they were able to correct their pocket watches and then carry that current time back to the towns with them.[22]

Butter played a big role in the Irish calendar as well. New Year's Day was known as the "Day of the Buttered Bread"—bread-and-butter sandwiches were set on the front stoops of the houses, and young people would go door to door like American kids do for candy on Halloween. Moving forward four months, May Day has historically been the day in Ireland when, it's said, your "butter luck" is determined by the fates. If the fairies make off with it, you're doomed to have difficulty with your buttermaking for the rest of the year. Per the luck of the Irish, perhaps, Irish butter remains excellent. I recommend eating it aplenty. The late Ivan Allen shared an Irish saying with me on my first visit to his country, smiling his huge smile and flashing his ironic Irish twinkle: "By the time your teeth hit the bread, the butter better be hitting your gums."

A Modern Take—Buying Time

The days are just as long (or short, depending on how you look at things) in the 21st century as they ever were. What's changed is the way we relate to them. As it did for so many elements of Western life, the Enlightenment and the shift to centralized nation-states changed the way time was talked about and perceived. What was once tracked in broad swaths, tied primarily to nature, became clearly divided into carefully measured slots—hours—which were overseen by state-mandated supervisors and logged into central business offices from whence pay was dispensed. The same efforts to quantify, standardize, measure, and create order from the perceived chaos and disorder of daily life that were applied to agriculture, forestry, language, and taxes were also applied to time. Time became a commodity to be tightly tracked and traded the way one would money. With the coming of the Industrial Revolution in the West, what had once generally (or at least ideally) belonged to each person —except in the case of slaves and servants—began to belong, for a good part of the week, to one's boss. Time, it turns out, was as important a product in the Age of Industrialization as anything being made in the world's burgeoning factories. Today, the concept of "time as money" is a commonly accepted one, but a few hundred years ago, that supposition would likely have gotten a very strange look.[23]

Early in the 19th century, American factories began the mass production of clocks. One of the many ironies of this subject is that the men and women who were giving up ownership of their hours—workers on the production line— were the same people making the machines that put them into this new form of indentured servitude. Clocks came into the average person's life as a result of the rise of capitalism. Unlike the ones on church towers or in the homes of wealthy aristocrats, these smaller, mass-produced, more mobile "time machines" could be mounted anywhere and everywhere, making it much easier to measure time when you weren't standing in the town square. Where labor overseers might previously have pulled out whips or weapons, capitalist factory owners added clocks as one of management's most powerful tools. For the first time in history, hours were tracked to determine workers' wages and used to calculate costs. At the same time that serfs and slaves around the world were being "freed," to survive, they often had to sell off portions of their newly found freedom.

This new set of timeways had a major impact. To quote 20th century Canadian anarchist historian George Woodcock, "At first this new attitude to time, this new regularity of life, was imposed by the clock-owning masters on the unwilling poor . . . gradually the idea of regularity spread downwards among the workers. Nineteenth century religion and morality played their part by proclaiming the sin of 'wasting time'. . . . In the church and in the school, in the office and the workshop, punctuality was held up as the greatest of the virtues. Out of this slavish dependence on mechanical time which spread insidiously into every class in the nineteenth century there grew up the demoralising regimentation of life which characterises factory work today." Woodcock continues, "The problem of the clock is similar to that of the machine. Mechanical time is valuable as a means of co-ordination of activities in a highly developed society, just as the machine is valuable as a means of reducing unnecessary labour to the minimum. Both are valuable for the contribution they make to the smooth running of society, and should be used insofar as they assist men to co-operate efficiently and to eliminate monotonous toil and social confusion. But neither should be allowed to dominate men's lives as they do today."[24]

In the Time of Slavery

Looking back to the era before the Emancipation Proclamation, slaveholders literally *owned* their slaves. Time was tied into the institution of slavery; while others could opt to treat time as they so chose, slaves didn't have the option to decide. All of a slave's time belonged to their owner, who was legally entitled to do what they wished with it as with their wagons, water mills, and the other property they possessed. Aside from an occasional holiday or short stints of time "off" each week, *a slave's time was not his own.* The fortunate ones were "given" time to themselves to engage in work free from the master's direction, during which they might occasionally make and save enough money to eventually buy their freedom. In essence, they were granted time to do extra work to earn money to buy back the time that they should rightly have owned in the first place.

GUIDING TIME

Times, of course, have changed. For hourly employees today, time is a product, a natural resource they can sell off to support themselves; essentially, they contract to sell their time to their employers. Whatever they don't bargain to give their boss still, of course, belongs to them.

But Woodcock got me thinking. Is our focus on time just another means of squashing creativity and restricting people's freedom? Does teaching time management just encourage people to cram ever more onto their calendars? Am I making another (unwitting) contribution to the cacophony and constant worry that's spread through modern society? Have I allowed time to take over and dominate my own life? And am I then destructively encouraging others to do the same? Is time management a bad thing?

Having spent a lot of time considering questions like these in the last few months, I actually think the answer to all of the above is no. *Time management is merely a tool*—like business in general, it's what we do with it that's the key. Going back to Woodcock's worldview—"Mechanical time is valuable as a means of co-ordination of activities in a highly developed society"—whether it's with minutes or by watching the sun slide across the sky, contemporary time tracking helps us to communicate and collaborate more effectively. Keeping time as we do establishes a common language that everyone can work with. In that sense, it's all become far more egalitarian. In the old days, only the elites could keep time; today, almost everyone has access to timekeeping devices. Time provides us with a tool we can use to frame what we do, to weave the way we work into the operations of the rest of the world. Keeping time helps us make music, follow recipes, and reach our destinations at the agreed-upon hour.

On the upside of the balance sheet, a positive approach to time could be the start of a better relationship—accepting time as it is, gaining good things from it, and contributing positively to others in the process. Making peace with time's limited nature is clearly conducive to a more mindful approach to life. The more mindful and respectful we are of time, the more at peace we are with its rhythms, the more we appreciate every little bit of it we have, the more likely we are to have a rewarding life. That said, we know that many people today allow time to take over their lives—they relate to it in ways that can be unhealthy, unproductive, and certainly unrewarding. The key, coming back to Woodcock's context, is to get comfortable with time and to avoid attaching value judgments, life lectures, and unhelpful guilt to it.

To wit, I'm sure you're familiar with the judgmental ways of the world that lay time trips on many folks, and really help no one. "Why are you working weekends?" "Don't you have anything better to do with your time?" "You need a time out!" "You're wasting your time on that art stuff when you could be out in the world doing something productive!" are value judgments that really help no one. "Nine o'clock" is neutral, but in our society, "working nine to five" says something about the person who does it. Controlling time by deciding which days are "holidays" and which aren't, making clear that the "day shift is better than a night shift," that working Sunday is somehow worse than Monday, etc. are intrusive strictures if you don't happen to agree with the suppositions that support them.

Having calendars and clocks with which everyone concurs is similar to using agreed-upon street numbers, street names, neighborhood designations, etc. There's certainly nothing wrong with having them—they allow us to give directions, share locations, get where we're committed to going, etc. But addresses can also be used destructively. People may place value judgments on others based on the street they live on. Certain people may not be allowed into certain neighborhoods or allowed out of others. One's access to a loan, a livelihood, or a decent education can be helped or severely hindered based upon these distinctions. The classification of one's time, too, can greatly affect one's quality of life.[25]

exercise **A Few Minutes for Reflection**

Given all of the above, take pause for a bit. What does time mean to you? How do you feel about it? Who manages your time? Or in some cases, who actually owns it? Are you mindful of it as it moves forward? Are you expending your energy tracking time while forgetting to really read the natural rhythms of life?

DATING TIME (EXPLORING A MORE MEANINGFUL RELATIONSHIP)

You read that right—if we're going to have a positive long-term relationship with time, it only makes sense that we'd begin by doing some dating. Working on this essay, for me, has marked a move to a much more serious, far more intimate relationship. Earlier I'd known time casually, as most everyone else around me did. Today, having spent six months reading and writing and becoming more mindful of it, I feel like we've gotten far closer. Personally, I've come to really like time. I'm drawn to it. Fascinated, actually.

In many ways, our relationship with time is a lot like any other we might have. It's greatly impacted by how much energy and effort we invest in it, and what we give is closely correlated with what we get. The more time we spend making peace with, understanding, appreciating, and enjoying time, the more positive our relationship with it is likely to be. On the other hand, if we're intimidated by it, the relationship will rarely be good. Each person, of course, has their own dynamic with time. Some flee from it, others are oblivious, and others still are angry at it. Ultimately, though, our relationship with time will be what Martin Seligman defines as a "reflexive reality": the better we feel about time, the better our relationship with it is likely to be. As Seligman says, "Optimism helps love, pessimism hurts." It's true with our significant others, it's true at work, and it's true with time, too.

All that said, I know that our relationship with time is pretty one-sided. Relationships generally blossom when each party gives of themselves and is willing to adjust their behaviors to meet the needs and desires of the other. But time, I'm afraid, is rather unyielding; no matter what we do or dream, time will not alter its course. While it's true that time doesn't stand still, it is incredibly consistent. We can change the way we measure it or the way we relate to it, but at the end of the day, time is what it is. Although people frequently profess to have "run out of time," it's actually the other way around—time runs out on us. When our lives end, we're left behind, but time continues on apace. Time, as I know it at least, will long outlive me. Others believe that our presence on the planet (or at least in its orbit) is practically infinite, through rebirth, an afterlife of the spirit, spoken word, or written memory.

On an upbeat relationship note, I know that time will never be reactive. Unlike others in my life, it won't reprimand me for being late. No matter how erratically I act, it stays steady as can be; time won't be baited into behaving badly or acting out in anger. Its stable nature gives us a great opportunity—we can modify our moods just by mindfully managing the way we relate to it. And, because time stays so steady (whereas most everyone and everything else is changing in response to what we do), we have a decent shot at making meaningful modifications to our lives by improving our relationship with it.

Making peace with time, for me, means not complaining about getting older because the alternative is "not getting older"—i.e., dying—and I'd prefer aging to exiting. I want to make the most of as much of time as I get, to enjoy and appreciate every element of it, to embrace each passing minute. Although on occasion I do say things like, "It'd be great to have another few hours in the day," I know full well that I'm not going to get it. Making this statement involves smiling at the silliness of my impossible wish. I'm working on making peace with the reality that other freethinking folks can and will choose to use their time differently than I do. When I work with others, I know we need to collaboratively decide how our shared time will be spent. If we can't come to an agreement, we'll need to agree to spend our time separately.

THREE TYPES OF TIME FROM A RUSSIAN CHRISTIAN ANARCHIST

The other day, I was reading an essay by late 19th and early 20th century Russian Christian anarchist Nikolai Berdyaev, when I stumbled upon his rather unique take on time. I loved it—see what you think. In a nutshell (see his 1916 essay, "The Meaning of Creativity" for the detailed explanation), Berdyaev believes that there are actually three types of time, and that we would benefit from being mindful of all of them. The first is what he calls "cosmic time"—the natural cycle of the sun rising and setting, which occurs each and every day in perpetuity. Berdyaev sees this type of time as visually represented by a circle. The second sort, he says, is historical time—the unfolding of days and years, marked, of course, by whatever events we perceive as meaningful. Historical time is represented by a line; while each event falls into the circle of cosmic time, each incident is actually unique and unrepeatable, and can only be revisited via memory.

The third type is the one that really caught my attention. Insightful, intriguing, and, for me, immediately intuitive, it's what Berdyaev refers to as "existential time," visually represented by a dot. An existential moment, he makes clear, may take only a minute or two by the clock, though it could also go for much longer. But for the person who's experiencing it, existential time will feel, for better and/or for worse, like an eternity. We all know those moments—the short stint where something so intensely positive was happening, so rewarding, so enriching, that we felt submerged in it. It could have been a really great date, an intellectual epiphany, hitting a home run, watching the birth of a child, falling in love, or finding the answer to a question you'd been asking for a lifetime.

Conversely, existential time could be something so terribly hard, so emotionally draining, that we can't get it out of our heads. Seeing someone get shot or being hit by a car, watching your spouse get struck down by a heart attack, experiencing an earthquake, seeing a tidal wave rushing towards you during a tsunami, or any other set of circumstances so severe as to be almost inconceivable. Like the bliss of the better side of existential time, these moments of horror might feel like they'll never end. Most everyone has been through both of these sorts of experiences, formed not by the clock or the calendar but, as Berdyaev says, by "the intensity of experience." They inspire the phrase, "It was like time was standing still." The more intense the situation, the "longer" it lasts existentially. "Eternity," in Berdyaev's conception, doesn't mean going on "forever"; rather, it's about the greatest intensity of experience imaginable. A rich life then is about going as deep into those "dots" as you can get. I love the concept, and now that I have the context, I can quickly think of any number of moments that would qualify. They are, without question, the most memorable moments of my life. I smile and squirm, alternately, as I remember them now, one by one.

I'm fascinated by this idea of existential time. Clearly, I can't live forever, at least not chronologically. But now that I have Berdyaev's insight in mind, I've realized that one of my life goals is to experience as many marvelously enjoyable existential moments as I can. Unlike the other two types, existential time really cannot be measured, at least not from the outside in. It is, in the context of the modern state, strictly untaxable and untrackable. What it does have is passion, power, positive energy; it's a source of inspiration and insight. As Berdyaev says, "The creative act takes place in existential time." You can see why I'm so eager to make room for even more existential moments.

Mindfulness, by the way, sets the table for life to serve up those existential events. The more I'm "present" in each moment, finding the joy and appreciating what is, the more likely I am to have a deep existential experience. A taste of an amazingly delicious piece of just-caught fish cooked on the grill and eaten with friends while the sun sets off the coast of Spain could qualify. So too could your child's first steps, or a single sip of a truly superb wine. If we can put enough of them together, the result would be almost otherworldly. As Berdyaev writes, "Heaven, the interior spiritual life, is not a remote transcendental and unattainable sphere; it is part of the inner depths of our spiritual life." Henry David Thoreau, another anarchist, wrote in *Walden* in the middle of the 19th century, "Time is but the stream I go a-fishing in. I drink at it; but while I drink I see the sandy bottom and detect how shallow it is. Its thin current slides away, but eternity remains."

Part 2: Four Ways to Enhance the Quality of Your Relationship with Time

The four principles that follow, I believe, are universal; they're timeless. The way I see it, they form the basis of our relationship with time and, for that matter, every other relationship we have as well.

1. Devote Meaningful Time to Time
2. Draft a Positive Vision of the Future
3. Make the Most of Every Minute
4. Be Appreciative—Make Every Day a Holiday

1. DEVOTE MEANINGFUL TIME TO TIME

If the main focus of all this timely activity is to develop a more positive relationship with time, then the first place to start, as with any relationship, is by devoting some quality time to it. Seriously, how many really rewarding relationships of any sort have you had that you didn't devote meaningful time to? Getting to know time, quite simply, takes time; if your connection with your kids, your significant other, your work, or anything else you care about were merely something you squeezed into the spare moments that may crop up here and there, the quality of that relationship wouldn't likely be very good. The same is true with time. Treat it like an unwanted stepchild, and the odds are that tension, frustration, and trouble are pretty sure to follow suit.

Building a good relationship with time feels, to me, a lot like what it takes to work out effectively. We all know that we won't get in shape by *worrying* about our health; nor will we improve our relationship to time by lamenting how little of it we have. Making time for either is rarely urgent, but it's almost always helpful. Even if it's awkward in the moment, you're pretty sure to feel far better in the long run. We get away with not doing either when we're young, but the older we get, the more we have going, the harder it is to move forward in a healthy way without making some commitment to do better. There are always about eight hundred good reasons not to work out on any given day, but everyone knows that we'll feel better for it if we do. The work we invest in exercise usually results in increased energy going forward, better grounding, better health, and lower stress. The same is true for time; put some time and effort in up front, and pretty soon you'll bring better energy and efficiency to almost everything else you do. And whether it's working out or spending time on time, once you get used to it, it's unlikely you'll go back to the haphazard ways of old.

One of the most effective ways I've learned to spend time on time is by engaging in reflection. Taking a few minutes to look back on what's happened, to assess what your actions have attained, how they correlated with your intentions, and how you felt about the whole thing, can be a great help. If we don't know what's worked well and what's been less than ideal in the way we've managed our time to date, it's tough to make major improvements going forward. In essence, I suppose, it's a self-review on how you spend your time. Since you're ultimately your own boss, it's up to you to manage the messages you send yourself. We also need to take time to consider the time to come. How much time is left in the day? In the month? In the year? In our lives? What do you need to erase from the to-do list in order to give yourself a good shot at completing what you want to get done? Is there anything really meaningful we want to add to our list before time, for the period we're considering, comes close to running out?

The journaling I do every morning helps me get my mind around what I need to do for the day, how I'm feeling, what I've done, what I appreciate, what's happened around me, and what I see coming up on the horizon. As I put down random thoughts and feelings, I'm pretty much always reminded of something I want to do, someone I want to appreciate, or something I can positively contribute that wasn't in my mind when I began writing. When I start to worry about running out of time, I try to quiet my mind—I know that worrying is energy expended unproductively. Attempting to appreciate each moment and everything in it has helped me significantly—it's turned my relationship with time into a positive, rewarding experience I like being part of, rather than an effort to escape from someone else's idea of a rat race.

2. DRAFT A POSITIVE VISION OF THE FUTURE

If you've read anything else I've written about business (in particular, Secret #35 in this very book), then you'll understand why I'm adamant about the importance of taking time to write a vision of what we'd like our relationship with time to look and feel like. With that in mind, I'll go ahead and ask the same question I ask about everything else we engage in: "When your relationship with time is as close to ideal as you can imagine, what will it look like?" Pushing deeper, "How will you measure your success? How will you feel about it yourself? And about others you interact with around time? What are some stories that will tell you it's working?"

If you want a more in-depth look at the visioning process, go back to Secret # 9 in *Part 1* of the *Guide to Good Leading* series or on page 191 in this book. But in the moment, in the interest of reducing the amount of time you'll need to devote to doing this, I'll offer a simple two-step version of it here. First, write down all the positive supports you have in your life that can help you make your relationship with time a rewarding one. That should take you maybe two minutes. Then sit down and quickly draft your vision.

For the actual vision-writing work, do the following:

Pick a time frame. For this work with time, I've found a year or two in the future to be fair. It gives us time to make changes, but not so much time that we forget what we've said we were going to do.

Write in the present tense, as if it's already happened.

Follow the "hot pen" technique. Just start writing and keep going for a good ten or twenty minutes.

Make your first shot a draft. You'll later come back to it to refine what you've put down the first time through, but for this first version, it's imperative that you just write straight through without stopping to assess what's viable or not, or how you're going to get what you want to happen. It's just a first draft—the key is that it be from your heart! Don't edit at first. Just keep writing until your allotted time is up!

Whatever you put down, remember that all you're doing is describing how you'd like things to work for you, not dictating how others should live their lives. It's your relationship, and you can design it most any way you want. There aren't any right and wrong answers. If you don't mind being mad at time for its limited nature, or frustrated with it for repeatedly running out on you, or sad that it slipped away when you weren't paying attention, then, by all means, keep at it.

A vision is, of course, a picture of the future towards which we're working. It's what we desire, a waking dream of what we'd like our lives to be like at a particular point in time in the future. To get you thinking, here's a draft of my vision for my relationship with time:

> *It's two years into the future. My relationship with time is better than ever. I really do love it. I appreciate each little bit of time that I have to work with, and very much enjoy being with it. Although I still slip, now and again, into frustration with time's seeming shortness, I*

recover now more quickly than ever. I never fight time the way I used to when I was younger. And if I feel tension around time building up, and feel myself starting to blame time for my problems, I get myself quickly regrounded to avoid sliding into an emotional abyss.

While I take great advantage of pretty much every tick that time has to offer, I fully accept—often even embrace—time's limited nature. Just as I know that I won't be able to be with the people, places, and pets I love for as long as I want to be, just as I know that I'll never read every good book, meet every interesting person, see every exotic place, or taste every bit of traditional food that I want to try . . . the same is true of time. I'm at peace with the idea that no matter what I do—or don't do—there will never be more minutes in each hour, more days in the week, or more weeks in the year than there always have been. And my commitment to effective acceptance dictates that I'm at peace with time's limited nature in all its natural beauty. Like a beautiful sunset, I can only enjoy it for the short window in which I can see it moving past.

Given my desire and drive to do so many things, I go out and make as much happen as I can in the time that I have. I like to be busy, to move quickly with the flow, to feel the rush of time moving through me and around me every minute. I appreciate every hour and every day that I have to work with. I take in as many details as I can. I breathe as evenly as I'm able. I appreciate the people, things, nature, and everything else around me every day. I share generously with the world. Courteously but effectively, I manage to stay as far from people and activities that drain my energy and take up time in ways I don't want to use it. Conversely, whatever I do engage in, I usually manage to make the most of it. I'm always on the lookout for some new learning or insight, and I've trained myself to value even the most mundane of moments.

More than ever I take ownership of my choices around time. When I sleep, I do it soundly. When I eat, I eat food I like to eat. When I do run out of time—really run out, in the final sort of way—I won't have too many regrets about how I used the time I had. I know that although how much time I have is ultimately out of my control, I do have a lot of influence, that there's an abundance of time to engage with and employ in any number of wonderful ways. That like everything else, the more I work at my use of time, the more I'm going to get from it. Which I suppose leads to a paradox—I want to move with urgency but never so fast that I forget to appreciate all that's around me. 'Tis truly the ride, the journey, the path that's the point.

When I'm dealing with time, I've learned to really watch my language—I've almost completely stopped using phrases like "I have to . . ." "I can't . . ." or "I should." Instead, I own my choices, and I understand that everything I opt into doing will have (both intended and unintended) consequences. I've pretty much completely stopped complaining about not having enough time. I understand that my desire and commitment to learn as much as I can is my own choice, and not a value judgment from, or about, anyone else. I figure that the time I've been given by the fates, god, or some secret underground central time agency amounts to X days to work with in my life. I believe that the more I work at making my time on earth a positive experience, the more positive that experience is going to be.

In the spirit of my approach to anarcho-capitalism, my connection to time is one of equals. I want to have a positive, peer-to-peer, non-hierarchical relationship with it. I don't want to dominate it or whip it into some strange new shape. Time and I respect each other. I want to work with it, not warp it. A spirit of generosity seems to apply—when I devote time to time, time does right by me. While we each have our issues, we work well together as peers. We each embrace what the other has to offer, and we collaborate to co-create positive things for the community around us. We support each other as well. I'm committed to myself and to making the most gentle and positive use of time's presence that I can. Throughout it all, I have fun with time; I enjoy doing all that I do and will do.

Once you have your vision written for the way you're going to relate to time in the long term, I'd recommend repeating the process at most every level at which you're working. You have a clear picture of long-term success, but what's your vision for this week that we're in now? Or for today? What will you get done? How will you feel about it? What are the challenges you've likely steered clear of? If this suggestion irks you, then as always, exercise your anarchic option to skip it. I share my approach only in the hope that it will help you, and because I know it's helped me to put it on paper. The truth is that the act of sharing it has actually significantly increased my odds of successfully making it happen.

The same, I would argue, will hold true for your vision of time. Writing and sharing any vision you've done with others will always improve the odds of your realizing it. But of course, you still have to do the work. Interruptions will come, distractions will develop, and frustrations will certainly follow. Let's face facts—the unexpected will almost surely arise at some point to mess with what we're working so hard to achieve. As Monsieur Servan-Schrieber said, "The path of our lives is more like a twisty mountain road than a straight flat interstate across the plains." But the beauty of having our vision documented and reading it regularly is that no matter how lost we may get in the mountains on any given moment, our destination is never in doubt. Only time, of course, will tell, but if you're a high achiever (which I'm betting you are), you're highly likely to get there.

3. Make the Most of Every Minute

This, I suppose, is very 21st century of me to say. But here's the thing. When I say, "make the most of every minute," I *don't* mean that you have to get a lot of financial return for what you do. All I'm advocating is that you get what *you* want from what you have. This isn't about anyone's judgment but your own. That might mean you're playing video games; going fishing; getting an MBA; running for Congress; reading a good business book; reviewing the minutes of the First International Anarchist Conference in Amsterdam (in 1907) as I recently did; or just ambling around aimlessly. My point is merely to mention how important it is to correlate what we do with the results that we really want to get. You want time to drink beer and watch TV? Have at it. You want to spend more time with your kids? Have at that too. You want to work? Great, go for it. You want to meditate, watch a football game, walk in the woods, chop wood, or work out—make it happen. These are all totally legitimate uses of time. My point is just to be mindful of how you're choosing to spend your time, and then make the most of the time that you have.

The idea of making the most of every minute, appreciating and actively engaging, is one of the keys to making every day like a holiday. Most people in the world don't get to choose exactly what they want to do all day. But acknowledging the good things going on and maximizing every minute, even if you're doing something you weren't all that high on doing in the first place, will still make a positive difference. Seth Godin, who's written extensively on creativity in business, says, "Investing in the wrong place for a week or a month won't kill you. But spending ten years contributing to something that you don't care about, or working with someone who doesn't care about you . . . you can do better."

Time, I realized twenty years ago, is a nonrenewable resource. No matter what we do, or don't do, it's never coming back. I want to spend each minute in a way that adds to the quality of my life and the lives of those around me. If I'm standing in line, I try to stretch, or read, or watch other people and see how they're behaving in order to learn something about human behavior. If I'm walking across the street in front of the Deli, I try to pick up paper out of the gutter—it takes pretty much just as long to walk past it as it does to bend over and pick it up. If I see someone at work who's doing a good job, I might as well tell them. If I'm near the computer, why not email someone I care about to say hi? It's not complicated but every little bit really does count! I try to remind myself, as dancer Martha Graham wrote, "Make the moment vital and worth living. Do not let it slip away unnoticed and unused."

In/On/Self

If you're a manager and are having a hard time figuring out an effective way to invest your time each week, take a look at the essay I wrote on beekeeping as a metaphor for management in *Zingerman's Guide to Good Leading, Part 2,* and do this little exercise.

On average, roughly what percentage of time are you spending each week:

Working *in* your department?

Working *on* your department?

Working on *yourself?*

The key is to find the allocation that works best for you. Most of us, in my experience, tend to short *ourselves.* The amount of time we devote to working on our own development is usually rather minimal—and in many people's lives, nonexistent. That said, as is clearly the point of this entire book, focusing more on our self-learning, self-growth, and reflective solitude probably has the biggest benefit of anything we can do. Every hour we spend improving ourselves (count the time you spend reading and reflecting on this book!) is likely, if we put it to work, to pay positive dividends in other parts of our lives as well.

In your department versus *on* your department? Both are important. Generally, the bigger your organization gets and the more people you're managing, the more sense it makes to devote more time to working *on* your business. Unfortunately, without mindful redirection, most of us will slide steadily in the other direction; the busier the business gets, the more time we tend to spend *in* the business, even as it's becoming more important to work *on* it.

The "secret" for me is that as much as possible, I try to do all three—*in, on,* and *on myself*—simultaneously. If I'm working *in* the business, I want to also be thinking about systemic ways to improve it at the same time. If I'm working *on* the business, that doesn't mean I can't be greeting coworkers or customers as they come by, or picking up trash while I'm talking about long-term visions and strategic plans. And in anything I'm doing, I can pretty much always be working on managing myself, trying to coach and coax myself into having more meaningful interactions, being a better listener, stretching, breathing, working to be more sensitive to myself and to the world around me.

From an organizational standpoint, I try to look at where my time is going to bring the biggest return for the group. Am I spending it on things that are going to make a difference? Making time for things that get bottom-line results (whatever those bottom lines may be)? If I'm standing next to a new staff member, I try to take the time to learn about their life, or to teach something that will help with success down the road. If I'm walking past a customer, I check to see if they're being helped. If I'm standing in line, why not say "Hi!" to someone I care about via phone, email, or text, rather than just stand there being frustrated with how long the line is taking? Or maybe better still, I'll just stop and mindfully manage my breathing. If I'm preparing to interview a job candidate who will report to a manager in our organization, I'll frequently suggest that the two of us interview the candidate together. I can get to know the applicant and have the opportunity to coach the manager on their interviewing skills at the same time.

Good Time Investments at Zingerman's

Looking at where we spend our time is often a far better measure of what we truly value than where we spend our money. It's worth taking ten minutes to examine the way time is used in all the various elements of your life.

When I started to assess time use in our own organization, I was a bit fearful that I wouldn't like what I found. But that proved not to be the case. I was actually quite impressed with how often (in both our systems and our culture) we devote generous amounts of time to things that the rest of the world would likely consider crazy. That investment of time has, for us, proven to contribute greatly to the quality of our workplace, our service, and our products. Our efforts have paid back plenty; they're manifested in most all of what we now do and experience here at Zingerman's. Here are a few of the things that come to mind:

While most call centers are trying to reduce the amount of "talk time" they have with Mail Order customers, we're working to raise ours. We've long believed that the more time we spend on the phone with guests the better our relationship with them, the more we know their needs, the better we can serve them, the higher our sales ultimately will be.

• We expect everyone in a leadership role to make time to talk to any staff member who asks to chat.

• We regularly take time to talk to interested job applicants even if we aren't hiring at that moment. Some of the best people in the organization came in that way. They were willing to wait a couple months, or even years, before something opened up that was a good fit for them here.

• We spend a lot more time interviewing people at every level of the organization. Almost everyone gets two interviews, and some get three or four. Applicants for upper level positions go through a round robin "tilt-a-whirl," where they interview with a dozen different people over the course of half a day. Many applicants also do a "trial shift," where they work for a few hours or even a whole shift to see if they like the work and if we like working with them.

• We put way more time into training than most other food service organizations. It's part of our investment in the people we bring on board, and we're big believers that this time investment pays off big time.

• Our organizational change process moves very slowly by most businesses standards. But by investing a lot more time up front to get most everyone involved, we gather more insights and build buy-in, leading to far more effective and lasting long-term change.

• We ask everyone in a leadership role in the organization to do two hours of formal learning per month, on average, plus an additional hour a month teaching within the organization.

• We begin every big project by writing a vision of greatness. By investing time in getting clear on where we're going, we far more effectively inspire and organize ourselves to do what we want to do. Having failed to convince so many colleagues around the country to do the same, I've come to think of their refusal to write one as the vision version of "penny wise, pound foolish." They might save half an hour by not drafting a vision, but they'll then spend it sixty times over struggling to make decisions without a clearly defined end in mind. It's akin, I've realized, to not pulling over to ask directions because you think you'll be late if you do. Chances are, if you don't ask, you'll end up being later than if you had. Vision writing is easily some of the best time we spend. It's time invested in helping each of us get clear on what's important in our lives, what we want for the future, what it means to us to feel like our lives have meaning, what we want to achieve in our work and with our relationships, how we'll engage with the world, and how we can feel good and fulfilled.

• Time is a key ingredient in our food as well as our work. One of the "secrets" to our (or any) traditional country breads are their long rise times— eighteen hours from start to finish for many of them. The same goes for our cheese. We allow longer times for the starter cultures to develop, increasing the cost but improving the flavor of the cheese.

• And we end every meeting by setting aside time for "appreciations"— a few minutes of round robin appreciation by anyone for anyone.

Please understand, it's not that we're not mindful of the importance of efficiency or speed. In many areas of what we do, working quickly is super helpful. Our Mail Order production crew uses the LEAN approach to systems management to gradually and consistently push unhelpful inefficiencies out. We've just finished spending many millions of dollars on a renovation at the Deli, in part so that we can make sandwiches more quickly and with far less wasted time. A speedy response time to customer complaints is, of course, critical. Eliminating wasted motion, I think, is really a sign of respect for both the individual's and the organization's time. But the point is there's more to time management than just making haste!

4. Be Appreciative—Make Every Day a Holiday

Being appreciative of time and of all the players who are active on its stage is the best way I know to make the absolute most of what we have available to us. There are still twenty-four hours to the day, but they feel far better when I go into them with a grateful attitude.

When we're young, most of us feel like we have all the time in the world. But if we take things (and people) in our lives for granted, trouble—and at the least, regret—are pretty sure to follow. The way I see it, every minute I don't mindfully value is a minute wasted. Since they never come back, there are no second (or minute, or hour-long) chances. Every minute, hour, or day I can move onto the positive side of my life's ledger sheet, the more rewarding things will be, the more effectively I can add to the lives of those around me, the lower my stress, the longer my life is likely to be. There are never any guarantees, but when I leave the planet, I want to go having worked hard and devoted serious time to great appreciation of all that's around me.

I try to relate to time according to my own anarcho-capitalist ideals about equality. Holidays are all well and good, but I want to treat every day as if it were special and bring out the best in each as it comes along. While I'm happy to enjoy all those days that get high social play, I don't like to downplay the ones that get no special credit on the calendar. I love them all equally. In essence, I decided a decade or so ago to treat every single day like a holiday. To celebrate it, to do special things, to live the way I want to live, to actively get around people I want to be around. I try to wake up each morning like a kid on Christmas morning—excited to find out what gifts the world has given me.

With all this in mind, I work hard to actively appreciate everything: each of the great people I get to work with, the really wonderful customers who come to us every day, the kids who experience their birthday with us, the amazing foods we get to sell. I could go on at length about my appreciation for the rich flavor of the rye bread from the Bakehouse, the slightly spicy crunch of the fried chicken at the Roadhouse, the positive energy of the crew at the Deli, the artisan cheese made by the folks at the Creamery, and the way the women at Zingerman's Press work to get the recycled paper in this book just right, and how that feels every time I turn one of these pages.

Appreciations add up. I wrote a whole Secret on the subject in *Part 1*. You know about my Three and Out Rule (see page 80). Martin Seligman has his version in the positive psychology world, which he calls "Three Blessings," or, "Three Good Things": writing down three things you're grateful for every day for a week. Seligman recommends that for each item we also respond to the questions, "Why did this thing happen to you? What does it mean to you? How can you have more of it in the future?"

What's so great about these questions is that he's basically guiding us into conscious competence about making good things happen in our lives. Seligman suggests that if we start paying attention, "the odds are that [we] will be less depressed, happier and addicted to this exercise six months from now."

Some simple ways to add appreciation to your day:

End all of your meetings with "appreciations."

Live and teach the 4 to 1 rule: four parts praise for one part
constructive criticism.

Say thanks whenever you can.

Write thank-you notes.

Look to the "SBA" for help: When in doubt or distress,
Stop, Breathe, and Appreciate.

Part 3: 15 Practical Tips on Making Better Use of Your Time

The tips that follow have helped me enormously in making the most of my time over the years. Obviously, I can't tell you what will or won't work for you. But hey, what's the risk of trying 'em out. When you find other tips of your own, by all means, send 'em my way! I'll take all the help I can get!

1. Get organized

2. Budget your time

3. Write effective to-do lists

4. Just do it—the quicker you get to something, the less time it takes

5. Tackle the tough stuff first

6. Move forward mindfully, not carelessly

7. Make it easy to maximize your time

8. Make your meetings as effective as possible

9. Don't let perfectionism slow you down

10. Remember that poor quality will cost you

11. Honor your commitments

12. Hold others—courteously and considerately—to their commitments

13. Learn to say no

14. Avoid the time wasters

15. Finish up by *putting things in writing*

Plus 1: Plan for the unexpected

1. GET ORGANIZED

A small bit of organization can make a *big* difference. In one of my favorite business books ever, *The Corporate Mystic*, Gay Hendricks and Kate Ludeman propose that "If you have a life any more complicated than, say, a sheepherder's, be sure to write agreements down." As Jim Munroe, author of the comic book *Time Management for Anarchists*, says, "When you develop a habit of writing down stuff, and referring to it often enough, you'll find out an amazing thing: you can let it all go. You can forget about missing appointments, not getting stuff done, and have your brain back to think about creative, interesting stuff."[26] This sounds good to me. I'll take every bit of brainpower I can get for fun and creative activities.

If you've written a personal vision (see Secret #35), this will be infinitely easier. You know where you want to be at whatever point in time you've chosen in the future. You can break things down from there into what needs to happen in the next year, and from there into the next few months, and then consider this very week. If I push myself to get consciously competent about it all, it looks something like this:

> Long-term vision
>
> Key goals from the vision
>
> Objectives to accomplish in the next year
>
> Action steps I need to take to get 'em done
>
> Plus, all the new things I've committed to doing in the moment—i.e., "Get back to Bill about book cover," and that sort of thing

To Jim Munroe's point, if you get good at this stuff, it will seem to come naturally. If you're not good at it now, you absolutely can learn to be—but like any other skill, you have to work at it long and hard, with a vision of greatness for your relationship with time clearly embedded in your mind.

There are hundreds of software programs and books on how to do this. I still use a list (see below) on a yellow legal pad, a paper calendar, and a back-up calendar on the computer. I know lots of other people who use index cards, apply "stickies" to their computer screens, etc. Whatever you do, take time to reflect, get focused, document your short- and long-term desires, and then, as per below, budget your time accordingly. Reflection and attention to detail will help make all or any of these more effective. No method will compensate for not making time to see where you stand, where you're doing well, and where you're behind, and coming up with a course correction going forward. Getting off plan is pretty normal. The problem most people who struggle with this have isn't so much getting off course from what they intended, but rather not going back and adjusting what they're doing accordingly.

Beware Time Biases

This entire essay is, as I've suggested, inevitably biased towards my Western timeways. Even when I try to compensate, they're so ingrained in me that some of them bleed through. Not that that's a terrible thing—it's just helpful to know where and when our biases begin to get in the way of doing the right thing. One fairly easy-to-identify Western worldview when it comes to time is the common American and European belief that things that *look* neat and organized are, by definition, more efficient. The Midwestern farm with acre after acre of straight rows of corn; the forest with only one kind of tree (generally a Norway Spruce); the factory with clean and efficient production lines, making a single standard product. These constructs may at times be good for near-term time management. But once we move beyond the bias, we find that what might appear to be chaotic can actually be more effective.

Here's a snippet from James Scott's fascinating book *Seeing Like a State.* Scott shares the example of an old-style Guatemalan garden, judged absurd by European "experts" because of its chaotic, confusing, multicrop construct. "It is frequently said by Europeans and European Americans that time means nothing to an Indian. This garden seemed to me to be a good example of how the Indian, when we look more than superficially into his activities, is budgeting his time more efficiently than we do. The garden was in continuous production but was taking only a little effort at any one time: a few weeds pulled when one came down to pick the squashes, corn and bean plants dug in between the rows when the last of the climbing beans were picked, and a new crop of something else planted above them a few weeks later." To Scott's well-taken point, when it comes to time (or agriculture or business for that matter), straight lines may look good, but they're not always the most efficient way to get where we want to go.

2. BUDGET YOUR TIME

Nearly every healthy business does some sort of financial budgeting; those that don't usually spend money haphazardly. The latter almost always end up expending even more time and money down the road to make up for mistakes missed by not giving a more mindful thought to their spending decisions. While that model can certainly be made to work, investing a bit of time into thinking about what's coming up, what you want to achieve, what your long-term vision is, and how you're going to allocate resources en route tends to be hugely helpful. The more people you involve in your organization, the more important it becomes to allocate resources in advance, and then do some work to keep track of how things are going through the course of the year.

The same sort of budgeting approach can be equally effective with time management. Doing a time budget isn't all that hard, nor is it particularly time consuming. But without one, you're setting your schedule adrift where it's basically at the mercy of the world's madness and other people's manic behaviors. Forecasting the resources available and contrasting that with expenditures to see if there's anything left over (i.e., profit and/or cash) can only help with long-term visions and short-term goals; promote more proactive decisions; and in the process, reduce stress and increase mindfulness.

A budget gives structure that can help us avoid the "Wow, where did the time go?—I just spent four hours making a sign that should have taken ten minutes" feeling. It's not rocket science and it's not a perfect solution to all our problems. It just pushes us to make mindful decisions about where we'd ideally like to invest our hours and days. For example, I could easily spend the next two years finessing this essay, and likely the rest of my life working on one book. And while there's theoretically nothing wrong with these endeavors, the problem is that neither will fit with the other time commitments I've got in mind.

A budget basically designates how we spend our resources to get from where we are today to our vision for the year, the week, the day, life, etc., that we've drafted (if we're living out Tip #2). Sure, a time budget—like any other budget—is based on estimates, past experience, etc. But a decent estimate is almost always more helpful than flying blind. If you become at all mindful of time, and blend that with your ever-higher awareness of your own abilities, you can usually tell yourself roughly how long various pieces of your day are going to take. And by the way, that can include screwing-around time. It's your budget and you can do what you want with it!

3. WRITE EFFECTIVE TO-DO LISTS

There are likely about eight million words written about effective list making, but here are a few tips that have worked for me. I should say up front that I'm a list person. If you're one too, you'll know what I mean. We're the people who write everything down and who take great pleasure in crossing it off when it's done. If you're like me, you live from, and for, lists. Lists bring freedom, and they add support and structure to life. And when we're having a really bad day, we write down a couple things we've already done, and then cross them off in order to get a bit of positive momentum going.

Separate the long term from the short term. One issue implicit in any meaningful list management is how to keep track of work that's due next September *and* the smaller stuff that's supposed to be done by this coming Saturday. What works for me is usually breaking the longer-term items into smaller tasks—the latter make my to-do list; the bigger goals are on my monthly calendar. That helps me remember that we're supposed to have a proposal finished next spring, but it doesn't have to be on my to-do list every week for the entire year leading up to its completion. What does show up there are the small things: "finish redrafting," "call printer to get quote on book," etc.

Start keeping follow-up lists. One thing that used to trip me up regularly was following up on stuff other people had committed to do. When I knew that I needed to talk to someone to ask them to take on the work, I'd write the item on my to-do list, i.e., "Talk to Tom to have him redo training plan for bussers." As soon as I talked to Tom, I'd cross the item off. I was "done," and happy for it. The problem was that the actual work was not yet done. What I figured was now "finished" was actually all too often still incomplete. My mistake? Asking someone to take care of something is a fine first step, but it's *not* the same as the work actually being completed. To remedy this problem, I put together a separate "follow-up list" for work I'd asked others to do but wanted to be sure to check up on later to make sure it was finished. Super simple, but it sure helped me a lot.

Take care of items lingering on the list for too long. If something's been on my list for more than a week or two after I'd wanted to have it done (or whatever time period works for you), it's generally either time to get it done asap, or to take it off the near-term list altogether.

4. Just Do It—The Quicker You Get to Something, the Less Time It Takes

I know that "Just do it!" is from a big ad campaign for shoes, but it's at least as true for time management as it is for Nike. While it may sound counterintuitive, more often than not the *sooner* you complete a new piece of work you've decided to take on, the *less* time it will take to get it done. I can't really explain this phenomenon scientifically, but it's proven true way too many times for me not to take notice. The longer I wait to tackle a task, the longer it takes me to accomplish it. While I'm not advocating racing mindlessly into action without thinking things through first, my experience is that the more I move away from taking care of business soon after my decision to do something, the longer everything seems to take. If I'm looking at an email that I can compose a good response to in my mind, it's generally better to just answer it immediately. (There are exceptions—I'll get back to those in a minute). When I get a phone message, it's usually most effective to return the call right away. Or if I think of a new idea and spend five minutes with it, I can frequently sketch out the first draft of a vision in ten minutes of straight, uncensored writing. And usually what I throw down quickly is remarkably right on.

If you, like me, are someone who worries about acting too hastily, this is a tip that's well worth considering. But of course, not everyone is like me. Some people are wired the other way—they tend to be so impulsive that they'll act on just about anything instantaneously, which, we all know, can often get them into trouble.[27] If you're one of those impulsive types, or if you're afflicted with Shiny Object Syndrome (being attracted to new ideas but failing to follow up on them), my suggestion is simple. Check your vision and your values, and, in this case, your time budget before you begin! *If your action isn't going to help you get closer to your vision, or if it's out of line with your values, that's a pretty sure sign that the action you're about to embark on probably isn't a good move.*

5. Tackle the Tough Stuff First

This is, I know, standard wisdom in the time management world. I hate to be in the mainstream, but I find that it works. I almost always tackle the things I like least early in the day and save what I'm more eager to work on for later. Of course, I'm a delayed gratification person and I'd always rather do what needs to be done first, even if I don't love doing it, so I can free my mind and my day for more interesting things. My general rule of thumb is that if I've put something off for more than a week or two after I told myself (or others) that I was going to get it done, something's wrong. That long a wait usually means it's time to either a) ask myself some bigger questions (like, Why am I putting this off? Am I afraid of something? Do I really care about it as much as I thought I did? Am I just procrastinating or trying to push myself to do something I shouldn't?); or b) kick my energy up a notch, caringly confront the issue, and get it done quickly before my relationship with time, myself, or my integrity starts to suffer, or I alienate anyone who's been waiting for me to finish it.

6. MOVE FORWARD MINDFULLY, NOT CARELESSLY

This tip is really about pace—moving steadily forward, neither too quickly nor too slowly, but as a good marathoner would do, maintaining her pace throughout the race. It's about staying away from the extremes of either abandoning something altogether or racing forward so quickly that you make more trouble than you might have had in the first place. Other than in extreme emergencies (when you want to go quickly, of course) or when dealing with compulsive behaviors (try to back off as best as you can), you'll want to stay steady, measured, in the middle.

Being mindful of feelings—and frequently not acting on them—can help here. My experience is that the best pace to move at often runs completely counter to the one that we *feel* like we need to follow. If you feel internal pressure to act impulsively and in the moment, you're generally going to do better to back off. If you're a procrastinator, move more quickly. In either case, it's about shifting away from unneeded extremes of action and back towards the middle.

Important work takes time to unfold, but getting moving more quickly than slowly helps—I can draft a rough outline or a preliminary write-up for most projects in under half an hour. And the risk of drafting—not *acting*, mind you, but *drafting*—is next to nil. The longer you put off that first round of action, the further you get from your true feelings, your creativity, and your insight. Mind you, this first shot at things is just a beginning—don't race right out and send what you've done to headquarters, or trigger immediate action. But if all you do is draft, I think you can have the best of both worlds. You clear your mind by getting moving quickly and follow your intuition, but you integrate safety into the system by waiting a while to gather input before you pull the final trigger on anything too controversial. If in doubt, wait a day, talk to two friends, do a quick vision and values check, and then go with your gut. Steady as she goes might be a good motto for our work styles, as well as our ships.

7. MAKE IT EASY TO MAXIMIZE YOUR TIME

This one is incredibly simple, yet so many people fail to do it. No matter where I go, I always have something with me that I want to do. Please understand here that it's not my intent to get you racing through life more rapidly than you want to go. My interest is only to increase the odds of your time being used in ways that *you* want it be used. I know I have a *lot* that I want and like to do, and since time will never be any longer than it is today, I want to be ready for whatever's available to me. I bring a book almost everywhere I go. I keep cards with me to write thank-you notes and postcards to send to friends and family. I take note of any phone messages I need to return so that I can make a call or two if I get stuck waiting somewhere. Sometimes I stretch or do wall sits to strengthen my quads. When I'm driving by our local massage place and I'm early for a meeting, I'll sometimes head in for twenty or thirty minutes. For you, it might be having a flower in hand to smell or poetry to read or . . . you get the idea. Just think about what you want to have with you to make it easy to maximize a few free minutes that might appear unexpectedly in your day.

With all the electronic devices available today, this is easier to do than ever. That said, you don't need a fancy phone to make the most of your time. Emma Goldman was arrested so often that she started to bring a book to every speech she gave so she'd have something to do when she was sitting in the jail cell waiting to get bailed out. I still take my journal (that fine-lined yellow legal pad I wrote about earlier) almost everywhere. Similarly and inspiringly, I once saw a guy working behind the counter in the Delta lounge at the airport in Memphis who had a small set of single arm weights to work out with. When he had a quiet, customer-less moment behind the counter, he lifted weights! His energy was very positive, and his biceps were very big!

The idea of being ready to maximize my time at any moment really took hold for me about twenty years ago. At the time, someone I worked with was prone to getting pulled out of our conversations by almost anything that came up. We'd be talking and then, bam, he'd walk away to answer a call or he'd just disappear to do something else for a few minutes. I was always frustrated, but really what could I do? One day it dawned on me that, rather than getting mad, I could just get to work. When he got up to go do something, or put our conversation on hold to take another call, I just started on other tasks. I understand this solution won't work in all cases. But in this instance, it worked great for me. Instead of wasting energy being angry with my colleague and complaining about *his* lack of focus, I increased my own output instead. From that simple shift in approach, I lowered my stress, improved my productivity, and made my energy and our relationship more positive. And by the way, because he's worked hard to manage himself more effectively he rarely does it any more anyway. [28]

8. MAKE YOUR MEETINGS AS EFFECTIVE AS POSSIBLE

Although it's never been discussed at a national level, I'm adamant in my belief that badly run meetings make for more economic and emotional problems than many of the issues that get raised in political forums. I'm convinced that, if all we did was to make American meetings more effective across the board, we could increase gross national product by 10 or 15 percent. Seriously, regular and effective use of six or seven simple strategies in all our meetings would make a major dent in the deficit.

You know the feeling, I'm sure: sitting in a long one, feeling frustrated and helpless, like your precious time is being wasted. Now you may be thinking, "I wasn't the one running the meeting, so there's not really anything I could have done." But given my belief that everyone in the organization is responsible for leadership, if we don't collectively take charge of a bad situation, then we're each consenting to squander our own time. Rather than being frustrated and wasting an hour or two (or more) a week, why not volunteer to lead the meeting yourself? If your offer is spurned, you'll at least feel better for having actively tried to be part of the solution. At the very least, for the sake of your own sanity alone, don't leave the meeting without knowing what was decided, who's doing what, and when they're doing it.

Regardless of who leads it, by contributing a modicum of work to improve meeting effectiveness you can make a major difference in how people feel about the workplace and how much time you have available to do other things, as well as, perhaps, the quality of your life. If your meetings lack structure or clarity, then doing any or all of these seven things will put you way ahead of the rest of the world.

- Hand out an agenda in advance, with budgeted times for each agenda item.
- Get clear on the objectives for each part of the meeting before it starts.
- Assign relevant homework in advance and have it completed by attendees before the meeting.

- Clarify roles: know who's facilitating and keeping the group on track, who's keeping time, who's taking notes, etc.

- Document specific commitments made during the meeting. (I hate having to spend half of the next meeting arguing over what we actually already agreed on the week before.)

- Follow up! If things are agreed upon in a meeting but never actually implemented, our integrity falls, energy flags, rumors fly, and frustration follows.

- End with "appreciations." Five minutes of random appreciation, of anything or anyone, at the end of any session will successfully send folks back into the business in a better mood, a big energy win for them and for the organization, taking everyone's effectiveness up half a notch for almost no cost.

While it would be easy to dismiss spending time on meeting management as a waste of precious minutes, it's actually the opposite. If you work in an organization with more than four people, a bit of time spent improving meeting structure will pay big dividends to the entire business. I stand by the rule of thumb I learned years ago—for a meeting of a good-sized group, spend one to two hours planning for each hour of meeting time. It's a worthwhile investment, not just to make the time spent in actual meetings more productive, but also for all the impact the participants will have on other people after it's over. Think about what happens if people emerge from a bad session angry and frustrated. That negativity will cost the company, bringing down the mood of others who weren't even in attendance at the meeting.

The good problem that will come from doing this work well is that like good chocolate, good coffee, or good anything else, it's very hard to go back to bad meetings once you've been in one that's well run. Frustration with other people's meetings is probably one of the top three or four complaints I hear from former staff members who've moved away and are now working elsewhere. In their time here, they became accustomed to being part of reasonably productive sessions, and struggle to return to the poorly run meetings that unfortunately tend to be the norm in the work world.

Writer Peter Block calls meetings "the family dinners of organizational life." With Block's metaphor in mind, bad meetings are akin to serving fast food—you won't drop dead from eating it, but we all know that it takes its toll over time in the form of bad health and bad feelings that eat away at your energy.

9. Don't Let Perfectionism Slow You Down

Anyone out there besides me tend to get hung up trying to get things *just right* before we let them go out into the world? Having wasted way too much time worrying about making everything perfect before I did anything, I've learned to *drive for long-term perfection* (where appropriate), while still, in the moment, being glad to just get going. I'm not saying you should settle for so-so—it's just that waiting for the ideal to arrive before we do anything is dooming ourselves to failure. Things that could have already been improved will lie dormant, diminishing organizational energy while you wait.

On the other side of this coin are those who struggle with what's been called Shiny Object Syndrome: the tendency to run after every exciting new idea, while seeing few if any of them through to fruition. Learning to stick with things until they're finished, or at least fairly well implemented, is no small achievement if your mind is used to moving more quickly than completion is likely to come. But it can have a hugely positive impact on our sense of achievement, the contribution we make to others around us, and our self-esteem and vibrational energy.

Over time, I've come to accept that for me, at least, *excessive fretting only brings failure and frustration.* Doing my best and achieving steady, if imperfect, improvement is ten thousand times more productive than waiting, and waiting, and waiting to get it just right. Believe me, I know—just letting this book go to the printer is an exercise in self-management. I've been writing long enough now to know full well that a week after we send it in, I'll have found five quotes, had two new insights, and come up with one more concluding point that I desperately want to add. I truly want to make everything perfect, and I hate, hate, hate making mistakes. But making mistakes is totally human and can be a healthy way to learn.

If you tend to perfectionism—and many high achievers do—all I'd ask is that you consider what's really worth more to you: agonizing over imperfection or imperfect action? I've learned to live happily with the latter and I far prefer it to the former. But there are many people out there who let their drive to make everything perfect put them off of really doing much of anything. Charged with teaching a new training class, they'll spend months worrying about it, working at it, and reworking it over and over again without ever actually teaching it. But if you have sufficient experience in doing the work the class will cover and are willing to quickly knock out a draft outline, then run your ideas by others who know the material too, make efficient revisions, and then pilot the class (saying up front that it's a test run, not your nomination for "new training class of the year"), you have far more to gain than you'll ever get by waiting.

Here's the math: If you put down 80 percent of what comes quickly to your mind, that will almost certainly be 80 percent more than 80 percent of your staff knows without you having taught it yet. If you wait until you've got the perfect class (which may take forever), you make no progress. If you go forward, you get a very meaningful, if imperfect, improvement. If you invite the people who come to the pilot to help you make the class better, you're using your time even more effectively—you're teaching, you're learning, and you're getting them engaged in the business all at the same time!

Driving steadily for improvement is an imperative for anyone who wants to get to greatness. But by being a perfectionist, we'll probably just drive ourselves and others crazy. As Julia Cameron writes, "Perfectionism is not a quest for the best. It is a pursuit of the worst in ourselves, the part that tells us that nothing we do will ever be good enough—that we should try again." Ultimately, she says, it is "a refusal to let yourself move ahead."

10. REMEMBER THAT POOR QUALITY WILL COST YOU

Moving quickly and combatting perfectionist tendencies does *not* mean that it's good to go for mediocre. Sloppy, error-filled, failing work is never good. I will vouch, both from firsthand screw-ups and from studying business practices, that it's more effective in every way to get it all right the first time. Balance, of course, is imperative; we want to say no to both perfectionism and poor quality. Steady, careful, collaborative work means we can deliver high quality that's both problem- and procrastination-free!

A quick note: While poor quality is often associated with inaccuracy, remember that, in a service context, the customer's perception of what's right may not be the same as what's accurate. Which, in the case of time, is why we long ago came up with the 55/05 Rule in order to avoid the service equivalent of an emotional train wreck. The rule is simple, but I stand by it as one of the best little things we do. It's so subtle I doubt that very many customers even mindfully notice it. But I can guarantee you it will register (if unconsciously) when they go elsewhere and have a less satisfying experience.

Here's how it works. If we say we open at 8:00 a.m., we actually turn on the lights and unlock the door at 7:55. If we say we close at 10:00 p.m., we don't lock the door until 10:05. Why? Because not every customer's watch is going to be correlated to ours. And even if their clocks do read the same as ours, the reality is that they might still be frustrated if they miss us by minutes. Imagine running a few minutes late, driving as fast as you can to get to us, getting caught at three long lights, and finally arriving on the other side of town two minutes after we've closed. You don't need an advanced degree in customer relations to realize that, even though it's not our fault that the customer failed to get there on time, they're going to be upset. Through the simple act of waiting an extra five minutes to close, or opening up early on a cold winter morning, I know we've made an emotional impression on many customers.

11. HONOR YOUR COMMITMENTS

I feel fairly confident in saying that every adult human will have failed to honor at least a couple of commitments they've made in their lives. I know I've fallen short on many. I also know that when I do, my integrity is diminished, my energy flags, my anxiety rises, I fall further and further behind, and really nothing good ever comes from my shortfall. Here's the cycle I used to go through: the more I'd let commitments slip, the more I'd get mad at myself, the more energy I would waste, the less I would get done, the more I would over-commit to compensate—suffice it to say, that cycle was not much fun.

In our catering department, we track on-time deliveries. At the Roadhouse, we keep track of late orders. Why not do the same to self-manage around commitments? Keeping track of how well we do at meeting them isn't really that complicated. If you just list each commitment as it's made, write down the time frame in which you've said you would do it, and then measure how well you do against that list, you'll have some down-to-earth data to draw on. If you set an inspiring but still strategically sound goal or a percentage to be completed and track it over time, and if you're willing to adjust the way you work in order to improve, I'll bet that you'll hit your target. Before long, you're likely to be known as one of the most timely folks around!

12. HOLD OTHERS—COURTEOUSLY AND CONSIDERATELY— TO THEIR COMMITMENTS

If others who work with us consistently fail to come through on what they said they were going to do, and if we consistently fail to bring up the issue, we become the equivalent of an enabler of an alcoholic. I don't mean we need to get nasty about it, nor to call them out in public, but somehow, in a caring and considerate way, we'll find it more productive to engage the issue. Although the conversation may be awkward, in the end, everyone will become more effective for it.

13. LEARN TO SAY NO

Learning to courteously *and* appropriately say no is a critical component of effective time management and also one element of meeting commitments. While well intentioned, volunteering for every possible project that comes up can quickly turn from a helpful move to a hopeless mess. None of us, no matter how well organized or hard working we are, can possibly do everything. Saying yes whenever you're asked for assistance or involvement can only mean that you'll fail to come through on a significant number of projects. Yes is meaningless if you don't do the work—saying you'll do something just to make your boss or your coworkers happy in the moment is rarely a productive strategy. Rather, it often leads to the inverted integrity spiral I referenced above: you say yes too often, you can't get things done, you beat up on yourself, your energy flags, you feel like you're failing—you get the idea. As Servan-Schreiber reminds us, "Saying no may be an unpleasant moment, but it passes quickly—especially when we have the grace to use a little tact with it."

Of course, saying no every time you're asked to do anything is unhelpful and unreasonable. If you're at a "lower level" of an organization, it will probably get you fired. If you're at the top, it makes for a pretty unproductive environment for others to work in if 99 percent of the time the response they're going to get to a proposal is no. I once worked with a person of whom it was said, "You have to know that the first three times you ask him about something he's pretty sure to say no. But then the fourth time he'll almost always come around to yes!" Once his colleagues all figured this out, they were able to arrive at a workaround. "You just have to learn not to give up that first time he shuts you down," one of his crew told me. While it's nice that they were loyal and persistent enough to power through, it would really have been so much nicer if the no's hadn't been used in such a consistently obstructionist way.

14. AVOID THE TIME WASTERS

Nineteenth century French philosopher Louis de Bonald once wrote, "There are people who do not know how to waste their time all by themselves. They are the scourge of active people." I'd guess he was correct back then, and his statement is most certainly still true today. I hardly think the "time wasters" he refers to are malicious people—they don't get up in the morning intending to detract from others' effectiveness. They just have a high affinity for unproductive action, seemingly unending uncertainty, or irrelevant distractions.

Seriously, it may sound mean, but learning to successfully steer clear of the time wasters in life can be one of the biggest time gains you'll ever make. Setting a second appointment to follow hard on the heels of a previous one with a time waster can work wonders. Learning to move effectively past with a pleasant, "Hi! How's it going? Gotta get to a meeting!" works well too. If you find yourself cornered, and nearly unable to escape, that's usually a spot for a friendly, "Oh wow! I just remembered something I need to do for a guest/client/customer." The truth is, given the complexity of life and the large volumes of clients we (fortunately) have, I can pretty much certainly make that statement come true. There's rarely a moment where I can't think of something I should do for a customer. And really, no one will ever argue with you that you shouldn't take care of a client.

15. Finish by Putting Things in Writing

This, I'm sure, portrays a Western bias on my part. There are cultures in which what's said orally in casual conversation has all the veracity of an ironclad legal document at the Supreme Court. But here in the 21st century US, at least, what's said and what's remembered are only rarely the same thing. Rather than get into long arguments, I just try to write things down to reduce the time it takes to sort it all out.

I'm not talking about documenting every single in-the-moment comment we make, only conversations that conclude with some sort of action being agreed upon. While this will seem overly formal for many people, the failure to confirm in writing is the cause of countless problems and an enormous drain on the nation. How many times have you completed a conversation feeling relieved, only to realize later that you didn't know what you or anyone else had committed to doing? How many times have you been to a planning session where you spent a good 60 percent of your time trying to remember what you all agreed to at the last meeting? It's not hard to understand why this happens. Humans are . . . human. We forget, we misunderstand. We make mistakes. I say "a," you hear "b." It happens every day all over the world.

Taking time to confirm the details of your conversation later in writing, over email, or in whatever form works for you, can contribute huge time gains to your week. If everyone is really on the same page, fabulous—it took two minutes to make sure. In the more likely situation that there are two somewhat (or significantly) different interpretations of a previous interaction, isn't it better to discover the discrepancy the next day rather than to work down diverging paths for three weeks before uncovering the error? Think of how much time and energy you can save, how much stress you'll avoid. Two minutes of slight awkwardness traded against two hours, or two weeks, or even more, of ineffectiveness avoided. I'll take that trade any time.

Even if done orally, it really does help to reconfirm. Years ago, we had a very effective supervisor who ended every conversation with a staff member by saying, "OK, tell me again, what are you going to do?" It's not my style, but it was hers, and she sure made it work well. Confusion in communication was almost *never* an issue in her area!

Plus 1 Tip I Hadn't Thought of Earlier— Plan for the Unexpected

A while back, we had a manager who had a hugely difficult time getting her work done on time. No matter how many hours she put in, she was always way behind. One of her biggest problems, I discovered, was that she was scheduling up literally every hour of her day. While that may work in some places, in the hectic world of food, it's guaranteed to make a mess of even the most well-meaning of time managers. If you've never worked food service, let's just say that about the only thing you can truly count on is that every day some new problem (or combination of problems) will arise that you hadn't previously thought of. At least that's been true for the first thirty years of my career.

What was obvious to me (but not to her—she was just trying to get a lot done) was that, by scheduling her entire day to the max, she left herself no room for the unexpected issues that always arose. To make matters worse, she was so "busy" that she "never had time" to organize herself, no time for time, to reflect, or get re-centered. As soon as one thing pulled her away from her plan, she was behind permanently for the day. And since her next few days were pretty much packed too, the problems just piled up until she was buried under an avalanche of unmet expectations.

To avoid falling into that hole, I work hard to schedule only about three-quarters of my time. Most days I leave a few free slots to deal with the unexpected things that come up, so as not to be thrown completely off my game. Add in an hour for getting grounded in the morning, some time to work out, and time to pay attention to all these other tips, and I can usually get through most unexpected events fairly well.

Time to Close

I've never liked the idea of living each day as if it's your last. It seems to encourage a rather irresponsible, good-people-gone-wild kind of mindset, a careless and chaotic, if not downright cataclysmic, approach. The other extreme—putting off all pleasure until you reach some far-in-the-future date with desire—isn't all that helpful either.

The middle ground is more my style. I approach things as if I have only a couple years left to live. Mind you, it's a rolling two years, so each day I move the deadline out a bit. And I don't act like I'm really dying, just as if my time might be running out in a few years. For me, at least, that time frame keeps me focused on doing the right things for the longer haul, while still accomplishing some of the short-term stuff that scores high on my life list. The mental window for you might be longer or shorter, but you get the idea. Having an end gently in mind helps me stay focused on doing the things that are important to me; keeping that time frame reasonably at bay in the future keeps me from fixating on the urgent at the expense of the important and interesting.

As I stress everywhere in this book, we can all initiate meaningful improvement without waiting for the world to change around us first. The place to begin is usually by looking inward, reflecting, and then actively finding ever-more effective ways to work with ourselves and with the world. As you begin to devote even a little more time to time (you're already off to a good start by reading this essay), as you draft a vision for your relationship with it, as you become more mindful of every minute, and as you work to be ever-more appreciative of every hour and every day, I feel confident that the quality of your life will significantly improve. None of this, of course, will fix all your problems overnight, nor will it allow you to overcome every obstacle that arises in your path. But if you figure that these techniques might gain you a bit of time each day, improve your effectiveness by 7 or 8 percent, and increase the amount of joy and appreciation you experience by a factor of four, that's a pretty positive improvement.

The point of all this work with time, of course, isn't really to move faster; it's to feel better. And to help those around you feel better as well. Ultimately, I've come to see time management as a creative act. As Julia Cameron writes, "Art is the act of structuring time." And at the same time, I would say structuring time is an art. Either way, the message is the same. Whatever you do, be mindful, make something special out of every minute you get, and have a good time with time!

A Problematic Philosophical Postscript:
My Struggle with the Idea of Hourly Pay

Although I don't really know what to do about it just yet, I think we still have a seriously flawed hierarchy of time in American culture today. The vast majority of the people who work here at Zingerman's are still scheduled and paid on an hourly basis. Legally, it's very difficult for frontline folks to work any other way. Bosses, by contrast, are on salary—society has somehow decided that we "at the top" should have the freedom to manage our own time. We get to decide when and where we're going without having to track it all to the minute. Granted, we have commitments to meet, but when it comes down to it, *we* can determine what we do with our days. We can work more, or less, when the workload, the world, and we ourselves dictate that we want to.

While in our anarcho-capitalist setting here at Zingerman's, staff members probably have more influence on when they work than they would elsewhere (and definitely a lot more influence on what the work experience is like when they're here), they're still essentially scheduled at our whim. Like it or not (and I don't really), we're basically buying their time, and this creates an odd imbalance, one that I'd rather do away with. As David Graeber writes in *Fragments of an Anarchist Anthropology,* "Instead of people selling us [as in the time of slavery] or renting us out we rent out ourselves. But it's basically the same sort of arrangement."

Paying people by the hour this way seems such an old-school way to approach work. Labor codes say that we're supposed to compensate an hourly employee for anything they do that's "work related." Think about the absurdity of that within our holistic approach. When everything they learn about food, history, language, culture, writing, nutrition science, social studies, or themselves has meaningful value for work performance (which we believe it does), that means we'd have to provide compensation for every article they read, as well as every time they talk about food with friends, take a class of almost any sort, appreciate great art, or learn something while listening to NPR. Right now we're probably violating some legal code by not paying them every time they cook a new recipe, read a book, meditate, or make time to talk to a friend about how to improve the quality of their lives.

Frustratingly, the way the codes are interpreted in the courts, we aren't legally *allowed* to let a frontline person be paid on salary. The law says that salaried positions, though, are reserved only for those we can prove are at the "top," somehow entrusted with managing their time responsibly. Everyone else is relegated to the lower ranks of the time pyramid. I can remember back to when I was an hourly line cook getting more and more engaged in the running of that restaurant, and I was regularly really frustrated that I wasn't allowed to come in and do more when I wanted to. I wasn't trying to milk the clock—I just wanted to contribute more. But my effort and good intentions were irrelevant. As an hourly person, I was part of a class clearly cut out from the important stuff. The real work—what I thought was the fun part of it all—was reserved for the folks who were on salary; the rest of us were stuck punching in and out with shift work. In this situation, you're excluded from actively learning as much as you possibly can, coming in when you want to work on new ways to run the business, having the opportunity to think with others in the organization about the way you work, and to work on new ways to think.

What can we do about all that? Honestly, I'm not sure. I'm gonna spend some time on it and see what I can come up with. Stay tuned.

Take Stock of Your Relationship with Time

Getting a good sense of how you currently relate to time can give you food for thought as you begin to make your relationship more mindful. Here are a few questions to get you thinking.

In one or two words, describe your current relationship with time.
What's working about your current relationship with time?
What's not working about your current relationship with time?

notes from the back dock

Luke Bromberg, Busser, Zingerman's Roadhouse

I love working at Zingerman's. I think it's a perfect match. Here is why. I was a happy customer before I began working there. First of all, Zingerman's has the best sandwiches in the whole Midwest. It is also the role model for restaurants in Michigan. There is also a saying, which is "Zingerman's is too good to be true." Zingerman's also makes more than 45 million dollars in sales annually. I bet if you ask anybody in the Midwest if they have heard of Zingerman's, most of them would probably say yes, it is in Ann Arbor. Another reason why I love Zingerman's so much is because they let other businesses buy their food and sell it to their own customers.

Then I went to a job fair at the Center for Independent Living. I spotted Zingerman's and they spotted me. Now I am a busser at the Roadhouse. If it is great to be a customer at Zingerman's, it is just as great to work there. I am constantly learning new things and trying to be as good as I can be so that the customers can see my service is as good as their sandwiches. When I eat at other places, I now see things that they could do better—if they learned from Zingerman's.

Orientation—that was fun. I traveled around the world with my passport—and no customs agents! Huddles—a great way to learn more and sample the food, so I can know what the customers will be eating.

In my opinion Zingerman's treats all of their employees with respect. When I go to the Bakehouse and the Deli, they recognize me as a coworker, and I feel at home while eating more great food. Another reason why it is exciting to work at Zingerman's is because you get to meet great people who also have fun doing what they are doing.

early morning journaling at the deli

Thinking About Thinking

Why the Way We Think Alters Our Organizations

What follows are a series of (I hope) provocative and productive thoughts about thinking: the way we do it, why it matters, and how we might work to change it in the interest of running more effective organizations. I'm not a neurologist, so I can't talk intelligently about brain cells or the chemical workings of neural synapses. My experience is all, shall we say, hands on. But while I know next to nothing about neuroscience, I have done a great deal of thinking about thinking over the years, a lot of it directed towards how to become an ever better leader and manager.

What I've been mulling over in my mind of late is this: *The way you and I think as leaders, the way we process the details of what's going on inside and around us, is going to be reflected in the way our organizations work.* It's an insight that's changed the way I work and the way I think. And as per the idea behind the piece, as I think differently, that, in turn, will change the way our whole organization works. Bear with me as I explain; my mind works in sort of strange ways. But that, I guess, is part of my point. Letting that strangeness surface—rather than pretending it doesn't exist or exiling my off-the-wall ideas to some walled-off corner of the mind—is one of the keys to building the sort of free-thinking, creative, constructive, frontline-focused organization we're after.

How Writing Leads to Thinking, Connections Lead to Creativity, and the Two Together Took the Lead on This Essay

It's always interesting for me to hear what ideas people attribute to me. Alex Young, our partner and the chef at the Roadhouse, has taken to quoting me fairly regularly: "Like Ari always says," he explains, "you don't know what you want until you write it down." I don't honestly remember when I might have first said that to him, but the quote and the content are both correct. If I didn't say it before, I will definitely say it now. The way I learned to write (with a lot of credit to Brenda Ueland)—being willing to begin writing before I know what I'm going to say, working relatively quickly, not self-editing everything as it first emerges—is almost guaranteed to get good stuff from my, or anyone's, mind. This belief has been backed up time and time again by the very effective "hot pen" process that we use to do our visioning work: once you start writing, just keep writing. The key is to keep the computer keys or the pen moving! Speaking from my own experience and from watching others work in a similar way, I can tell you with confidence that if we write in this manner, things will come out that we didn't know were going to get said when we started the process.

In her amazing book *If You Want to Write,* Brenda Ueland explains that so many of us struggle when we write because we've "been taught that writing is something special and not just talking on paper." Having lived by her advice ever since I heard it, I've learned to just write the way I talk. ("Forget convention—just have a conversation.") The learning flows in both directions at the same time. When you work the way Ueland teaches it, I'd say that *writing frequently comes down to thinking on paper.*

In fact, that very thought just came to mind for the first time right now, while working on about the 18th draft of this essay. When I sit down at the computer, or with the yellow legal pad I use for journaling, I really just do a take-off on that old Yellow Pages ad: *I let my fingers do the talking!* It's a very good way to get at what's in my gut and to encourage good things I hadn't previously thought of to come to the fore. As art historian Lynn Hunt puts it in "How Writing Leads to Thinking," "writing is not the transcription of thoughts already consciously present in my mind. Writing is a magical and mysterious process that makes it possible to think differently." This is one of the big reasons why the way we do visioning work here at Zingerman's works so well. One doesn't need to know what one will write into the vision in order to begin writing. To the contrary, what comes out is often way better than the vision writer ever consciously imagined it would be.

The process is actually so simple that many people are adamant it won't work. But it almost always does. If you just start writing, and then keep writing while letting your inner critic stand aside, good things will show up. When you write steadily, without stopping, what appears on the page is almost always an accurate, if often un- or only semi-conscious, reflection of what's long been sitting quietly in our minds for months, and often years. It probably would never have emerged if we were asked to deliver a more thought-out, carefully analyzed, and very "properly prepared" PowerPoint presentation.

Being patient with the writing—and thinking—process is imperative. If I don't let my mind wander while I'm doing it, if I try to keep everything that comes out constrained and on the corporate side of straight and narrow, if I don't let the writing have time to work its wondrous written magic, connections are missed. But when I let the words flow, when my fingers really do the talking, ideas and images emerge that just weren't clear to me before I began. Things that I'm anxious about at first often end up being the best parts of the final essay. The key, for me at least, is to avoid worrying and to just do the work; overthinking and unneeded analysis will almost always get in the way of the art.

To quote Brenda Ueland, "No writing is a waste of time . . . With every sentence you write, you have learned something. It has done you good." That's for darned sure. Pretty much all of what follows flowed from writing about things that I didn't know I was going to write about. Honestly, I've probably had nearly a hundred insights or new ideas emerge over the course of writing this essay, ideas that I'd never given conscious thought to until I was typing away on the computer, often working on only slightly related subjects. But as Ueland understands, and I now believe as well, the magic in the writing brought out new thoughts, which, in turn, have evolved into a series of insights that have changed the way I think. Which means that if I'm right in my supposition—that the way we as leaders think is almost always fully manifested in the way our organizations operate—I will have in the process changed (for the better) the way that Zingerman's works as well.

One of the things that comes out with this style of thinking by writing (or maybe it's more appropriate to call it "write-thinking") is connection. In the process of writing, pushing myself to go faster than my critical thinking mind might be able to do, I often stumble into connections between ideas, insights, problems, processes, people, or products that I hadn't worked out previously. This act of connecting the previously unconnected, it turns out, is one of the keys to creativity. (For much more on that subject, see the next Secret.) By learning to let my mind be and allow it to wander a bit, I can meet my dead-lines but not get all stressed out over things while they're working themselves out. If I can wait, watch patiently, and walk through the fields of the various facts and feelings that are all around me, letting ideas from left field come to the fore, then good things are almost guaranteed to come!

Anarcho-Capitalism:
When Seemingly Conflicting Concepts Come Together

With all that in mind, let me tell you a story. It's a bit about writing, and a lot about thinking. It brings together creativity and connection. Communication. Community. Crazy ideas. Collaboration and abundance. Hierarchy, or lack thereof, and also a bit of happenstance. It's about anarchists and capitalists and bringing them together in ways that Mark Twain (or anyone else at the end of the 19th century) would never have imagined the two would meet. It's about connecting them—in my mind, at least—to converse about creative and caring ways to do business in the best interests of all involved. Ultimately, though, it's a story about thinking, and how the way that we as leaders do it will impact the way our organizations work.

The story starts out with a small slip of an idea, something that, on its own, didn't seem particularly poignant in the moment. With the benefit of hindsight, I can mindfully remember the path it took, the way it moved from a silent mental step into a significant (for me, anyway) intellectual innovation. It may sound a bit like a fable, or a rerun from an old showing of the *Outer Limits*. But to quote from one of my favorite books, *Why the Bee Is Busy, and Other Rumanian Fairy Tales* by Idella Purnell and John Weatherwax, "Once upon a time what happened did happen, and if it had not happened, you would not be hearing this story."

Several years ago, I stumbled on a connection serendipitously, only because I'd agreed to speak at the Jewish studies department at U of M. Deborah Dash Moore, who runs the department, had invited me and titled my talk "Rye Bread and Anarchism." As the date for the presentation approached, I realized that I'd never spoken about the anarchists in any kind of venue in which anyone besides me really knew anything about them. At business conferences, they were just some obscure historical bogeymen and women, and it seemed like most audiences responded to hearing about them with a combination of uncertainty and minor discomfort.

Going to speak to Jewish studies, though, was a different story. These were people who were well versed in the wonders of Emma Goldman, who would know if I had any of my facts and figures out of order. Anxiety started to set in. The talk was mostly meant to be about the story of Zingerman's and my personal path from history major to nationally known business figure, but if I was going to get into anarchism's influence on me, I figured I should bone up on the subject. I didn't have to be the world's biggest expert; I just needed to brush up enough so that I wouldn't embarrass myself. In business conferences sometimes, the bolder and less data-driven your beliefs, the better the response. But not so with historians. So I got out a bunch of my old anarchist books and started studying.

And something funny happened as I prepared to speak to the scholars. Reading anarchist stuff for the first time since I'd been fully engaged in my new business context, things came clear that I never could have imagined. Having spent over twenty years studying progressive business writing had changed my frame of reference; the works of the old anarchist radicals still rang true to me, but this time in a very different way than they had when I was a student. I was caught by parallels I'd never expected to uncover; for someone like me, who loves to learn and is energized by surprising connections, it was like finding buried treasure in a stack of old books.

My epiphany was to realize the surprising number of parallels between much of what anarchists like Emma Goldman were saying about a century or so ago and the ideas of contemporary, progressive business writers. While I'd certainly looked at plenty of both business books and anarchist essays in my life, I'd never before studied the two in tandem. The anarchist work was what I was immersed in while I was in school at the University of Michigan, sitting on the 7th floor of the Graduate Library, reading century-old pamphlets and such in the Labadie Collection. Back in those days, there was no web—studying meant sitting at long tables reading rare books and documents with a note pad and a pencil (no ink pens allowed) for hours. I was totally energized. The anarchists' emphasis on independence, self-direction, freethinking, and creativity really resonated.

Business books came later—within a few years of opening the Deli (in 1982), it become clear to me and Paul that we'd better start studying positive leadership practices if we wanted to have a shot at creating the special sort of business we had in mind. By this stage, all I remembered from my anarchist studies were the names of the key "conspirators"—Emma Goldman, Peter Kropotkin, Voltairine de Cleyre, etc.—and a few of their major theories. The only reason the anarchists would have come up at any of the business conferences I went to or in books that I read would have been to blame them for causing chaos or wreaking havoc, not to consider them as models for mindful organization management in the 21st century.

Traveling in Different Worlds Makes for More Creative Connections

As you can read about, in detail, if you skip ahead to the next Secret, one of the keys to creativity is to gather info and input from diverse sources. A willingness to think about things that seemingly have nothing to do with what you do, and then to think about them all again in new and different ways, can work wonders for your life. Gutenberg's work with the first printing press drew primarily on what he knew from the way the wine press operated. Getting outside of one's field—reading, traveling, studying the experiences of different industries—can provide the raw material for a breakthrough or insight that might literally change your world.

The reason it works is really quite simple—what's second nature in one part of the planet is often unknown in others. Although the web makes accessing this sort of information infinitely easier, one still has to go out and get it, and then mindfully make the otherwise unmade connections. There are thousands of documented examples of this kind of creative thinking—see Atul Gawande's *The Checklist Manifesto* to learn how he took a standard operating procedure among airline pilots and applied it to great effect in operating rooms.

The possibilities are limitless. I can almost guarantee that if you spend a decent bit of time studying another industry of almost any sort, or another culture, you will find some technique, approach, or insight that can be adapted to the area in which you already operate. The results can be big!

The similarities between the anarchists and contemporary progressive business theorists were sort of stunning. If I pulled out the overtly political parts of what Emma et al. were writing about, I found some amazingly beautiful parallels. There are a couple dozen compelling quotes I could share to demonstrate my point, but my favorite is still Emma Goldman's great line: "[Anarchism's] goal is the freest possible expression of all the latent powers of the individual . . . [which is] only possible in a state of society where man is free to choose the mode of work, the conditions of work, and the freedom to work. One to whom the making of a table, the building of a house, or the tilling of the soil, is what the painting is to the artist and the discovery to the scientist—the result of inspiration, of intense longing, and deep interest in work as a creative force." Sub in "business" when Goldman says anarchism and you can see why I got so excited. What she was writing about in 1910 *exactly* described the sort of organization we were working so hard to build a hundred years later.

Clearly, Goldman and the other anarchists were far more radical in their politics and desire to destroy government than modern management gurus like Robert Greenleaf, Peter Block, or Jim Collins. But beneath that political, get-rid-of-government piece of anarchist writing was a whole stream of thought that sure sounded eerily similar (after making slight adjustments for century-old writing styles) to what I was reading about in the high-powered business books I had piled up in my living room. Stuff about how you can't have a great organization without great people; how an organization needs to serve its community; how important diversity is; how a healthy organization ought to serve the needs of its members; why when employees have no sense of the big picture, they lose their drive to do great things; that when people don't believe in what they're doing, they lose heart; why free, conscious choice and intrinsic drive for greatness will always outperform organizations that depend on the use of external authority; how the old model of command and control is unjust and ineffective; how, by contrast, when leaders appeal to the hearts and intelligent minds of a workforce, they're so much more likely to get an organization to excellence. Strikingly, though, the anarchists were often incarcerated for their ideas, while Paul and I were on the cover of *Inc.*

The idea of bringing together my previously unattached interests in the anarchists and my passion for progressive business models was exhilarating. I was totally jazzed. Not only, it turns out, am I good at making otherwise unrecognized connections, but I really enjoy the process. Once I had the connection in mind, parallels seemed to pop up at every turn. Russian anarchist prince Peter Kropotkin's century-old advocacy of growing and buying local; Alexander Berkman's arguments about how frontline workers have been alienated and depersonalized; Gustav Landauer's insights about personal energy, freedom, and spirit, and his belief in starting free communities that had disconnected themselves from the painful reality of the status quo. These anarchists were envisioning a better life for men and women in an anarchist society, but what I was reading was clearly "better business." As Goldman and her creative colleague Max Baginsky said at the 1907 anarchist conference in Amsterdam: "Organization, as we understand it, . . . is based, primarily, on freedom. It is the natural and voluntary grouping of energies for the achievement of results beneficial to humanity; results which should endow life with meaning, worth and beauty." Narrow the focus (only for the moment) from "humanity" to "our organization," and the idea is perfectly applicable.

I had to wonder though: why did I seem to be the only one making the connection? And why did it take me so freaking long to find it? My answers are pretty simple, really. Having spent some time now studying what the so-called experts have to say about creativity and innovation, the connection clicked, I believe, for the same reason so many other seemingly big insights are eventually uncovered: a) I was dabbling in two different worlds, studying two streams of seemingly disparate (maybe even antithetical and antagonistic) thought; and b) I was open in my thinking to the possibility of strange things connecting.

No offense to either 19th century anarchist historians or contemporary business people, but the two groups just don't travel in the same circles. While the *Harvard Business Review* has probably written a lot about Goldman Sachs, I'm pretty sure it's never reprinted any of Emma's Goldman's great essays. Nor, I would guess, are there many contemporary, community-minded anarchists reading *HBR*, *Inc.*, or *Fast Company*. It was really only through my long-standing interest in (and spiritual alignment with) the old anarchists that I ended up with the opportunity to read books and simultaneously make connections that anyone else in the world could easily have accessed at any time.

Being Open to Odd Thoughts Opens More Doors

The good news about any good idea is that once you have it, all sorts of other stuff starts to follow in its intellectual footsteps. It was while I was writing up an explanation of the connection between progressive business and the anarchists that the idea of us at Zingerman's being "anarcho-capitalists" came to mind. I wrote the term at the end of a long list of various streams of thought that included anarcho-syndicalists, anarcho-communists, anarcho-individualists, and anarcho-everything elses. I wasn't sure in the moment whether or not the term was a good one, and I almost took it out right after I wrote it.

When you publish your own writing, when words carry as much weight for you as they do for me, when you're in the public eye every day, when you have nearly six hundred staff members and seventeen partners all tied (for better and for worse) to things you write, well . . . the pressure is on when you're going to put something in print. I'm generally averse to making claims, and I try to stay away from political groupings; saying we at Zingerman's were "anarcho-capitalists" did worry me a bit. I didn't want to provoke problems. I could hear the voices chattering in my mind. An anarchist activist accusing me of being a callous capitalist, attempting to lay claim to an idea or a title that I had no right to be writing about. A mainstream businessperson questioning my sanity for siding with a group considered to be the bomb-throwing, chaos-causing, evil enemy of every upstanding American at the turn of the last century. Added to that was my concern that a business book about anarchists wasn't exactly poised to win wide acclaim in the entrepreneurial world.

Fortunately I cut my worrying short and let the moniker remain in the draft. In hindsight, I would say that I just needed to give the concept some space to develop. Ideas, it turns out, usually need a good bit of time to come to fruition and find their rightful place in the world. I decided to override my self-doubt and stick with it. The book went to press in late August of 2010. The process, I think, is typical. Ideas occur, sometimes they go nowhere, sometimes they sink roots, on occasion they actually get implemented. One day someone puts something in print, and the rest, really, is history!

The Case for Congruity:
Anarchism in Action in the Privacy of My Mind

As I was processing the idea further, it dawned on me one day that *if I really wanted to help create an anarcho-capitalist organization, I needed to manage my brain in an anarcho-capitalist way as well.* If I wasn't thinking in a way that was in synch with what we were supposed to be doing, I was going to be hard pressed to get things working the way I wanted.

This concept as well is fully congruent with the key tenets of anarchism. The spiritual center of that work was always to free people from the externally imposed constraints, judgmental thinking, and biases that were quashing their natural spirit, instincts, and abilities. If the machinations of my mind were constricting my innate creativity, I wasn't going to be able to help shape the kind of creative organization I wanted us to be. If I wasn't allowing my own out-there ideas and oddball insights to flow freely, if I was dismissing ideas just because they didn't fit with the way people thought things were supposed to work, well then we weren't very likely to have the kind of freethinking, inclusive, cutting-edge business I was after.

There's no question about it—congruity counts. Landauer, Goldman, Abraham Maslow, Anese Cavanaugh, and all sorts of other high-achieving, well-grounded, spiritually sound freethinkers all say pretty much the same thing: the more congruity we can create among the various elements of our lives, the more rewarding those lives are likely to be. *And* the more effectively we're going to lead our organizations. As Goldman wrote, "No revolution can ever succeed . . . unless the MEANS used to further it be identical in spirit and tendency with the PURPOSES to be achieved." Again, plug in "organization" where she says "revolution," and you have a progressive business essay instead of an anarchist call to action. Actually, you'd have both—a call for revolutionary action in leadership and in organizational behavior as well. Apply that approach to everyday living and the concept is clear. *What happens inside my mind needs to be congruous, aligned and allied with whatever it is I'm trying to achieve personally and organizationally.*

Imagine, for instance, that you're thinking in command and control context but trying to manage collaboratively—it's got to be hard, if not downright impossible, to pull off. The two are in total conflict; one of them must, by all rights, be untrue to who we are. Which means we're stuck with some seriously unpleasant playacting at least half the time we're at work. It'd be like working for both sides in a game of international espionage. You have to be on guard all the time, and sooner or later even the best of secret agents is sure to slip up.

Allowed to go for too long, incongruity can be literally life threatening. As Brother David Steindl-Rast says in David Whyte's *Crossing the Unknown Sea: Work as a Pilgrimage of Identity,* "[Being] half here will kill you after a while." Stress goes up, energy goes down, job satisfaction decreases, and dissonance comes to dominate. All of which will lead, I think inevitably, to problems in the performance of the business. By contrast, if the way I think is the way I want us to work, then I can move through my day and move around my mind—intellectually, emotionally, ethically, and strategically—far more effectively and enjoyably. Better results in all areas of one's life can't help but follow.

Thinking Like We Work, Phew, Phew, Phew (To the Tune of "Whistle While You Work")

Take a minute and write out the characteristics you'd like to have as hallmarks of your organizational culture. If you take the exercise to heart, it can't help but inspire some serious reflection. My instinct was to begin by assessing the way I was thinking about things, but I quickly realized that was kind of backward. Since everything we do here starts with the end in mind, the key question isn't really how I think now—it's how I *need* to think to get us to where we want to go. If the organization is going to reflect the way we think, then it seems clear that the first question would be, "What kind of organization would we like to have?"

So in no particular order, here's what I quickly came up with for our desired cultural characteristics here at Zingerman's:

positive and upbeat

high energy

inclusive and welcoming

open to new ideas

supportive

fun

out of the box

continuously improving

egalitarian

collaborative

effective

pushing the envelope

caring

values driven

diverse

community focused

mindful

delivering on commitments

creative

Looking to the middle of the list, let's pause for a moment to consider the idea of being "collaborative." What's become clear in the process of writing this piece is that I don't just need to work collaboratively; I need to be sure I'm thinking collaboratively as well. Most of the time, nowadays, I do. I don't think I was naturally wired that way, though—I've just worked at it for a good twenty years now. Today, without even thinking about it, I started sending my draft list of cultural components out to others for input. As it always does, the dialogue paid dividends. Others I asked all added things that I'd overlooked. Thanks to them, the list above is about a third again as long (and three times as rich) as the one I originally outlined on my first quick pass.

For me, collaborative thinking has become a habit. I don't think I ever make any meaningful decisions about the business (other than on-the-spot, urgent customer- or quality-related decisions) without first sharing my thoughts with others. We could, I've realized, start to interview applicants for this skill, seeking people who strive to tap others' expertise before they arrive at a significant decision. We could also train everyone who works here on the technique—"six steps to effective collaborative thinking" or something like that. It's an idea I'm going to write down somewhere for safekeeping. It may yet come to fruition in the future. Openness to new ideas is, after all, one of the characteristics of the culture I'm working to help create.

 Culture Klatch

Your assignment, should you opt to accept it, is to write out descriptors for the way you'd like your organizational culture to be. There's nothing that needs to be on it—it's your list, your life, your organization, and your culture, so you can write what you want to. It is, in essence though, the start of a vision of greatness for your organizational culture. If "collaborative" is on your list too, try showing the draft to others to gather their input as well. Once you've got a good list going, give yourself a bit of time to do some self-exploration and reflection around each item on that list. Think about how these qualities relate to the way you think, process ideas, and make decisions. Your descriptors of the ideal organizational culture for you would, it only makes sense, have implications for the way you want to think as well.

The more you can think in synch with the way you want the business to be, the more likely it is that both you and the business will do well, learn from each other, and support each other's growth and development. Take each item on the list and look into what goes on inside your head on each count. In some cases, I'm guessing you'll be in good shape—the way you think is already aligned with the way you want your organization (or in the immediate context of this book, your life) to operate. But there may be other areas that need work so your mental processes better calibrate with the way you want your company culture to look. With that in mind, the next issue up is an obvious one—can we alter the way our minds work to make our businesses, and our lives, more of what we want them to be?

Can We Change the Way We Think?

If the answer to that question were no, it would be awfully frustrating—it would mean we were stuck working and living in exactly the same way that we currently think. Fortunately, the correct answer to the question is a very clear *yes!* It's not easy and you can't do it in a day, but we absolutely can change the way our minds work. Which means that we can also change the way we live our lives and the way our organizations operate.

Both the evidence of my own life and learning *and* a great deal of emerging data from a series of very sound studies show that, if we work at it, we can alter the way we think. Which is why the exercise above isn't just informative or academic; it's actually highly practical and hugely helpful. If you're clear (now) on what sort of culture you'd like to have, then the best way to attain it is to start working at aligning your thinking processes with how you'd like your organizational culture to look.

Over the years, I've taught myself to think significantly differently than I was raised to do. I've learned to think positively where I was raised to find fault; to pursue visioning where I was raised to focus on near-term tactics; to be a better listener where I grew up having learned to interrupt; to accept myself as I am where I was rooted in self-criticism; to think about choices I'm making rather than feeling that I'm being forced into things. I've got a long way to go, but even I can see that I've come a heck of a long way. I have changed my thinking a *lot* and it shows in the way I live and in the way Zingerman's looks and feels.

Clearly, my belief in people's ability to shape their lives has been one of my strengths. Paul taught me a lot about the importance of this many years ago. I've worked hard and have many successes to share. As Bob and Judith Wright put it in their very revealing work, *Transformed!*, "It's tremendously empowering to be told that you're capable of doing or being a way that you've always assumed to be beyond you." But over time, I started to worry. If strengths lead to weaknesses (as per Natural Law #10), is this good quality causing me problems too? For example, has the strength of my belief in people's ability to change caused me to stick too long with staffers who weren't wired to change?

The answer is no—we all have the ability to alter the way our minds work. Positive psychologist Martin Seligman summarizes it: "Habits of thinking need not be forever. One of the most significant findings in psychology in the last twenty years is that individuals can choose the way they think." The keys, it turns out, are already embedded in the Natural Laws of Business and Life. I've referenced this in the sidebar on page 257, but I think it's so powerful I want to reiterate it here.

The first requirement is our attachment to a better future. It's not enough to just set a goal; to change our thinking, *we've got to bond into and visualize a different way of being*. This is the emotionally engaging, strongly held vision of greatness that we use and teach so extensively here at Zingerman's. When we have designed our own futures, we believe in those futures. When we write a vision of our own choosing, we are actively and creatively imagining ourselves successfully living (or in this case, thinking) in this new way, and thus the odds of getting there go up significantly. As the Wrights explain, "Dedicating and living with intent activates the most highly evolved part of our brain—our frontal lobe." That's also the part of the brain in which visioning is done, so the two—living mindfully while moving towards the future we want—feed the brain and bring results. "Our consistent focus on our highest values increases blood flow to the frontal lobe, and the more we focus on our yearning and our values, the more we transform."

Secondly, we need to do the work to get there. As someone who sticks with things long and stubbornly hard, I realize now that I was unconsciously competent at this. Coming from my own doubt, my drive to compete with myself and not fail, and the good study habits I'd had imbued into me as a child all seem to have served me well. Once I decided to think more appreciatively and find more joy in the world, I worked long and hard to make this a reality. The same is true for every other mind change I can remember. It was a lot of work, but my determination to change and my diligence paid off.

Similarly, once I realized how destructive it was for me to be saying "I have to," "I should," and "I can't" all day long, I was able to eventually change my mindset. I've told the story many times—it took me a good three years to change, but I did eventually make it happen. If you figure that I was working at it, say, thirty hours a week, that'd be almost 1500 hours a year. Within those three years that I was pushing myself so hard, I would have gotten halfway to the 10,000 hours of mindful practice that Anders Ericsson's studies show are necessary to achieve excellence. Having now taken what I've learned to the next level by teaching and writing about choice, discussing how much these changes have impacted my energy and my existence, I'm probably not that far from those 10,000 hours.

Maggie from ZingTrain and I have often discussed over the years why we at Zingerman's have been able to succeed with so many new approaches when other organizations seem to struggle and never get to greatness. Long ago we came up with a simple, almost self-evident answer. Most people give up way too soon. At Zingerman's, we both agreed, we're probably not any more intelligent than anyone else out there in the world. We just stick with stuff long after most other organizations would have given up. This same pattern, it turns out, also holds true for personal change. As the Wrights write, "There's no such thing as a quick fix; transformation is gradual . . . It's one thing to learn a valuable lesson; it's something else to put it into practice. Transformation takes time and practice—a lot of both."

If we put our minds to it, any of us who are willing to work at it, then, can develop a couple new habits, abandon some old and ineffective ones, train ourselves to see things through different "lenses," learn to manage ourselves more effectively, and process information differently than we have in the past. The changes probably won't be quick, but that's ok—if you've been thinking one way for thirty years, you can't just pop in some new software program and change the way your mind works in a matter of minutes. But it can definitely be done! In the words of the Wrights, "With focused attention and repetition —the requirements for liberating—[we'll find] new patterns of thinking, feeling and doing." And in a similar manner, we can alter the way our organizations work.

While the science behind all this is new, the idea of it is not. Here's what the anarchist writer Henry David Thoreau had to say on the subject a century and a half ago: "As a single footstep will not make a path on the earth, so a single thought will not make a pathway in the mind. To make a deep physical path, we walk again and again. To make a deep mental path, we must think over and over the kind of thoughts we wish to dominate our lives."

The Downside of Being Able to Alter Our Thinking

I don't like to even bring it up. But to be clear, the same process I've described above can also play out in destructive and undesirable ways. If we are schooled hard for ten (or more) years in a setting that promotes an "everyone's out to get you" mentality, we're highly likely to become cynical ourselves and suspect everyone of being up to no good. If you're told that you're incompetent over and over again, you internalize that message. If you're raised in a racially or ethnically bigoted setting and have heard about the inferiority of (fill in the group) for forty years, it's not easy to stop seeing the world that way. It's no wonder, then, that entire countries and communities can seemingly go crazy—raised with enough off-base, negative, hateful teachings, one can come to believe almost anything. And the way we think will have been shaped accordingly. While I still always like to think positively, the odds seem small that people who've had their minds actively trained to be suspicious and hateful will decide to live and think more equitably.

The Power of Positive Thinking

It's a cliché, to be sure, but trendy or not, it's true. Thinking positively is one of the single most meaningful ways known to improve the quality of your life. Natural Law #12 says successful people are more appreciative and have more fun. Be cynical if you want, but I tend to think that means you're missing the point.

There's a wealth of data on the subject. In *Flourish*, Martin Seligman cites findings demonstrating that "Positive mood produces broader attention, more creative thinking, and more holistic thinking. This is in contrast to a negative mood, which produces narrowed attention, more critical thinking, and more analytic thinking." If we want organizations in which people think the best of their customers and coworkers, we as leaders need to think positively first.

Can those of us who were raised with a lot of criticism pull off this positive mindset? I can say very positively that I've radically altered my approach to life on this front. I come from a caring, well-meaning family whose number one way to give attention, nevertheless, was to offer criticism. Finding fault is easy for me, second only to "sitting alone reading" on the list of behaviors that come to me "naturally." But I learned (the hard way, through failure and frustration) that in organizational behavior, constant criticism simply doesn't work. A steady stream of it from the leader will lead, inevitably, to more criticism throughout the organization. While it's true that some achievements can come from a consistently critical mindset—it's not like I was a total loser before I learned to think positively—it's just not a whole lot of fun to live that way. My life is more rewarding, richer, and certainly more fun if I focus on finding the good rather than finding fault.

The day-to-day details that helped me change my thinking? In no particular order:

I started to teach, write about, and institutionalize visioning, which is all about going after a positive future that we're passionate about putting in place.

We built appreciations into our organizational culture—every meeting ends with them, our staff newsletter is full of them.

I started to list good things in my journal almost every day.

When I'm feeling down, I write about the good things around me to get me refocused.

I came up with the Three and Out Rule as a way to self-manage myself out of bad days.

I learned about positive energy from Anese Cavanaugh and then started to teach and write about it.

We wrote "fun" into our guiding principles and our 2020 vision.

By focusing on the idea of free choice, I rarely feel required to do anything, which is of course a far more rewarding way to live.

When I catch myself being overly critical in meetings, I try to recover with grace.

I start with the positives when responding to new ideas or proposals.

Anese also taught me to use the "yes, and" technique to replace the "yes, but" framework in order to encourage others to go after their ideas and implement their insights.

I keep working hard to accept myself, to stop the steady stream of self-criticism that coursed through my brain for most my life.

Almost everything we do at Zingerman's is focused on the positive: visioning; open book finance; forecasting; authorizing everyone to fix a complaint; expressing faith in people's ability and desire to do well and do right; and promoting the belief that everyone is creative and everyone cares and that together we can achieve almost anything we envision. When we follow the fun, smile and laugh, and strive for positive contributions, it adds up to good things. Work in this setting is supportive, inspiring, invigorating, and energizing. We get better results, we enjoy life more, and our lives—to paraphrase the late Chris Peterson—are more worth living.

We're not alone. In *Flourish*, Seligman cites a study that shows the difference between positive and negative strategies in companies and the impact that makes on how well those organizations succeed. Psychologist Barbara Fredrickson reported that "There is a sharp dividing line. Companies with a 2.9 to 1 ratio for positive to negative statements are flourishing. Below that ratio, companies are not doing well economically." This ratio is known in the study of psychology as the "Losada" ratio. I had to laugh when I read about it. Fifteen years ago at Zingerman's we wrote down that one of our expectations of ourselves as Servant Leaders was to set our sights on a target of 4 parts positive feedback for 1 part constructive criticism. According to Fredrickson's study, it looks like a ratio of 5:1 is what's needed for a strong loving relationship. So in the interest of living Natural Law #8—to get to greatness you've got to keep getting better, all the time—I think I'm going to propose that we up our organizational expectations by 25 percent.

Losada Yourself

About a month or so after I'd finished reading Seligman's work, I was reflecting on the impact and importance of that ratio. It dawned on me that it likely works in reverse as well. In other words, when I take in a very harsh criticism from a customer, colleague, or casual observer, if I want to rebalance myself, I would do well to try to access at least three equally adamant positive comments. If the study and my own inverted logic are right, then it would take three compliments to offset one complaint. And if I wanted to get myself into a really positive, loving place, then I'd do even better to find five meaningful compliments in order to correct my course.

POS in A2

Here at U of M, we're fortunate to have the Center for Positive Organizational Studies led by Wayne Baker, Bob Quinn, Lynn Wooten, Chris White, Kim Cameron, Jane Dutton, and others. We also happen to have a big center of positive psychology, led by the late and much-loved Chris Peterson and the very passionate Nansook Park. The focus of all their work is on the positive impact that an upbeat, optimistic, abundance-oriented approach can have on a business or organization, as well as on individuals. All of the folks I've just listed are regular Zingerman's customers; people who think positively like to be in settings that support and spark positive energy. Which is part of the point—the more positive stuff we can start up, the more good things come to us, the more we can achieve, the more positive stuff and the more positive people come to us. Which in turn helps us improve our performance, which then draws even more positive and creative people our way.

Thinking Free: Openness to New Ideas

Paul and I have, I believe, always been open to anyone who comes calling and wants to share thoughts or suggestions with us. In truth, we regularly listen to ideas that don't seem like they're going to be of much help. One could probably make a case that we waste excessive amounts of time talking to people we don't need to be talking to. But for us, this sort of openness and engagement with ideas is essential to what we do. Any idea, we've long believed, might turn out to have merit; if we don't hear it out, we might well be leaving intellectual money on the table.

This openness to ideas is fully in synch with the way we want to work with people. We welcome everyone into the organization, look to connect people on the periphery with what's going on in the center, and are dedicated to treating everyone with respect and dignity, regardless of background, age, race, gender, tenure, or spot on the org chart. If we do things well, we're ready to spend a lot of time and resources to help nurture almost anything that might show potential for improving the organization. Do we get this right all the time, though? No, of course not! Sometimes I slip, with ideas and with individuals. I get reactive and judgmental when I would do much better to be patient, judicious, and respectful in my responses. But the good news is that thinking about thinking has led me to self-improvement. When I find myself getting harsh or defensive, I can usually double back and reengage before too much is lost.

My plan for further improvement is that if and when I start to get defensive or argumentative about someone else's idea, I'm going to self-manage my way to success. I'm going to work to greet the idea like I would a guest—to welcome it, to be appreciative that it came my way, and to act sincerely happy to see it. If I do a good job of it, I'm confident that the service sequence I've internalized so well when it comes to customers will eventually be triggered subconsciously as soon as someone starts to speak. In a year or two, I'm pretty sure that I'll be smiling every time someone says something new and different, just as I would with any customer! It makes good sense. Don't we want more and more good ideas to come to us in the same way that we always want more customers? *Yes!* It's one of the keys to having a creative, compassionate, and engaged organization. Welcoming in an odd idea might end up helping me embrace many others I might have unwittingly dismissed in the past. I'm already excited about what I've learned here just from writing this down! Maybe five years from now, this will be quite the trend. Effective idea meeting and greeting will be getting enormous national attention!

Crazy, Kooky, and Ultimately Compelling Ideas

One of the first things I realized from my efforts to think in synch with my anarchist orientation was that I needed to encourage my intellectual and emotional edginess; to push myself even further "out there" than I already was; to consider what initially seemed like it would never work; to cultivate the arguably crazy; to track the silly and seemingly slightly insane ideas inside my own mind. Just as an organization will be far healthier for bringing in a diversity of people and personalities, so too my creative output will be far more powerful if I can keep myself from squashing these ideas in their early stages.

Freethinking isn't something that someone else can grant us; it's a choice and a discipline that starts in our own heads. It sounds simple but I know I'm not the only one for whom eliminating the influence of internal critics has been difficult. It's not easy to leave the slightly kooky ideas in play. To the contrary, most of us are trained to weed out the "impossible," "inappropriate," "unthinkable" (a contradiction of a term if there ever was one), "childish," "silly," "stupid," or whatever, for fear of facing a barrage of disapproval. What we would benefit from is actually the opposite—classes in kookiness. Sadly, as anarchist Gustav Landauer wrote a hundred years ago, not enough people encourage our "right to wildness and boundlessness."

Carrying the thought further, I've become ever more mindful of how crucial it is that we, as leaders, choose to live freely within our own minds. If I could effectively open my mind to my own healthy and constructive oddities, then the organization overall would be way more likely to up its creative ante as well. After all, the best, most creative ideas anywhere usually come from the parts of our minds that we and/or others are apt to consider "crazy." It's what pours in from the periphery, what lives in the intellectual margins, the out-of-hand humor, the out-of-the-box thinking, the off-the-cuff comments, the things that get lost in most straightlaced settings . . . that turn out later to be darned good ideas, to be game changing or even life altering insights.

I don't want to suggest that you aren't already doing this well. Hey, you might be. For all I know, your mind is as free and unfettered as the anarchist society Emma Goldman always imagined. In my case, though, I had to do some serious work to remove the constraints, to shut out all the "shoulds" and the "can'ts" (and their cousins, the "should nots" and "can't dos") from my internal conversations.

Of course, we don't necessarily want to *act* on everything that comes to mind. We just want to own it, engage with it, give it a shot at success before it gets squashed. See, if we edit out everything that seems strange for fear that we'll act on it, we will inevitably lose the good with the bad. Not that the status quo is necessarily sterile, but if we want to be creative and cutting edge, we must, by definition, do what others don't do. And when we quickly rule out what doesn't seem to fit, we're going to greatly reduce the odds of coming up with interesting, exceptional ideas. Which, by the way, are often the ones that will become "all the buzz" in the future.

As Sam Keen says in *Inward Bound,* "If we listened to our fantasies we would discover that each of us has a thousand forbidden lives. The trick for freeing the imagination and reawakening sleeping desires is to begin by granting yourself permission to indulge in fantasy without any obligation to act out anything you imagine." If we want to have a free country, free speech, and, in our case, a "free company," then we clearly have to think freely too. The burden to begin is, of course, on us as leaders. While I'm sure I was never told *not* to be creative, the truth is that staying true to oneself within the context of society, family, religion, and social norms of all sorts is far harder than it's made out to be by those who tend to embrace the status quo. The pressure to perform and to conform, to find "the correct response" and the "right way," starts really early on.

Whether it's in writing a vision, drafting an essay, working on a new system, or crafting a job description, it's imperative for me to be open to those secrets Keen alludes to. To be patient, to see how things will unfold, to avoid forcing them into preconceived constructs. The truth is that I often doubt myself, and my intuition, before I actually begin to work on whatever it was I thought of in the first place. As Jonah Lehrer says, "The lesson of letting go is that we constrain our own activity." Decades of dealing with social standards and learning to conform usually means that it's not easy to again access that with which we arrived in the world. But we have to start somewhere, right? As Keen advises, "If you have been out of contact with your imagination, you will need to be patient and clever to lure it back. Think of your imagination as a frightened and disappointed child who has been told no too many times. Invite it into your awareness as you would any shy person. Gradually you will win its trust and it will begin to tell you secrets."

The anarchists were all over this issue. Freethinking is at the heart of everything anarchism is about—encouraging people to be themselves, to tap their natural abilities and insights, to connect and collaborate freely without interference from authorities. Lucy Parsons, best known to historians as the wife of executed Haymarket anarchist Albert Parsons, was a powerful writer and presenter in her own right a century ago. Speaking of the same sort of self-censorship that Lehrer referred to more recently, Parsons wrote, "There is always a limit; some imaginary boundary line beyond which (society says) the searching mind dare not penetrate." In Goldman's words, we must strive to liberate "man from the phantoms that have held him captive." Italian American anarchist Errico Malatesta defined an artist as "someone with visions and rhythms that form a separate inner world; someone who can manifest this world on the outside."

Really, no one can be harmed by my having these thoughts and setting them down, in the moment at least, for my own enjoyment and edification. The risk, really, would be in not releasing them, holding them hostage, confining them in intellectual captivity. Businesses today, I would argue, are filled with folks who are holding back, afraid to share their ideas, afraid to voice concerns, afraid to go after what they believe is right. If we bury our ideas inside our own brains, what are the odds of getting ourselves and the people we work with to do things any differently as they go through their days at work?

Sidebar Sum Up

It goes like this: "If we as leaders aren't organizationally open to edgy ideas, it's highly unlikely that we'll be open to ideas that come from the edge of the organization." This line came out of my mouth as I started to explain the key point of this essay to Michelle Moran, former editor at *Gourmet Retailer* magazine and now an organic farmer in Florida. Once again, collaboration came through—the words are mine, but they came to the fore only because I was sharing the concept with a colleague.

How One of America's Best Cheeses Began by Getting Hung Up On

If you love cheese and you haven't yet tried Rogue River Blue, you might want to add it to your long-term vision to do so. It's pretty amazing stuff. David Gremmels and Cary Bryant have been making it at Rogue Creamery in Oregon since 2002. Its first year out it won best of show at the Cheese Championships (in London, no less—no small accomplishment when American cheeses are generally looked down on by Europeans). It's a raw milk blue cheese, aged for over a year in Syrah grape leaves that are macerated in Clear Creek Distillery pear brandy. Anyway, the cheese is fabulous, but David Gremmels' story of creating it is almost as delicious.

"We really wanted to develop a cheese that was our signature and have it be something special. Something totally different than what anyone else was making. So we were thinking about the idea of using grape leaves to wrap the cheese—it's done in Europe in some places, and since we're located in the heart of Oregon wine country, we thought that sounded good. Then I had the idea of using another local product—this really delicious brandy from Clear Creek Distillery. So I looked up the number of the Distillery, called and asked for the owner, Steve McCarthy. I explained who I was and what we wanted to do, and he just hung up on me."

Determined to see his vision through, David waited a few days and then called back. "I explained again what we wanted to do, and again, he just hung up on me." Like so many successfully creative (or is it creatively successful) people, David was intent on making things work. "I decided I'd just go around and buy up all the Clear Creek pear brandy I could find in the local stores," he told me.

David's determination paid off. "About a week later, I get a call from this guy who says, 'This is Steve McCarthy. Are you the guy buying up all my brandy?' I explained again what we were doing. This time he listened and agreed to start selling us brandy, with approval from the state liquor board so that we were able to save some money as part of the process." Later that year, the cheese went to London and won! A decade down the road, it remains one of the country's (and really the world's) best cheeses. But as with so many creative successes, it started with a wacked-out idea to make something different, a good bit of dissonance, and the willingness of the person whose idea it was to stick with his dream despite others' opposition. Add in high quality—a critical component without which even the wackiest idea will never work—and sometimes you get a world-class winner!

Thinking in an Egalitarian Way:
How We Think Hierarchically and Don't Even Know It

While it's easy to say that we're open to ideas regardless of origin, I'd guess that most of us are influenced a lot by the way that a concept comes to us, as well by who's doing the delivering. In the same way that it's easy to dismiss an employee or customer because of their background, accent, or other superficial stuff, the same goes for ideas and information. I know I'm vulnerable to that myself. I could apply it personally to the way I've responded to the writing of Murray Bookchin. Born in NYC in 1921 to Russian Jewish immigrants, he was one of the most prolific, and probably one of the most provocative, of 20th century American anarchist writers.

But from afar at least, Bookchin was not an easy man to love. The passion, intelligence, drive to learn, and intense focus on righting our social and ecological ships, which were his strengths, also led to what I'd guess were some of the challenges of being around him. He seems to have alienated any number of smart, caring people over the years. One opponent, also an anarchist, said that Murray handled criticism the way stereotypical Americans talked to foreigners who didn't speak English—when they don't understand you, just talk louder! On top of that, for me his writing can be sort of academic—loaded with big ideas but also very heavy on big words. Bookchin's books are not easy reading.

Beneath the bluster, though, there's a whole range of worldview-altering approaches that, as best as I can tell, Bookchin alone was advocating for. Here's a bit from *On Spontaneity and Organization*: "The self in hierarchical society not only lives, acts and communicates hierarchically; it thinks and feels hierarchically by organizing the vast diversity of sense data, memory, values, passions and thoughts along hierarchical lines. Differences between things, people and relations . . . are organized hierarchically in the mind itself and pitted against each other antagonistically in varying degrees of dominance." His writing style is more academic than mine, but it's almost exactly what I've been thinking in my own space, way, and time: people in our society, instinctively and unconsciously, think hierarchically. They also often process and organize information in competitive and opposing (as opposed to supportive and collaborative) ways. And they do that, quite understandably, because that's how we're generally raised to think.

While Murray's quote caught my attention when I first read it, and made good sense, I was having a hard time translating it into practical application until I was handed a perfect illustration of this point one day at a ZingTrain

333

seminar. I was teaching with managing partner Maggie Bayless, who was reviewing what in the training world are called "the levels of learning a skill." I learned this from her, and we've been teaching it regularly at ZingTrain seminars for fifteen years or so. It's been hugely helpful, so much so that I think I'll just offer it to you now. When we teach the Four Stages of Learning a Skill, we draw a chart on a white sheet of paper on the wall that looks like this:

Unconsciously	Competent
Consciously	Competent
Consciously	Incompetent
Unconsciously	Incompetent

With any skill that we know nothing about, we start at the lowest level of the chart. Maggie uses the example of teaching a teenager to drive. Before they start learning, they're "unconscious" (they don't know what they don't know) in their incompetence (although they might think they do, they don't really know how to drive). If you take them out and give them a lesson, showing them all the details that go into it, most of which they've missed while being a passenger, they move to the next level—they become "consciously incompetent." In other words, they now know a lot more about driving, but they still don't know how to do it.

If you keep teaching and the teenager keeps practicing, they will move to the next level to become consciously competent. They know how to do it, they're paying a lot of attention to their newly learned skill, and they're pretty good at it. And then, if they drive daily for a decade or so, it's pretty likely that they'll end up (as almost all of us do) becoming unconsciously competent. In other words, they're still good at driving but they do it (as most of us do) almost instinctively, without paying any mindful attention while they're engaged in the activity.

There isn't really a "good" or "bad" place to be on the chart. The key to working the stages of learning a skill are, much as Edgar Schein insightfully pointed out, all about matching the level with the needed application There are ups and downs to all the levels. Unconscious incompetence has its benefits—we're not bothered by what we don't even know exists. Conscious incompetence is the first step forward towards learning a skill. Acceptance, as in so many parts of life, is essential to moving productively forward. The best teaching work, and I believe the best active learning, will happen when one is consciously competent. But unconscious competence is a positive state too. It allows us brain space to take on other tasks—for example, we can easily carry on a complex conversation while driving a car. As positive psychologist Martin Seligman points out in *Flourish*, "The more components of a task you have on automatic, the more time you have to do the [intellectual] heavy lifting." Each level, then, has its benefits, and each one has its challenges. The key is comprehension—understanding how the learning moves, and then matching the level of learning with what you want to achieve.

Anyway, I was listening to Maggie teaching all this for about the two-thousandth time. As she was wrapping up, one of the attendees asked a question that caught me off guard, and helped me enormously to understand the point Bookchin was making. I don't tell the story to embarrass—the question was a totally reasonable one, and the asker is a smart, caring guy who studies leadership very seriously. As Maggie finished teaching the chart, he raised his hand and said, "I just don't understand. If 'consciously competent' is so much better, why do you guys put 'unconsciously competent' at the top?"

"Well, that's just the way the stages are taught," Maggie said. "It's used regularly that way in the training world." "Yeah," he responded, "but you guys are always adapting things to your own way. I don't understand why if the conscious competence is better, you don't move it to the top of the chart." Both Maggie and I answered in the same moment. "But it's *not* better. It's just one of the stages of learning a skill." And then a million-kilowatt light bulb went off in my head. I actually thanked the guy later for speaking up—his well-meaning, and not at all unreasonable, question helped me really understand the idea of hierarchical thinking at a much deeper level than I ever had previously.

Our guest had, as would many Americans, made a couple of assumptions, both of which turned out to be inaccurate. His mind was unconsciously organizing the four categories into exactly the sort of hierarchy that Bookchin was writing about and which is so common in the world. One of the four levels *must* be the best. He decided that "conscious competence" was the winner. With that first assumption (inaccurately) in place, he continued apace. If "conscious competence" was best, he couldn't then understand why it wasn't "at the top." If you're thinking hierarchically, it makes sense that the "best" category should be at the top of the stack. The fact that it wasn't had him all flustered.

I, on the other hand, was fascinated. A professional trainer like Maggie will tell you that none of the levels is better or worse; they all have upsides, and downsides as well. They're just the stages that we all go through, naturally, as we learn a skill. Like shifting gears on your car, all have a positive place in the process. You move through all of them as you drive through a life's worth of learning.

So taking that long story and turning it around, what would the kind of non-hierarchal approach that Bookchin and I are both after look like? Well, first, there'd be no assumption of superiority or inferiority tied to position. There wouldn't be any kind of competitive, win-lose working relationship among the four levels. Nor would there be a correlation between the spot that a particular level sits on the chart and its value to the world. Instead you would start with the assumption that all the levels are equally important.

I hope this makes sense to others; for me, it was an amazing educational moment, in which, to adapt the title of Jonathan Safran Foer's fine novel (and the subsequent film), everything was illuminated. If, in our organizations, we think and order things hierarchically and competitively, as our client unconsciously did, then our culture is pretty inevitably going to be organized this way as well. Most situations will have winners and losers, and the winners will go "to the top" while the losers are left behind at the bottom.

What does this mean for you? It really just comes down to the way you want your organization to operate. If you're good with hierarchy, and most people in the world seem to be, then don't stress on it at all. But if you're open to a thought-provoking thought, coming from a guy who worked at the fringes of intellectual society, then give it a bit of time and see what it might mean to you. Or better still, talk about it with a couple of other out-of-the-box thinkers and see what they say. There is, in any case, no "correct" answer here. Only the clear correlation between our thinking and the way we work and lead.

A Not-So-Great Take on "Employee Ownership"

As per Secret #32 on the subject of Choice, the way we speak has a lot to do with how we think. Conversely, the way we converse is often a good way to get a read on what's going on in our heads. As we work to assess and perhaps adjust our thinking, our language is often a good place to look for insights.

One of those clues is summed up in what follows. It has to do with the unconscious implication of ownership. We're very mindful here at

Zingerman's of our use of pronouns. Although there are some situations in which it's unavoidable, I really work to avoid acting like I'm the lord of some medieval organizational manor. We're doing a lot of work right now to develop ways for Zingerman's staffers to own a share in our business— we're all about that form of employee ownership. But I'm not big on the sort that implies—through certain kinds of language—that we "own our employees." Take a look—or maybe a listen—to the phrases that follow, and see what you think.

What's commonly used	What we say here
"My business"	"Our business," or "We"
"My managers"	"Our management team"
"My people"	"Everyone in the organization"

The words on the left imply that I own everyone and everything, commanding from my corporate castle. Think how people feel when an owner or an executive talks about them as if they're property. "My people" has implications of indentured servitude, not independently minded team members thinking freely and feeling like leaders in their own right. The words in the right column, by contrast, share the power—we are all in this together. The sense of collective ownership, shared stress, and also shared success, makes an enormous difference. While the feeling behind the words will also make a difference, even just changing the words alone will work wonders.

I also work hard to make sure that new staff members (not, of course, *my* new employees) use language that implies collective ownership of our organization and places them, accurately, inside the collaborative process. If a new staff member makes a comment like, "I like Zingerman's because they . . ." I will politely but firmly set them back on course. "You mean, 'we,' right?" The question stumps them for a second, but eventually they get it. Once they choose to work with us and we've chosen to employ them, *they are* Zingerman's. And it's imperative that their language and internal mindset reflect that reality. It seems, perhaps, a small thing, but I will argue that it's actually huge.

What new staffers often say	What I ask them to say instead
"At Zingerman's, they . . ."	"At Zingerman's, we . . ."
"Zingerman's does . . ."	"We . . ."
"You guys give really great service . . ."	"We give really great service . . ."

Thinking About Thinking Collaboratively

Speaking of talking to others to inform our ideas, let me come back to the idea of thinking collaboratively that I touched on earlier. The insight on this one came to me courtesy of an article by Kenneth Bruffee, English professor emeritus at Brooklyn College, called "Collaborative Learning and the Conversation of Mankind." Like Murray Bookchin, Bruffee's approach is a bit more academic in style than mine, and it took me a couple of read-throughs of his article to really get it. But after turning the essay around in my mind a few times, and talking to a few friends to get context, another really big light bulb went off in my head. What Bruffee suggests is brilliant: the way we dialogue with others around us is really just a reflection of the way the conversations are generally already happening inside our heads.

To quote Bruffee directly: "because thought is internalized conversation, thought and conversation tend to work largely in the same way . . . If my talk is narrow, superficial, biased, and confined to clichés, my thinking is likely to be so too." I'm still sorting out exactly what all this means for interviewing, hiring, training, etc., but I think the insight is enormous. It gives me a much better understanding of why some folks who like the *idea* of collaboration still have a hard time working that way. If you're accustomed to processing ideas and making decisions on your own, it's likely that you're going to struggle to work well in an inclusive, collaborative context.

Luckily, according to Bruffee, thinking collaboratively is a teachable and learnable skill. "To think well as individuals," he says, "we must learn to think well collectively—that is, we must learn to converse well. The first steps to learning to think better, therefore, are learning to converse better and learning to establish and maintain the sorts of social context, the sorts of community life, that foster the sorts of conversation members of the community value." In other words, if you want to become more inclusive in your thinking, start by practicing an inclusive conversation with real people, and allow that dialogue to impact what you decide. While you will still, of course, come to your own conclusions, the conversation can only help—the more we open ourselves to input and insight from diverse sources, the more we're likely to learn to think more openly and inclusively as well.[29]

Paul and I make very few meaningful decisions without bouncing them off any number of others who we think are knowledgeable on the subject. That's probably true of most leaders in our organization. It is, as per Bruffee's point, a collaborative conversation that goes on in, and out of, our heads. When an idea presents itself (or is presented), we process it a bit on our own. But then we move quickly into collaboration—we start asking others we respect for their opinions and use that information to adapt what we're thinking. Honestly, other than in a crisis where command decisions are called for, I don't know if I could even make a big decision without that kind of collaborative conversation.

In fact, what you're reading in these pages (and throughout the entire book) is a reflection of collaborative thoughts, filtered through my own instincts and judgment, and then brought together into one—hopefully coherent—piece of prose. I've probably consulted with thirty or forty folks just during the writing of the early drafts: everyone from an internationally known professor of organizational studies to a couple of teenagers working at the Deli. Each person has given me some insight into the issues at hand. Collaboration doesn't guarantee success, but when it's well managed, it will pretty much always make for a more effective decision, better implementation, and a more resilient organization. What does well managed mean? It means that we stay true to our guts throughout, and that we include the voices of recognized experts as well as those who are traditionally left out of the conversation.

It's not for me to say here that thinking on one's own is an unproductive process. What I do know, though, is that this sort of limited-spectrum conversation is not effective for us here. What I know with ever more clarity (the more I write and bounce this concept off others I care about, the more I believe it to be true) is that collaboration is the way we want to work here at Zingerman's.

Finding a Constructive Community with Which to Collaborate

One difficult part of this collaborative thinking thing is that if you connect with the wrong people, your fragile, fledgling ideas are likely to get crushed like—well, you can make up your own ugly metaphor. The point is, it won't be pretty. If you don't pick the right people, the responses you'll get to your ideas are likely to simply reinforce the status quo instead of nurturing your slightly crazy-sounding intuitions.

So how do you know whom to go to as your collaborative partners? I'd go to folks who share your values, who think creatively and caringly, and who will be interested to hear your thoughts and then share their own. Colleagues like that can be hard to find, but it's worth the effort. I look for people whose energy is positive, whose egos rarely get in the way, and whose curiosity about the world is high. People who, to some degree, are aligned with what I'm doing but who still have enough of a different view that they see things I've failed to see or say things I've failed to say. When an idea is just forming for me, I'm not going to send it straight to the board of directors meeting, nor will I call up those who will likely be opposed to it to ask for their response. At this stage, I need nurturing, not nuclear attack. Friendly voices that can give criticism and suggestions from a supportive and insightful place are resources to be treasured.

My loving and much-loved friend Daphne Zepos was one of those people. Sadly, she passed away while I was writing this book. You can read more about her, and what she brought to my life and others, in the epilogue. Expanding on the concept in the moment, let me quote the powerfully insightful poet David Whyte, from his book *Crossing the Unknown Sea*: "Each of us must identify in our personal history those who represented freedom in the world, those who managed to live just outside the rules, who seemed not beholden to the forces that held others in place . . . who seemed to exude freedom by the way they lived, who [weren't] slave[s] to all the truths repeated so easily by others, who had a breath of spontaneity in their lives."

Abundance Thinking

Here at Zingerman's we want to operate with an abundance mentality. We work with the belief that there's plenty of intellectual insight (and most everything else as well) out there for everyone. And that the more success others around us have, the more we and everyone else are going to have. All of which has made us a center for interesting ideas, which in turn seeds and breeds the kind of creativity that keeps us on the cutting edge.

Following this thread . . .

If we as leaders start our thought process from a position of scarcity, it's pretty likely that outlook will prevail within the organization overall. In other words, if we look at ideas as if they're a limited resource, one we need to protect, to be considered only in the proper time and place, it's likely that information will not flow freely through the organization.

If we look at the world in a win-lose way, then everything our competition gains must, by definition, mean our loss; that mindset will more than likely be manifested inside the organization as well. When information is held close to the vest, we start to suffocate the natural creativity in the organization.

If the way we respond to a new idea is to worry about how it could mess up what we've already got rather than imagining the successes we might gain, then we're likely to create an organizational mindset where potential new initiatives are minimized and marginalized long before they have a chance to really make a difference.

That sort of win-lose, zero-sum game mindset often dominates the world's worldview. And yet, as Steven Johnson says, "environments that build walls around good ideas tend to be less innovative in the long run than more open-ended situations." The more you restrict ideas, the lower the odds of more coming in.

To quote the most anarchistic of American presidents, Thomas Jefferson, "it is the action of the thinking power called an idea, which an individual may exclusively possess as long as he keeps it to himself; but the moment it is divulged, it forces itself into the possession of every one, and the receiver cannot dispossess himself of it. Its peculiar character, too, is that no one possesses the less, because every other possesses the whole of it. He who receives an idea from me, receives instruction himself without lessening mine; as he who lights his taper at mine, receives light without darkening me."

Staying True to Yourself—the Insight of the Individual

While working with others is a critical skill, it's imperative to remember that it's each of us as individuals, not some theoretical team acting in lockstep, that leads us forward. Creative ideas and insights come from individuals, operating often in a group setting, but not from a group acting as a single entity. Effective leaders learn from extensive interaction with others and their thinking is meaningfully informed by input from colleagues, customers, and others. But greatness, significant insight, and out-of-the-box ideas will still almost always come from a single strong-minded, focused individual.

From a strictly personal standpoint, that means we need to guard our gut feelings, stay in touch with and stay true to ourselves, and not bail immediately on what we believe in just because the rest of the organizational body doesn't rise up in unison and say "amen!" From an organizational standpoint, it means we need to protect and nurture the ability of every person in the business to think for themselves. To nurture new staffers so they don't feel their voices are irrelevant. To keep those of us who've been here longer and can unconsciously and quickly dominate a conversation from quashing others' views, while still speaking up for what's right. Speaking from experience, that's no simple challenge!

Does it make sense to say that being *in* the group, connected and collaborative, is generally a very good thing, but that groupthink is always bad? Or that getting input from others is integral to effective leadership, but that leaders (at any level) still need to step up and take the lead? Or that getting buy-in is a beautiful thing, but en route to securing it we as leaders will likely take flak from nearly every direction while we go for greatness? Should I just quote Steven Johnson, who says, "[Creativity] is not the wisdom of the crowd, but the wisdom of someone in the crowd . . . It's not that the network itself is smart; it's that the individuals get smarter because they're connected to the network." Or maybe I'll go back to Emma Goldman, who was adamant on this subject: "Every effort for progress, for enlightenment, for science, for religious, political, and economic liberty emanates from the minority, and not from the mass."

In the context of this essay, that would mean that the most effective and innovative leaders need to *think collaboratively*, but also, even when the rest of the world thinks we're a bit mad, *we still need to speak our minds with passion and purpose*. The paradox, the problem, the challenge is that to be more creative, we need to circulate among others, yet at the same time we need to stay true to ourselves. Poet David Whyte says it so well: "One of the distinguishing features of any courageous human being is the ability to remain unutterably themselves in the midst of conforming pressures. The surprising realization is that our friends can try to make us conform as much as our worst enemies. The excuses to fall away, to lose courage, to be other than ourselves are ever present and incredibly intimate."

To the same point Peter Senge says, "The most effective people are those who can 'hold' their vision while remaining committed to seeing current reality clearly." I say, think big, involve others, travel widely (intellectually, emotionally, and physically), absorb all you can, make a multitude of connections, but still stay true to yourself throughout.

Thinking About the Case for Diversity in Thinking

If you run with my belief that the way we, as leaders, think is going to be significantly reflected in our own lives and in the way our organization operates, you'll also realize the inherent dangers this all implies. To wit, any organization is likely to have their leader's thinking patterns—and problems—embedded into its culture. Given that we all have strengths and weaknesses; given that it's a Natural Law that the two are actually connected on a continuum (see Secret #36); given that even if we're working on our weaknesses, it takes a long time to make them less of a problem—what's a good leader to do? Well, one thing I know from experience is that we can bring other brains into the mix, people that probably have very different and also hopefully complimentary ways of thinking. It's totally true for me and Paul. While we share vision, values, and work ethic, we also approach many (if not most) issues from opposite ends of the thinking spectrum. While that can feel frustrating in the moment, it makes, I believe, for a healthier organization.[30]

But the benefits of diversity don't need to be limited to the owners or top executives. One can use the positive impact of different thinking styles by bringing even more brains into the mix as well. When one thinking pattern predominates, the organization is likely to be vulnerable to anything that attacks its areas of weakness. Different thinking styles may cause discord in the short term, but when there's a commitment to shared values, shared vision, and ongoing collaborative dialogue, those differences serve to make our organizations more resilient, healthier, more sustainable, and more successful. As anarchist author Eunice Schuster said early in the 20th century, "Diversity in unity, unity in diversity is the ideal."

Murray Bookchin makes a good case for diversity in an organization as well, though as per usual, he does so in less-than-simple language. "Ecological wholeness is . . . a dynamic unity of diversity. In nature, balance and harmony are achieved by ever-changing differentiation, by ever-expanding diversity. Ecological stability, in effect, is a function not of simplicity and homogeneity, but of complexity and variety. The capacity of an ecosystem to retain its integrity depends . . . on its diversity." It's a natural and healthy way to work.

Hold That Thought: the Importance of Sticking with an Idea

If our organizations reflect the way we think, then the attention span we show for ideas that have—at one time at least—inspired us is surely going to have a significant impact on our organizations. While sticking with something to the finish comes more naturally to some of us than others, ultimately we need a way to make sure our minds don't drift off too soon, before our insight has been followed up on and implemented. Worse still, if most of the things we think up are never finished, the organization is essentially eternally stuck spinning its wheels on intellectual ice. There may be a lot of noise but almost no meaningful movement forward. Ultimately, integrity implodes, disillusionment and distrust dominate the culture, and poor performance follows. Being able to stick with an idea—both in your mind and in your management work—until it's been successfully put into place is an important skill if you want a business where big things actually get done.

Another downside of not sticking with your intuitive insights is that you really can't tell which of your gut feelings is good. In other words, if all your intuitive sparks stay as ideas without ever being implemented, you have no data on which to assess your own intuitive ability. As Robert Greenleaf wrote in *On Becoming a Servant Leader,* "Unless insights are acted on, they don't speak with assurance."

This struggle to finish is a great example of how our strengths will generally lead to our weaknesses. The good news for folks who have a lot of ideas is that they're bringing their creativity to the fore; the bad news is that they frequently abandon these ideas long before they arrive at effective implementation. As Paul told me 30 years or so ago, "professionalism is sticking with things long after the initial glamour is gone!" This essay is, in itself, a testament to the idea of sticking with stuff. I started it three years ago, restarted it more than once, then began again, divided it into two, and only now am finalizing it. Soon, it will hopefully be woven into our regular teaching routines and will help us be more mindful about the way we think. I'm glad I persevered.

It occurred to me while writing this wrap-up that perhaps the reason I never noticed the parallels between the anarchists and the progressive business world until recently is that I wasn't ready. It's not that I wasn't smart enough. I just had a lot of work to do to set my spirit free to find the connection. David Whyte, writing in *The Heart Aroused: Poetry and the Preservation of the Soul in Corporate America*, tells us, "The alchemists maintained that we can create only in our own image. That is everything takes form according to the consciousness that shaped it . . . It is essential, then, to know what is vital and alive inside us and shape our lives in its image." Quite simply, it took me a long time to begin thinking like an anarcho-capitalist.

I was still too constrained, too reactive, too fettered, too focused on the negative, too quick to judge, not free enough to see a connection that was actually close at hand all along. The concept is simple: *Before someone else's work or words can inspire you, you have to be ready to be inspired.* It makes sense, then, that only in the last few years, when my mind has been less weighed down with worry and more inclined towards having fun, was I ready to bridge two schools of thought. I'd been drawn to anarchist beliefs intellectually but never internalized them; only after years of mindful self-management, after I'd already been thinking like an anarchist for a while, could the idea of anarcho-capitalism come clear so quickly one day. After all, as anarchist Gustav Landauer wrote, "a goal can only be reached if it is already reflected in its means." Or in the words of the more contemporary anarchist Peggy Kornegger, "As we speak, we change, and as we change, we transform ourselves and the future simultaneously." If I can make a slight tweak to this formulation: as we think differently, we change, and as we change, we transform ourselves and our futures, simultaneously.

Let me just close out my thoughts on thinking with one last comment said about—rather than by—Emma Goldman. Just after Goldman's death in Toronto in 1940, her friend Frieda Diamond said of her, "She opened your mind and made you think about things you never thought about before." I hope this piece sparks some strange thoughts of your own!

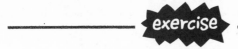

Mindful Thinking

1. Track your reaction to new ideas as they come in. You can list the idea, followed by how you felt when you heard, read, or thought of it. And then write down what you said and/or did immediately after coming across it.

2. Pick a couple of ideas that you like and then keep track of what happens to them. Note how and when you thought of them; who, if anyone, you talked to about them, and the responses you got; and if you decided to go forward with the ideas, how you attempted to implement them. One workable way to do this is to keep a separate list, journal, or file on the computer where you can track all your actions and interactions around each idea. The chart may extend out for any number of months, or even years, to see how the process fares.

notes from the back dock

Heather Kendrick, Sandwich Runner, Zingerman's Delicatessen

I was fortunate to spend a weekend last spring at the Institute for Musicianship and Public Service offered by Community MusicWorks, an arts organization, in Providence, Rhode Island. Throughout the seminar, I became increasingly aware and thankful that I could communicate with professional musicians and organizational specialists because of my experiences at Zingerman's. I was by far the youngest person in attendance, but felt comfortable and confident participating because I understand community, visioning, and our guiding principles. I was able to contribute because I have been exposed to business and leadership training since my first day at the Deli. I was hardly conscious of how much and how thoroughly I had internalized these ideals because our training is so FUN! It was fulfilling to draw parallels between what we do at Zingerman's and what great community music programs are doing. I'm so grateful to Ari, Paul, and the ZCoB for preparing me for my future—a career sharing the gift of music through performance, teaching, and arts advocacy.

Brandon Clark, Line Cook, Zingerman's Roadhouse; Farmer, Cornman Farms

I won't lie. Working for Zingerman's has its highs and lows. Unfortunately when I began my career here, I was more concerned with chemical highs. I managed to fool a lot of people. Hardly anyone knew the extent of my drug use. I still worked hard—when I showed up. Sadly, though, my addiction got the better of me and I managed to miss one too many shifts. I was fired.

My boss clearly recognized that I needed extensive help. I was given one glimmer of hope upon my firing—that I may return upon completion of a substance abuse program and maintained significant clean time. Chef Alex held out hope for me at a time when I had very little. He recognized that when I wasn't screwing up my own life, I still had potential value to the company.

I've been back at Zingerman's for over a year now. I treat every day as an opportunity to show how grateful I am to be given a second chance. Getting fired for my actions was the best thing that could have happened to me. It has helped me reevaluate my life's direction and strive to be a better person to myself and others. I truly love working for such a great organization and I look forward to many more years of service to the Zingerman's Community!

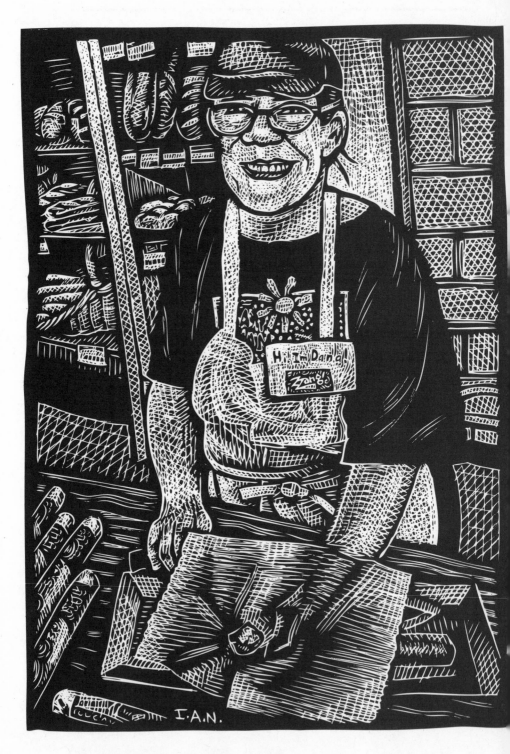

dana Laidlaw brightening up the counter at the bakehouse

Creating Creativity

Falling in Love With Your Inner Anarchist

Creativity is a nearly universally sought-after attribute. I really can't think of anyone I've ever met that didn't want to have more of it. The funny thing is that unlike baking a cake or building a cathedral, you can't really design and create creativity—it kind of just happens. What you can do, though, is actively build an environment in which creativity, encouraged rather than encumbered, is much more likely to occur. We've done a great deal of that sort of work here over the years, and with really good results to show for it.

The interesting thing, though, is that until I started work on this essay, I really couldn't have explained to you what it was we were doing to make that happen. Paul and I and other leaders here have prided ourselves on being creative thinkers, and the organization has, as per the last Secret on thinking, followed creative suit. But having given it much more thought of late, it's clear to me that we were all, by training standards, unconsciously competent: good at being creative but clueless about what we were doing that was making it happen.

What follows, in essence, brings together all the other work in this book. It's an exercise in self-awareness, a move towards mindfulness, and a tribute to the power of living the Twelve Natural Laws. In the context of the essay on Edgar Schein's stages of organizational development, the creative constructs that follow could help you lead your organization from the intuitive and instinctive creative work of a successful start-up straight on through to mindfully designing a culture and systems for a much larger, but equally creative, organization.

One caveat before we begin. Although everyone is interested in the idea of being in a creative setting and living a creative life, I'm not sure that all of us are ready to do what it takes to really increase the odds of it happening: sharing information widely; releasing control; encouraging the crazy, can't-quite-figure-out-what-to-do-with-them kind of ideas that challenge the status quo and our existing realities. As poet David Whyte writes, "When it comes to the moment of truth, both the organization and the individual are equally afraid of the creativity, the passion, and the courage that accompany those powers hidden within them and that are central to their vitality." But if we push past the fear, we can realize wonderful things!

The essay that follows, then, is my only recently realized take on how we, and other creative companies and individuals I know, have cultivated our minds and our methods to make creativity an everyday, even kind of ordinary, occurrence. If you're drawn primarily to the practical, skip straight to Part 2, *which gets into the how-tos of taking creativity to the next level.* Part 1 *is mostly about the theoretical background—how and why creativity works, and why it's lacking in so much of modern American society.* Part 3, *at the end, offers a bit of reflection, with the benefit of hindsight aplenty, on why and how what we do here has created such a creative and innovative culture at Zingerman's. Pick any part, read in any order you like, learn as you will. I trust your creative instincts to inspire you to ever-greater heights.*

———

Part I: Connections, Missed and Made, and a Quick Look at the Contemporary Creativity Crisis

CONNECTING COMPLIMENTS

About ten years ago, my partner Paul Saginaw paid me a compliment. It's hardly the only one he's given me over the last thirty years, but for some reason, what he said that day has stuck in my mind ever since. It wasn't any of the standard stuff one might really want to hear—about being smart, hard working, handsome, fun, patient, or blessed with a good palate. What Paul said was: "You have a rare ability to draw a meaningful connection and find the common theme between almost any two things." I really didn't know why, but his compliment struck a chord. I don't think anyone else had ever said anything like that to me.

What happened after Paul passed on his observation actually kind of contradicted the compliment he'd given me. Because in the ten years that his words have been resting quietly and comfortably in a back corner of my mind, I'd never made a single meaningful connection between his compliment and anything else. Oddly, his comment about my ability to connect the seemingly unconnected was one insight for which I'd failed to find an intellectual collaborator. Until now. A decade down the road, I think I've figured out what it was about that compliment that was so compelling to my subconscious. I didn't know it at the time, but I do now—the skill for which Paul praised me turns out to one of the critical components of creative thinking.

As with many creative insights, Paul's remark lay dormant for a long time before something else came along to complete the thought. In this case, the connection came when I read Steven Johnson's book *Where Good Ideas Come From: the Natural History of Innovation.* The number one thing on Johnson's list for creative thinkers is "A capacity to make new connections with as many other elements as possible." It's not exactly the way Paul presented it, but it's clearly the same concept—the prime force behind creativity is the act of connection! And with that understanding, I finally realized why Paul's previously unattached comment had resonated. I greatly value creative, cutting-edge, out-of-the-ordinary thinking. Paul's compliment was one of the best anyone could have given me.

CALLING FOR CREATIVITY

Before we delve more into creative connections, let me take you back a few years, to the dark days of the economic morass of 2009–10. After fifteen years of doing ZingTrain work and speaking all over the country, we suddenly started getting a whole mess of requests for me to present on a subject I'd never ever spoken on. You guessed it—the calls were all about creativity. Each was some version of "With the economy tanking like this, we really need to crank up our creativity! You guys are so great at it. We want you to come speak and share your secrets." Or "We want you to help our people learn how to build an innovative organization the way you guys have!" I was honored, but at the same time caught off guard. I didn't doubt that Zingerman's was a creative, trend-setting business. That I knew. The problem was that we'd never done a day—or an hour, or even ten minutes—of training, teaching, or writing specifically focused on the subject of creativity.

Over the years, we'd developed effective organizational "recipes" for service, quality, and complaint handling. I'd presented extensively—both within our own organization and around the country—on visioning, customer service, Servant Leadership, open book finance, training techniques, marketing, and management. But we had nothing—not even an idea of an outline—on innovation. How, I wondered to myself, could we have been so out of it that we'd completely missed such an important concept? Stumped, I then decided I'd spend some time talking to the clients from whom we'd gotten the inquiries to find out more about what they wanted.

The good news was that they were quite enthused about the idea of me coming to talk. "You guys do such a good job with it," one said. "Just tell 'em what you do!" Others asked more specific questions. One guy who runs an innovation department at a big company wondered, "Who at Zingerman's is responsible for innovation?" Heck. I had no idea. It seemed like a reasonable question, but it threw me off. Today I could answer it confidently and calmly in about two seconds. But back then, I really had no idea what to say.

Who was responsible for our creativity? It's as if he'd asked me who was responsible for breathing. I stuttered and stumbled a bit before muttering, "Everyone, I guess." (It turns out that was totally the right answer, but at the time, I was very unsure of what I was saying.) "Do you give people dedicated time for innovation?" another woman wanted to know. That really left me feeling foolish—we didn't set aside any time at all. I'd never realized we should. "But don't you teach classes on it?" still another person asked. "Well, no," was my honest answer. "We've never taught one at all."

I was starting to feel like an innovation imposter. Clearly, our clients were convinced that we were really creative, and that we had the kind of caring-capitalist-cool they were looking for. And yet, here I was basically coming up empty when it came to talking about it. "When do your people innovate?" one client asked. "Well," I managed to get out, "I guess they innovate all day long. That's what we all do. All day. Everyone innovates, every day. I can't really imagine how we would work without it."

I stayed stumped for about six weeks. I couldn't really figure it out. We were just trying to do good work, and somehow, almost unwittingly, what we'd come up with was considered a hugely creative way of working. I kept looking for insights into our innovation, but I kept coming back to basics—we weren't teaching or preaching creativity, yet every day there were dozens of creative ideas being brought up and implemented all over our organization. We had no constructs designed for creativity, no corporate program for it, no classes to teach it. Somehow, though, we'd made it happen anyway.

WHY GOOD WORK CREATES A CREATIVE CULTURE

In truth, I couldn't understand how it could be otherwise. How could you have an even kind of successful company, or employees who you thought were doing a good job, if creativity weren't involved? The question caused me consternation, but it also made realize that we must have a different definition of what it means to do a "good job" than most mainstream organizations. The difference, I realized, was partly in the wording. When you hear about someone who does a "good job," more often than not they're being praised for following orders, completing tasks they've been assigned by their "superiors." Having (and doing) a good job is way better than having (or doing) a bad job, which, in turn, is still a bunch of times better than having *no* job. But, I realized, what we're trying to do here at Zingerman's is to provide more than a good job—we've set our organizational sights on *good work!*

Good work like this is, by definition, all about creative energy. It's work that helps people be themselves, that taps their natural abilities it's work people care about, in a workplace that cares about them. When people do good work, they're enjoying what they do and feeling fulfilled and rewarded by it. As Sir Kenneth Robinson writes in *Out of Our Minds*, "Real creativity comes from finding your medium, from being in your element." It happens best, I believe, when we work in harmony with the Natural Laws of Business. *Good work is, by definition, creative; it can't but bring out the creativity that's innately present in each of us.* When people are doing *good work*, feeling good about themselves and what they do, in an environment that encourages them to think freely and be frank about both their fears and their fantasies, creativity comes naturally. So much so that most people who are doing good work in this context don't even know they're being creative! They, like me and most of the folks who work at Zingerman's, probably can't imagine life any other way.

Everyone Is Creative

On the surface, at least, nearly all the social credit for creativity seems to be given to the superstars. Media focus is almost always on the talented artists, the brilliant writers, the record-breaking musicians, the prize-winning scientists, the world-class "creatives," the people who cut the edge and then sew it back together in unique, attention-getting, world-changing ways. In the corporate world, creativity is often attributed to "R & D," "marketing," or maybe a carefully cultivated "innovation team." These folks are treated as if they're some special "creative class," privileged enough to have been given—whether by god or genetic chance—some innovative gene that the rest of us don't have access to. While much of what comes from that upper class of creativity is certainly worth admiring, I'm far more focused—as I usually am—on everyone else. The creative organizational edge, I would argue, isn't to be found by CEOs getting more brilliant or by innovation experts being more insightful—it's in tapping the generally underutilized creative force of the folks on the frontlines.

Although skill levels in most fields may range widely from one person to the next, we're actually all pretty equally endowed when it comes to creativity. I like the way writer Hugh MacLeod, in his excellent book *Ignore Everybody*, puts it: "Everyone is born creative; everyone is given a box of crayons in kindergarten. Then when you hit puberty they take the crayons away and replace them with dry, uninspiring books on algebra, history, etc. Being suddenly hit years later with the 'creative bug' is just a wee voice telling you, 'I'd like my crayons back, please.'"

Which is hilarious, because one night not too long ago, a guest at the Roadhouse told me that when they got seated for dinner, the hostess gave her artistically oriented child three or four crayons to draw with. When the hostess walked back by a few minutes later, the kid politely asked for a few more. And, his mother explained, "She came back and gave him a *whole* box! He was thrilled. And I realized right then that that was my metaphor for coming to Zingerman's. Everywhere else you go, they just give you a couple of crayons to work with. But when you come to Zingerman's, it's like you get a whole box of crayons to color with every time you come in!"

Science fiction writer Rod Serling, who I'm sure knew more about UFOs than IPOs, said much the same thing: "Ideas are probably in the air, like little tiny items of ozone. That's the easiest thing on earth, to come up with an idea." Brenda Ueland, whose insights changed the way I write, had this to say on the subject: "Everybody is original, if he tells the truth, if he speaks from himself. But it must be from his true self and not from the self he thinks he should be." Children left to play on their own consistently prove themselves way more creative than the average adult; playfulness provokes positive energy, which in turn cultivates creativity.

Which brings me back to Emma Goldman's great line: "Anarchism is the spirit of youth against outworn tradition." Thinking creatively, she clearly knew, need not depend on chronological age. It's all about attitude. Acting young, thinking youthfully and anarchistically, without the standard constraints of a conservative adulthood, consistently brings about the kind of positive energy that underlies pretty much everything good you can imagine. When it comes to creativity, the people really do have the power!

UNCONSCIOUSLY COMPETENT CREATIVITY

While teaching this approach to creating a creative organization for the first time, it struck me that the stages of learning a skill (see page 334) actually operate in reverse when it comes to human creativity. With most skills, we start out "unconsciously incompetent." In other words, we don't know what we don't know and we don't know how to do the task at hand. With a training demonstration, we move to "consciously incompetent." We still can't do it, but at least we sort of know what "it" is. With a lot of mindful practice, we move to "conscious competence"—we know what we're doing and we're mindfully good at it. And then over time, with a great deal of repetition, most of us will become "unconsciously competent." We no longer think about what we're doing—we're good at it, but we no longer pay much attention while we're doing it.

It dawned on me, though, that with personal creativity we actually move through those levels in reverse. Because everyone is born creative, we actually come into the world unconsciously competent in our creativity. As kids we all have it, but we can't explain what it is we're doing or why it works. As we grow up, socialization and "training" in the family and school move us to conscious competence—we can still be creative, but we're pushed into constructs that require us to be much more mindful. Told to draw a dog, Jimmy might draw a giraffe. "That's not a dog, Jimmy," the teacher makes clear. "Now try again." As we get older, a select few are allowed to pursue their art, but most of us are told, subtly or directly, that we're not "creative types," and that we need to get serious in thinking about how we're going to make our living. With enough outside pressure and an increasing sense of self-doubt, I think most of us actually slide into being "consciously incompetent." We know that there is creativity at work in the world, we hear it and see it and taste it prepared by others, but "we're not creative." At that point, our self-consciousness starts to erode our natural abilities. The result is the sort of creative apathy I allude to on page 360. For the majority of us who were told we weren't all that creative, the challenge then is to relax enough and let our natural abilities reemerge—to stop thinking and just have some fun connecting the creative dots!

How Hierarchal Thinking Hurts Creativity

It seems reasonable to assume that experience and education would make for better-rounded, more effective individuals. But when it comes to creativity, the data is that advanced degrees, seniority, and impressive titles make no difference whatsoever. Steven Johnson shows statistically that there's absolutely no correlation between creativity quotients and any of the usual credentials that earn people social and organizational status. Moving up the org chart, growing older, having a bigger office or a fancier car may matter to some, but they count for naught when it comes to being creative.

To the contrary, if we're not careful, creativity levels can actually decrease as we mature and move up the corporate ladder. From the outside looking in, at least, that may seem strange. But a deeper look makes it clear how that happens. Old-school organizations still tend to confine creative activity to a certain department, or to owners and managers; everyone else is instructed to just implement the ideas the elites initiate. Since so much is filtered out and lost as it moves up through the hierarchy, there's actually limited access to real-life information from the frontlines. As people grow more attached to the status quo, it becomes harder to bust out and break down barriers everyone has accepted for so long. If you sketched out a creativity pyramid, it would probably work in reverse to the way the hierarchical organization operates. Decisions are mostly made at the top, but the potential for innovation and insight are more readily found at the wider base.

Jonah Lehrer, in his book *Imagine,* makes a comparable case. "The people deep inside a domain often suffer from a kind of intellectual handicap. As a result, the impossible problem stays impossible. It's not until the challenge is shared with motivated outsiders that the solution can be found." In the old model, the people "inside the domain" are those at the top of the organization. The "outsiders" are all around them—the frontline folks they employ but rarely engage with. Instead, upper level execs hire high-end firms and spend big bucks to gain innovative insight. I'd suggest at least experimenting with a lower-cost option: creating a constructive framework in which everyone in the organization is involved. As David Whyte writes, "Companies need the contributing vitality of all the individuals who work for them in order to stay alive in the sea of changeability in which they find themselves. They must find a real way of asking people to bring these hidden, heartfelt qualities into the workplace." Or as Pablo Picasso famously said, "All children are artists. The problem is how to remain an artist once he grows up."[31]

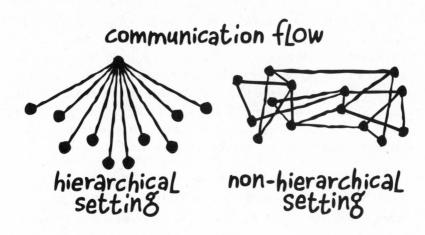

communication flow

hierarchical setting

non-hierarchical setting

What all of this comes down to is bad organizational algebra—if all of the insights are supposed to come from the top of an organization (small or large, for- or not-for-profit), then by definition, we're missing out on the majority of our collective creative ability. As Sir Kenneth Robinson says, "The role of a creative leader is not to have all the ideas; it's to create a culture where everyone can have ideas and feel that they're valued." Business writer Steven Johnson (sounding very much like an anarchist) maintains, "Hierarchical filtering of ideas constricts creativity . . . No matter how smart the 'authorities' may be, if they are outnumbered a thousand to one . . . there will be more good ideas lurking in the market than in the feudal castle." And anarchist Colin Ward (who sounds like a colleague of Steven Johnson's) warns, "the knowledge and wisdom of the people at the bottom of the pyramid finds no place in the decision making leadership hierarchy of the institution. If ideas are your business, you cannot afford to condemn most of the people in the organization to being merely machines programmed by somebody else."

ANARCHIST INSIGHT

To Ward's well-taken point, creativity is really at the core of what anarchism is all about: helping individuals remove the emotional, intellectual, and socioeconomic constraints that crimp their natural, inspirational, creative styles. Basque performance artist Esther Ferrer frames it beautifully in her 1991 letter to avant garde composer John Cage: "Anarchism shall always have a future, and a present, for the basic reason that I associate it with creativity. Please, I don't mean art, which is something else, much more limited. I am talking about creativity in the sense that it comes from rejoicing, from pleasure."

This theme of freeing people's hearts and minds and encouraging natural innovative ability runs throughout anarchist activity. Earlier in the last century Sam Dolgoff wrote, "What is needed is emancipation from authoritarian institutions *over* society and authoritarianism *within* the organizations themselves. Above all, they must be infused with revolutionary spirit and confidence in the creative capacities of the people." Colin Ward, writing in *Anarchy in Action,* argues much the same thing: "knowledge and wisdom are not distributed in order of rank, and they are no one person's monopoly in any undertaking."

INTELLECTUAL AND EMOTIONAL ATROPHY: THE ANTITHESIS OF ANARCHIST CREATIVITY?

Getting people involved at every level of an organization of any sort will, almost certainly, mess with the modern model of hierarchy and order. But if we let conformity trump creativity, we'll never have an innovative organization. Sure, life will be safer, on the surface at least, more stable and more predictable. But it will pretty certainly be slipping steadily towards stagnation and failure. Which is why, I believe, all these well-known companies started calling ZingTrain to inquire about our training on innovation when the economic crisis came down. After years of playing it safe, they were caught, suddenly, creatively unprepared. That old-school, in-the-box way of doing business doesn't work well in the 21st century. To quote positive psychologist Martin Seligman, "In the modern world, I believe we have finally arrived at an era in which more creative thinking, less rote following of orders—and yes, even more enjoyment—will succeed better."

The problem for so many organizations, though, is you can't play it safe for a decade and then suddenly demand instantaneous innovation. Well, you can demand it, but I seriously doubt you're going to get it. "Planned spontaneity" and "forced creativity" would probably make a good match in a dating service for bad organizational idioms. As Sir Kenneth Robinson writes, "Companies are keen to promote [creativity] but they're not sure what it is or who has it." Sure, as I've been saying, everyone is born creative. But you can't immediately get in shape after eighteen years of idleness just by deciding you want to be and then willing it be so. When we don't use what we've got, we lose the ability to use it. Can it be regained? Of course! It just requires major effort in emotional rehabilitation.

This image—the connection, I should say, since we're talking about creativity—came clear to me while I was doing some rehab of my own. I was recovering from a series of surgeries, none of them life threatening, but still serious enough to mess with my physical and mental state. One unintended short-term consequence of the surgeries was that I started to suffer from what's known in the physical therapy field as "frozen shoulder." Essentially, my shoulder had atrophied; it became nearly impossible to reach my arm above shoulder height. It's hard to explain to someone who hasn't experienced it, but it's a pretty painful and incredibly awkward state to be in. I never knew how much reaching I did every day until I couldn't do it.

And yet people can learn to compensate pretty quickly. It's amazing how much you can rearrange most everything you do in order to avoid having to reach for anything too high up. Not sure what to have for dinner? Why not make something from stuff stored lower down, so you can stay away from the top shelves? Wondering what to wear? How about that shirt on the bottom shelf? Seriously, it doesn't take that long to reorganize your life so as to avoid any activity above shoulder height. The problem is that, in essence, this eliminates at least half of our natural range and reach. And one day, in a crisis, when we need to access something important that's high up, we simply can't do it.

Fortunately, for me, the problem was pretty short lived. Within a few months, I was back to about 90 percent of my previous capacity, and today my shoulder is fully functional. But as it happened, my shoulder problems coincided with all these queries about creativity. And one day it dawned on me that, in the same way my shoulder muscles had atrophied and normal, unconscious movements had become painful, awkward, and even at times impossible, so too the creative skills of much of the corporate world have atrophied. While everyone is born creative, organizations have tapped into these skills so infrequently that the people who work in them have lost their abilities. Even in time of crisis, they simply couldn't access them. And so they'd called ZingTrain.

Part 2: Restoring the Spirit:
Keys to Creating an Environment Conducive to Creativity

So how do we help people bring their atrophied creativity back? Or closer to home, why had we at Zingerman's (and others of our creative organizational ilk) kept alive what others had so clearly lost? Innovation and creativity were so much a way of life in our world that we had no real sense of what we were doing or *why* it worked. And like anyone who's unconsciously competent at anything, we weren't able to really explain to others how to re-create our success.

What follows, then, are a dozen and a half different connections, insights about innovation and quirky creativity that have come to me from studying the subject. Each one has contributed to building the creative culture we have here, as well as, no doubt, many other creative settings all around the world. If you're looking to increase your creativity quotient, here are some good ways to start the work. They are all very much about moving from unconscious competence to high levels of consciousness. I'm no longer stumped about how to nurture creativity and innovation. In fact, by the time you read this, I will surely have taught my first class in organizational creativity![32]

1. GET AROUND CREATIVE PEOPLE

It turns out that the biggest thing anyone can do to increase their innovative ability is to go hang around in a creative environment. Quite simply, if you work in an organization that's highly invigorating and regularly innovating, it's very likely that you'll soon be coming up with cool stuff too. Which means that the direct answer to everyone's question about how we got people working in such creative ways here at Zingerman's was simply that we had provided them with a creative environment in which to work. It's straight out of Natural Law #4—People do their best work when they're part of a great organization. So it only follows that people do their *most creative work* when they're part of a *creative* organization as well.

Of course, on a practical level, this isn't very helpful. It's a bit like answering someone's query about how to increase profitability by saying, "Make more money." And yet, as circular as the logic seems, it's clearly an accurate statement. You don't have to have a degree in anthropology to figure out that cultures are generally self-reinforcing—over time, any culture is likely to do more of what the culture already does, which in this case means acting creatively. As Sir Kenneth Robinson writes in *Out of Our Minds*, "Creativity is related to culture. Cultural conditions can kindle or kill creativity." I'm focusing on the kindling—the more someone works in a creative setting, the more creative stuff they're likely to do. Which means, in turn, that the place they work is going to be—you guessed it—more creative too, which in turn means its members will act in more innovative ways.

Healthy, innovative ecosystems are then, to some degree, self-sustaining—creative people (both staff and customers, and now that I think about it, suppliers) are drawn to them and deliver unto them all sorts of new, ever-more innovative activity. And, not to be underestimated, they're cooler still because the cultures are more receptive to the creative ideas when they show up. Which again makes them more creative and successful still. To wit, the reason I started reading Steven Johnson's book on the history of good ideas was because it was recommended to me by a good—and I'd guess very creative—customer.

It's like some sort of law of karmic creativity: the more innovative you are, the more you share what you create, the more creativity is likely to come your way. I shouldn't have been surprised then when, a week or so after I started reading Johnson's book, Deli staffer Chad Hayes brought me a second tome on the same subject: *Imagine: How Creativity Works* by Jonah Lehrer. A lot of people had recommended it to Chad, so he got himself a copy and picked one up for me too as a gift. Lehrer's work enhanced my thinking and understanding of the subject still further.

So if the number one thing to do to build creativity in an organization is to establish a creative setting for people to work in, then the big question is clearly, "What can we do to design a creative setting in the first place?" You can get going as follows.

2. LIVE THE NATURAL LAWS OF BUSINESS (AND LIFE)

This one's kind of obvious after that long intro above: people who work in organizations that operate in harmony with the Natural Laws are almost always going to have higher energy. By definition (see Natural Law #12), the people in these kinds of organizations are having more fun and are far happier.

And when that happens, guess what? The data in both Johnson's and Lehrer's books shows very clearly that when people are happier and are having more fun, they're also far more creative. It's not rocket science. In settings that are in synch with the Natural Laws, innovation and idea generation almost always go way up. Live in harmony with nature and naturally occurring abilities—like creative thinking—come fairly quickly to the fore. You don't really have to do anything all that radical—just be you!

Living the Natural Laws both builds a healthy business and brings out the best in everyone in it. Which is why, I believe, if all you do is live the Natural Laws, you're very likely to be more creative. And if you're doing it well on an organization-wide level, you're pretty sure to be collectively more creative and successful still. As Englishman Herbert Read writes in his book *Poetry and Anarchism,* "The rule of reason—to live according to natural laws—this is also the release of the imagination." It's in this setting that people find their passion, vision out a vocation, pursue a life they love, and drive towards their dreams. And it's when the passion is high that we're often at our most creative.[33]

Why Startups Are So Conducive to Creativity

Having now studied a lot about creativity, I've made a new connection. Startups are so often creative because the almost inevitable reality is that all of what I've written about here are part of what life in a startup is all about. As Sir Kenneth Robinson writes in *Out of Our Minds,* "The most creative periods in the lives of organizations are often in the early stages of its work, where there was a rush of excitement about possibilities." People in those crazy early days of getting a business going are generally really bought in or they wouldn't be there. They're living the Natural Laws, which means their energy is high. And because almost everyone in a startup learns each other's work in order to assist wherever needed, connections happen far more quickly. A good startup is, in many ways then, an ideal setting for a surfeit of creativity. It's only as we gain success and grow, and then start to separate staff into areas of specialty, where people become bonded to the status quo, that the creativity so often starts to erode.

3. SHARE *LOTS* OF INFORMATION WITHIN YOUR ORGANIZATION

The third element of the equation is access to information within the business, and lots of it. The problem is most workplaces won't—or don't—do that. Most do the *opposite:* information isn't freely distributed, it's safeguarded. "The strange fact," Johnson explains, "is a great deal of the past two centuries of legal and folk wisdom about innovation has pursued the exact opposite argument, building walls between ideas . . . patents, digital rights management, intellectual property, trade secrets, proprietary technology." Keeping people tightly trapped in departmental silos without giving them a sense of how the business itself works and how it's doing is likely to drastically diminish creative thinking. Holding information and ideas close for security or other reasons is pretty sure to create the antithesis of a creative setting. On the other hand, open and active sharing of information encourages insight and innovation. Finding systemic and also unstructured ways to keep everyone in the know will work wonders. Granted, it takes time, but it's clearly an important investment in long-term innovation and effectiveness.

Here at Zingerman's that information is freely flowing in every direction almost all the time. All our meetings are open and agendas and notes are widely circulated to everyone in the organization. Open book finance helps every employee make sense of dollars and cents that most businesses would never allow a frontline staffer to see, let alone let them manage. Our expectation here that leaders be teaching at least an hour a month makes sure we keep putting information out into our organizational universe. Our organizational change process systemically sticks information about impending changes in front of everyone that might be impacted and involves them early on in the effort. Our annual strategic planning process gets almost everyone involved in figuring out what we're going to do in the next year. Our promotion of 1 + 1 work—where we encourage anyone interested to get involved in a second (+1) piece of work, like participating on a committee, taking responsibility for "owning a line" in our open book finance work, teaching a class, etc.—means that ZCoBer's are regularly reaching out to folks outside of their own area all the time. And that's really the tip of the information iceberg for us. Information and ideas move regularly across business and department lines, without having to first pass up to the top of the organization, wait to get clearance, and then in very limited amounts be allowed back out the other side.

I'll make mention here of the value of attention to nuance and detail. The more we encourage everyone here to be aware of what's going on around them all the time, the more information they're taking in. The sad, but very serious, reality is that in most settings, even when information isn't freely shared, many people could pick it up for the asking if they were encouraged to actually ask. Mindfulness at every level means people are listening, inquiring, being attentive to an array of otherwise ignored information. Connections, and creativity, are pretty sure to follow!

4. Bring In Lots of Information From the Outside

The next big contributor to creativity is the inflow of information from other sources, stuff that comes in through activities like industry benchmarking, traveling, reading, and engaging in other positive pursuits of knowledge. In other words, if we want to successfully and effectively put pieces together in new and creative ways, we have to have a lot of interesting pieces to play with.

It's easy to see how so many people who get stuck in their ruts—the small business owner who can "never get away," the manager who's too busy to move outside day-to-day duties, the line worker who's completely disinterested in their work. But the lack of outside insight in your daily life deems you less likely to be actively creative. Which in turn means you're more likely to be stuck in the status quo, less likely to innovate your way out of what you're stuck in, and more likely to lose energy and excitement.

Gathering information from outside our everyday existence has been a critical component of our culture since our very first days at the Deli. To compound the flow of outside info already in place, with the Zingerman's Community of Businesses we're formally engaged in eight different businesses, and probably active in about twenty different industries. Which means that every time we have a ZCoB-wide meeting, we're bringing together minds that have had access to different tools, different ways of working. Candy bar making and coffee brewing have enough in common to engage in a conversation, but they're clearly in very different industries. Running a restaurant and shipping stuff across the country both share some of the same struggles, but of course each endeavor brings its own issues and insights to the intellectual table.

ZingTrain takes all that up a few notches still. We probably share thoughts with people from over 500 diverse businesses in a hundred different industries each year. And although we're teaching others our way of working, in the process we are, naturally, exposed to all sorts of new information and ideas. Add to all that our internal expectations (see the essay on Servant Leadership in *Part 2*) that everyone in a stated leadership role here does, on average, two hours of formal learning a week, and teaches at least one hour a month within the organization, and you've got a whole lot more info to throw into the mix. On top of all that you can add in the rather large number of conferences, nonprofit boards, symposia, and such that we're part of. And I don't want to forget the hundreds of hours a month of travel we all do, gathering info and insight from other countries, companies, and cultures.

The information icing on the culture cake of creativity for us, and others who do this work well, is that interesting organizations like ours have a big edge in the business world. Simply by giving great service and engaging in meaningful connections with customers, we're taking in a couple more tons of interesting outside information. The whole idea of "third places" (see Secret #14 in *Part 1*) and the way we try to construct them here is all about creating connected communities, places where people meet folks they'd otherwise never have interacted with, in the process sharing insights and information that in turn will help form otherwise unlikely connections. By coming into a creative environment, our customers connect in new ways too, with each other and with any number of out-of-the-box ideas we advocate, use, or present. Which, in turn, helps them to lead their own organizations more effectively, which in turn makes it more likely they'll want to keep coming back to us.

You don't have to be in a learning organization to be doing this sort of learning. Want to increase your creativity quotient? Simply doing more reading and traveling; getting active in a community organization; surfing the web for interesting information; or, for that matter, taking a surfing class will expose you to new ideas and people. Heck, even just hanging out with well-read and well-traveled, artistically oriented individuals will make a big difference. When new information is coming in from every angle, you can't help but make new connections. Speaking of which . . .

5. SYSTEMICALLY AND CULTURALLY SUPPORT CONNECTION

Steven Johnson says there are "two essential properties to the 'innovation engine.'" The first is "a capacity to make new connections with as many other elements as possible." Second in Johnson's scheme is to "provide a 'random-izing' environment that encourages collisions between all the elements in the system." In other words, feed as much information into your system as you can from as many diverse sources as you can access, and then create systems and a culture in which bits of that info are consistently connected in new and compelling ways.

As per point 2 above, when we live the Natural Laws of Business, we create a fertile field for creativity. When we do 3, sharing information internally, and 4, regularly gathering up outsider insights and experiences, we plant a creative and diverse set of seeds in our soil. All of which increases the odds of doing 5, building new connections between otherwise unrelated insights, thoughts, wonderings, and mental wanderings. The equation is easy to understand: 2 + 3 + 4 = a lot more raw material in the form of positive ideas, observations, and insights circulating in our community. Then with systems in place that bring together people from diverse backgrounds and places in the organization, the connections are likely to generate unusual ideas, creative insights, inspiring and strategically sound visions, etc.

It's important that we, as leaders, actively cultivate and promote connections across the organizational boundaries that typically block communication. The more you can connect minds in ways they wouldn't normally work, the healthier the organization is going to be. It's right out of anarchism 101—stop organizing things hierarchically and know that a meeting between the general manager and the new kid working the counter is probably more likely to yield creative output than a meeting of the same six managers who've talked together every week for the last two years. Connection across every line you can imagine will improve the odds of creativity (and organizational coherence and resilience) coming to the fore.

I've listed a bunch of the ways we do that in point 2 above: open book finance, open meetings, our organizational change process, work groups, 1 + 1 work, etc. You can do some of the same things on a personal level as well. Getting into regular discussion groups, making a point of reading a magazine or blog from a different industry each month, talking to people of different ages who work in different fields and come from a diverse set of backgrounds, etc. are all sure to help open up the connective channels.

exercise Connection Comparison

List all the places and systemic ways in your life and/or organization in which you connect information and people across "party lines."

Working with your colleagues over the next week or so, see if you can come up with a few more. If each month for the next year you add one more systemic way to connect information and people, you'll have come a long way on the road to greater creativity.

Creative Acts and Innovation—Forward, Sideways, and Back

As I've begun to teach more and more about the subject of creative organizations, I've come to view our creative acts in three broad categories:

Creativity that moves forward—Technological innovations are the most obvious example of this—smart phones, new apps, software, etc. are all generally new ways to take tasks that people have become accustomed to doing one way and turning folks on to a new, and ultimately more effective, process. In the food world, moving forward might manifest in the form of things like gas flushing of olive oil storage tanks or the development of refrigeration.

At Zingerman's, although we've certainly taken advantage of the forward-thinking creative work of others (I'm typing this on a computer, after all) this isn't generally the sort of creative work we do. At least not with our food—there we focus on the old ways, not on technological breakthroughs. It is, though, very much what we've been doing with our approaches to our organizational life and business. What we're working on, I believe (see the Introduction to *Part 2*), isn't a revival of something from the 16th century, it really is a new way of work. Granted, it pulls pieces from the past, but a blend of them comes together to make a cultural cocktail that I think is completely different from anything offered up before, and is different even from those of the many other progressive companies out there that I consider our peers and that I hold in high esteem.

Creativity that shifts sideways—This generally seems to come in two forms. Often, it's merely finding something that's commonplace within its own culture but, when introduced into unfamiliar territory, is transformed into an attention-getting, creative act. I remember the first time I went to the famous Parisian specialty food shop, Fauchon, and was shocked to find a large window display featuring a mass-market American brand of salsa and taco shells. Clearly, what was considered mundane here in the American Midwest was almost magical if you moved it to France. We do a lot of this sideways creative work at Zingerman's. In Wisconsin, fried cheese curds are anything but unusual. But in Ann Arbor, they're an inspiration—many loyalists now come every Wednesday to get them. The Hungarian foods (see page 369) we're working on at the Bakehouse would certainly fit as well. In fact, most of the food we sell at Zingerman's would fit this bill.

The other sort of sideways shift of creativity comes when two already well-accepted ideas or ways of working are put together in a totally new way, resulting in an innovative approach or product. This is very much about the concept of being open to connection between otherwise never-before-linked elements. The classic historical example is of Gutenberg using wine press technology to print books. In the modern food world, the Sonoran hot dog that's such a favorite out in Arizona was created by simply connecting Mexican taco toppings with all-American bacon-wrapped hot dogs. Neither bacon-wrapped hot dogs nor taco toppings are anything to write home about—but when you put them together, you get a unique (and tasty) regional specialty, both oddly familiar and totally new at the same time. The same would apply to using Emma Goldman's ideas to help run a progressive 21st century business. Or the whole idea of thinking of business as an agricultural ecosystem.

Creativity in reverse—This is what we do at Zingerman's with so much of our food—we don't "invent," we just go back and find the old ways. Our cream cheese is crafted the way it was made in the 1890s. My favorite Bakehouse bread—what we call Roadhouse bread—is a mix of wheat, corn, and rye, sweetened a touch with molasses; we found it under the name of "rye 'n' injun" bread in 18th and 19th century New England cookbooks. The hand-sewing of the little books we've published recently with pieces I've written about Wisconsin cheese and sardines would be another example—two hundred years ago, there was nothing in the least innovative about hand-sewing a book. Today, it's totally a product of, and for, special attention.

Another good example, for me, that's very literally at hand is the old-school phone receiver I carry in my shoulder bag to plug into my smart phone. (If you remember, it's the one that our young customer Eli is so excited to play with every week—see page 114.) The receiver, itself, is essentially identical to the ones that everyone had when I was growing up. All that's different is that it's made to plug into an iPhone! It works beautifully. Interestingly, it gets almost everyone's attention immediately. Old-school stuff stuck into a totally modern setting makes it into something special.

Push Down and Turn

When it comes to creative work with products and services, there's a big difference between being creative and copying. On occasion, we find something that literally no one else seems to be doing. But more often than not, we're not the only ones out there who are doing something, even if it's old and obscure. In that case, I think it's important to make some adjustment to make the innovation our own. Stas' Kazmierski always taught us to "adapt, not adopt." In other words, adjust what you learn to your own ecosystem and environment. I've come to look at it in the same way as I do the directions on the lids of pill bottles, the ones that say, "To open, push down and turn." In other words, to find the item in the first place, we need to do a bit of digging (the "push down"), but to make it our own we want to give it just a bit of a twist to make it special and unique to us (the "turn"). And when we do, we effectively unlock the creative "cures" that we're after.

Building Change and Innovation, One Patient, Thoughtful, Creative Layer at a Time

One thing I realized from my reading is that, although innovations often seem to be sudden game changers, in truth even the most out-of-the-box creators can still generally shift only one (often quite small) connection at a time. It turns out that no matter how brilliant somebody is, ideas are still combined much like bricks in a cathedral, one layer atop another. Later, when the cathedral is complete, it looks remarkable and majestic, but in the moment, it's more mundane. The credit usually goes to the "capstone" concept that's seen as completing the work, but the cap will never be put on until the other parts have all been put in place. In other words, elements of ideas appear in an instant, but the finished form rarely is ready to be implemented for quite some time.

This understanding doesn't help one be more creative, per se, but it did help me understand the way creativity works. Johnson calls the concept "the adjacent possible"—everything "new" is almost always just another layer of nuance added to a foundation that already existed. Even exceptionally creative people can only extend an insight a single level at a time; you can't connect with, or capitalize on, something you can't conceive of. By contrast, if you have a piece of raw material with which to work, you can pretty quickly come up with any number of ways in which to enhance it or apply it in alternate environments. Each insight, each new connection, is then installed on top of the one placed previously, helping to create "new" things, innovation, and, again, more insight.

Which brings me to an illustrative example within this illustrative story. Five years from now, I forecast, Zingerman's Bakehouse will be famous for its amazing array of Hungarian baked goods. While it may seem random that we'll be known for now almost-unheard-of-around-here pastries like pogacsa, Rigo Janczi, retes, flodni, and other fabulous stuff, this didn't all just appear one afternoon in a fit of creativity on the part of managing partners Amy Emberling and Frank Carollo. To the contrary, our fascination with Hungarian baking is actually the culmination of a long story of earlier creativity and connection, in which each new idea was built, as Johnson points out that it must be, on the parts that preceded it.

It was back in 1992 when we first started talking about opening the Bakehouse. I happened to tell my good friend Lex Alexander, who'd worked in the food world for many years, that I had this idea for us to start baking our own bread. Lex immediately connected me with master baker Michael London—as per the point above about gathering resources from outside the organization—who, in turn, trained managing partner and longtime friend Frank Carollo in how to bake the breads for which we're now nationally famous. At the time, there were really no other artisan bakeries in the area. Which is why even the act of opening, I suppose, was a creative act. Back when we began, though, hardly anyone (other than us, of course) was particularly high on the idea. The Deli was already well known and sold a significant amount of other bakeries' bread. Customers were happy with what we already had and weren't clamoring for a change. Fortunately, we went ahead anyway. The Deli's high sales level made it much easier for the fledgling Bakehouse to get a solid market on which to build. From whence, thanks to the hard work and high skill of everyone there, the business grew and got ever better with each passing year.

Not long after we opened the Bakehouse, we developed our approach to visioning, learned from ZingTrain co-managing partner Stas' Kazmierski and put in place primarily because we'd started doing our seminars at ZingTrain. In 2010, we wrote a new long-term vision for the Bakehouse, in which (among a range of other things) we identified that, by 2020, we'd have become famous for some as-yet-unknown-to-us area of baked goods. That unknown area of expertise emerged quickly from our post vision writing work—we chose to focus on the bread and pastry of Hungary, which has long had one of the best baking traditions in the world. The cafes of Budapest are beautiful and so is the pastry they bake and serve. We knew little else about it, but clearly it was (for us at least) a fascinating culture and history, a place we were eager to investigate. So we decided to pursue Hungarian baking as the "next big thing" that we'd written into our vision. The rest, shall we say, is in the process of becoming intellectual and culinary history.

The fame and national acclaim hasn't really happened yet, but given the effectiveness of the visioning process, and the terrific track record that

Frank and Amy and everyone at the Bakehouse have put together, I'm confident that it eventually will. At which point, when pastry lovers anywhere in the US get a hankering for something Hungarian, they'll know they can place an order with us. When journalists write about us, they'll regularly refer to our Hungarian baked goods, and when the reports come in about the foods of Hungary hitting homes across America, we'll be listed as the go-to source. In fact, by then, the baked goods of Budapest will be considered cutting edge on the American culinary scene. Chain bakeries will roll out their own versions of Hungarian classics, and the most progressive minds on the R & D team of some national fast food franchise will argue that adding Hungarian baked goods to their drive-up menus is clearly the way to go. But it'll be a point of pride for Zingerman's that we had the Hungarian goods in our sights long before they entered the mainstream.

My point is not that we're so hot, but that this happy future will never have happened without all of the organizational pieces upon which our Hungarian dream could be developed. Innovative ideas are rarely implemented as isolated activities—while one element of an innovation may seem to the outside eye to have happened in an instant, it's actually a long, steady, piece-upon-piece creative construction project to take an initial insight to fully formed fruition. No matter how creative you are, you can't put the top layer on until the other ideas that serve as its base are in place. It takes time and a lot of good, hard work to make it happen. In the process we create a veritable philosophical phyllo dough of ideas, layered around plenty of tasty, well-spiced content. As anarchist Murray Bookchin writes, "Every revolutionary project is, above all, an evolutionary one."

6. THINK DIFFERENTLY

Most of the subjects I've written about over the years—visioning, Servant Leadership, customer service, collaborative thinking, etc.—have been learned behaviors for me. I wasn't particularly good at any of them growing up, but in the years since we opened the Deli, I've studied hard and gradually taught myself to do all of it pretty well.

Thinking differently, though, is *different*. Best I can tell, I've been actively working at it since I was about six. For whatever reasons—DNA, upbringing, early exposure to anarchist influence during my academic career, or something strange in the water in the city of Chicago—I've always had a high attraction to doing things my own way, and generally not following the path that most people were on. While this tendency can cause some problems in parts of one's life, it can be a big strength in others, especially in business—it's hard to create meaningful, mind-engaging work and exceptional, compelling products if all you're doing is what everyone else has already done. I seem to have the ability to walk into almost any trade show booth, find the product the owners of the company are really excited about but that no one else can sell, declare my love for it, and then figure out how to sell a lot of it over a long period of time!

If you dare to do it, thinking differently and doing what others aren't doing can open up doors, markets, minds, and pocketbooks. Spiritually, strategically, and instinctively, I far prefer this route to going with everyone else's flow. By the time a trend is being touted in the press as "the next big thing," I figure we'd better have already been doing it for five or six years or else, in the interest of being exceptional, hold off for another five or six so it can start to fade some before we begin. To wit, when everyone in the country seemed to start making bagels in the mid '90s, we stayed away. By the time bagel shops were on every block, and many were being shut down due to oversaturation, we started to bake our own. I'd far rather be either first or last in the market than to get stuck stranded in the middle.

7. Cultivate the "Crazy"—Think Like an Anarchist

Taking the drive to be different a bit further, I want to encourage you, myself, and anyone else who cares about creativity to let our minds take regular little walks with our wild sides; to acknowledge and honor those seemingly out-there, almost-impossible-to-implement ideas that most of us self-regulate out of our consciousness. I keep coming back to Emma Goldman's remarkable statement, quoted earlier, that "Anarchism is the spirit of youth against out-worn tradition." I loved that line when I first read it a long time ago, and I love it now. It's quite clear to me from reading Johnson's and Lehrer's books, and from thirty years of practical Zingerman's experiences, that the spirit of youth is the font of enormous creativity. Lest you misunderstand, it's not age related. I've met eighteen-year-olds who were so stuck in convention they could barely disagree with anyone, and eighty-year-olds still happily and creatively pursuing their passions in unique ways. I'm working towards being one of the latter—trying to let my mind continue to meander through meaningfully out-there ideas and insights as long as I can.

What we all want, I think, is the opposite of constraint. Most everyone would like to be part of a culture so rich in creativity it's like a rain forest full of interesting ideas. To build a business in which people dream big, think differently, drive for out-of-the-box solutions, and don't get totally stuck in the status quo. This work must begin with us. If we, as leaders, don't let our crazy ideas free in our own minds, it's highly unlikely that our organizations are going to do so. Constricted thinking at the top creates a constricted—and not very creative—organizational culture. We have to catch hold of the wild stuff, the ideas that others are likely to dismiss as impractical. We don't necessarily have to act on them—we just need to be open to explore the opportunities they present. But great ideas rarely come from the middle of the market. In Emma Goldman's words, "the extreme thing is generally the true thing."

And, Emma writes, "The true criterion of the practical, therefore, is not whether the latter can keep intact the wrong or foolish; rather it is whether the scheme has vitality enough to leave the stagnant waters of the old, and build, as well as sustain, new life. In the light of this conception, Anarchism is indeed practical. More than any other idea, it is helping to do away with the wrong and foolish; more than any other idea, it is building and sustaining new life."

To think like an anarchist, you don't have to be all that serious. I'd say a solid share of our best ideas here have been surprises. We'll be messing around at a meeting and someone will say something they think is sort of silly. Everyone laughs, we start to move on, and then, either a moment or a month or so later, someone else says, "You know, that's a good idea. Maybe we should actually do it!" Letting ideas in from the periphery, giving them the time of day even when you might want to just dismiss them out of hand can be a big contributor in helping develop an inclusive, creatively oriented organization. Let people err on the side of silliness, if only to help them learn that they can make a difference, that they can have hope for their ideas, that someone might listen, that what they dream might actually get done.

Many an innovation at Zingerman's has started as someone's only semi-serious, often sarcastic, throwaway thought. Our annual Camp Bacon fundraiser happened because Pete Garner, who manages our marketing, suggested we go with the silly concept I'd made up in *Zingerman's Guide to Better Bacon*. Gary Snyder writes, "Wilderness is a *place* where the wild potential is fully expressed." And, "I for one will keep working for wildness day by day." Once we let the wildness out, we have a more than reasonable chance to make it real. As Tina Seelig, author of *inGenius: A Crash Course on Creativity*, says, "Essentially, if you believe something is possible, then it is."

One thing I know for sure—tentative, self-conscious uncertainty is *not* a productive mindset for generating creative and compelling work. I love what

Lewis Carroll wrote in *Alice in Wonderland*. "Alice laughed: 'There's no use trying,' she said; 'one can't believe impossible things.' 'I daresay you haven't had much practice,' said the Queen. 'When I was younger, I always did it for half an hour a day. Why, sometimes I've believed as many as six impossible things before breakfast.'" Coming back to business, the late Anita Roddick, founder of the super successful The Body Shop, wrote, "Creativity comes by breaking the rules, by saying you're in love with the anarchist."

Teaching Staff to Break the Rules

Thinking about thinking creatively and anarchistically, I realized that we've actually been overtly asking our staff to break our own rules for decades now. You read that right—we actively instruct them to break the rules. Paul and I go over the practical application of this at every new staff orientation class. Near the end of the two hours, we tell people that with four exceptions (don't come to work in an altered chemical state; never be rude to a coworker or guest; don't steal; and don't be rude to our food), we WANT people who work here to break the rules when they need to in order to get better service to a guest.

In essence, then, encouragement for breaking out of the mainstream and going constructively and creatively against the grain is written into our Guiding Principles. We're teaching people to bust through the boundaries—even the ones we ourselves erected—in the interest of doing the right thing. That little sidebar of a statement in a two-hour class may not change the world, but I'm sure it's caught the attention of a couple of new employees who'd previously worked in the standard "follow the rules or find the exit" environment. Right from the get-go, people here get the idea that being creative in the interest of doing good work is not only ok, it's actually expected!

8. Make Solitude Part of Your Routine

While I'm all for thinking collaboratively, I don't want to imply that creative work is only done in group settings. To the contrary, there's a lot to be said for solitude. In fact, many experts argue that great innovation and creative work originates with someone working alone on an issue. It may well be later enhanced by others, evolving as the group works on it. But the original insight—the idea, the spark of sudden creativity—generally comes from an individual or, at most, a small group working within the larger group. I'm with Emma Goldman, who articulated, "My lack of faith in the majority is dictated by my faith in the potentialities of the individual."

Apple CEO Steve Wozniak said, "Artists work best alone . . . I don't believe anything really revolutionary has been invented by committee." It's certainly true for me that a lot of what I come up with comes when I'm on my own—reading, writing, or running. Of course, like Wozniak, I'm an introvert. And the nature of diversity means that there is no one single way in which all creative people (which, by definition, is all people) create most effectively. Wozniak's advice? "Work alone. You're going to be able to design revolutionary products and features if you're working on your own. Not on a committee. Not on a team."

It's likely that the most productive things will happen if we move back and forth between both solitude and group settings. For me, the group serves as a way to work out my thoughts, to get input that helps me see where I've gone astray, to gather insight that leads me to alter what I've come up with or, at times, just to see that I'm not completely off-base with the ideas that are forming in my mind. The most productive path for me is usually a spread of time to myself interwoven with group engagements. I bounce my ideas off others, reflect, revise, re-bounce, reflect, revise, re-bounce, and gradually improve what I'm thinking, build my sense of what's right. Even disagreement sheds light on what I believe and helps me get grounded. What's most important is to know which ways work best for you so you can do your best to make them happen. Effective self-management always serves us well.

9. Act Really Confident (or Constructively Crazy)

Both professional studies and my own personal experience have shown the same thing: great creative insights almost never gain immediate support. As Hugh MacLeod makes clear in *Ignore Everybody,* "It's more like, the better the idea, the more 'out there' it initially will seem to other people, even people you like and respect. So there'll be a time in the beginning when you have to press on, alone, without one tenth the support you probably need. This is normal." Which is why to push for creative activity and attempt to initiate what might later be seen as a super innovative idea, we usually have to have very high self-confidence, to be willing to ignore what most everyone around us says when we start to share our ideas.

Trying to build our own self-esteem so we can hold onto what we believe in the face of ongoing opposition isn't easy to do. I can't tell you how to know when it's time to stay true to your instinct, to honor your intuition, when everyone else is wagging fingers and telling you you're crazy. Somehow, in your heart, you have to feel strongly that you're onto something special, no matter what. In the encouraging words of 19th century French anarchist and geographer Elisée Reclus, "Whether we succeed or not, it doesn't matter, we will have been at least the interpreters of [our] inner voice."

It's hard to stick with it. But that's what it takes. Paul and I have arrived at an informal understanding on the subject, which goes something like this: when everyone tells us what we're doing is crazy, we figure we're probably on the right path. Conversely, when lots of people respond positively to what we want to do, we start to wonder what we're missing. There are certainly exceptions to this theory—it's a loose guideline, not standard operating procedure. But the key often is, as MacLeod makes clear, "Nobody can tell you if what you're doing is good, meaningful, or worthwhile. The more compelling the path, the more lonely it is." For me, it's *always* better to risk failure going after what I believe in than to stick to the mainstream, go against my own beliefs, and give up on my dreams.

Brenda Says
From *If You Want to Write*

As I've mentioned, Brenda Ueland's book *If You Want to Write*, published in 1938, has been a major influence on the way I write, think, and live. Allow me to quote her at length:

> The creative power and imagination is in everyone, and so is the need to express it, i.e. to share it with others. But what happens to it?
>
> It is very tender and sensitive, and it is usually drummed out of people early in life by criticism (so-called "helpful criticism" is often the worst kind), by teasing, jeering, rules, prissy teachers, critics, and all those unloving people who forget that the letter killeth and the spirit giveth life. Sometimes I think of life as a process where everybody is discouraging and taking everybody else down a peg or two.

You know how all children have this creative power. You have all seen things like this: the little girls in our family used to give play after play. They wrote the plays themselves (they were very good plays too, interesting, exciting, and funny). They acted in them. They made the costumes themselves, beautiful, effective and historically accurate, contriving them in the most ingenious way out of attic junk and their mothers' best dresses. They constructed the stage and theatre by carrying chairs, moving the piano, carpentering. They printed the tickets and sold them. They made their own advertising. They drummed up the audience, throwing out a dragnet for all the hired girls, dogs, babies, mothers, neighbors within a radius of a mile or so. For what reward? A few pins and pennies.

You can see a lot of the core principles of creative work at play, literally, in this account. Little girls, untrained in the formal techniques of dramatic theater, regularly wrote entertaining plays. They connected otherwise unconnected things, putting their mothers' fancy dresses to work as costumes. They installed unexpected participants—dogs, babies, neighbors, etc.—as audience members, which in turn added to the creative energy of the event. Clearly, this was work. But as with all "good work," the initiators of it were inspired and excited, and creative constructs followed. As Ueland adds:

These small ten-years-olds were working with feverish energy and endurance. If they had worked that hard for school it probably would have killed them. They were working for nothing but fun, for that glorious inner excitement. It was the creative power working in them. It was hard, hard work, but there was no pleasure or excitement like it, and it was something never forgotten.

But this joyful, imaginative, impassioned energy dies out of us very young. Why? Because we do not see that it is great and important. Because we let dry obligation take its place. Because we don't respect it ourselves and keep it alive by using it.

Why not keep the creative spirit alive by being in touch with ourselves, by following Anita Roddick's recommendation that we love the anarchist in each of us?

9. TAKE NOTES

Little did I know when I started to do daily journaling twenty-five years ago that it would turn out to be such a "secret" to leadership success. Mostly, I just did it to keep myself from going crazy. Taking time to reflect regularly helped me keep my mental feet on more solid ground. But everywhere I turn these days, journaling seems to show up! Robert Greenleaf recommends it highly as an aid in reflecting. Martin Seligman suggests writing down three good things a day, which I've also done, if not quite that consistently, in my journal work for years.

You probably won't be surprised to hear then that according to Steven Johnson, journaling is a very helpful tool if you're trying to be more creative and innovative. In *The History of Good Ideas,* he writes about the early modern era tradition of keeping notebooks of randomly collected thoughts. Called "commonplacing," the idea was to get one's insights, ideas, and intellectual oddities down on paper where one could later look them up, consider them anew, and maybe connect them with some other idea to complete what the first half of the hunch had begun. In essence, the practice of commonplacing gives ideas the time and space they need to develop while saving them so that they can be accessed where needed! It also frees the mind to focus on other things. Once the oddball idea has been inscribed in your journal (or whatever you use), you can begin working on other issues. Contemporary education expert Edward Davis advocates this in his book *Lessons for Tomorrow*: "Journaling ought to be a skill that develops commensurate with the ability to write."

Journaling isn't the only way to do this, though. Technology makes it easier than ever to track your insights. In fact, while I was writing this essay I had the idea to create what we've gone on to call Zingerman's "idea exchange." We actually piggybacked it onto another project we'd just begun: an online Zingerman's Resource Exchange. It's sort of like Craig's List but solely for people who work at Zingerman's. That idea, by the way, was taken from an off-hand comment made at one of our regular Partners' Group meetings by Tom Root, one of the very creative trio of managing partners at our Mail Order business. Tom threw it out in passing and I loved it. And now, two years later, we're doing it in earnest. People can list either work-related things they need or want (looking for someone to work a Saturday catering event, looking to pick up more hours) or personal projects (looking for someone to paint my back porch, looking for a dog-sitting opportunity). The idea is to . . . drum roll . . . make connections that help people in the organization do things and do them better.

So when the idea of an idea exchange emerged from the work on this essay, it seemed a natural fit for the Zingerman's Resource Exchange. Ideas, after all, are the ultimate raw material for innovation. So the hunches and unfinished insights are all there, easily available for others to access, waiting for someone else around here to take them through to fruition. Listing things in accessible places makes it all the more likely that some other caring and insightful individual will close the loop by completing an unfinished thought that's been sitting around for a long time.

The Theory of Relevantivity

Speaking of collecting off-kilter concepts and storing them up for later use, here's one I've been sitting on for about six years. I was going to write an entire essay on it, but that hasn't yet happened, so for the moment, I'm going to let it make its intellectual debut as part of this discussion. In the spirit of any new idea standing on the shoulders of another, this is my take-off on Einstein's Theory of Relativity. My version has little to do with physics but a lot to do with philosophy.

This model is called the "Theory of Relevantivity." What it means is that pretty much anything that happens in our lives is going—to a greater or lesser extent—to be relevant to everything else that's going on. I think the Theory of Relevantivity is likely a natural law from time immemorial, but in the past, it would have been much harder to see it in action. Ten centuries ago, the information flow that would have made existence of the law clear would have taken, literally, ages to arrive. But today, with the world as connected as it is via technology, there's really very little that can happen—anywhere—that won't have some meaningful and visible impact on what we do.

I know it's true for us at Zingerman's. Pick a change in the world, any change, and I can probably show you how it's going to have some meaningful impact on our business. To wit, a change of regime in Bali could bring swings to our supply of sea salt; new scientific discoveries can alter the way we eat; teams win championships and consumer interest is piqued in products from those areas.

To quote Aldous Huxley, writing in his classic novel *Island,* "Never give children a chance of imagining that anything exists in isolation. Make it plain from the very first that all living is relationship." I'd simply insert "anyone" where Huxley says "children." The point is the same. Everything is relevant to everything else. In fact, even the act of accepting that this theory is true could change your life. And, with that, those of the people closest to you, and then the people closest to them, and so on.

Knowing the Theory of Relevantivity doesn't really change all that much in the moment. By definition, everything is already impacting everything else, whether we know it or not. What it does do, though, is alter the way we view the world. When we recognize that earthquakes in Africa or bee mites in California can cause major crop shortages, then we start to tune in more directly to what we hear, read, see, smell, and smile at. When we realize that every action we take will impact a whole host of others, we become more mindful, more caringly considerate.

10. Sound Systems and Structure Yield Creativity

One of my early misreads on anarchism was the erroneous assumption that any, or all, organizational structure would impinge on the creativity of the individuals within it. Man, was I mistaken! In fact, it turns out the total absence of structure is just as constricting as a series of autocratically instituted, ironclad codes of order. Maybe more so. Given a total blank page, most of us will be paralyzed or perhaps even start to panic. The more productive approach, I've learned both from reading and from three decades of doing, is to create structures that essentially encourage people to bring their creative selves to the fore without quashing that self-same creative spirit. The key that keeps the work in line with the anarchist belief in autonomy is that the people who are working within the structures need to have the freedom to constructively change or improve the systems within which they're working.

Although I was oblivious, the anarchists were fully aware of the positive role healthy organizational structures can play. They weren't opposed to organization, only to externally imposed, authoritarian ones run really only for the benefit of those in charge. Errico Malatesta, the eloquent Italian American anarchist, wrote, "The large scale organizations, anarchistically oriented . . . are THE VERY ESSENCE OF ANARCHISM AS A VIABLE SOCIAL ORDER." The caps are Malatesta's, so you know he meant it: healthy organization is at the core of effective anarchist existence.

The key is to create constructs that make it more likely that all of us will get to good outcomes, while still leaving loads of space within which each of us can apply our own insights, experiences, and intuition. (For much more on how we do this, see Secret #3 in *Part 1* on Organizational Recipes, and Secret #29 in *Part 2* on Anarcho-Capitalism.) Though they don't necessarily require it, all of our recipes clearly call for collaboration. The 3 Steps to Great Service, 5 Steps to Effectively Handling a Customer Complaint, 3 Steps to Great Finance, the recipe for visioning, etc. all fill the bill. They lay out tried and true paths that will get anyone who follows them close to a good (and often a great) answer to a question or dilemma. But at the same time, they never actually *give* the answer—they just get you close. To finish the equation, each of us has to think for ourselves.

To wit, our 5 Steps to Handling a Customer Complaint, for instance, asks us to "make things right for the customer" but doesn't dictate how to do it. Every situation is relatively unique and requires a relatively unique solution. One customer who doesn't love his sandwich wants me to call him personally. Another wants a new sandwich asap. A third one with the same problem wants a replacement, a refund, and a piece of peach pie. Determining what the right "answer" is can only be done by using good service skills, which in our case always calls for creativity.

It's with these loose but life-giving, effective, and energizing formats that we encourage people to think freely, to put their minds into action, and to go for greatness in all they do. Tina Seelig writes in *inGenius: A Crash Course on Creativity* that "constraints sharpen your imagination and enhance innovation." Which, connecting the dots again, is clearly one reason why the time limits we use when we have people write their visions in ZingTrain sessions are so constructive. The constraint creates urgency and avoids the unproductive worry, time wasting, and obsessing that all too often block people's natural creativity. The visioning recipe, for me, is probably the ultimate in systemic assurance of creative greatness. It gives a construct in which to write out the future you dream about, but it never tells you what "should" be written into it.

It's clear to me, then, that we'd do well to come up with comparable constructs for our minds. That is, to adopt healthy regimens, repeatable systems, freely followed processes, etc. that we find will help us tap our own creativity. In fact, that's what journaling does—it's flextime for the brain, but with no agenda other than writing down what comes to mind. Resolutions like "I will write ten thank you notes a week," or "I'll do a dozen extra miles for coworkers" leave freedom to decide exactly what you'll do in the moment, while still compelling you to take constructive action. They may not be fancy but they do work well!

Time for Hunching Season?
Getting Good at Gathering Gut Feelings

Having hunches and, more importantly, honoring them when you have them is one of the keys to creativity. And if creating structures and systems that leave us freedom to move and encourage us to get out of the mainstream is a good way to go, and if I have a proclivity for provocative puns and a lot of alliteration, then how can I resist suggesting that we start to have an annual "hunching season" here at Zingerman's?

I can already see it in my mind's eye. We would model it after the annual autumn activities in the Michigan north woods. You know, where everyone gets dressed up in hunching outfits, wears goofy looking hunching hats, brings all their intellectual weapons to bear, and spends a whole week or so doing nothing but hunting for hunches. I love it. You could tell tales of ideas that were never implemented—you know, the big ones that "got away." You could bring your favorite friends and sit around scoping out hunches. Sometimes you'd get little or nothing, of course, but other times you might score some significant insights. And just like people do when they go hunting, we could bring back what we've bagged, clean it and dress it up some, and then serve it, well prepared, to the rest of the organization. Or maybe you want to mount your hunches and hang them above your mantle.

No hunching licenses required—given everyone's innate ability to be creative, we're all already qualified! You can go hunching any time you want to! You might even catch some oranga boogas. Never heard of 'em? Neither had I until our then-five-year-old regular customer Maia brought me a drawing of one on a late summer Saturday morning. Never having seen an orange booga before that, I was curious. "Where do they come from?" I asked Maia. "This one came from my imagination," she said matter of factly.

11. CONSIDER PROBLEM SWAPS

Way back in the early years of the Deli's development, I remember being perpetually frustrated with how much each department manager seemed to know just what their colleagues ought to be doing to improve, while at the same time seeming unable to address the problematic issues they themselves were responsible for. I remember threatening at times that I was going to simply shift everyone one department over—maybe we'd have all our issues resolved in no time!

It turns out that my sarcastic "solution" was actually more appropriate than I imagined. Jonah Lehrer suggests what he calls "problem swaps." The idea is simple and it makes sense. When people are stuck, give them a new issue to work on, one they've never really paid attention to, at least at that level. In essence, it's another appeal to tap diversity: new people looking at an old problem will frequently find a creative solution that those of us who are around the issue all day are oblivious to. The risk of asking is low, and the reward of engaging can be high. For very little investment, we might reap really big rewards. If everyone comes up with some quick, easy-to-implement solution, it's basically like hitting the jackpot at a creativity card game. And, as Sir Kenneth Robinson writes, "There is no substitute for putting people in situations where their abilities may be tested differently or where different aspects of their potential are called upon and revealed."

12. GET IN, AND OUT, OF CONTEXT

I've always known that by and large, the people who come to ZingTrain are the most out-of-the-box thinkers in their industry. Now I know why. By regularly moving out of our normal contexts, we see things we'd never see, or hear them in ways we never would otherwise experience them. When we come back into our own contexts, this allows us the opportunity to look like creative geniuses. The mundane in one setting is often marvelously spectacular in another. As Steven Johnson says, "The movement from box to box forces the mind to approach intellectual roadblocks from new angles, or to borrow tools from one discipline to solve problems in another." Which is why creativity tends to come more often from people who explore other worlds, either intellectually through reading or physically by traveling to distant and different places.

13. QUIT WORRYING!

Don't worry. I'll be quick about this one. Cutting to the core of the issue—when it comes to increasing creativity and building a better organization, worrying is never helpful. I'm not talking about constructive concern and the appropriate planning and prep work that come from it. I'm talking about worrying—about what we might have done wrong, about what might go wrong in the future. *The negative energy we create when we worry never works.*

Concern tied to appropriate corrective action can be very constructive. But worrying usually only leads to more worrying, an erosion of creative energy. When it gets really bad, we end up making dumb decisions because we can't stand the stress of the worrying any longer. When we worry about what's already over or what might yet take place, our creativity is caving in. To quote Ueland, "Creative power flourishes only when I am living in the present."

This kind of overthinking and high anxiety always gets in people's way with the visioning work. I've started to ask people to invite their worries to wait outside while they write. At the ZingTrain Creating a Vision of Greatness seminar, we now post a big white sheet on the wall where attendees can sign their various critical voices up for a tour of the Bakehouse while they're busy working on their visions. I did it at first as a bit of a joke to prove the point, but people took it seriously and one after another wrote various "voices" on the sheet. One woman wrote about ten. She looked very relieved when she sat back down to start writing her vision.

Coming from a family of worriers, I've worked hard to change the way I think in this regard. As I would a difficult customer who comes in three or four times a week, I've learned how to handle my worries calmly, with a deep breath and a reliance on well-tested routines for gently turning them aside. I can let them be as they are, but not let them take me off my game or delude me into doing something that would cause significant harm to the business or myself. If and when the worry starts, I can usually now work my way out of it fairly quickly with a little journaling, a long run, the Three and Out rule (see page 80), or a quick call to a good friend. While I can't say I've completely eliminated worry from my existence, I will say that I no longer worry about it.

14. PAIRING THE PRODUCTIVE USE OF STRESS WITH HIGH PERFORMANCE

Speaking of healthy intellectual ecosystems and how they attract even more good insights and ideas, the chart below came to me courtesy of a ZingTrain seminar attendee, Clay Garner. I think it provides a nice visual model of the healthy use of stress (as in making sure you're properly prepared, covering all your bases, etc.) vs. worry that undermines other constructive energy.

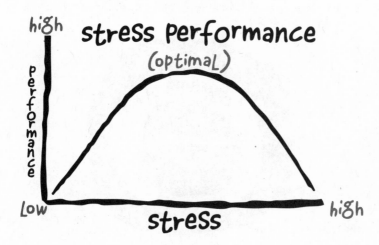

Another take on the same subject is The Learning Zone Model, developed by German educator and "adventure pedagogue" (there's a career!) Tom Senninger in the year 2000. I like this model a lot for its simplicity and, I think, nearly universal applicability. He draws three concentric circles, the innermost of which he calls the "comfort zone." We're all familiar with that one. It feels fine but, other than respite and rest, rarely leads to anything exceptional. The outer ring he refers to as the "panic zone." (I like "danger zone" better myself, but the point is the same—when we're in it, we're so stressed and disoriented that we don't behave well.) The key, as you'll likely already have intuited, is to stay as much as we can in the middle ring, which Senninger calls "the learning zone." In this region, a certain amount of stress acts as a trigger to make growth and creativity happen. Here, we're too unfamiliar with what we're doing to be comfortable, but not so far from success that we have no hope. Effective self-management, if you're going for growth and learning, means managing ourselves to stay in that zone as much as we can. Which means understanding that, although stress is generally blamed for being the source of everything from bad energy to a bad economy, it's desirable (if we want to learn and grow) to have some stress in what we're doing.

The concept is simple even if effective implementation is not. When we feel flat or stagnant, we need to move towards the middle. If we get too wigged out and can't get good work done, then we're in the danger zone, and somehow, through breathing, better self-management, working our way through the stress, we need to move back from life on the brink, into the learning zone.

15. Open Your Mind to Connection

When it comes to creativity, Steven Johnson says, "openness and connectivity may, in the end, be more valuable to innovation than purely competitive mechanisms." In other words, making positive and meaningful connections between things that most people pass up as unrelated will frequently result in something special. There's more, it turns out, to connecting dots than a kids' game; creative breakthroughs occur most often when we break the current molds and find new associations. Bringing otherwise unrelated things together in new ways will often be the opening that results in a breakthrough, an insight, an epiphany, a leap forward into excellence, or whatever else you want to call it. Kudos to Paul for figuring that out, and for seeing my ability to do so long before I actually understood it for myself.

Significant applications of new ideas seem to come along not in overwhelming tsunamis of innovative thought or sudden flashes of brilliant insight, but rather in small, steady, often slightly off-center steps towards a more meaningful and more positive future. It's true really of everything we've done with food here at Zingerman's over the last three decades. (See the story of our Hungarian adventure on page 369.) As Jonah Lehrer writes, "The act of innovation [is] really an act of recombination." Paul, once again proving himself pretty darned bright, told me back when we were getting going in 1982, "There's not really that much that's truly new in the food world. All we can really do is put things together in different ways."

Zingerman's is regularly cited as an example of creative, out-of-the-box thinking and a place that sets the tone for others trying to find an alternative path in the world. People come from all over to learn about what we do. But the truth is that nearly all of the elements of our activities are things we learned from others who were talking about, if not doing, them somewhere else. By adding one piece at time—visioning, Servant Leadership, open book finance, devotion to traditional foodways, great customer service, community giving, diversity work, the influence of the anarchists, etc.—we've managed to emerge with a management model that's completely unique.

16. Don't Focus (Too Much)

Jonah Lehrer writes, "One of the surprising lessons of this research [on creativity] is that trying to force an insight can actually prevent the insight." This is right in line with the research on preferred futuring (what we now call "visioning") that Ron Lippitt did at U of M fifty years ago. People who are focused on "fixing" something may succeed, but more often than not, they'll be stuck in various shades of the status quo. "Deep focus actually decreases the odds of creative intellectual connections," Lehrer tells us. This is one of the main reasons why the visioning process is so powerful. It stops us from getting stuck worrying about what we "should" do this second, and sets us to dreaming in a well-outlined but otherwise anarchistic way.

Other formats that foment this sort of structured focus-through-unfocus might be yoga, walking, running, rowing, meditation, or other primarily physical activities that free the brain to be engaged in unplanned ways. Improv training could contribute a similar experience. Lehrer suggests long showers as well. "When your brain is supposedly doing nothing, it's really doing a tremendous amount," he says. Establishing a regular regimen around this sort of stuff increases the likelihood of our minds wandering into wonderfully unexpected insights. Lehrer quotes world-class cellist Yo-Yo Ma: "It's when I'm least conscious of what I'm doing, when I'm just lost in the emotion of the music, that I'm performing at my best."

Brainstorming, Zingerman's Style

Brainstorming has been taking a bit of a beating lately. I've seen more than one article that argues that it "doesn't work," because it doesn't get groups to good solutions. I think it works really well—but as we do it here, brainstorming *isn't supposed* to get us to solutions. At Zingerman's we do brainstorming in order to a) get everyone in the room engaged and active; b) get people's minds and mouths moving quickly so that there's no time to assess, analyze, or critique; c) through both of these, increase the odds of coming up with seemingly strange but often ultimately very effective ways to approach an issue; and d) do it all in a matter of two or three minutes.

In other words, brainstorming isn't designed to solve problems (which might, I suppose, explain why it doesn't). It's just supposed to get people's minds moving. And for that, it works fabulously well. When we feel a meeting going flat, a three-minute brainstorm is a great way to break up the bad energy. Or when one of us is super stumped, we know that asking the group we're in for a two-minute brainstorm is an easy and efficient way to get assistance. Having participated in a few thousand brainstorms over the years, I can say the odds are very high that the group's list will include at least two or three useful insights. The risk in either case is next to nil—even if you don't get a single good idea out of it (which almost never happens), you still get the group talking and the energy up. And as Nobel Prize–winning scientist Linus Pauling said, "The best way to have a good idea is to have a lot of ideas."

Here are the rules of brainstorming at Zingerman's:

Pick the topic. The person asking for the brainstorm first needs to get clear about what question they're asking, e.g., "What are some ways we can increase sales of olive oil?"

Choose a time frame and then get someone to track time once we start. Here, we usually do two or three minutes only, but you can do whatever you like. I've been involved in brainstorms that went on for up to fifteen minutes, but most are much shorter.

Quantity counts more than quality. That means that any idea is a "good" one. It matters not if it's practical, achievable for the organization, or even possible on this planet as we currently know it to be.

Get someone to transcribe the "storm." Usually, we do that on big white sheets on the wall to raise our visual energy, but you can do it on the computer too. If it's a big group, you'll need more than one person to act as scribe when people shout out their thoughts.

No judging. During a brainstorm, there's no discussion, evaluation, critiquing, or name-calling allowed. This is just about getting as many ideas on paper as we possibly can in the allotted time.

Piggybacking on others' ideas is encouraged, as is repetition of the same idea.

Spelling doesn't count. Spell-checking during the brainstorm only serves to slow things down and diffuse the positive energy in the same way that judging does.

The timekeeper tells everyone when time has almost expired, and then announces the end of the "storm."

The finished list is given to the person who initiated the brainstorm to do with what they will.

Note: We also do what we call "introvert's brainstorms" in order to make the group engagement a tad bit more comfortable for those who, like me, like to work in their own heads. First, we give everyone a minute to write down as many ideas as they can. *Then* we start the actual out-loud brainstorm session. The "moment of silence" helps get introverted groups moving more effectively.

17. Get Emotional

Data seems to show that creativity and innovation, out-of-the-box thinking, and significant artistic activity come when emotions are running at more extreme levels. As writer and all-around interesting person Anaïs Nin noted, "The richest source of creation is feeling, followed by a vision of its meaning." It's generally when our emotional energy is either very positive (because we're having a great time) or really down (we're depressed, or grieving, or in some other form of mental anguish) that creativity comes most quickly. More often than not, I'm operating at the more positive end of the spectrum. But the epilogue of this book, about my friend Daphne's death and the inspiring way she lived the life that preceded it, came very clearly out of grief and sadness. Having published it already in a few places, I can say it's gotten more response than almost anything else I've written over the years.

While I can't imagine trying to get emotionally down in order to incite an internal burst of innovation, it's hard to argue with the realities of creative history. A brief look at the art world will show you hundreds of famously creative people who struggled through depression and emotional crisis for most or all of their lives. From Sylvia Plath to Kurt Cobain, it's a pretty compelling list. The problem, of course, is that while dwelling in the emotional depths may inspire creativity, it's a crappy way to live, and an almost impossible place from which to lead an organization. Personally, I'd prefer to have my innovative energies powered by being at the positive end of the emotional spectrum—if I'm living the Natural Laws; bringing good energy to my daily life; staying in settings in which people feel empowered and excited about what's to come; reading and learning and laughing a lot; and enjoying regular stints of running, writing, and solitude, I'm far more likely to score high on the creativity scale.

There's data to back up the belief that people who are feeling really good are more creative. Jonah Lehrer cites studies showing that "people who score high on a standard measure of happiness solve about 25 percent more insight puzzles than people who are feeling angry or upset. In fact, even fleeting feelings of delight can lead to dramatic increases in creativity." I know that when I'm feeling good and having fun, when my energy is upbeat, creativity comes quickly. Why even before breakfast (to echo the Queen in *Alice in Wonderland*), while laughing loudly with half a dozen staff members working the coffee counter at the Deli, I "invented" a Zingerman's musical café, with a Hungarian ambience and emphasis; a toothpaste company making traditional toothpastes with really wild flavors (like one of our Zzang candy bars); and Zingerman's gift cards for kids that "come from the tooth fairy." Whether we'll actually do any of them I don't know, but they sure were fun to think of in the moment. And if we had fun doing it, don't you think that might also increase the energy of the people behind the counter, in turn increasing the odds of them thinking creatively, improving service, and increasing sales as a result?

18. BE PATIENT: INTUITIVE INSIGHTS AND IDEAS TAKE TIME TO PLAY OUT

It's a Natural Law of Business that great things take a lot longer to happen than you'd think. I stand by Joe Linley, a seventh generation North Carolina miller, who once told me, "Nothing good ever happens in a hurry!" In studying all this stuff around creativity, what I've known instinctively and experientially for a long time turns out to be statistically true too. Hunches, intuitive insights, epiphanies, or whatever you want to call them need time in order to move from their initial intellectual inception to implementation. If we judge them too quickly, if we let our impatience get in the way of our innate wisdom, we will likely have forgotten the idea long before it has a chance of being successfully implemented.

As Steven Johnson says, "Most hunches that turn into important innovations unfold over much longer time frames. They start with a vague, hard-to-describe sense that there's an interesting solution to a problem that hasn't yet been proposed, and they linger in the shadows of the mind, sometimes for decades, assembling new connection and gaining strength. And then one day they are transformed into something more substantial." He continues, "Sustaining the slow hunch is less a matter of perspiration than of cultivation." Community-minded anarchist Peter Kropotkin said much the same thing in the late 19th century: "A great idea does not germinate in a day, however rapid the elaboration and propagation of ideas during periods of revolution. It always needs a certain time to develop, to spread throughout the masses, to translate itself into action." Speaking of strange ideas and crazy connections, we've done well in the world with the work of the Slow Food initiative. Maybe it's time to give some thought to a similar initiative for the intellect. A Slow Ideas movement might make sense as well.

19. DO IT: FROM INSIGHT TO IMPLEMENTATION

It's an interesting question to consider: how much value does a creative thought have if no one ever does anything with it? I'm gonna argue that an idea left unimplemented has about the same value as a vegetable left on the vine, a book that's never read, or a recipe that's never cooked. Clearly, it's far better to have them available than not, but the benefit they actually bring when they're unused remains next to nil. Granted, we've learned that an idea unfinished in one area (or era) may later be picked up and pushed forward by someone in another, so there is some merit I suppose in just having it handy. But I would

391

argue that the value is mostly in making connections come alive—ultimately, it's the ideas that get implemented that matter most. As anarchist composer John Cage said, "Ideas are one thing and what happens is another."

 Thinking About Implementation

If you run with what I wrote in Secret #38, that the way we think will have a huge impact on the way our organization works, then there's really great value in looking inward to assess how we view this part of the process. Take some time to reflect on the following:

Which parts of the idea-making process provoke the biggest sense of achievement? On a scale of 0 (I don't like it at all) to 10 (I want to celebrate!), score each of the pieces of the implementation process:

Inception (i.e., the first time you have the idea)

Initial discussion (i.e., the first time or two that you share it with others)

When the action plan is being produced

When the first steps towards implementation are initiated

About halfway through the implementation process

When the last piece of the project is successfully completed

As always, there are no rights and wrongs in this reflective exercise. But mindfulness here, as everywhere, really does matter. Personally, I'd place my highest scores at the beginning and the end of the process: with inception, and then again with effective implementation. Learning about open book finance from Jack Stack and energy management from Anese Cavanaugh, along with connecting the anarchists and our approach to business, were particularly exciting points of the idea development process. Fortunately, I'm equally attracted to the finish line. The pieces in the middle are less exciting for me, but I've learned to appreciate, work hard, and enjoy them more over the years as I've improved in my own self-management.

By keeping my energy relatively positive throughout, I can help others see how to effectively take ideas from inception through to fruition, which means that they're learning the logistics of how to make their dreams come true. Which, in turn, is very inspiring for me. On top of which, if I get super excited about completion, then it's kind of clear that I have to do at least decently well in the middle of the process to get to where I want to go at the end. *The big sense of achievement for me is when we've successfully sunk a new idea deeply into our organizational culture.* When it has an ongoing positive impact that no longer requires me to personally push on it, then I know that the idea has really meaningfully made a difference.

Keep in mind that any sort of significant idealization takes time. While an insight or an epiphany may make itself apparent to our conscious minds in an instant, it usually takes much, much (much) longer before the idea is converted into a meaningful change. Here at Zingerman's, I generally figure about two to three years before something new will really take root in our culture. As long as that seems, it's only at that point that we've started to make a difference, to move past dissonance and discussion into change that will have a deep impact on the way we live and work.

What this means for managers is that we need to stay intellectually engaged with an idea (and, for that matter, as per the Secret on thinking, with the people involved as well) long enough to see it through to fruition. Having ideas is fun, like being a kid cruising through a candy store. The possibilities seem limitless, the attraction is high. Implementing an idea, on the other hand, is like owning and operating the candy store instead of just coming for a visit and ogling the sweet opportunities it presents. Ultimately, managing a successful candy business can be hugely rewarding, but it requires a whole lot more work and stick-to-itiveness than it does to simply stand in the shop thinking about how great it would be to eat one of those really amazing looking red and white lollipops lying on the counter.

Sticking with an idea through to effective implementation is a lot, I think, like any successful long-term relationship. It's about finding ways to stay engaged, to rediscover its wonders, to stay focused on the fun, to love the possibilities, to believe in who you are and what you're doing, and to put up with the frequent drudgery of daily details, all the while looking forward to new discoveries still to come. There's no value judgment implied here; have any sort of relationship—as short, long, chaotic, or calm as you like. My point is only that if we leave our new ideas or insights behind after a brief flirtation, we're likely to end up with the sort of flavor-of-the-day management that's so ineffective at any level.

When it comes to creativity, there's a big difference between the idle daydreamers wondering what might be possible one day and entrepreneurs who start successful businesses, or scientists who see their insight through from invention to practical application for the general population. I'll bet the same ideas that someone eventually makes big money from, or wins an award for, have often also popped into the minds of many others. The work we want to do here is about turning a daydream into something that makes a very real difference for real people in the world. Which has led me, of late, to consider an alternate view of the acronym ROI. Rather than the standard, financially focused "Return on Investment," I've started to think about the "Return on Insight" as a way to consider how well we can take creative ideas and turn them into tangible realities. I'm not sure yet what my formula will be, but I'm increasingly confident that this kind of kooky formulation might turn out to be a really effective way to track an organization's creative output.

20. Go Wild—Fill in Your Own Way to Get Creative!

I have no illusion that, even in this long essay, I've come up with everything there is to convey about creativity. You, I'm confident, will have much to add, whether small, large, silly, or seriously stupendous. I'd love to hear what you think on the subject. If you're feeling inspired, how about writing me at ari@zingermans.com to share whatever cool, creative stuff this piece has prompted you to do? Who knows what great connections could come of it?

Two Reasons Why We Had No Recipe for Creativity, and One Reason I Don't Want One

1. You can't force it. As much as you may want your creativity to increase, you really can't just cause it to happen on the spot. What you *can* do is increase the odds of it happening. In other words, do your best to create the right conditions and then wait and see what emerges. Which is why, I also realize, we went so long at Zingerman's *being* creative but failed to write up one of our now almost routine organizational recipes to make it happen.

Given what I know now, this actually makes good sense. All our other organizational recipes are designed to take us, one step at a time, closer to success; if we follow them all the way through, the final step is almost certain to bring a positive ending to the process. Our 3 Steps to Great Service are pretty much guaranteed to get us to a good customer experience, and our 3 Steps to Great Finance will lead us closer to better finance. None of our recipes are foolproof, but there's a clear result that we're after, and we've been able to map out the steps to take in order to very regularly make it a reality.

While the recipes always leave room for surprise, adaptation, and innovation, they're still remarkably direct and to the point: "if we do this, we get that." Creativity, however, is different. You can't guarantee that you'll arrive at it by following a simple plan. Innovation is like wild fruit— you can only create the conditions in which it's more likely to do well. All of this was driven home even more effectively through a visit with a very progressive business school professor. She showed me a great book on creative organizational models, commenting that the Zingerman's Community of Businesses really ought to have been in the book. I chuckled, thanked her for the compliments, and said, "Of course you realize that if we'd set out to develop a creative business model, we'd probably never have come up with anything that would have qualified us for the book."[34]

Creative business models, like other creative results, are almost always arrived at by accident, obliquely and indirectly. If we'd tried too hard to be creative, we'd probably have failed. What we did do was to actively envision an organization that we would want to work in, that would help us live our mission and contribute to our community, one that we thought would enhance entrepreneurship, high quality, and great service, and provide a positive workplace with plenty of room for growth. We did well to achieve all of that. Inadvertently, in the process, we happened to develop a creative and innovative model for our business.

2. The more often you make something, the less you need a recipe. When you study cookbooks and their role in the cultures that create them, what you find is that the frequency with which recipes appear in books is generally *inversely* related to the familiarity with the dish in the everyday kitchen of its era. In other words, the more something is made regularly in homes, the *less* likely it is to show up in a cookbook. The reason is simple—there's no need to document anything about a dish you make every day, because nearly everyone already knows how to make it. If you learned it from your grandmother, you don't need to look it up in a cookbook. It's only as the knowledge of how to make the dish erodes—for example, when people who grew up in the country move to urban areas away from their culinary roots—that formal recipes are documented and published.

The connection to creativity struck me as obvious. We've had no written recipe for innovation at Zingerman's, because it's a "dish" we prepare without really even thinking about it, all day, every day, in our cultural kitchen. But in corporate America, with a mainstream manager's mindset, it's a different story all together. The creative insights that our employees offer up every day without even thinking about it would be challenging, if not impossible, to incorporate in that other world. In creative settings, innovative ideas appear like wild mushrooms in the woods. (It's worth noting that, using modern agriculture, you can, of course, cultivate mushrooms en masse under controlled conditions. But while they're clearly related to their spontaneously appearing wild cousins, and will work in recipes, they really don't even come close to the full, complex flavor of their "out-of-control" forebears.)

In a tightly controlled, highly regulated workplace, people become more focused on following along and fitting in. Wild mushrooms are likely to be plowed under before they ruin the main cash crop. As Deanna White, who's always making spiritual connections with the work she does selling baked goods, said to me one morning, "Most places you work, creativity is considered dangerous. Here, it's rewarded." Staff members in other organizational cultures may be well meaning, but they often don't know what to do without a way to "cook up" the creativity that happens more spontaneously in healthier cultures. Like the city kid who can no longer prepare their grandma's favorite dish, but longs for it regularly, corporate staff members struggle without some sort of formal process. They might even need to call in caterers to cook for them. In which case, they might just, I suppose, contact ZingTrain and ask us to come in to teach a class on creativity.

Plus, even if you had a recipe, it won't really work. Here's the real kicker, though. Trying too hard to fix the creativity deficit diminishes creativity! It's ironic, but according to both Johnson and Lehrer, *the more you focus on a problem, the lower your creativity is going to be.* Which means that the more people profess the need for creativity in the corporate setting and try to push their crew to quickly find their creative feet, the less likely it is to happen.

Mind you, that doesn't mean we should never focus on a problem. Problem solving certainly has its place; if we're short three people on tomorrow morning's shift, creativity is generally not what we need to set things straight. In that case, there's a pretty straightforward situation, one that generally (though not always, I know) calls for quick, straightforward solutions.

Worrying about not being creative enough creates awkward self-consciousness, not creativity. It's like stressing out trying to write "a great poem," rather than just letting go and letting the words and rhythms emerge naturally from your heart and your head. It's no wonder so many well-meaning companies are struggling. Trying to fix a creativity problem by focusing on it too hard only exacerbates the problem. They might do better to take that old Brooklyn approach and just Fuggetaboutit for a while.

Part 3: Transforming the Ecosystem of Business?

ALTERING OUR OWN ECOSYSTEM

In Steven Johnson's *Where Good Ideas Come From,* he mentions what environmental scientist Clive Jones calls "ecosystem engineers." Jones isn't referring to a new advanced degree program at the Cary Institute of Ecosystem Studies, where he teaches, but rather to any number of naturally occurring organisms whose behavior alters the entire ecosystem in which they "work." I'm not talking small stuff, but rather major cultural change—think about the Theory of Relevantivity on steroids. Beavers are his big example. They chew down trees to make dams, which in turn transform whole forests into wetlands in a relatively short time. Everything that was living in the woods when the bucktoothed rodents took down their first logs will then be significantly impacted afterward.

Speaking of the Theory of Relevantivity, reading about Jones's work made me look anew at the impact our work here at Zingerman's has had on the world. I don't know if I'm reading things correctly, but it dawned on me during the writing of this piece that the Zingerman's 2009 vision that we wrote back in 1994 actually filled the bill: we didn't just open a new business, *we radically altered the business ecosystem in which we were working.*

The Zingerman's Community of Businesses that came to exist as a result of that vision has, I believe, had a huge impact on the local environment in which we operate. By designing and implementing an entirely different organizational architecture—*a connected and collaborative community of businesses rather than the usual path of opening various branches of the original business*—we didn't just change what we did every day, we remade the entire way we live, work, and think. Rather than the mainstream 20th century model of narrow focus, franchise, or, replicated models run through fairly central staff services, we created an organization that operates in an entirely different way. Instead of trying to cash out or go public, we preferred to stay local and go for it for the long haul.

Knowing what I know now, it's pretty clear why our implementation of that vision was such a game changer when it came to creativity, and hence to our long-term viability and vitality. What we wrote in 1994 really institutionalized all of the key components of creativity that I've outlined above. If four of the biggest factors involved in building an innovative organization are a) living the Natural Laws of Business; b) sharing information across organizational lines; c) bringing in a steady stream of info and ideas from outside the organization; and then d) encouraging offbeat connections between otherwise unconnected things, with the benefit of hindsight, the model we made up for our Community of Businesses starts to look like Frank Lloyd Wright–quality design work.

In fact, it's clear to me now that *the way we designed the organization— having a community of different businesses all operating collaboratively—means that simply by talking to other people in the ZCoB, almost everyone here is exposed to new and different ideas every day*. In theory, although it didn't dawn on us when we wrote the vision in 1994, it's designed to be creatively sustainable: the bigger we get, the more we will diversify, and the more creative our company is likely to be.

Bo Burlingham's *Small Giants* has helped to make us look like ecosystem engineers on a national level now. The book was based on the story Bo wrote about us in *Inc.* magazine in January of 2003. But over the last ten years, it has evolved into a mini movement of people seeking to build organizations in synch with their values and dreams rather than following mainstream business models. It's the rare week now that I don't get a call from a businessperson somewhere who's considering growing using a model of separate but still connected businesses operating as one coordinated community. One friend even heard someone at a board meeting of a nonprofit organization in another state suggest the group look into what she referred to quite weightily as "the Zingerman's model." A surprising (to me at least) number of organizations have decided to actually pursue this. While the concept has hardly gone mainstream, there are a lot more "communities of businesses" around the country today than there were when we wrote the vision.

Add to that all the things that have evolved out of our ecosystem shift, things we didn't invent, but which have thrived here where they might not have elsewhere—visioning, our service recipes, an emphasis on traditional food, open book finance, Servant Leadership, energy management, my interest in the anarchists, etc.—that have all gone on to contribute to a plethora of other workplaces around the country. All of which tells me that this one bold, unintentionally creative, collaborative, caring, and ultimately very effective vision for 2009 (written and embarked upon in 1994) has altered the way many people think about business in this country. That kind of broader change was hardly the goal of the vision, but it seems to have happened in the process.

The Big-Time Benefit of ZingTrain

While it's only one small piece of our organization, it's clear to me that ZingTrain has contributed significantly to our creativity. Johnson writes, "There are good ideas, and then there are good ideas that make it easier to have other good ideas." ZingTrain was one of the latter. While its product is most properly defined as training, it's pretty clear to me that exchange and incitement of ideas, insights, and inspirational learning are its most immediate impacts.

Maggie Bayless's original vision of a small Zingerman's training business that might actively teach the world about our ways of working has proven itself exceptionally productive. The active sharing that she initiated and that ZingTrain now routinely runs has benefited thousands of organizations around the world. It's really raised the bar on our own learning here at Zingerman's as well—when you teach something, you learn it at a far higher level than if you only need to understand it. ZingTrain has radically improved the way we share ideas and information within our own organization.

Bonus of bonuses, although ZingTrain's work is about training, in synch with a spirit of generosity it's actually brought a wealth of good ideas from others. Over the course of the twenty years since ZingTrain came into being we've created an intellectual community of thousands of creative businesses around the world, most of whom are happily sharing ideas with us and, in turn, with each other. Not surprisingly, when you start to share your ideas actively, others will begin to share in return. It's a very sustainable, supportive, creative cycle. To paraphrase Thomas Jefferson, light one candle with another, with that one another still, and on and on and on. In the end, everyone and everything is increasingly illuminated!

Why Community Giving Trumps Corporate Profit in Pushing Creativity

One of the most interesting insights I gleaned from Johnson's book is the data he did on what he calls the "Fourth Quadrant." Studying innovations over the centuries, he tracked the course of significant innovative developments in order to determine what the driving force behind them was, as well as who it was (whether individual or group) that was doing the driving. Which inventions, he wanted to know, were motivated mostly by the idea of making money? And alternatively, which were driven by the act of doing good deeds for society? Which inventions tended to be individual efforts, and which were arrived at more collaboratively? He put his findings into the form of a graph, sorting them into four quadrants:

1. Innovations achieved by individuals with the intent of making money from them.
2. Collaborative innovations done to make money.
3. Individual innovations done for the common good.
4. Collaborative innovations created with community rather than corporate profit in mind.

Surprisingly (or not, I guess, depending on what you believe about the world), there were far more innovations in category 4 than any other category. The ideas that came from collaborative processes, driven primarily for the purpose of doing good for the world, are by far the dominant domain over the course of the last few centuries! In other words, doing good and contributing to the world seems to have contributed more creativity than the drive for cash. It makes good sense to me. And it also speaks to contemporary New Zealand writer Helen Richardson's statement that, "[anarchism] at its heart promotes creativity. Creativity that is not profit driven but respects the individual's need of autonomy and job fulfillment and care for the environment." Or as Emma Goldman said a century ago, "The rejuvenation of mankind needs the inspiration and energising force of an ideal."

Conclusion: A Quick Look at Leaders and Creativity

Clearly, if you've made it this far in this piece, creativity is a high priority for you. I hope I've given you enough intellectual food for creative thought to keep you going for a while. I'm pretty confident that any of the ideas I've listed will be of help in your own creative cause. I hope you'll pursue any or all of them, regularly, and that you'll get back to me to share how your efforts unfold.

Personally, I've started to focus particular attention on how we attempt to spread our creative mindset, optimistic outlook, and openness to ideas to people we've newly hired into our organization. The way we welcome them into the organization makes an enormous difference. So many of them seem to be coming out of severely limited settings, and many seem to suffer from what psychologist Martin Seligman calls "learned helplessness." They've been trained to believe, through the process of growing up or by being emotionally beat up out in the work force, that their views and their work make little or no difference. Most will unknowingly have been taught that they have no influence over anything. In which case, why get creative? Both animals and people in test groups where they had no influence on delivered pain just "took it," Seligman reports, waiting it out "with no attempt to escape."

This helpless feeling is, unfortunately, endemic. It appears in the form of the energy crisis in the workplace that I wrote about in *Part 2*. It feels more and more to me that the most important creative work we can undertake is an effort to encourage those who are new to our organizations, our social circles, or our families to undo that difficult state of mind. We can teach people that rather than wait for their bosses to make things better, they'd do better to think boldly, to go for greatness, to wonder why, and to release a bit of their natural wildness into the world. Whether your organization employs five people or fifty, five hundred or five thousand, think of what amazing things might happen if we could unleash all of their naturally occurring creative abilities.

Pulling a couple of my favorite themes together, maybe I'll leave you with this thought from Basque performance artist Esther Ferrer. Writing to composer John Cage, she articulated that anarchism, like creativity, is "choice, which engages only yourself and which you decided to practice . . . One can practice it alone, even if others are not at all interested . . . These ideas, John, at bottom, are simply natural creations of free thought . . . capable of inventing imaginative and joyful solutions."

So, I say, let's get to work and have some fun while we're at it. Go wild, read books, connect all the dots you can, and "embrace the anarchist." Whatever you do, don't worry—the creativity will come. And, when it does, it's sure to raise our spirits, our effectiveness, and our enjoyment of life. At the least, we'll breathe better. As Julia Cameron says, "Creativity is oxygen for our souls."

List of Things to Do to Increase Creativity

Brainstorm: Pick any issue you're working on and spend three minutes listing ideas for how to improve it. You can follow the rules of brainstorming (page 388). While they're particularly effective in groups, I've done them on my own on my yellow legal pad. The results can be similarly energizing in either setting.

Read something new: If you don't have anything intriguing in mind, my personal reading list is in the back of the book on page 455. Reading anything interesting is pretty sure to spark new insights, especially if you pick up something that's far from your normal field—an anarchist essay, something on the history of Hungary, a study of chocolate, or almost anything else is bound to get you thinking.

Read something old: This afternoon I stopped by our Coffee Company to get a cup of Ethiopian to keep me going while I worked on the book. When I walked in, the crew behind the counter (Erin, David, Rebecca, and Chris) were asking each customer who came in for the name of a book that had changed their life. Which, in turn, triggered this thought in me. Think back to a book, a poem, an article, or an essay that made a major positive impact on you. Go back and reread it. The chances are it'll trigger many of the same positive feelings it did the first time around, and with all of the input you've gathered from reading this far in this book, I'm guessing you'll find even more insightful messages to tap into as well.

Run, walk, row: If you don't have meditative exercise of some sort in your week, give it a try. The mental "free time" often works wonders. As Brenda Ueland says, "For me, a long five or six mile walk helps. And one must go alone and every day."

Listen to new music, go to a poetry reading, admire amazing art: Really, any medium that you're not used to being in, mindfully attended to, will add richness to your world and probably provoke a couple new and interesting connections.

Travel, either in person or online: Getting into a new cultural setting is sure to shake you up a bit, generally in good ways! Travel doesn't have to be to distant lands. Even a day trip to the small town nearby can give you a new perspective. Sit in the coffee shop on the corner and take it all in, see who you see and see what you learn.

Open up your meetings: If you're at work and you want to shake things up and inspire some new ideas, try inviting some frontline people, or maybe some colleagues from a different department, a client, or a supplier, to sit in. The new perspectives are sure to make the session more interesting.

Move: I don't mean to a new apartment or a different city. Just move into a new spot in the same environment you're already in every day. Literally, just going into a new space at work can change the way you see the world. Move the couch to a new angle. Shift your desk to a different spot in the office; change your office; or better still, go sit in the lobby or by the back dock and work from there for a while. If you attend a regular meeting, try sitting in a spot that's different than the one you usually go to. Better still, get up and move to a different spot in the room every hour or so in a long meeting.

Reflect: Try journaling regularly. As you know, I do it every day, even if it's just for fifteen minutes. Julia Cameron recommends the same, doing what she calls "your morning pages," a minimum of three pages per day (see page 136 for more on journaling). If you don't want to write, try Martin Piszczalski's visual journaling process instead (see page 139).

notes from the back dock

Dana Laidlaw, Retail Staffer, Zingerman's Bakehouse

Creativity Is NOT . . .

• Complacent! If you are satisfied, why do things differently? My creative moments come when:

I am not satisfied with the choices presented
I don't have the usual tools I need to do the job
I have to figure out a different or better way
There are almost always constraints to work around

• Something you can turn on or off. Creative thoughts need a little pressure or time constraint but don't come on demand. Your mind will mull things over and pop out answers when it is ready.

• A free-for-all. You can't just decide to change how we do things. That is what Bottom Line Change [our process for organizational change] is for. Getting others' cooperation and approval is necessary to make anything work and to ensure you haven't missed some big glaring problem with your idea. You also still have to work within our existing rules, standards, vision, etc. Knowing the limits makes it easier, since you have a base of good decisions to work from. You can't have a jam session until you have mastered your scales.

Creativity IS . . .

• Creative. You pull together items or ideas or tools that others haven't thought to use, or you put your own spin on them.

• Open. Closed minds can't be creative. You have to be willing to see connections between things that aren't normally linked together, like Anarchists and great business practices, for instance.

• Diverse and collaborative. I was listening to a television writer and producer talk about his craft. He said he likes to have a group of writers to work with because you never know who will know the piece of info that will make the story better. It is the same with creativity in any business. The more diverse group of people you get together, the more likely the group will generate ideas that one person could not make on their own. That is why creativity and our Bottom Line Change process go hand in hand. The more people you consult, the better and more creative the results are likely to be.

a happy moment: randolph hodgson of neal's yard dairy and daphne zepos

EPILOGUE

Daphne's Death, a Fascination with Friendship, and Owning Our Lives

What follows is both the end of this book and also the story of the death of one of my best friends. Daphne died while I was writing, in the summer of 2012. While it's not the kind of thing one usually includes in a business book, I think a reflection on her passing is appropriate here. Managing ourselves well through life also means, by definition, preparing for a graceful and good death.

Daphne was seven years old when, in the spring of 1967, Greek colonels took over her country and cut out democracy for seven years. A few months earlier, in January of that year, American anarchist poet and prodigal rock star Jim Morrison sang very slowly and very somberly:

> *This is the end, beautiful friend*
> *This is the end, my only friend*
> *The end of our elaborate plans*
> *The end of ev'rything that stands*
> *The end*

It's still hard for me to say it out loud, but between the time I began drafting this epilogue and the time you arrived at this page to read it, my very dear friend Daphne Zepos died. Her cancer, which came on seemingly out of nowhere in early April of 2012, took her away a mere three months later. As she was a revolutionary in both deed and spirit, it's fitting that Daphne's entrance and exit from the world took place within a day of the anniversaries of two of the world's most famous revolutions—she was born on July 13th, one day before Bastille

Day, the anniversary of the French Revolution. And she died just shy of 53 years later, on July 3rd, the eve of American Independence Day.

As hard as it is for me to tell it, it seems fitting to include her story here: effectively managing ourselves, eventually, inevitably, means managing through death, our own or those we love and live with. On a professional level, we may also need to manage through the death of a business, a project, or an idea we cared deeply about. Although there's no funeral to attend or flowers to send, the struggles can be similar. It might be helpful to consider the words of the Indian mystic Osho: "Death is an organic, integral part of life, and it is very friendly to life. Without it life cannot exist . . . If you really want to live you have to be ready to die."

An epilogue serves a similar purpose in a book, encapsulating and high-lighting what is past, bringing a formal end to a long and organic process. The word "epilogue," like "Daphne," comes from the Greek. One formal definition explains that an epilogue is "the concluding part of a speech or discourse, in which the speaker or writer recapitulates the principal points and urges them with greater earnestness and force." Considering Daphne's life—and now death—here is a sad but sure way for me to attempt to do that.

Daphne was diagnosed with cancer in the spring of 2012. The news was rather sudden—her symptoms had been minimal. The cancer worked quickly. In late June of 2012, knowing there was no way to stop the disease from careening through her body, Daphne opted to cut out the chemo. She decided to exit the earth as she'd lived—on her own terms. I had the privilege of watching Daphne manage herself with extraordinary grace and insight even while dying of cancer. In the process, she modeled positive psychologist Martin Seligman's belief that "People who live well, die well. The more peace you culti-vate in your life, the more peaceful your death is likely to be."

In those final months, as well as throughout the nearly two decades we had together as friends, Daphne lived in a way that really exemplifies every-thing in the ten Secrets that preceded this piece. This epilogue, this bittersweet ending, ties together the key content covered in the rest of the book, and at the same time serves as a tribute to someone I opened my own heart to, someone from whom we can all learn a lot about managing ourselves into more mean-ingful, more rewarding lives. By living her life with passion and poignancy, Daphne touched many people; I hope that by sharing her story here, she can touch many more.

A Life of Her Own

I am, as you know by now, fully aligned with the anarchist belief that we're all unique human beings. But Daphne was somehow more unique than the rest of us. Whatever she did, she did quite simply by being Daphne. Which is really the whole point of this book and, I think, the point of life: to be true to ourselves; to pursue our passions and to be passionate; and to the best of our abilities, live a life of our own design, all the while helping to make the world around us a better place to be, but always by doing it in our own way. As Miles Davis said, "A genius is the one most like himself."

Daphne's upbringing was rich in the sort of diverse experiences that can contribute to a creative life. Born and raised in Greece, she had lived in four international capitals by the time she turned 18—Athens, London, Geneva, and Brussels—as her diplomat father moved around for his work. I remember her telling me tales of obscure boarding schools, reading books, writing poetry, and eating bread and chocolate in fancy sounding places in France, Switzerland, and England. She later studied medieval history at the University of Kent in Canterbury, England, and then architecture at the Architectural Association in London. At some point, I know, she made her way across the Balkans on a motorcycle. In 1987 she moved to New York and enrolled at Peter Kump's New York Cooking School. At the time we met, in the mid-'90s, Daphne was living in San Francisco and working as a sous chef in the kitchen at an upscale hotel on Union Square.

One thing Daphne never was in the twenty years I knew her was docile. Her energy was expansive, a natural wonder, a forceful inspiration, and a thought provoking presence. When she entered a space, everyone knew it. Even if she stood off to the side, the energy in the room shifted when she stepped into it. Long, bold, black curly hair; fierce, focused, loving dark eyes behind oblong red-framed (rather modernist) glasses that I think only added to the sense that you were in the presence of someone special. Whatever she did, Daphne had style and an especially great smile. She spoke like no one else I know—defiantly, with a tinge of self-doubt, but always with great dignity, and always from the heart. Her accent was unique—definitely Greek, but significantly influenced no doubt by her fluent French and excellent English learned in those continental boarding schools.

Walking one's own way, following one's beliefs, and adhering to a path even when it wasn't the easiest to traverse was clearly a family trait. When the colonels took power in the Greek junta in 1967, Daphne's father refused to serve the new government, earning himself the moniker, "the Red Diplomat." He and his wife, Daphne's mother, sheltered political prisoners in their home. When the junta fell seven years later, Daphne, only 14 at the time, disappeared for a few days in the middle of the madness. It turned out she'd tracked down some of the demonstrators and was working to restore the same freedoms her father had fought for on a more professional political level.

Daphne was probably way too direct to have succeeded at diplomacy the way her father had. Her passions were far more powerful than her politics. You might not have always heard what you wanted to hear, but you definitely heard what she was thinking. She said it so poetically that even when she was putting you down or really, I should say, putting you back in your place, you sort of didn't mind. It was like getting sent to jail knowing that the portrait for your prison ID was being painted by Picasso.

Daphne and I met twenty years or so ago, in the mid-'90s, on a trip to the town of Metsovo in northern Greece, organized by the American Cheese Society. Another food writer I knew told me that this amazing woman was going to be on the trip, and gave me very clear instructions: "You MUST meet Daphne Zepos!" It didn't take long. That friend had told Daphne to meet *me* as well. Without being formally introduced, we figured out on our own who each other was from across the airport. Our vibrational energies were running on similar wavelengths—it's pretty clear that we were wired to be connected in the world.

Wendell Berry writes, "The old and honorable idea of 'vocation' is simply that we each are called, by God, or by our gifts, or by our preference, to a kind of work for which we are particularly fitted." Daphne's calling, as everyone who knew her knows, was curd, cheese, a field of study that she unofficially but majestically presided over for the last decade of her life. She bonded with it, stayed with it, lived it, loved it, taught about it with terrific passion, and of course ate it with great gusto. If the cheeses of the world wanted to choose a spokesperson, they'd have done well to have decided upon Daphne.

I'm still not exactly sure how to describe what Daphne did for a living, but I like the name she made up for it, "pastoral anthropology." As her sister Amalia said, "She invented the profession she wanted and made it work."[35] If successfully managing ourselves means that we leave the planet better than it was when we arrived, and that we've thoroughly enjoyed our travels en route, then Daphne was as successful as anyone I know. The world is a far better, more flavorful, more fun place for having had Daphne in it. If vocation, as Paul Goodman says, is a love story, then Daphne lived it well.

Anarchists and Friendship

The word *anarchism*, like *epilogue*, is also from the Greek. Its root—"anarchos"—means "without rulers." Which is, upon reflection, what friendship as I'm writing about it here is really all about. Because there's rarely a ruler, and so also no ruled, a good friendship might be the ultimate in anarchistic relationships. Unlike blood relatives, friends become and stay friends purely by choice. Despite outsiders' occasional efforts to the contrary, we can't really be forced into a friendship. And friendships are freely traded—they're formed only when both parties are in favor of the arrangement. They're not taxed, there are no trade restrictions that limit them, and there's no paper you have to sign to acquire or to end one. Good friendships, like all anarchist activities, are based on free choice, mutual support, hope, belief, generosity, and a win-win way to work together. As Massimo Pigliucci says in *Answers for Aristotle: How Science and Philosophy Can Lead Us to a More Meaningful Life*, "It makes perfect sense that you could be in love with someone who doesn't reciprocate your feeling, but it is incoherent to say that one has a nonreciprocal friendship."

To quote early 20th century German film critic and anarchist Siegfried Kracauer, "Friendship expands the soul. [It] presents people with treasures they could hardly have attained on their own." What we achieve together is quite simply shared; it makes the notion of intellectual or spiritual "property" seem kind of silly. Friendships are about treating each other as equals regardless of one's formal standing in the world, honoring and encouraging the unique personality and spirit of each and every person we befriend. As Professor Pigliucci writes, "Friends, then, share a similar concept of *eudaimonia* [Greek for the phrase 'having a good demon,' which many refer to as 'well-being'] and help each other achieve it. So it is not just that friends are instrumentally good because they enrich our lives, but that they are an integral part of what it means to live the good life, according to Aristotle and other ancient Greek philosophers . . ."[36] They end when one or both of the friends decide it's time to move on. Or when one of them dies.

Life, Love, and a Bittersweet Bit of Liberty

Wherever she was, Daphne was the epitome of liveliness. She had a fierce love for learning, traveling, teaching, and tasting. I doubt that I'll ever meet anyone else like her. She fit into no box; she always made her own mold. She was Greek all the way through and yet, at the same time, completely international. She was a cheese aficionado without being a cheesemaker, poetic without being a poet, a leader without ever really having been in charge of anything other than her own life. She never owned a big company, but she could well have been the president of something significant or, I might say, the queen of a country so compelling it doesn't yet exist. She was unique, unselfish, unrelenting, unequalled in her love for cheese, her passion for life, and the way she shared those passions with those she loved and cared for.

Throughout her years Daphne demonstrated with great consistency that the more love you can bring to your life, the richer it—and the world around you—will ultimately be. We were never lovers in the way the world at large likes to use the term, but her husband Brad told me, "You were one of the loves of her life." The first day we arrived on that original cheese trip to Greece, we went to the village of Metsovo, up in the mountains. Metsovo is not a big town—I'm sure we traversed most of it in a few hours. About halfway through our walk we came to a church atop a small hill. The panorama was spectacular. Down the slope, looking out to the valley, we saw the village cemetery. Gravestones glistened white and gray in the sun, the sky was blue, and we were enjoying the energy of our new friendship. Daphne explained to me that graveyards in Greece were always positioned so that the dead would have the best possible view of the world. I hope that the view from wherever she and her spirit now reside is even more beautiful than what we saw in the village that sunny afternoon.[37]

Daphne was always a great friend, but she was a terrible communicator when you weren't sitting or standing right next to her. We both knew it and laughed about it often. Over the years, I pretty much made peace with the reality that I needed to call Daphne about fifteen or twenty times before she would call me back. Part of my ongoing acceptance of her death is that no matter how many times I call or write her, this time I know there will never be a response. I told her, a week or so before she passed away, that I would keep on calling her after she'd gone. I left her a voicemail a month after she died. Knowing her, I wouldn't be surprised if she got it. Her lack of response doesn't necessarily mean that it didn't get through. Mostly the message was just me telling her how much I missed her.

Daphne's Recipe for Owning One's Life

It still makes me sad to think about not having Daphne in my life, to no longer be able to laugh and taste and talk and travel together. Part of managing oneself through something as dark as the death of a dear friend is to share the struggle, to own that it hurts, to say to anyone that's interested that I'm incredibly sad, that I miss Daphne now, and that I will miss her deeply as long as I'm alive. Thinking back to the Natural Laws, first of Business and now of Life, I have to work very hard to remind myself that my deep sadness around Daphne's death is a good problem. I'm lucky to have had many great friends in my life, and Daphne was one of the dearest.

A few months before she died, Daphne agreed to spend a small bit of time with me sitting by her bedside. It was, for me, one of Nikolai Berdyaev's "existential moments," the painful kind that feels like it's going to go on forever. Watching my friend failing, significantly thinner, weaker and paler than I'd ever seen her, the fifteen minutes I was with her seemed like months. Her spirit was still solid but sickness had taken hold of her body and her breathing had become shallow. It was a painful, awkward, uncomfortable moment that I didn't want to end. Sad as I was, I knew it was the prelude to even greater sadness. And yet it was an amazing few minutes, which Berdyaev himself might have appreciated. "I've lived my life!" Daphne said, with a force almost incongruent with her obvious weakness. "I went against the grain of success in many ways. But I have no regrets. I've lived a good life. *I owned my life.*"

I wanted to write this piece to honor Daphne, and also to honor everyone who works hard to create a life that is their own. Or perhaps I should say, to own a life that they've created, that's stayed true to their own spirit in spite of the pressures to perform and conform that come at us so hard, it seems at times, from nearly every direction. By Wall Street or world press standards, you couldn't really say that Daphne was a success; she had neither formal fame nor fortune. If you were to look at her balance sheet, it probably wasn't all that strong. But if you turn your attention to what she was most proud to have owned, she could be considered one of the world's wealthiest women. She lived the Natural Laws of Life as well as anyone I've ever met, and she brought love and passion everywhere she went.

If you travel and study the food world, I think you'll find, as I have, that although the formal credit and kudos frequently go to fancy restaurants and food stores, the true soul of a community and its cuisine is to be found in the homes. While the chefs can write recipes and put out books, and retailers can sell enough to survive or even thrive economically, it's the women (and sometimes men) in the home kitchens who truly get it, who have internalized the cooking and culture in ways that better known industry stars can't quite pull off. Home cooks rarely write out recipes—they just make the food, and they do it well. There's far too much nuance, instinct, emotion and below-the-surface insight involved for them to bother with formal instructions. They teach by doing, not by drafting detailed directions.

Having watched many talented cooks in action over the years, I've gotten pretty good at figuring out what it is they're doing when they're working. Even if they don't hand me a detailed recipe, I can usually recreate a pretty good version of their best dishes. Having known her for twenty years, I think I can also come up with a pretty reasonably accurate version of Daphne's recipe for a good life. I'll probably miss an ingredient or two, but at least I'll come close.

So here's my take:

Find something you're passionate about and then give yourself
    to it.

Find people you're passionate about and then give yourself
    to them.

Don't give in to demands to live in a way that's out of synch
    with your self.

Study with passion and learn like crazy.

Travel widely and mindfully to where you want, and need, to go.

Embrace your feelings and share them freely and joyfully with
    the world.

Laugh a lot, especially with those you love.

Believe in anything big you do, or don't bother doing it.

Always hope for the best and have fun in the process.

Be generous of spirit and everything else.

Bring love, passion, poetry, and the flavor of great cheese
    (figuratively if not literally) to everything you do.

Own your life!

One thing I know for sure—Daphne's recipe for a good life wouldn't include any halfway measures. She had a habit, a gift, of seeing the best in everyone she loved, and of identifying what they were good at, even if they themselves were in denial. The bottom line is that the people she loved felt better in her presence. Whatever it is you're about, I know she'd have said to go all out. And to keep going, to push beyond the staid stuff in which much of the world so often wallows. To put as much love as possible into your life, and where you have love, to let it loose as extravagantly as you can.

The End

While I was working on this essay, extracting the epilogue from an ending I never dreamed of, nor desired to write, I came across a note Daphne had sent me many years ago. The last line stopped me cold, stunned me really, with its simplicity and with her exceptional ability to say what is in a wonderful, if in hindsight chillingly sad, sort of way. At the end of an otherwise unimportant email she wrote: "I never see you enough. There is always so much more to say."

Some day when you taste a particularly great piece of cheese, or when you're surrounded by good friends, or when you start to doubt yourself and feel you've lost your way, I hope you'll think of Daphne, or of the "Daphnes" in your life. Don't dally. Life is short. Live it well, going for greatness throughout, sharing thoughts and feelings, liberally and lovingly, with family and friends. This is, it seems, where the epilogue ends. I want to go on, but I'll stop here. As Daphne said, there is always so much more to say.

the black bench out front of the delicatessen

Extra Bonus Stuff

Notes from the Front Porch

As I'm sure you've noticed while going through this book, I'm adamant that all of these "Secrets" work well in all sorts of settings. They can, as you'll see below, be organization-altering experiences. What follows are stories from folks who've adapted our ideas and approaches to their businesses. They offer, I hope, a different but productive perspective on what it means to put all this to work in places that are far afield—geographically or professionally—from our Zingerman's Community of Businesses in Ann Arbor.

About a year ago, Ari called me, out of the blue. He asked if we could talk. Zingerman's was engaged in a process of transitioning to employee ownership and he had some questions.

I didn't know Ari. But I was a long-time admirer of Zingerman's. And I had met Paul once. I heard him speak at a conference and he said something that impressed me, and stayed with me. He was talking about principled business, and he said, "But principles aren't principles until they cost something."

Isn't that the truth?

Anyway, we talked—Ari and I—and we talked again, and then I went to a Zingerman's partners' meeting to talk about the SMC cooperative ownership structure. Ari and Paul were appreciative. Ari suggested that I come to ZingTrain for their two-day Zingerman's Experience training session and graciously extended an invitation for a free session. By this time, I had become friendly with Ari and I was knocked out by the whole Zingerman's thing.

Meanwhile, Maggie Bayless, who runs ZingTrain, wrote me and said she was coming to a two-day class I do called "The Art of Small Business." At first I was a bit intimidated: she runs ZingTrain and she's coming all the way to Vermont to take my two-bit class? But I was excited too.

She came, and her presence made my class much better than it would have been without her. So my colleague Deirdre Bohan and I decided to go do the Zingerman's Experience. There would probably be a lot to learn.

ZingTrain is end-to-end superb—a beautifully designed and executed program. No detail is overlooked. It's well-organized, takes place in a comfortable space, it's full of humor, the food is great—you name it, they got it covered. Wonderful model. I came away inspired and I learned more than I expected.

One of the exercises Ari gave us was five minutes to write a vision for our business in 2025. Just spill it out, he said. No editing. Straight from the heart. What you want. Here's what I wrote:

> It's 2025. South Mountain is celebrating its 50th anniversary. I'm 75. I'm starting to wind down but I'm all wound up too! It's just a day—like every day—and I'm walking into work, like I do every day, around dawn, looking forward to the coffee I'm about to brew, or maybe Peg already has—even better. And I've got that feeling—you know—that feeling that "Here I am again, heading to work, amazed—again—that I get to go to work with all these people—these remarkable people—and get paid for it?" I've been saying that for decades, but suddenly it feels new—just born—like omigod now I'm REALLY here. So what's up?
>
> I stop, dead in my tracks, before I reach the steps, and look at the sky that's just beginning to get light. I wonder. Then I've got it. I remember back to 2013, when I thought we had made just about as wonderful and important a company as there could be. But that was the year I learned that nothing could be further from the truth and that this business—wonderful and important to be sure—could be so much more that it would clearly take lifetimes to make it so. And that was when I decided to devote myself, during the time I had remaining, to teaching and training, inside the company and out.
>
> And now here we are, all these years later, changing the world, changing ourselves, being the best in the world at what we do, getting better all the time, treating each other well, knowing what to do, engaged in our work, because we have devoted ourselves to learning to make sense out of what we know, and to communicate that to others through teaching and training.

That was straight from the Zingerman's Experience.

We learned a lot about exceptional customer and employee service. Ari said, "People always ask: what's the secret to your success? There is none. It's everything. Everything matters. Every moment, every part, they all fit together. It's like diverse organic farming compared to mono-cropping."

And "Everyone has dreams. In a healthy work environment they invest their dreams—or some of them—in their work. If the workplace is unhealthy, they will invest their dreams elsewhere."

At Zingerman's, they are training all employees to think like leaders. They trust each employee to solve problems on their own and then review solutions with a more senior person. They provide independence, and room to take chances and make changes. They feel that we all have the opportunity and responsibility to help create the organization we want to be a part of. "When you walk in the door, everything is 100 percent your responsibility from then on—you are fully responsible for the quality of everyone's experience."

Ari and Maggie talked about employee orientation, and how important it is to tell the whole story. We expect them to know it, but they don't. We expect them to have read everything that's available, but that's unrealistic. And they said that people often ask them, "What if you do all this training and invest so heavily and then the person leaves?"

The answer is, "Aah, but what if they stay?"

Zingerman's does not shy away from radical business measures. Ari quoted Jim Hightower, the former Texas Commissioner of Agriculture: "There's nothing in the middle of the road but yellow stripes and dead armadillos."

Zingerman's is anything but middle of the road. They are charting a course to the Next Economy. We learned a lot, and we will continue to learn a lot as our relationship with this extraordinary group grows.

John Abrams, CEO, South Mountain Company,
Martha's Vineyard, Massachusetts

Very often entrepreneurs are lonely at the top. We think we need to have all the answers or don't have time to find help, even if we knew how to ask. When I found ZingTrain I knew I had found the help to support me AND my staff.

From the time I took my first seminar or have been a member of the ZingTrain Executive Roundtable, I have constantly been renewed and supported with: a new book from Ari, my favorite is *Being a Better Leader* (I have taken it apart and stuffed it in my purse so I can have chapters to read when I have extra time); to making a call when I have a big or small problem; to seeing the training program expand and grow.

I can count on ZingTrain always being willing to help.

But the very best thing is the key people are ALWAYS walking the walk, working on new (Ari would say "better") problems, ideas, and concepts. There is nothing static, outdated, or unexamined.

It's the most reliable source of information and support I have in my business.

It constantly renews me.

P.S. I've been pouring a lot of water lately!

Sharon Watkins, Owner, Chez Zee American Bistro, Austin, Texas

Warning: Don't go to Zingerman's. Don't order from Zingerman's Mail Order. Don't read this book (or any of Ari's other books). And certainly don't attend a ZingTrain event! That is, don't do any of it unless you are ready to have your *world of possibility* completely turned upside down.

What makes any interaction with Zingerman's (whether food, a book, or training) so much different? The world today is filled with "experts" espousing theories that you should follow if you're going to build a great business. The problem is that often these theories are untested in the real world.

Zingerman's is completely different! Unlike most, they don't just teach theory; they implement theory into their culture. They turn theory into methodology, and then generously demonstrate and teach others how to do the same. They are remarkable!

I could literally spend hours telling you all the things that we've learned and implemented from Zingerman's in our business. But instead, let me condense it down to one simple sentence for you: our company is far more successful, growing quickly, and far more remarkable as a result of Zingerman's!

Go, read, implement! You, your business, and those you interact with will never be the same.

Wayne Mullins, Chief Daydreamer,
Ugly Mug Marketing, Alexandria, Louisiana

I don't think that it would be a wild exaggeration to state that Ari Weinzweig, Zingerman's, and the ZingTrain experiences we have been privileged to attend under the tutelage of Maggie, Stas', and innumerable Zingermans staffers—

who gave up their time to share their secrets—have fundamentally changed the way we think about, execute, and live our business.

We are an investment company. We buy businesses and own them, usually outright, but always as substantial partners, with an entrepreneurial stake in the outcome. I have a finance background and my roots in a family who have been commercial operators for generations. My father once said we were congenitally unemployable. Often the businesses we buy are broken or hurting or dying. We started, as all investment professionals do, with a vague notion of "creating value" through our ownership, which is investment bullshit for buying at what one hopes is a reasonable price, letting growth take care of the rest and hoping nothing goes seriously awry before selling it on at a profit. This was never a particularly fulfilling proposition and even if it works (which it does quite often—look at private equity), it begs the question "Why? Why is the world a better place for your period of ownership of this business? Exactly?"

My quest as an investor—particularly in a world awash with capital looking to buy businesses and "create value"—has been to answer the question "What, exactly, can you, as an owner of a business, into whose hands and stewardship the livelihoods of possibly hundreds of individuals have been placed, do, exactly, to ensure that their efforts, futures and income security are rewarded and allowed to develop to their full potential, in order, at the end, to be able to say 'I discharged my duty well'? Exactly?"

The answer first suggested itself to me in May 2009 in a fairly undistinguished building in an industrial estate on the outskirts of Ann Arbor. It came softly initially, I heard it, and something registered. I heard it when Ari spoke, I heard it when I talked to the staff at the Bakehouse and the Roadhouse and the Deli. I heard it when Stas' and Maggie explained visioning and I heard it loud and clear when I visited my first huddle. And I kept coming back—pretty much once a year—catching up with Ari at conferences and visiting ZingTrain sessions on everything from the Zingerman's Experience to Visioning, and the message was consistent and reinforced each time. Great Products, Great Service, Great Finance. Treat people in the way you would want to be treated yourself; give them the tools, the education they need to do the best job they can; explain the purpose of the business; craft a vision of success; and dedicate your life to serving as a leader to release the full potential of each individual—and by doing that, the full potential of the company itself.

So that became our mission: to create an environment in every business entrusted to our care in which the managers of those businesses were given every possible support, training and freedom to develop their chosen business to the fullest human potential. To steal a phrase from Bo Burlingham and the Small Giants Community: we seek to maximize Mojo. We do this by selecting our responsible managers very carefully with our most critical focus being on their ability to grasp leadership as a service, not to us, but to their staff and to the business. Then we serve them: we provide methods and teachings to improve strategic thinking to focus on the purpose of the enterprise, to create a vision, to nurture first-class service, to build and maintain excellent finances, to establish a "Great Game of Business" transparency and operation, and above all to learn to grow, as people, as leaders, as creators of value. We support and nurture and act as vigilant sounding boards and encouragers. We work through their failures and celebrate their successes and ensure that they in turn are carrying out their duties to the individuals entrusted to them.

At every turn of our business, in every handbook and strategy paper, every vision, every huddle, you will find Ari's fingerprints and DNA all over them. When it works, much of the credit must go to Zingerman's and their extraordinary contribution to the compendium of knowledge on management, leadership, and business, upon which we continue to study and reflect. Where it fails to live up to expectations, you will probably find my footprints all over the crime scene and plenty of evidence to deduce that I was less than rigorous, cut corners, or missed critical signs that the wheels were starting to wobble.

Ari's reflections and recipes on the business of leadership are enormously valuable and I hope fervently that, when I am done, I will be able to say that "I discharged my duty well" and if I did, it will be no small thanks to Ari, his example and his simple generosity in sharing that example with us. God (yours or mine) bless you for that.

Steven Wilkinson, CEO & Founder, Buchanan, Germany

Adding Vision and Purpose to Businesses

My discovery of ZingTrain and its Creating a Vision of Greatness Seminar was just what the doctor ordered for me in the fall of 2011. At the close of these two days, Ari and Maggie helped me unearth two critical treasures: rekindled passion and direction for my new business venture; a mission to get as many of my Vistage members as humanly possible to also make the pilgrimage to Ann Arbor.

One year later, 60 members and their executive staff had experienced

Creating a Vision of Greatness and its transformative effect. Entrepreneurs now understood where they would drive their businesses. Partners got back on the same page. Staff members collaborated for the benefit of their entire company. Family Owners found a means of agreement after years of conflicting arguments. And it didn't matter whether their visions were 3, 5, 10, or 15 years out.

Today, the real satisfaction comes from watching these Vistage members purposefully involve their managers and staff in their company vision quests for growth, for profitability, for community involvement, and for the benefit of everyone involved.

Clay Garner, President of Growth Resources Inc.
& EnSellopedia.com, Chicago, Illinois

Signing up for my first ZingTrain seminar is one of the best decisions I ever made for my business. The class itself was hugely helpful; however, the best part is that it was my gateway into the community of people that I now consider mentors—my "business best friends."

Through the Zingerman's community, I've learned so much, grown as a leader, and become a better person all around.

Visioning especially is a powerful tool that I now use in both my business and my personal life. It's become typical in my household for us to drop into breakfast table conversation, "So, what's your vision for that?" whether we're talking about the bakery or a home improvement project!

Ari, Maggie, and Amy especially have been so generous in sharing the wisdom they've gained through their own experiences; my life is much richer for knowing them. I fervently hope that someday I can be for someone else what they have been for me.

Kat Gordon, Founder, Muddy's Bakeshop, Memphis, Tennessee

Often in medical practice, the emphasis is on great expertise, not great service. For the patient who can't get through the phone tree, is treated rudely on the phone, and sits in the small exam room waiting patiently for the doctor who is always behind, it is hard to feel the expertise when the feeling of the experience is so bad. Patients above all want to feel the doctor and his office care, not "could care less." The Zingerman's Experience captured our imagination. Could we upgrade our services so patients could actually say they were glad they came, even if it was for a serious medical problem, because they knew we genuinely cared? Could we give our patients a "wow" experience?

We created a vision for our organization, Michigan Multispecialty Physicians (MMP). We defined metrics around service areas like the "MMP phone experience," we taught the principles from the *Guide to Giving Great Service*, and we worked to rebuild our culture using the model of "teach it," "define it," "live it," "measure it," and "reward it." It worked. Our "customers" (patients, staff, nurses, physicians, etc.) noticed: more smiles, a greater sense of a collective purpose, and a happier business. Oh, and more referrals, more phone traffic, and patients telling us "my friend, neighbor, coworker, family member sent me here."

Thomas R. Gravelyn, MD,
Michigan Multispecialty Physicians, P.C., Ann Arbor, Michigan

Pouring into the lives of others is inherently the duty of those working in the nonprofit world and especially in early childhood education. Interestingly enough, we as members of this service-oriented community often care for ourselves with much less deliberacy. Learning and practicing the management of ourselves is critical if any nonprofit plans to stay in business long term. Many nonprofits go out of business due to staff burnout, yet Child Care Network has been in this community for more than 40 years with staff who had been dedicated to the mission for over 15 years. Upon accepting the position of executive director of this well established organization, I realized the true meaning of the statistics . . . I felt the burnout . . . observed the exhaustion in their body language, saw the monotony in their eyes, heard the frustration of financial concerns in their conversations with clients, experienced the negative energy in the interactions with each other with broken spirits, witnessed the mundane goals lacking purposeful direction and thought to myself . . . where has that laughter gone?

What could I do as a new leader? Then I reflected on the experience of fun, visioning, and positive energy of a ZingTrain training (Customer Service) back in 2008 . . . remembering a feeling of an unexplainable energy that excited me, embraced me, and invited me to partake of great food, quality service, happy people, and much more. It was the first time I had been to or ever heard of Zingerman's. Not knowing what to expect, I quietly observed as we were trained . . . I watched the trainers . . . the responses of the participants . . . observed . . . documented and reflected on it all . . . paid attention to the mannerisms and patterns of interaction . . . and attempted to relax in the experience of learning in this new way.

After this reflection, I took a deep breath and thought . . . we (CCN) need a cultural and visionary overhaul. Through many strategic efforts, referencing the *Guide to Good Leading* series, and with the consultative support of the awesome Stas', our leadership team began working feverishly on bringing a climate change within our organizational walls. We focused heavily on leadership development and unity, positive energy renewal, authentic relationships, and visioning. Since that time, people are laughing again, sincerely enjoying their work experience, approaching constituents with a new light of passion in their eyes, and owning their leadership responsibilities for the success of the organization. And as if that wasn't enough, we developed a five-year vision of success and improved operational processes.

Of all the recent accomplishments, I am most proud of CCN staff willingness to develop personal visions of success. Visioning is the one key component that I think will ensure staff to see their personal value in fulfilling the organizational mission. It seems the world sometimes can strip us of our true selves or compresses us into something other than our true selves . . . maybe because we needed income so we chose a job we had no personal passion for . . . or we went to college and selected a major that had absolutely nothing to do with what we enjoy doing. In my aspiration and dedication to be a transformational leader . . . I thought the new knowledge would transform me into some new, exciting, totally different being . . . and as I learned and grew on my journey . . . I realized the process actually brought me "back to myself." That truth is why I proudly commit to the work of helping others within this organization find themselves once more . . . it is that hidden treasure within that makes us all so individually special and unique! And a ZingTrain training back in 2008 helped me to more easily and concretely imagine "in writing" a better me, which enabled me to now work with a team of people to innovatively develop a new and improved Child Care Network . . . Thank you!

Camarrah Morgan, Executive Director,
Child Care Network, Washtenaw County, Michigan

Theodore Roosevelt is quoted as saying "Far and away the best prize that life has to offer is the chance to work hard at work worth doing." Entrepreneurs are in a unique position to create and offer the prize that Teddy referred to, and thus enhance people's lives. Zingerman's is a model for those with such a goal in mind—if it's something you have a passion for.

I was introduced to ZingTrain through my Vistage [CEO organization] chair. I was of course skeptical about yet another workshop on how to improve your business. But I finally discovered an author who not only writes great books and delivers a great workshop, but does so in a way that is intertwined with his living and breathing business for all to experience. It finally comes all together, in a business "laboratory," so to speak, with Ari and Maggie cast in the roles of "science professors" whose students are hopeful that the results of their experiments are reproducible in their own business "laboratories." The professors mix different ideas and people into the test tube (code named ZCoB) in the infinite quest to create the ideal, organic ecosystem called work.

Ari admits that not every idea worked. Mistakes are part of the growth. But what I have taken away mostly is the concept that information can and should be pulled from many sources, old and new. It is the role of the leader to seek and adapt information that is already out there in order to improve the business. Ari is constantly citing sources for concepts that he applied to Zingerman's, and this was robust confirmation for me to hear something that I already had an intuition about. No one person, book, or seminar is going to transform my business. The idea of constantly learning new materials, adapting them to my business, and applying that information is what is going to make the huge difference over time. No magic bullet. Natural Law #11 applies here: "It generally takes a lot longer to make something great happen than people think."

So I attended my first workshop with three leaders in my company, and we left with a cohesive company vision that was finalized with the rest of the company two weeks later. I was pleasantly surprised that we were all on the same page. We proceeded to have our nine departments create their own specific vision statements. Now even smaller projects start out with a vision. Such a simple idea—yet so powerful!

At the end of the day, we learn more from observing our mentors than listening to their lectures or reading their books. I urge anyone and everyone who is serious about making significant change to make an effort to attend ZingTrain, see their operations in action, and learn from what you observe.

I want to end off with the most striking ingredient that I feel gets mixed into the ZCoB test tube, and that is how successful you are likely to become when you develop (or inherently have) a passion for growing people. And it's not just people within the company, but even people outside the company.

There were even folks in the food business attending the workshop, but they appeared to be of no threat to Ari. I learned that not only is transparency, caring, and kindness not a weakness, but it actually strengthens your business and leads to success.

Returning to Teddy's quote about "work worth doing," that is now an even higher calling for me than a particular financial goal. Since I got to meet and chat with ZCoB staff, I've realized that the reward for such achievement is not even measurable.

David Michael, MD, North Shore Pediatric Therapy, Des Plaines, Illinois

I was driving back to Boulder, Colorado with my family from a vacation in New Mexico, and for the first time since our business was founded over 8 years ago I had the feeling of not wanting to go back to the office. Usually, I'm fired up and ready to roll after time away, but this was different. Business was feeling like a slog: what were we doing, where were we going—why were we struggling with the easy things? That first day back, I had lunch with my business partner Jason and told him I was dreading coming into work that day. He said he had a very similar feeling from his recent vacation and we knew we needed to do something, but what?

It just so happens the week I returned from vacation I visited a friend, John Fisher of StickerGiant.com, to pick up an order of stickers. He walked me through his office and I could sense the sky-high energy the moment I entered the building. John was fired up, his people were focused, most were smiling, some engaged in conversations with each other—it was the business equivalent of a playoff atmosphere. We ended up in the area where John's desk is and I saw this big huge whiteboard on the wall with all these numbers and colors and I had to interrupt John and know what it was. He explained to me it was a Huddle Board for their open book management and began to tell me how it all operates. BINGO, this was the remedy to our ills.

I read *A Lapsed Anarchist's Approach to Building a Great Business* and it resonated with me the same way *London Calling* did when I first heard it. It had a force to it I felt like I could live off.

Soon after, four of us went to ZingTrain's The Zingerman's Experience seminar, and after two days with Ari and his team the gloves were off. We went full steam ahead with visioning and then attended the Fun, Flavorful Finance seminar. In a matter of three months as leaders, we went from wandering to focused, and from trudging to exploring.

428

Sharing the 12 Natural Laws of Business with our staff and implementing open book management has released a creative and emotional energy in the agency unlike anything we ever expected. The love and passion each employee brings to work each day is visible in our weekly agency and business unit huddles.

Ari and Paul are very much realists too; there is no sugar coating. They clearly state this is a process, a continuous learning experience, it has its ups and downs, but stick to it and trust in each other. I would say the ups far outweigh the downs and the downs are only opportunities to get better.

I'm profoundly grateful for the Zingerman's Experience framework. It has not only changed our agency, but it has changed my life and the lives of everyone associated with our business.

Oh, one thing about ZingTrain seminars, okay two: 1) Ari, Gauri, Maggie, and Paul are brilliant, and 2) nowhere in the world will you be trained by people living the ethos and in the same day be connected to, and immersed in, the culture where you see the embodiment of the teachings. Most of the time it's some supposed guru giving a blueprint and you having to trust it works. Ain't that way at Zingerman's. Fear not, you know you want this.

James Clark, Co-Founder, Room 214, Boulder, Colorado

Liz wanted the "Draft" to be on here because it helped her get over her drive to make these notes perfect. She figured if it worked for visioning, it would work for Notes from the Front Porch.

DRAFT

Ari (The Humble Giant) and his terrific team have taught us so many things and we are grateful to have the opportunity to learn from the Lapsed Anarchist and his entourage. Ari translates conceptual and philosophical "hoo ha" into real world practical advice. Zingerman's willingness to merge spiritual ideologies with sensible business systems makes magic. The art of visioning is the single most important business practice that we have learned from Zingerman's. The concept and practice of visioning has enabled our team to play an active role in building a tangible and exciting future, has opened new avenues for success, and strengthened our culture of ownership and "servant leadership."

We not only use visioning for our strategic planning but we also use it on simple everyday tasks like writing a vision for the outcome of an upcoming meeting. The effect is that we have attracted a better reality: better projects, better people and better mindsets, which have all lead to better service, better systems, and a better future.

One other important lesson we have learned from Ari is . . . staying true to yourself! On that note . . . our company's introduction to ZingTrain was a memorable one. I attended a one-hour seminar where Ari was the speaker and was so impressed by the power of that hour that I knew I needed to share the experience with everyone in our company. I scheduled Ari to speak to our company (and three peer companies) about Zingerman's 12 Natural Laws of Business. I was initially concerned that we had an all-day session scheduled and Ari's only audio/visual request was for paper and a marker. I even called him beforehand to explain that we would need to keep "this crowd" engaged, and that I wasn't sure if flipchart paper was going cut it. He insisted that it was all he needed (along with special permission to wear a t-shirt and jeans to Congressional Country Club!).

On the day of the seminar, time flew by. Every single person was engaged, motivated, and inspired by simple, practical advice from the Humble Giant, in a t-shirt and jeans, armed with a marker, just being himself. Ari is the most powerful speaker and friend we have ever heard.

What Ari did for us that day was priceless, but what made it so special were his message and his delivery. He does not assume a guru-like superiority and that is part of his magic. He doesn't just inform . . . he inspires . . . and teaches you how to do the same—to generate this energy on your own. He has a way of making ethereal things do-able! Ari and Zingerman's take the esoteric, hippie stuff that usually turns people off in a work environment and translates it into relevant, relatable, usable material that inspires and incites action.

Elizabeth Wilder, Co-Owner,
Anthony Wilder Design/Build, Cabin John, Maryland

We found Zingerman's at a pivotal time in our young company's life. Our first business had been open long enough to develop our culture and general way of doing business, but learning about ZCoB and reading Ari's books both overwhelmed and exhilarated. Overwhelmed because it was clear how far we had to go in building our business to where we wanted it to go. Exhilarated because they very articulately and pragmatically spell out the concepts that make them the amazing businesses and community they are.

We studied their methods and implemented such core business foundations as a vision statement, our employee guide and our approach to open book management. I glance over these tools not to diminish their worth since they are each individually invaluable to our company, but because we had a larger problem on the horizon.

Our first business was a boutique hostel. While the heart and soul of our business was born there, the timely repayment of our investment wasn't plausible. That is, without the previously planned phase two of adding a bar and restaurant to the equation. While this second business would provide the margins and cash flow to repay both businesses, it offered its own set of unique challenges, not the least of which was our utter lack of restaurant experience. Details, details! At the top of our list was how to take this incredible culture exemplified by our three employees at the hostel and translate that to the bar staff that was literally ten times the size.

Enter ZingTrain. Last July I went up there with our GM, Al, and operations manager, John, to take the Customer Service Express workshop. We'd read their books and knew most of the material, so I suppose by "take their workshop" I meant "steal their wonderful training tools and make our own course on The Crash Pad way of doing business." Sounds kind of harsh saying it like that, but these guys actually like it like that and said as much during the course.

Over the next months, Al and John created what would become our Crash Pad Hospitality training. Cut to late April of this year when we had our first day of employee training for the bar. Most intriguing to me, if you'd closed your eyes, what was being taught could apply to any business: our culture, our core values, how we do business, and how we treat our guests and each other. It's now the end of May and we have gone from teaching our new people Crash Pad Hospitality to them teaching us the basics of every position in the house. I am living my dream.

I'm not saying this wouldn't have been possible without the work we did with ZingTrain, but I sure am thankful for the time and effort that was saved not having to reinvent the wheel. They themselves admit that what they do isn't magical. It's just that they do the little things every day, long after the glamor has worn off, and they do it with a smile. That's magic. Thanks for the inspiration, ZCoB.

Max Poppel, Co-Founder, The Crash Pad, Chattanooga, Tennessee

Experiencing Success—Taking Responsibility for the Effectiveness of Your Own Small Business's Development

We used to talk a lot in the Bread Department at Zingerman's Bakehouse about being set up for success. In a system as detailed as theirs for producing hand-crafted breads in a traditional fashion, there were many opportunities every day to set others up, and to be set up by others, for success. As we set up Niedlov's Breadworks in Chattanooga, Tennessee, 10 years ago, this became our operating motto: "The best way to ensure that we are successful is to set ourselves up for success." In reflecting recently on the last decade, I realized that Niedlov's owes a lot to Zingerman's for helping prepare us for our own entrepreneurial endeavor.

Seeing failure is informative. Experiencing failure is educational. Seeing success is encouraging. But experiencing success is empowering. The success that I experienced as a leader at Zingerman's equipped me for my own entrepreneurial adventure in a way that no school, or curriculum, or case studies, or even failures of my own, could have. Niedlov's remains indebted to Zingerman's for the model they have been, and continue to be. Ten years later, these experiences still resonate, as we lead an organization that aspires to be like Zingerman's, in our own unique way.

John Sweet, Co-Owner, Niedlov's Bakery, Chattanooga, Tennessee

My experiences with the books Ari has written and the class I took at ZingTrain are my secret weapons. Any time I'm feeling a little burned out, confused, or overwhelmed, I pick up my notes from class, grab one of Ari's books, spend a few minutes, and it's like a great big dose of Xanax and a clear map back to a good place in my brain. So much of what I've learned via Zingerman's has simply been an affirmation of that feeling in my gut as to what I know is the right way to treat people, treat myself, and run a restaurant. I'd still be doing the work I do without Zingerman's, but I'm way better at it and have way more fun doing it with them on my team!

Matt Hyde, Co-Owner, 715, Lawrence, Kansas

Dear Ari,

I ran into you over at the Southside a few weeks ago, and mentioned how your book *Building a Great Business* has seriously impacted my world. You gave me your card and said feel free to email. Where to begin?

For starters, the book connected a lot of dots for me. Not only has it explained some of what feels so magical whenever I visit a Zingerman's location, it reaffirmed the belief I held that you can work in an organization where even the "smallest" of positions feels significant. I was starting to think this was no longer to be found. Recently I decided it is time to make a change in my career, to become part of something that feels worthwhile regardless of the title.

So at some point I will be submitting my resume once I find where I can fit in the ZCoB. But that is a side note in today's correspondence. More importantly I want to tell you about something that happened at the Roadhouse, just hours ago, which will explain what a Labrador Retriever has to do with Zingerman's.

My two daughters (ages 13 and 11) and I went to the Roadhouse for a highly anticipated outing. What was supposed to be a lively time for the three of us took a bit of a somber note given that last night our 14-ish-year-old Lab named Sugar was suddenly unable to get up and walk. As with any older, large breed dog, we understand that this is part of the process of her dying. And we've been seeing other signs recently as well. This morning Sugar seemed to rebound a little, and our vet (Dr. Annie Staebler in case you ever need a phenomenal vet) spent a few hours at the house as she and I tried to determine if Sugar needed to be put down right then. Long story short is that we decided to give her some meds to make her comfortable for the next few days, and what will be the eventual outcome.

So my daughters and I were a bit tired and low energy as we ordered our lunch. I mentioned to our server, Kim, that we were all a little wiped out from a late night with our old Lab who doesn't have too much time left with us. She kindly expressed her sympathy, took the order, and went off on her way. Shortly she returned to our table with a small pink Zingerman's bag. She set it on the chair next to me; inside was a small, neatly wrapped package, a frozen bone. She told us she had gone in the kitchen and asked if there were any small beef bones that were not being used. She said "it wasn't much" but perhaps it could cheer both us and our dog, "hopefully, just a little."

I don't think Kim has any idea what a wonderful gift she gave us. What she did was so totally generous, so heartfelt, and so much what makes Zingerman's unlike any other place on the planet. It had nothing to do with our meal per se, but everything to do with us as people, not simply customers.

We had an outstanding meal and left smiling instead of downhearted. When we got home, I carried Sugar out to the lawn and gave her the surprise. Some may not believe that dogs express emotion, those skeptics should have seen the look of recognition and delight on Sugar's face. Her tail started thumping and she laid in the grass, enjoying the fresh air and a magnificent treat. We got to watch the pure joy of her enjoying a random act of kindness. It is probably the last time she'll have the energy for something so seemingly simple and normal for a dog to do. It took us, and Sugar, back to a much younger dog, one who has been a big part of our lives. It did so much more than cheer us all "just a little." It reminded us of the pleasure of the little things despite the sadness of this natural progression. We are so very grateful.

Today Kim, as a representative of Zingerman's, didn't just serve a delicious meal, didn't just make sure we had a positive experience, didn't just secure a great tip from people she had never met—she gave us a big dose of happiness in what is a sad process of saying goodbye, and for a dog she'll never meet. It was priceless and will not be forgotten.

We expressed our thanks to her in person. Now thanks to you for creating the environment that allows her to do more than a job, the kind of place that gives individuals the freedom to be a fantastic *people* as well as a fantastic employees.

While I look forward to future dialogues on all things Zingerman's, today I close with kudos to all of you, and much gratitude.

**Julie, Hannah & Gretchen Parrish, and, of course, Sugar,
Ann Arbor, Michigan**

I grew up in a small town in West Michigan, boxed in by wild apple trees and fifth generation farms. A town where folks go to work, attend church, and visit their neighbors with equal diligence; a place where people are born with roots deep in the land, and where everyone knows that the secret ingredient is almost always lard. I grew up in the homes of people who claim not to know a whole lot, but who know a whole lot more than most about being good to one another.

By the time I started working at the Deli in my third year of college, I had more than two decades of training in listening—really listening, in doing small favors, and in going out of my way to do what was right and good. What I didn't know until working at Zingerman's was that the lessons learned in my humble hometown were not only the key ingredients to a good life, but also to good business.

Zingerman's is a company with a conscience not unlike the moral compass guiding the village that raised me. From the time of their ZCoB infancy, employees are trained to put people first. As I reflect now on Zingerman's three steps to giving great service (Find out what the customer wants. Get it for them. Go the extra mile.), I realize they mirror, almost perfectly, some of the most fundamental values passed down in my hometown (Listen—really listen. Do small favors. Go out of your way to do what's right). It's not difficult to see why it feels so good to be at Zingerman's. It feels like coming home.

Less than a week after my college graduation and bittersweet last day of employment at Zingerman's, I moved back across the state to start a new job as the agriculture manager at the YMCA of Greater Grand Rapids. At twenty-two, I found myself managing elemental community programs. Programs that fed people. People who knew the consuming void of hunger. I found myself leading a team of an incredibly capable staff who craved and deserved gratifying work. I found myself balancing the budgets of dwindling grants and drafting sustainability plans to save what we were building.

In an early review, my supervisor was shocked to hear that I attributed my preparedness for these responsibilities to working at Zingerman's. "Isn't that where you served sandwiches?" she asked, bewildered. "What about that U of M education?" I laughed, considering the validity of these questions. I cherish my college experiences and education. However, there are some things you can only learn during an opening shift at the Deli, wearing a hairnet and already covered in pickle juice, smiling because it's your job to make everyone you encounter feel like they're the best part of your day.

I am so grateful to have built the foundation for my professional life at Zingerman's, a company proving with every valued customer, every gratified employee, and every dollar earned that you don't have to compromise morality to get ahead. I am grateful to know that sustainable organizational development and effective leadership can be as intuitive as being good to other people. Cultivating an invested, engaged team comes down to giving staff a stake in your success, and in having defined together what that means for you. Earning an exceptional reputation can be as easy as treating people how they deserve to be treated, rather than how they're used to being treated. It can be as easy as offering chairs to your hardworking farmers' market vendors, who tell you they've been coming to markets for seventeen years, and no one has ever offered them a chair. It can be as easy as walking the twenty-pound watermelon to the customer's car, and smiling when she tells you her plans to cut it up for her grandbabies when they come over to play in the sprinkler. It, honest to God, can be as easy as looking people in the eye, asking how they're doing this week, and pausing for their answer.

Zingerman's taught me that good business isn't just about what's happening behind closed doors in corner offices or, in my case, on a cluttered counter in a cramped cubicle. Good business is about listening—really listening, doing small favors, and going out of your way to do what is right and good.

Sara Vander Zanden, Healthy Living Agriculture Manager,
YMCA of Greater Grand Rapids, Grand Rapids, Michigan

I lived in Ann Arbor for 27 years before moving away to take a job 5 years ago. Every time I come home, and I mean EVERY time, I make it my business to either hit the Deli, Bakehouse, Roadhouse or sometimes all of them. My parents know to make reservations whenever I'm in town, and via mail order I'm already teaching my 18 month old the virtues of your bacon scones. To simply join in the chant: I love what you guys do. So without further dawdling, the story:

Last year I was the recipient of an award at my job, with the prize being $500 towards any sort of professional development activity—a conference, a workshop, software, etc. I like books, so I chose to start a library in my office. Ari, I'm the assistant director of student activities at the University of Kentucky Student Center, but I didn't know the FIRST thing about leadership as it's taught in a formal way. My whole experience in leadership was working at tech jobs and helping to start record labels back in '00s. "Leadership" as the traditional means define it, was not my forte. But with this $500, I figured maybe I would have a fighting chance against these polished people here that went to school on such matters.

Amongst the purchases of computer manuals, books by Godin, Belsky etc., etc., were your *Guide to Giving Great Service* and volume 1 of the latest series. I was immediately immersed and hooked. I made it a point to take a small group of students up to Ann Arbor in October, a ragtag bunch of creative kids who work for our University Cinema Program. Energetic, hungry (mind the pun), and wanting to learn more about Ann Arbor and Zingerman's, I was only TOO happy to oblige in taking a small two-day jaunt home to show them what I had been raving about for years.

We met with UM's Screen Arts and Cultures Department, took a tour of campus, and during down time the kids became obsessed with finishing the Zingerman's tour so they could get a t-shirt. Some of them still wear it as badges of honor nearly a year later. But the real joy was what they got to see in action. All of that August and September, we had been practicing what you preach. We sat in a group and wrote out visions for each academic semester and our yearlong goal of what we wished to accomplish and where we envisioned ourselves at the end. Some were skeptical, as some students can be, but I think after the visit in October, they were all converts to the method.

As the year went by, ever so slowly and subtly our energy went up, our interest in one another's well-being grew, our ability to work as a team in both times good and bad improved and our bonds had never been stronger in the two years I have served as their advisor. Things became embedded in our culture that spread to our marketing and our service to students attending the films. Our ideas became wilder and more inventive, and the student body responded positively. We thought of new ways and new ideas to influence not only each other, but how the program is run. We worked hard at implementing them and if someone was slipping made them accountable in our weekly meetings, always resolving things in a positive manner. Things felt good and by the time I picked up *Part 2* during my trip home in early April (apparently the book had just come out) to visit friends, most of what you wrote about felt second nature already. I was surprised to learn we were already on board with much of what you write about in terms of servant leadership, energy, and effort. Which isn't a bad thing (there was still plenty to learn, and I'm sure *Part 3* will expand on that. So hurry up!) at all. Like you said: bigger success leads to better problems!

As the programming year concluded last Friday, it came time yesterday to accumulate all of our data and reports for assessment of the year as a whole. I knew we had done well in Fall, but was a little bit unsure of how we did this Spring semester. I tabulated the numbers up from our event logs and had to do a double take. I'm pretty sure I also uttered a "holy shit" after running the numbers three times to make sure I was reading things correctly.

Before I get to the numbers, here were our targeted goals for the academic year:

Stronger marketing
Increased attendance of 10-15% per semester
Better graphic design (note: we've since won two awards for our work)
Stronger social media presence
Weekly meetings, stronger communication between staff and students

Term	Number of Movies	Overall Student Attendance
Fall 2010	30	2708
Fall 2011	36	5137
Spring 2010	32	2044
Spring 2011	39	4639

As you can see, the number of movies increased ever so slightly, but we had an 89.7% increase in attendance in Fall and a staggering 127% in the Spring semester. Not bad for a group of five kids showing films to a largely apathetic campus obsessed with basketball.

But the biggest part to me? The absolute proof in pudding irrefutable proof and validation that this system WORKS. Beyond the skepticism of others formally trained in leadership and student development, beyond even my own doubts that something like this could transfer from a working restaurant empire to a small group of University film kids. We've been asked by several student organizations as to how we've become so popular so quickly, several academic departments and colleges have asked to collaborate with us for NEXT fall, and we've been (tentatively) invited to work with the Governor's HS Honor Students program this summer, curating a week's worth of movies at their retreat.

I'd like to thank you for passing this wisdom on to the public for (nearly) free, thank you for making my job a pleasure to come to every morning, thank you for showing me and these kids things that are inside of them, but never really had an outlet to express it. Thank you for making a difference in our small little program. You have become the textbook from which I will herein teach so long as I'm in this position. If there was a way to send each of my kids up to ZingTrain each summer, I wouldn't blink twice about it. Hopefully one day I'll be able to convince my boss to let me come up as well. Until then, please put this letter in the piles of papers in the same chorus singing your praises, and know that you have my gratitude.

Keep pouring water and until the next reservation I remain in gratitude.

Rob Theakston, Assistant Director of Activities,
University of Kentucky Student Center, Lexington, Kentucky

The Inside Scoop on Working
at Zingerman's

What follows are some additional comments from real live folks about what it's like to work here.

I was once offered a chance to interview with Zingerman's Bakehouse when I was about 19 years old. I passed it up because I was arrogant and entitled thinking to myself, "Why the hell is any loaf of bread $9.99, those jerks!" Then I started learning about Zingerman's and firmly planted my foot into my mouth. I became an avid applier, re-submitting my application every 60 days. Then, one evening I was dining at the Roadhouse and the server, as if sent by the gods, said to me, "Can I get you anything else?" I dislodged my foot from my mouth and said, "How about a job?" Shockingly, she sent the restaurant manager over to me, and even more shockingly, I had an interview within a few weeks. Then my life changed. My entire life changed. I know that sounds trite, and really Hallmark-y, but it's the honest to goodness truth.

I quit my job as a restaurant manager to become a hostess full time, because it became harder and harder to live within corporate America where you're stifled and shoved into a one-size-fits-all uniform of unhappiness and creative desolation. I am grateful every single day of my life that I made the switch. I work in a business that wants ME, little old ME, to succeed. It wants ME to be the best I can be. Ironically, in turn, it makes me want to be all I can be for this business. The basic principles of this business have hit such a spot deep within my soul that I will never be able to leave and I want to shout from the rooftops that everyone should follow their passions and take the risks. Jump off the ledge, I promise that you'll never regret following your heart and I'm so grateful my heart found Zingerman's, because you can really feel the difference.

Allie Lyttle, Line Cook, Zingerman's Roadhouse

As a recent graduate from the University of Michigan, I am often asked about what moments defined my "Michigan experience." Without hesitation, I consistently rank my employment at Zingerman's Delicatessen at the top of my list. After joining the front of house team part-time as a sophomore, I quickly fell under the enticing spell of deli life, choosing to spend the majority of my free time at work. While the eclectic mix of coworkers, unparalleled food, and consistently positive workplace energy were impressive, what stuck out to me the most about Zingerman's was its beloved presence in the Ann Arbor community. Despite thirty-one years of growth and eager pleas from guests to franchise, Zingerman's remains a *local* business and a genuine reflection of its city's people and way of life. Whether it's greeting thousands of football fans on game days, preparing a regular customer's coffee drink of choice, or providing a hungry Michigan student with a taste of home, Zingerman's is the heartbeat of Ann Arbor, and I couldn't be prouder to be a part of it all. Given that I am now a full-time employee of the deli and permanent resident of Ann Arbor, I'd say the Zingerman's experience definitely cast its magic over me.

Maddie LaKind, Retail Staffer, Zingerman's Delicatessen

Vision of success as a ZCoB leader. Spring 2015

Biking home from work today, there was ease in the flow of energy through my body. My mind was humming with the ideas passing through it.

I was thinking about the time I've worked here, 17 years. Lived, learned, and grown here. How I started, and how my roles grew organically over the years as I adapted and was open to new possibilities.

Two years ago, I needed to reset. My body's immune system was failing. My mind was stuck in the mindset of "Why is this happening to me?" I was waiting to "get my life back."

I took a new approach. I stood back and looked in. Deeply. I became my own best advocate for my health getting back into balance. I did not resign to letting illness define what was going to happen. I began to live with a celebration of the joy I could be a part of, rather than what I could not have or could not do. My self-awareness is a journey that will continue throughout my life, though at the onset of this stage of it; I became more open to the energy I was putting into each experience I was a part of.

I practice a personal approach to seeing the full picture. I learn to embrace things more fully. I am working to constructively remain open to things I might have simply taken personally in the past. I recognize when a question needs to be asked by me, and when I need to hold it.

I feel more connected to the unique missions of each of the Zingerman's businesses than I ever have, and I see where they all align toward our overall mission. We are changing the world one interaction at a time, and I'm part of the whole. I've been able to live and act with the passion I feel for how we work here.

I am able to inspire creativity by opening a space for it to flourish. I remember to listen to the counterpoint. I am able to hear the messages there and can work collaboratively to help make surprising things happen. My coworkers feel encouraged with the support they feel from me. They feel the freedom to put forth their biggest hopes. If I hear myself thinking, "That will never work," I don't let that thought stick, and listen more. I welcome the sharing of new information and ideas. People who work with me feel their input is honored, and they value mine as well. They don't hesitate to call on me if they have a question—my enthusiasm and sincerity make them glad they did.

I come through on my commitments with a sense of ease. Even hard slogs and difficult decisions are a part of the work I do, and I face them with curiosity and vigor. I continue to find and ask for the support I need to help a project succeed. I see things through, and my coworkers value the level of engagement and presence I have with the work that needs to be done. I seek information and ideas from a global perspective and on a local level. I am no longer waiting for things to be defined *for* me—I am an active part in the collaboration of what creates the present and leads us toward our visions for the future.

I feel simultaneously energized and peaceful. The energy I bring to and from work each day holds a light of humility, gratitude, joy, playfulness, and confidence.

Jenny Tubbs, Beekeeper and Bookkeeper, Zingerman's Press

How a vision really can make things happen:
As a member of the Roadhouse's management team, I used to be the only single manager. At our yearly manager dinners, I was the one who went solo. Each year, I asked Chef Alex to hire a young sous chef for me. It was my vision to have the Roadhouse hire a new chef for me to marry; after all, what could be better, the front-of-house manager and the sous chef falling in love?

I remember the day Alex called me into his office many years ago and told me he thinks he found the right one for me. That Ari had met a young chef in England that wanted to come over here and work for Zingerman's. Alex said he was quite talented, really into technology (still not sure why that was relevant, but I distinctly remember him saying it) and thought he would be a perfect fit for Zingerman's and for me. Needless to say, I was quite excited. It took a couple of years, but in July of 2008, Kieron Hales came to work at the Roadhouse.

It wasn't instant, but after a couple of months, my vision came true—Kieron and I fell in love. We bought a house together, got married in 2011 (Paul Saginaw married us!), and then in December of 2012 we welcomed our first child together, a baby boy named Henry.

Could this have all happened if I didn't put my vision out there many, many years ago? Sure, maybe. But I like to believe it was the power of visioning.

Joanie Hales (formerly the single manager known as Joanie Mallory), Marketing and Events Manager, Zingerman's Roadhouse

I just wanted to take a moment to appreciate all of you for making the Roadhouse such an awesome place to work. Six years ago today I was hired by James: I was a shy, timid 16-year-old and never thought that I would still be working here, let alone in the capacity that I am now. I have grown exponentially not only as an employee but as a person, friend, and coworker. I have gained so many life skills that have helped me succeed in the past and will allow me to continue to succeed in the future. I cannot imagine working for a company other than Zingerman's, which frightens me as I am now starting to complete my second degree. You all have been amazing sources of information as well as catalysts for growth. I am truly grateful to be here, as well as to be working along side all of you. I would not be where I am today without you guys.

I think that being fully mindful in management is one of the hardest aspects of management. It's really easy to be so focused on helping staff members and giving great customer service that you forget to manage yourself:

being unaware of your own energy, vision, etc., not realizing that the way that you manage yourself can and will create a ripple effect of how others manage themselves and the energy level of employees as well as guests. It is also easy to forget that managing yourself can be as simple as being more positive, so that optimism is transmitted through the restaurant. This is why I think [our service measure] as well as staff energy trackers are important, because they make you think about your personal energy and how it is affecting others. A preshift meeting is also an important part of mindful management because it gives everyone a vision of things we want to focus on throughout the shift, tips for doing so, and creates an environment of teamwork and good energy. One of the greatest parts of working for Zingerman's is that you have an infinite amount of room for growth, allowing you to push yourself to go outside of your comfort zone to learn from anybody else, ask as many questions as possible, and be encouraged by more than just your manager. The environment gives everyone the power of shaping the atmosphere just by the vibes that you are giving off, even if you are just smiling at and saying hi to everyone. It seems crazy that these are things we have to learn because they are common sense, but I think that is why they are so easily skipped over. Having systems (and following them) and visions make it easy to get where you want to go and be the leader that you want to be because you already know where you want to go, and can therefore just make action steps to get there, being mindful of your mission in the organization. It seems so simple now that I know about visioning, but when I first started and something needed to get done, I had no idea where to start simply because I did not know what success looked like.

Amanda Imperiale, Supervisor, Zingerman's Roadhouse

The biggest difference for me at Zingerman's is that management asks staff questions and asks for help improving systems on an extremely regular basis. We understand that the staff is the knowledge goldmine that really makes us better and better. Having engaged staff helps all three of our bottom lines. It is the "good work" that keeps us in business.

Caitlin Doyle, Assistant Front-of-House Manager, Zingerman's Roadhouse

One thing that stands out is the idea of standing outside of myself. How does what I'm asking myself to do sound when I hear it with different ears? It's like talking to yourself when no one is listening. Then asking feedback-like questions. And then changing or making action steps in relation to time and actions. Better self-management for me has meant more visioning: writing them down, asking if it is achievable, and communicating it. When that all returns and I'm standing out of myself I get good learnings and directions. I know it's me I'm managing, but when I can refer to myself in the third person I think the idea of managing one's self becomes clearer.

Charlie Frank, Managing Partner, Zingerman's Candy Manufactory

I think that managing yourself in our environment presents a specific challenge in the sense that you want to encourage all people you manage to be themselves and have their own opinions— and you want to operate as yourself as well—but you also need to be able to see other peoples' points of view to get buy-in to get a project moving forward. This really requires a long-term view, I think, remembering that today you might be going along with something that isn't great or you don't agree with—but that tomorrow—or more likely months down the road—people will start to see things your way if you are saying the right things for the right reasons. There will still be naysayers even then, and your patience will still be tried, but the beauty of that is that you also have champions that are newer to the idea than you are and have a longer patience with the subject than you. You never know who your champions will be, and if you are willing to give them the credit and let them do some of the work, your leadership manifests through them in an almost magical way. So I think the managing yourself bit is about having real expectations in the moment—but knowing that the future is open if you let it get there at its own pace.

Kristin Wagle, Manager, Westside Farmers' Market

Suggested Reading

I have many more books that I like and have learned from than I'm going to list here. But below are a few of my favorites—some are new, others are longtime classics that helped form my thinking many years ago, but still seem just as relevant now as they were then. Happy to get your recommendations as well— send 'em my way at ari@zingermans.com.

ANARCHIST READING LIST

Carlotta R. Anderson, *All-American Anarchist: Joseph A. Labadie and the Labor Movement*

Ian Angus, ed., *Anarcho-Modernism: Toward a New Critical Theory in Honour of Jerry Zaslove*

Paul Avrich, *An American Anarchist: The Life of Voltairine de Cleyre*

Paul Avrich, *Anarchist Voices: An Oral History of Anarchism in America*

Mohammed A. Bamyeh, *Anarchy as Order: The History and Future of Civic Humanity (World Social Change)*

Alexander Berkman, *Now and After: The ABC of Anarchism*

Étienne de La Boétie, "Discourse on Voluntary Servitude"

Murray Bookchin, *The Ecology of Freedom: The Emergence and Dissolution of Hierarchy*

Murray Bookchin, *Remaking Society: Pathways to a Green Future*

Murray Bookchin, *Toward an Ecological Society*

Voltairine de Cleyre, Sharon Presley and Crispin Sartwell, eds., *Exquisite Rebel: The Essays of Voltairine de Cleyre—Feminist, Anarchist, Genius*

Candace Falk, *Love, Anarchy, and Emma Goldman*

Emma Goldman, *Anarchism and Other Essays*

Emma Goldman, "Anarchism: What It Really Stands For"

Emma Goldman, *Living My Life*

Emma Goldman, *What I Believe*

David Graeber, *Fragments of an Anarchist Anthropology*

Peter Kropotkin, *The Conquest of Bread*

Peter Kropotkin, *Fields, Factories, and Workshops*

Peter Kropotkin, *Mutual Aid*

Gustav Landauer, *Revolution and Other Writings: A Political Reader*

Peter Marshall, *Demanding the Impossible*

Erich Mühsam, *Liberating Society from the State and Other Writings: A Political Reader*

James Scott, *The Art of Not Being Governed: An Anarchist History of Upland Southeast Asia*

James Scott, *Seeing Like a State: How Certain Schemes to Improve the Human Condition Have Failed*

James Scott, *Two Cheers for Anarchism: Six Easy Pieces on Autonomy, Dignity, and Meaningful Work and Play*

Benjamin Tucker, *Why I Am an Anarchist*

Colin Ward, Damian F. White and Chris Wilbert eds., *Autonomy, Solidarity, Possibility: The Colin Ward Reader*

If you're looking to buy anything of an anarchist nature, check out Bolerium Books in San Francisco; they have a great collection. AK Press in Oakland and Black Rose Books in Montreal do as well.

BUSINESS READING LIST

The books that follow aren't likely to be found in any of the anarchist bookstores. All have helped me to arrive at where I am.

John Abrams, *Companies We Keep: Employee Ownership and the Business of Community and Place*

Ichak Adizes, *Corporate Lifecycle: How and Why Corporations Grow and Die and What to Do About It*

James Autry, *Life and Work: A Manager's Search for Meaning*

James Autry, *Love and Profit: The Art of Caring Leadership*

Warren Bennis, *On Becoming a Leader*

Peter Block, *The Empowered Manager: Positive Political Skills at Work*

Peter Block, *Stewardship: Choosing Service over Self-Interest*

Bo Burlingham, *Small Giants: Companies That Choose to Be Great Instead of Big*

Chip Conley, *Peak: How Great Companies Get Their Mojo from Maslow*

Stephen Covey, *Principle-Centered Leadership*

Max DePree, *Leadership Is an Art*

Max DePree, *Leadership Jazz*

Peter Drucker, *The Effective Executive*

Peter Drucker, *The Practice of Management*

Robert K. Greenleaf, *On Becoming a Servant Leader: The Private Writings of Robert K. Greenleaf*

Robert K. Greenleaf, *Servant Leadership: A Journey into the Nature of Legitimate Power and Greatness*

Paul Hawken, *Growing a Business*

Rosabeth Moss Kanter, *Confidence: How Winning Streaks and Losing Streaks Begin and End*

Gifford and Elizabeth Pinchot, *The End of Bureaucracy and the Rise of the Intelligent Organization*

Daniel H. Pink, *Drive: The Surprising Truth About What Motivates Us*

Tom Peters, *In Search of Excellence: Lessons from America's Best-Run Companies*

Ricardo Semler, *Maverick: The Success Story behind America's Best-Run Companies*

Peter M. Senge, *The Fifth Discipline: The Art and Practice of the Learning Organization*

Jean-Louis Servan-Schreiber, *The Art of Time*

Simon Sinek, *Start with Why: How Great Leaders Inspire Everyone to Take Action*

Jack Stack and Bo Burlingham, *The Great Game of Business: Unlocking the Power and Profitability of Open-Book Management*

Dean E. Tucker, *Using the Power of Purpose: How to Overcome Bureaucracy and Achieve Extraordinary Business Success!*

ON LIFE, MINDFULNESS, JOURNALING, WRITING, AND CREATIVITY

Kathleen Adams, *Journal to the Self: Twenty-Two Paths to Personal Growth*

Christina Baldwin, *Storycatcher: Making Sense of Our Lives Through the Power and Practice of Story*

Lynda Barry, *What It Is*

David Bayles, Ted Orland, *Art & Fear: Observations On the Perils (and Rewards) of Artmaking*

Sharon Begley, *Train Your Mind, Change Your Brain: How a New Science Reveals Our Extraordinary Potential to Transform Ourselves*

Robert Bly, *A Little Book on the Human Shadow*

Susan Cain, *Quiet: The Power of Introverts in a World That Can't Stop Talking*

Julia Cameron, *The Artist's Way*

Lucia Capacchione, *The Creative Journal: The Art of Finding Yourself*

Ram Dass, *Be Here Now*

Natalie Goldberg, *Writing Down the Bones: Freeing the Writer Within*

Daniel Goleman, *Emotional Intelligence: Why It Can Matter More Than IQ*

Steven Johnson, *Where Good Ideas Come From*

Jon Kabat-Zinn, PhD, *Mindfulness for Beginners: Reclaiming the Present Moment—And Your Life*

Jon Kabat-Zinn, PhD, *Wherever You Go, There You Are: Mindfulness Meditation in Everyday Life*

Sam Keen, *Fire in the Belly: On Being a Man*

Sam Keen, *Hymns to an Unknown God: Awakening the Spirit in Everyday Life*

Sam Keen, *Inward Bound: Exploring the Geography of Your Emotions*

David Kelley and Tom Kelley, *Creative Confidence: Unleashing the Creative Potential Within Us All*

Thomas Kelley, *The Art of Innovation: Lessons in Creativity from Ideo, America's Leading Design Firm*

George Lakoff, *Don't Think of an Elephant! Know Your Values and Frame the Debate*

Anne Lamott, *Bird by Bird: Some Instructions on Writing and Life*

Jonah Lehrer, *Imagine: How Creativity Works*

Harriet Lerner, *The Dance of Anger: A Woman's Guide to Changing the Patterns of Intimate Relationships*

Lawrence L. Lippitt, *Preferred Futuring: Envision the Future You Want and Unleash the Energy to Get There*

Hugh MacLeod, *Ignore Everybody: And 39 Other Keys to Creativity*

Dawna Markova, *I Will Not Die an Unlived Life: Reclaiming Purpose and Passion*

Debbie Millman, *Look Both Ways: Illustrated Essays on the Intersection of Life and Design*

Jim Munroe, *Time Management for Anarchists*

Osho, *Gold Nuggets: Messages from Existence*

Osho, *Life, Love, Laughter: Celebrating Your Existence*

Tristine Rainer, *The New Diary*

Lewis Richmond, *Work as a Spiritual Practice: A Practical Buddhist Approach to Inner Growth and Satisfaction on the Job*

Tina Seelig, *inGenius: A Crash Course on Creativity*

Gary Snyder and Jim Harrison, *The Etiquette of Freedom: Gary Snyder, Jim Harrison, and The Practice of the Wild*

Gary Snyder, *The Gary Snyder Reader: Prose, Poetry and Translations*

Gary Snyder, *The Practice of the Wild*

Brenda Ueland, *If You Want to Write: A Book about Art, Independence, and Spirit*

Brenda Ueland, *Strength to Your Sword Arm: Selected Writings by Brenda Ueland*

Bob Wright and Judith Wright, *Transformed! The Science of Spectacular Living*

What is Zingerman's, Anyway?

As I write this, the ZCoB includes:

ZINGERMAN'S DELICATESSEN

Newly renovated and expanded (for the fourth time), but still on that same spot at the corner of Detroit and Kingsley, the Deli is still unique, still crowded, still confusing for first timers, still hard to find, still short of parking, and still, I think (biased though I obviously am), pretty special. Now led by managing partners Grace Singleton, Rodger Bowser, and Rick Strutz, the Deli continues to deliver all the same sorts of sandwiches, traditional Jewish dishes, artisan cheeses, oils, and vinegars that it has for nearly three decades; along with other great foods from all of the Zingerman's producers (Bakehouse, Creamery, Coffee, and Candy). Only now, I think, it's better than ever.

ZINGERMAN'S CATERING AND EVENTS

From the far corners of the Deli kitchen comes catering for all occasions. We offer corned beef to caviar, potato salad to smoked salmon, for business meetings, bar mitzvahs, weddings, and whatever else—delivered down the block on Detroit Street or all the way into downtown Detroit.

ZINGERMAN'S BAKEHOUSE

We started the Bakehouse in 1992 with our partner Frank Carollo, to finally get bread for the Deli like the stuff I'd been bringing back from Paris and San Francisco for years. Working under the tutelage of master baker Michael London of upstate New York's Rock Hill Bakehouse, we learned to craft traditional, hearth-baked breads true to French, Italian, and old Jewish recipes. Later we added a whole range of butter-laden, full-flavored, know-fat (get it?) pastries and baked goods. Amy Emberling, who was one of the original crew of six bakers before she headed off to Denmark and from there to Manhattan (where she earned her MBA), later returned to the Bakehouse as a second managing partner. Today, the Bakehouse sells bread and pastries to more than a hundred different wholesale accounts across the state.

BAKE!

The Bakehouse's much-loved teaching kitchen, offering classes on breads, pastries, cakes, biscuits, croissants, pies, and much, much more. Not to mention the special week-long BAKE-cations.

ZINGERMAN'S CREAMERY

Just up the sidewalk from the Bakehouse, Ann Arbor's only creamery makes fresh, hand-ladled cream cheese, a variety of fresh goat and cow's milk cheeses, incredible gelato, and more. John Loomis and Aubrey Thomason are the cheesemakers and managing partners. The Creamery has one of the country's best little cheese shops on site as well.

ZINGERMAN'S MAIL ORDER

Ships all those full-flavored and traditionally made foods to people like you all over America. Led today by a trio of managing partners—Mo Frechette (the original Mail Order man, who packed boxes in the basement of the Deli nearly 20 years ago) along with Toni Morell and Tom Root (who together led the work to create the first Zingerman's website back in 1999). Check out their work by mail or online at www.zingermans.com.

ZINGTRAIN

Offers training and educational seminars on subjects like those covered in this book, as well as our approach to service, management, merchandising, and other engaging subjects. ZingTrain does custom consulting, too. Maggie Bayless is the managing partner who pushed the organizational envelope to create ZingTrain back in 1994.

ZINGERMAN'S ROADHOUSE

A full-service sit-down restaurant serving really good American food. Alex Young is the (James Beard award–winning) chef and managing partner who does everything from expert organic farming to very fine work on the fryer, to put together a well-crafted menu of ground-fresh-daily burgers, whole hog barbecue, Memphis-style fried chicken, Maryland crab cakes, and a wide selection of American beers, bourbons, wines, and cheese. The Roadhouse is also home to the Roadshow, a 1952 Spartan aircraft aluminum trailer permanently parked out front of the restaurant, where customers can get great drive-up coffee, homemade doughnuts, sandwiches, Bakehouse bread, and pastries. The Roadhouse also has its own farm. Cornman Farms is now up to 47 acres, located about fifteen miles to the west in the town of Dexter (next to where Alex and his family live). We grow a wide range of heirloom tomatoes, peppers, potatoes, and root vegetables; pasture-raise cows, sheep, goats, and hogs; and, as of late, host events in our soon-to-be-fully-renovated 1850s barn.

ZINGERMAN'S COFFEE COMPANY

Sourcing, roasting, and brewing really good beans right here in Ann Arbor. You can sip the Coffee Company's craft roasts at the Deli, Bakehouse, Roadhouse, and Roadshow, as well as at other leading cafes, restaurants, and retailers around the country, and now at our new retail space. Allen Leibowitz led the way as managing partner of the coffee company back in 2003, and was joined by co-managing partner Steve Mangigian in 2008.

ZINGERMAN'S CANDY MANUFACTORY

Our most recent arrival, the Manufactory crafts candy bars by hand, as they would have been made in the early days of the last century. Charlie Frank, now the managing partner, started making the amazing Zzang! bars while working as the pastry manager at the Bakehouse, and we later spun the idea out into a business all its own. Zzang bars are now sold in specialty shops all over the US, as is the peanut brittle, halvah, and other craft confectionaries.

9 KEY STRATEGIC ELEMENTS OF OUR VISION FOR ZINGERMAN'S 2020

1. Changing Our World
2. 12-18 Vibrant Businesses
3. Radically Better Food
4. Radically Better Service
5. Radically Better Finance
6. Intentional Technology
7. We Put the "FU" in Fun
8. ZCoB as an Educational Destination
9. Opportunity for Everyone; Responsibility for All

For the full write-up, see *Part 1* or www.zingermanscommunity.com.

A Handful of Organizational Recipes

Here are a dozen or so of our organizational recipes. Adapt at will!

4 elements of an effective Vision

Inspiring

Strategically sound

Documented

Communicated

5 steps to bottom-Line change

1. Create a clear and compelling purpose for change.
2. Create a positive vision of the future and develop leadership alignment around that vision.
3. Engage a microcosm to determine who needs to know and how to get the information out.
4. "Officially" present the vision and create an action plan.
5. Implement the change.

3 elements of energy

Physical

Mental/Emotional

Vibrational

4 steps to effective energy management

1. Read it

2. Vision it

3. Manage it

4. Repeat it

training compact

Trainer agrees to:

1. Document clear performance expectations

2. Provide the resources to do the work

3. Recognize performance

4. Reward performance

Trainees agree to:

Take responsibility for the effectiveness of their training at Zingerman's

decision Log

Current Situation	Desired Outcome	Decision	Implement- ation Date	Actual Outcome (After 3 Months)	Reflection/ Observations

twelve natural Laws of business
from zingerman's guide to good Leading, Part I: a Lapsed anarchist's approach to building a great business

1. An inspiring, strategically sound vision leads the way to greatness (especially if you write it down!)

2. You need to give customers really compelling reasons to buy from you

3. Without good finance, you fail

4. People do their best work when they're part of a really great organization

5. If you want the staff to give great service to customers, the leaders have to give great service to the staff

6. If you want great performance from your staff, you have to give them clear expectations and training tools

7. Successful businesses do the things that others know they should do . . . but generally don't

8. To get to greatness you've got to keep getting better, all the time!

9. Success means you get better problems

10. Whatever your strengths are, they will likely lead straight to your weaknesses

11. It generally takes a lot longer to make something great happen than people think

12. Great organizations are appreciative, and the people in them have more fun

Secrets 1–18
from Zingerman's Guide to Good Leading, Part 1: a Lapsed anarchist's approach to building a great business

1. Twelve Natural Laws of Building a Great Business

2. Contrast, Composition, Content

3. Creating Recipes for Organizational Success

4. The Zingerman's Business Perspective Chart

5. Building a Better Mission Statement

6. Revisiting the Power of Visioning

7. Writing a Vision of Greatness

8. Vision Back

9. An 8-Step Recipe for Writing a Vision of Greatness

Secrets 19 - 29

from zingerman's guide to good Leading, Part 2: a Lapsed anarchist's approach to being a better Leader

william marshall standing with his much-loved sardine display at the deli

Time to Eat!

Nine Recipes to Cook in Your Own Kitchen

Although the *Zingerman's Guide to Good Leading* series is clearly about business and life in leadership, I still like to stick some recipes into the back of each volume. It hardly seems like Zingerman's without saying at least a little something about food and cooking. While you didn't buy this book because you wanted to cook, the odds are that many of you like to do so, and that a healthy majority of men and women who are interested in progressive business practices are also interested in eating well.

It makes sense that good cooking would be a good metaphor for what we do in management. In our case, both can lead to a better life, solid organization, better food, and more self-fulfilled staff members and partners. To take the food angle further, I'll turn to my very talented friend Tamar Adler. While Tamar is a food writer, I've come to realize that her (very fine) book, *The Everlasting Meal*, is actually full of insight about the sort of self-management I've written about here. Respect for ingredients, the importance of good technique, having a clear sense of where you're going, combining components (often seemingly incompatible ones) in order to make something special happen, being able to adapt when needed, staying focused, and delivering timely and tasty results . . . it all sounds sort of familiar, doesn't it?

Cooking, I've come to realize, is a culinary equivalent to our approach to self-management. Take a look at Tamar's sound advice: "Cooking is best approached from wherever you find yourself when you are hungry." The same, I would say, goes for what we do at work. Managing yourself is best approached from wherever you find yourself—in this case, hungry not (only) for the wonderfully described pasta dishes, salads, and omelets that Tamar talks about in her book, but for self-growth and the desire to bring meaning to all we do in management. As Tamar writes, "We have different loves. Mine are food and words . . . I say: Let yourself love what you love, and see if it doesn't lead you

459

back to what you ate when you loved it." Which is, I would argue, an effective culinary metaphor for doing work that matters, work that qualifies as what Wendell Berry calls "good work" (see page 14).

Tamar describes *An Everlasting Meal* as her "attempt to hand over what I think matters. Then, whether you are hungry or anxious or curious, you can at least weed through and decide what seems right. I only mean to show what cooking is: an act of gathering in and meting out, a coherent story that starts with the lighting of a burner, the filling of a pot, and keeps going as long as we like . . . If your meal will be ongoing then our only task is to begin." It sure sounds like life in leadership to me.

"There is a prevailing theory," Tamar goes on to say, "that we need to know much more than we do in order to feed ourselves well. It isn't true." Tamar and I are in total alignment—it's my strongly held belief that anyone who wants to cook good food can do that as well. All it takes is learning some very basic techniques (with which her book will help), and buying the best ingredients you can buy (which we and other purveyors of fine food are happy to help with). Add in steady periods of mindful practice, regular rounds of tasting to train the palate, and a good bit of belief, and over time I'm betting you'll become a darned good cook. [38]

The same goes for managing ourselves effectively. Take out "feed" from Tamar's quote above and plug in "lead"—the message is strikingly similar. We don't have to be gifted—we just need to do reasonably good, creative work and help those around us do the same to accomplish something of value. I couldn't disagree more with the belief out there that says you have to be some sort of innately insightful, instinctively brilliant, natural-born superbrain of a businessperson to be a great leader. Anyone who decides they want to lead, or decides they want to manage themselves more effectively, can do it. Same is true in the kitchen. Most all of us have the resources and tools with which "we can do more good cooking," as Tamar says, or as I'd say, more good leading "than we know."

Like Tamar's meal, becoming a better leader is everlasting too. Here's to good food and good leadership! May both bring you great learning and great joy, and may both help you bring sustenance and delight to those you serve.

COLD BULGARIAN CUCUMBER SOUP

We've been making this cold soup pretty much since we opened the Deli back in the early '80s and it's been one of my favorites ever since. It's easy to make, delicious to eat, and it harkens back to the Deli's Eastern European roots. Here in Michigan, cold soup is more of a summer item, but because the ingredients are all available year round, you can make it any time you want. And, of course, if you live in warmer climes, cold soup is always in season!

1¼ pounds cucumber, peeled, seeded, and finely chopped

½ cup chopped walnuts

1 clove fresh garlic, peeled and minced

2 tablespoons fresh dill, finely chopped

2 tablespoons extra virgin olive oil

1 cup fromage frais or plain thick yogurt

½ cup sour cream

½ cup whole milk

Fine sea salt to taste

Freshly ground black pepper to taste

Combine all ingredients in a large bowl and mix until well combined. Adjust seasoning and serve chilled.

The flavors get fuller if you let it chill overnight.

CHOCOLATE CHESS PIE

As you probably know by now, my good friend Daphne Zepos died during the writing of this book. Sadly, she was not the only person I was close to who passed away that year. As the book was reaching its final stages, my friend Tricia Gatza died at the young age of 43. Tricia had a presence that turned heads everywhere she went, and one of the sweetest smiles I've ever seen. Unlike Daphne, Tricia didn't work with food professionally, but she had a great palate and a high appreciation for it. Our chocolate chess pie—luscious, creamy, sweet, and unique—was one of her favorites. I think of her now every time I see anyone eating a piece.

2 ounces unsweetened chocolate

¾ cup unsalted butter

1½ cups granulated sugar

4 eggs

1 egg yolk

½ teaspoon fine sea salt

1½ teaspoons vanilla extract

1 partially baked piecrust

Preheat oven to 325°F.

In a double boiler, melt the unsweetened chocolate and the butter over low heat.

Meanwhile, in a large mixing bowl, combine the sugar with the eggs, yolk, salt, and vanilla extract. Gently whisk only enough to make the mixture smooth and well combined.

Pour in the melted chocolate/butter mixture and whisk just until combined. Pour into a cooled partially baked piecrust.

Bake at 325°F for 45-50 minutes, until center is just set. Remove from the oven and cool to room temperature.

This pie can be stored at room temperature for several days.

ZingTRAIN

HUNGARIAN LECSÓ

Lecsó (pronounced "lehtch-o") has been on my mind ever since my first trip to Hungary in the fall of 2011. There it's a staple of everyday eating each autumn when the peppers and tomatoes are in season. To put at least some picture of the dish into your mind, lecsó is akin to ratatouille in texture, but with a Hungarian flavor all its own. Not surprisingly, as with almost every homemade dish, every cook seems to have their own version, along with strongly held opinions about the "right" way to make it.

In Hungary we had lecsó that was spicy and some that wasn't, so clearly not all Hungarians are in agreement on whether you should use hot peppers or sweet peppers. I've been doing a blend of the two, and you can adjust to meet your desired heat level. Bacon levels also varied a lot, and some of the lecsó had sliced sausage in it as well. You of course can adapt at will.

There are hundreds of ways to have lecsó for lunch or dinner. You can eat it as your main dish, side dish, or with pretty much anything you like. You can also add some beaten egg in at the end and let it set into the vegetables before you serve.

There's another version of lecsó you might make to use as a base for other dishes when peppers and tomatoes aren't in season. It basically says, using simple culinary subtraction, that it would be a lot of onions, cooked slowly in bacon fat, and then simmered with paprika and salt.

3 ounces double-smoked Hungarian bacon, chopped into small pieces

3 tablespoons bacon fat, sunflower oil, or olive oil (optional)

1 medium onion, halved and sliced thin

Sea salt to taste

1 pound (about 10) Hungarian hot wax peppers, seeded and cut in ½-inch slices

1 pound (about 3 large) tomatoes, cut into large chunks

2 teaspoons sweet Hungarian paprika

Lightly cook the bacon on moderate heat in a large deep skillet for a few minutes to render the fat. If the bacon gives off about 3 tablespoons of fat, you can continue to cook in that. If you're in need of more, and you have bacon fat standing by, you can just use that. Alternatively, you can use oil—in Hungary sunflower oil seems to be the choice, but I've been addicted to olive oil for so long, that's what I've been using.

Then add the sliced onion to the skillet. Sprinkle on a pinch of sea salt, and then cook over moderate heat for about 6 or 7 minutes until the onion is soft.

When the onion is soft, add the peppers. Sprinkle on a touch more salt and cook over moderate heat for another 10 to 15 minutes or so. (The salting makes a difference because it pulls the moisture out of the peppers.)

Add the tomatoes to the pan, along with a touch more salt and the Hungarian paprika. Stir well and simmer another 15 to 20 minutes. You can add a bit of water as you cook to keep the desired consistency. It should have the texture of a vegetable stew. To give you a sense of it, it will be moist, but almost spreadable. Taste for texture, salt, and spice level and adjust accordingly.

You can eat the lecsó right away, but it also cools and keeps really well too.

Zingerman's
maiL order.

DAPHNE'S WATERMELON, FETA AND ARUGULA SALAD

I learned this special salad from my good friend Daphne Zepos (for much more on Daphne, see page 407). I think it's an amazingly delicious combination—the sweetness of the melon, the salty tang of the feta, the richness of the olive oil, offset against the slight crunch and pepperiness of the arugula and black pepper. Toss in some roasted red pepper or toasted walnuts too if you like.

Before I give you the formal recipe though, let me give you Daphne's—her description of the salad will probably give you as good a sense of who she was as anything else I can tell you. Here's what she sent me when I asked her a few years ago to send me her favorite salad:

The salad is like a pyrotechnic.
Watermelon and sheep feta sitting on a few leaves of mature peppery arugula.
My sister's green olive oil from the island of Zakinthos.
Cracked black pepper.
4 black olives. They are all floating in the air. No plate. No fork.

If you're feeling creative and inspired, run, free-form, with Daphne's deliciously poetic instructions. With your creativity connecting with hers, I'm confident you'll come up with something spectacular. If you'd like a more specific set of instructions, here you go.

   3 ounces fresh arugula

   3 ounces Greek feta, preferably barrel-aged, broken into bite-size pieces

   8 ounces watermelon, cubed

   2 ounces roasted red pepper (optional)

   1 ounce toasted walnuts, chopped (optional)

   4 kalamata olives (optional)

   3 tablespoons extra virgin olive oil

1 tablespoon sherry vinegar or wine vinegar of your choice

Coarse sea salt to taste

Freshly ground black pepper to taste

In a medium bowl, gently toss the arugula, feta, and watermelon along with the red pepper, walnuts, and olives if you're using them. Divide onto salad plates, and drizzle with olive oil and vinegar. Sprinkle with salt and freshly ground black pepper.

LESLIE KISH'S SARDINE SPREAD

Leslie Kish, one of my all time favorite customers, passed away in the year 2000 at the age of 90. When I first met him, back in the early '80s, not long after we opened the Deli, I knew him only as a customer. He liked good cheese, good bread, and also sardines. Over the fifteen years or so I waited on him, I discovered that he'd been born in Hungary and had come here when he was fifteen. Later he fought in the Spanish Civil War (which probably contributed to his love of Manchego cheese), and was active in the International Peace Movement for decades. In 1947 Leslie was one of the original founders of the internationally famous Institute for Social Research in Ann Arbor, the same place that Ron Lippitt, the man who developed what we now know as visioning, also worked. In 1948, while pretty much every pundit was predicting a Dewey landslide in the presidential election, Leslie used his techniques for statistical surveying to predict that Harry Truman would triumph.

I, of course, knew Leslie mostly because he liked to eat good food wherever he went. Seemingly every time I would see him he'd have just returned from a trip to China or Italy or some other glamorous location where he'd received some new honor. Turned out his mother had one of the best pastry shops in New York, patronized, he told me, by people like Eleanor Roosevelt, Gypsy Rose Lee, Eugene Ormandy, and the violinist Fritz Kreisler, so his food fascination had been part of his upbringing. When we both had time, we'd sit over coffee and discuss everything from social movements to stuff like sardines and sheep's milk cheese. I learned this recipe from Leslie, who told me he'd learned it from his mother. You can use it on sandwiches or serve for hors d'oeuvres.

½ teaspoon sea salt

2 teaspoons fresh lemon juice

1 4-ounce tin sardines

8 ounces fresh cream cheese

1 teaspoon chopped flat-leaf parsley

1 teaspoon minced onion

In a large glass bowl, dissolve the salt in the lemon juice and mix well.

Add the sardines and mash them in with the juice. When the sardines are well mashed, gently mix in the cream cheese.

Add the parsley and onion and mix until well combined.

Serve chilled with slices of toasted rye bread or crackers.

For much more on sardines, see our little hand-sewn Zingerman's Press pamphlet *Sardines, What Can't They Do?* at zingermanspress.com

BUTTERSCOTCH PUDDING

I grew up with butterscotch pudding, but what we got as kids came out of a box. The packaged stuff pales in comparison to the homemade version we make at the Roadhouse. Fast becoming one of our most popular desserts, it's pretty darned delicious. As with everything we make, the quality of the ingredients is what makes it so special. In this case the key is the brown sugar. We use old-style muscovado brown sugar, which is radically more flavorful than the readily available commercial versions. The latter are made by industrially refining cane juice all the way through until it becomes white sugar, then adding a small bit of molasses back to it to give it some color. The old-style brown sugars are made by leaving in the natural molasses—they have much more flavor and are far less sweet. Think of the complexity of dark chocolate compared to the very sweet commercial versions. Better quality milk and cream will also add to the rich flavors of the pudding. And the fleur de sel sea salt garnish takes it over the top!

1⅓ cup whole milk

¾ cup plus 2 tablespoons dark brown sugar, preferably muscovado

¾ cup heavy whipping cream

4 tablespoons unsalted butter, broken into small pieces

¾ teaspoon coarse-flake sea salt

1 vanilla bean, split open and seeds scraped (or 2 teaspoons pure vanilla extract)

3 egg yolks

1 tablespoon plus ½ teaspoon cornstarch (you can up this a bit, depending how thick you like your pudding)

Fleur de sel, or naturally dried sea salt, for garnish

Whisk together the milk, brown sugar, cream, butter, salt, and vanilla in a heavy medium saucepan. Bring to a simmer over moderate heat, whisking frequently, until the sugar and butter have melted in.

Meanwhile, whisk the yolks and cornstarch together in a medium bowl until smooth. Remove the brown sugar mixture from the heat and pour about a cup or so into the egg mixture in a slow, steady stream; meanwhile, with your other hand, whisk the mixture constantly. Pour the hot milk-and-egg mixture back into the pot, and return it to the stove. Whisking constantly and getting all parts of the bottom of the pan, cook over medium heat until the first few large bubbles form and sputter. Reduce heat to low; still whisking, cook 1 minute. Be careful not to overcook or you will get bits of scrambled egg. If that happens, push the pudding through a fine-mesh sieve.

Remove from heat and pour into a bowl, then cover surface with buttered parchment paper (to avoid pudding skin) and chill until cold, at least 1½ hours.

Serve topped with a pinch of fleur de sel sea salt.

COFFEE JELLY

If you serve this dessert this weekend, you're pretty sure to get acclaim for your culinary creativity. This is a classic example of "creativity in reverse" (see page 368). Most modern day Americans would call this coffee "jello," but back before the brand name became better known than the traditional dish, it would have been known as coffee jelly. In the second half of the 19th century, "jellies" of all sorts were some of the country's most popular desserts. Heated up, and then poured into gelatin molds to cool, it's light, refreshing, low in fat, high in flavor, and a great way to bring coffee's flavor to the end of your meal in a new form. And of course because no one in your neighborhood has probably ever made one, you can look like an exceptionally innovative cook.

½ cup cold water

1 tablespoon gelatin

2 cups very strong hot coffee

5 to 6 tablespoons dark brown sugar

½ teaspoon pure vanilla extract or vanilla bean paste

Whipping cream

Place the cold water in a medium bowl, and sprinkle the granules of gelatin evenly over the surface of the water. Allow the gelatin to soften and bloom, about 5 minutes.

Meanwhile, prepare the coffee.

Stir together the hot coffee, sugar, and vanilla in a glass or metal bowl, then add the gelatin mixture, stirring until dissolved. Chill, covered, until set.

Serve with a generous dollop of softly whipped cream.

ZZANG BAR MILKSHAKE

Here's a good dessert for you. It's a great way to get your kids involved since there are only three ingredients and it's pretty safe to say the recipe will work out really well no matter what. The shakes will be very rich, so a little bit goes a long ways.

1 cup whole milk

2½ cups vanilla gelato or ice cream

1 Original Zzang Bar

Combine all ingredients in a blender, breaking the Zzang Bar into smaller pieces. Blend on high speed until all the ingredients are well combined. Add a little more or less milk for your desired consistency.

Zingerman's
CORNMAN FARMS

TOMATO AND VINEGAR SOUP

At Cornman Farms, we grow over two dozen varieties of heirloom tomatoes each year using sustainable methods. The yield of the old heirloom varieties is very low, less than 20 percent of their commercial cousins. But they have about twenty times more flavor—which, to state the obvious, makes for a marvelously delicious tomato soup.

This is a great way to enjoy summer tomatoes. If you can't get heirloom tomatoes in season, you're better off with high-quality canned tomatoes than to use out-of-season commercial varieties. The paprika I like to use is the smoked pimentón de la vera from Spain. The vinegar adds a wonderful lightness to the finished soup. Sherry vinegar, aged red wine vinegar, and balsamic vinegar all taste great.

As a fun alternative, you can skip adding the vinegar to the pot, and let your guests add it directly to their own bowls at the table—just set out three or four great vinegars and let folks experiment.

3 tablespoons full-flavored extra virgin olive oil, plus additional for serving

2 cloves fresh garlic, peeled and minced

1 small onion, diced

Coarse sea salt to taste

½ teaspoon hot Spanish Pimentón de la Vera paprika

4 pounds ripe tomatoes, chopped

2 bay leaves

½ cup short-grain rice, preferably Spanish

3 tablespoons wine vinegar

Freshly ground black pepper to taste

Heat the olive oil in a large heavy-bottom pot over moderate heat. Sauté the garlic and onion with a generous pinch of salt until soft. Add the paprika

473

and mix well. Sauté another minute or two. Add the tomatoes and bay leaves. Stir and bring to a boil. Reduce heat and simmer, partially covered, for an hour. Add a little water at a time as the tomatoes cook down if the soup gets too thick.

Add the rice and the vinegar and simmer until the rice is done, about 18 minutes. Season with salt and freshly ground pepper to taste.

Garnish with a ribbon of olive oil across the top and serve hot.

Endnotes

Foreword

1. *From Bob Wright:* 'I first met Ari through a phone call where he asked me about his late father, Bob Postel. Ari had heard that I was carrying on his father's innovative work, something Bob called Contemporary Adlerian psychotherapy. I first came across Bob through the work of people he had trained. I was consistently impressed by the forthright, clear-eyed way with which his students approached life. They were all highly competent at their work, but more than that, they were stellar, upright individuals. The next time that I ran across Bob's influence was at a group psychotherapy convention. He was part of a forum attended by over two hundred people. Audience members were passing written questions for these three prominent Chicago psychotherapists to answer. Two of the therapists had very good, impressive things to say, but the third, Ari's father, powerfully bottom-lined his responses with a minimum of words and a maximum impact every time. I was intrigued. Shortly after that, I went to a demonstration of his innovative group and individual technique and was blown away by Jane Myerson, one of the primary therapists on Bob's team, as I have been consistently blown away not only by Ari's insight and humanity but by the stellar humanity and service of his company.

In one of my latest email exchanges with Ari, I wrote, 'I really enjoy thinking of you and your father—two very remarkable men with whom I have been blessed to associate. Your father would be so proud of you. He is one of the few people I have known who could really appreciate the enormity of what you have done. His staff had the same zeal that I see in your staff. His approach was unique and grounded in that uncommon commodity, common sense. Just like yours.' Both Ari and his father stand as idealist rebel innovators. Bob Postel transformed stodgy Adlerian therapy into a practice that promoted vibrant, transformational growth. Up until that point, Adlerians had always done individual and group work. But they had never tied them together anywhere near as powerfully as Bob did. He systematically created a map for people's growth just as Zingerman's training passports provide a map for employees. He turned traditional Adlerian psychology on its head, as Ari and Paul and Zingerman's have turned traditional business upside down—insisting on a win for all concerned. Ari and his birth father are truly proof that the apple does not fall far from the tree. Zingerman's keeps bearing fruit—may our world continue to embrace their way of doing business."

From Ari: Connecting with Bob Wright and including his thoughts in this book successfully connects an important piece of my past with my professional and personal present. The philosopher I.G. Gurdjieff argued that we don't really become independent adults until we fully and freely forgive our parents. Finding and understanding who my father was—aided greatly by my connection with Bob—certainly played a big role in my own growth and development. It was one of those turning points that helped me become who I am today. Had I not done that work, it's safe to say that this book would never have been written.

The last time I saw my father was in 1963, when I was seven years old. He died fourteen years later, in 1977. Sadly, we had no communication at all during that period. Disconnected from him, and from my feelings about him, I spent little time grieving after I got the news. To fast forward another fourteen years, in the early '90s, while going to therapy regularly and doing a great deal of self-reflection, I decided to open that long-closed chapter and seek a better understanding of my father and the role he played in my life.

Although it was clearly impossible to connect with him in person, I figured I could at least learn more about who he was and what he did. I began my quest by calling a couple of relatives who I vaguely remembered had mentioned his name at some point. They gave me a few more names and phone numbers. Through those connections I got a few more contacts, and through them a few more still. Over the course of three years, I probably spoke to about 50 of my father's colleagues, clients, and relatives. Most of them agreed that he was very talented, innovative, and articulate, and often very controversial. Unfortunately, he doesn't seem to have ever written anything about his methodology. Bob Wright was the best source I had on the subject—he was the one carrying on my father's work, and with a great deal of success at that. Although it's hard for me to quite put it together with the fact that I never spoke to him after I was seven years old, Bob is adamant that my father was a genius who got little credit for his creative work.

I know it was 1992 when Bob and I first spoke—I found his name on the to-do list of one of my journals from the spring of that year. Fast-forward again, this time to the summer of 2012, when, out of the blue, I got a call from Bob. As you can see from his note above, my father's approaches to psychotherapy formed the foundation of the way that Bob and his wife, Judith, run their Wright Graduate University today. He was working on his forthcoming book, *Transformed!*, and he wanted to put something about my father into his version of "appreciations" at the end of it. As part of our conversation, I brought up ZingTrain and the *Zingerman's Guide to Good Leading* series. Neither had existed when Bob and I first spoke in 1992. I sent Bob copies of my books, and he sent me his. He came up to a ZingTrain seminar, where we had our first face-to-face meeting. With each interaction it became ever clearer that although our connection had begun twenty years earlier by talking about my father and *his* work, Bob and I actually had a great deal more to discuss about our own lives—we clearly shared many views on leadership, life, and business.

When I started thinking about who might write the foreword for this book about self-management and mindfulness, Bob was a natural fit. His contribution to my own inner work, his professional success in the world of coaching and personal development, his newly formed connection to ZingTrain, and our shared approaches to business were too perfect to pass up. As Bob says in his foreword, looking in the mirror can definitely lead to good things. Although it's at least a little bit awkward to share this story in public, it seems a fitting piece of supporting evidence for everything that this book, my life, and our organization are all about.

Secret #30

2. The commonly held belief that anarchism amounts to some sort of disorganized free-for-all is wholly inaccurate. As Emma Goldman wrote, "The general contention that Anarchists are opposed to organization, and hence stand for chaos, is absolutely groundless. True, we do not believe in the compulsory, arbitrary side of organization that would compel people of antagonistic tastes and interests into a body and hold them there by coercion. Organization as the result of natural blending of common interests, brought about through voluntary adhesion, Anarchists do not only not oppose, but believe in as the only possible basis of social life."

Secret #31

3. The ABCDE Model is a simple but helpful way to keep from getting overly worked up about something that feels far more important than it probably is. It was developed by psychologist Albert Ellis (the father of cognitive behavioral therapy, if you're interested in that sort of thing) in the 1950s. It works like this: A stands for Adversity—something challenging happens to us. B stands for Belief—we have beliefs about what's happening (i.e., "he said that because hates me"). C stands for the emotional Consequences—what we Believe about the Adversity generally drives the action that leads to those Consequences. D is when you Dispute, or internally refute, the misplaced Beliefs: Do they really make sense? Do they ring as real? Or am I ratcheting them way up beyond where they should be? E is the new Effect—what you learn from the reflection done during this process and how you alter your behavior accordingly. The key to the process for me is the clear realization that C (the emotional consequences) do *not* stem directly from A (the adversity) but rather from B (your beliefs about the adversity). If we manage those beliefs, we can, as Viktor Frankl recommended, alter our response for the better.

4. Mike Ganino started his company, Protein Bar, a few years back. He's been a big fan of ZingTrain and of the *Guide to Good Leading* series. Learning about energy management here at Zingerman's, he took the idea back to his own business and adapted it to come up with a recipe for his staff. I wanted to recognize it here because it backs up so much of what's in this book: teaching self-management to others creates good things; creative people like Mike are drawn to creative settings like ZingTrain, which in turn sparks even more creativity; as Mike helps his staff self-manage more successfully, his business is likely to do better. My hope—and Mike's—is that you riff off of his adaptation of our energy work and come up with ways to make everyday energy management a positive force in your business. If you'd like to take a look at it, drop us a note at zingpress@zingermans.com, and we'll send it right over.

Secret #32

5. Allowing a staff member to caringly and constructively say "no" to a request that we've made in this way is what *should* have happened with the not-so-great scenario I describe about Allie and the $10,000 turnaround on page 73.

Secret #33

6. Happily, Maia and Eli didn't move! Their parents, Brian and Cara, decided to stay in Ann Arbor, and they still visit Zingerman's regularly.

7. The dark chocolate from Vietnam is made by the folks at Marou Chocolate and is very highly recommended. You can read more about it at marouchocolate.com.

8. When I get too worried about all the stress of my job, or overly excited about something that's not ultimately all that important, I try to remember what anarchist Gustav Landauer wrote on the subject a century or so ago. "Passion," he said, "is no herring which one pickles." Landauer's line makes me smile every time I see it. His choice of fish says a lot about the society in which he lived; although we don't encounter too much herring in 21st century American life, in Germany, a hundred years ago, pickled herring was as common as hot dogs. Passion is not, Landauer is saying, something we prepare ahead of time and store in salt for future use. Rather, it's a "product" of living and appreciating in the present.

9. I don't know how many legal pads I've gone through over all the years I've been journaling, but I know it's a lot—I have them all stacked up in a cabinet, sans one, that I left on a flight from Detroit to Minneapolis a few years ago. While it probably seems silly to have gotten so screwed up over a pad of paper, its loss put me into a temporary tailspin; I take my journaling seriously, and losing a yellow pad was like losing a small piece of my soul. It was hardly life threatening, but I was seriously off center for the rest of the day. As had happened with not being able to run, a brief, unexpected absence increased my awareness of how much my routines around mindfulness mean to me. Despite a couple of calls to the airline, I never got the pad back. What had high emotional value to me looked like just a bunch of scrawled notes on a legal pad someone had left behind.

Secret #34

10. For more on Nashville Hot Chicken, see Joe York's fabulous film *Hot Chicken* at southernfoodways.org.

11. I learned the term "tradeskill" from Paul Hawken, who wrote about it in his great book, *Growing a Business*. "Tradeskill," he writes, "is really the set of skills that spell the difference between success and failure in a business. It is the knack of understanding what people want, how much they'll pay, and how they make their decision. It is knowing how to read the signals of the marketplace, how to learn from those signals, how to change your mind. Tradeskill gives you a canniness about how to approach a given product, market or niche. Tradeskill becomes a sixth sense that gives those who have it the ability to make decisions quickly, cutting through months of meetings, brainstorming, market studies and bureaucratic shuffling. Tradeskill is how to handle money, how to buy and how to pay."

Secret #35

12. For what it's worth, it's generally accepted practice in newspaper work that the person who authors an article is almost never the person who writes the headlines. I'm not sure about the history of that now-standard journalistic practice but it does reinforce my belief that the bullet points are likely to emerge from a different place in our brain than a more detailed, more richly engaging, poetically inspiring vision.

13. Ari's personal vision, written 2012.

It's June 2017, and Jelly Bean and I are heading out for a walk combined with a bit of slow running. She's seventeen, so the days of speedy sprinting in the sun have passed, but she's still going strong. We're living in Ann Arbor, enjoying the spring weather. The ZCoB is heading towards the final weeks of one of the finest years it's ever had. Sales are slightly above plan, combined ZCoB NOP is over 5.1, we have some great new partners, a couple exciting new businesses, a higher quality of workplace than ever, employee-owners, a working succession plan, and are well on our way to having that positive ecological footprint that we envisioned back in 2011. Our food and service are seriously better than ever—people regularly comment on how steadily we've improved. Growth has gotten us more focused on quality than ever. People in the community know what we believe in, and although there are always naysayers and cynics, the vast majority of the community cares and believes in us. It feels good to know that I've contributed positively to each of those things—and more importantly to the lives and careers of thousands of people who've worked and are working in the ZCoB over the last five years. It's a good feeling to know that I've been able to listen and be supportive through stressful times, impart some insight, help ZCoB'ers design a system or two, teach a bit about food, and help people get started on a vision or initiate a project or change that they've been thinking about for a while now.

More than ever, all of the ZCoB partners are feeling fulfilled in their work. They're actively working to attain their dreams and feeling good about what they're doing personally and professionally. I feel honored to have been able to contribute in some ways to helping make that happen. More and more often, the other partners continue to grow in ZCoB leadership roles as they have for the last decade—as they are all increasingly seen as leaders across the ZCoB, Paul and I can continue to be more and more just two of 20-something really positive, inspiring, collaborative and self reflective leaders. I'm working as much as ever, learning even more, contributing more to others, and enjoying it as much as I ever have.

More personally, I continue to feel really good about what I do. I've had probably the best job I could have for three and a half decades now. Though I have helped many others write theirs, I still haven't had to write a resume. I'm teaching, both within and without the ZCoB more than ever. I've finished Parts 3 and 4 of the *Guide to Good Leading* series and am working on Part 5. And I'm starting to sketch out a new food book as well. The business books have successfully become near-standard texts for alternative business people all over the country, and have gotten attention around the world. They continue to serve as handbooks and guide books for ZCoB partners, managers, and staff—the concepts, systems, values, visions, recipes, etc. are ever more accessible and consistently conveyed because they're effectively documented, and consistently used.

The ZCoB's approaches to visioning, appreciation, servant leadership, open book finance, anarcho-capitalism and more are now widely talked about and adapted in the world of sustainable business. And I've worked hard and long and with some success at getting better at living and modeling all of them every day.

Personally, I've worked hard to develop my listening skills, to exhibit more patience, to be slower on the trigger in conversation. I'm learning more than ever and sharing that more than ever through teaching and writing. It's exciting to see how much all the stuff we've developed, adapted, clarified, etc. over the years helps the people here and who come into contact with it around the country.

I've continued to travel and have gotten to some places I'd never been before–Lithuania, Croatia, Sweden, Maine, and Argentina are on the list. I've been back to Hungary and Tunisia again and have taught on both cuisines in any number of venues. The trip to Maui and our bond with our *ohana* there has become pretty much an annual event—good to get out of the cold in the winter.

I've read over a ton and a half of books, been to some new conferences, learned some new techniques, and then figured out how to adapt them to what we do in the ZCoB. I eat well, I'm more appreciative, I'm in shape and still running, if slowly, every day. I feel good going to work and I feel good going home. I feel good on the road and I feel good returning to Ann Arbor.

I've figured out how to teach our stuff abroad—the Zingerman's Academy overseas.

Speaking of the Academy, it's been super successful—more ZCoB partners are teaching than ever, we're bringing more great people from outside the ZCoB than ever, and we've helped to revive an understanding of anarchist approaches to life, education, etc.

Our governance plans (zingshares, decision making, etc.) have become models for others around the country and we now have ZingTrain sessions on them. I can see another book coming down the road.

We've helped to bring awareness of previously little-understood (or misunderstood) cultures to Ann Arbor through our food work—we're experts on African American, Native American, Hawaiian, Gullah, Hmong, and other contributors to the kaleidoscope of life.

I've continued to save money consistently so I have a solid savings account. My trust is in current working order, so should something happen, things are well organized and ready.

I feel very fortunate to have had the chance to work with so many great people, to have sought out, savored and sold so much great food, to have helped so many others to drive towards and often attain their dreams. And I look forward to much more of all those, a lot of good learning, and good laughing to go.

Secret #36

14. Early 20th century German writer and erstwhile Christian anarchist Eberhard

Arnold wrote of his friend, Gustav Landauer, "[he] expects to find the salvation in work—true work that is filled, guided, and organized by a brotherly spirit free from greed; work as the deed of honest hands and as a witness to the rulership of a pure and truthful spirit. What he envisions as the fundamental character of the future is work as an expression of the spirit, as provision for men's needs, as cooperative action. Side by side with the joy one feels in comradeship and in showing consideration to one another, man's joy in his work is to bring it about that he experiences his work as the actual fulfillment of his life and thus finds joy in living."

15. Abraham Maslow said as much in writing about the importance of self-actu-alization in *The Farther Reaches of Human Nature*. Maslow made clear that "the actu-alization of the highest human potentials is possible—on a mass basis—only under 'good conditions.' Or more directly, good human beings will generally need a good society in which to grow." In other words, if we join an organization—or family, club, clan, or conclave—in which self-development is considered a sign of success, we have much better odds of growing and developing, of going to great heights, both within ourselves and as part of our group.

16. Taking in harsh criticism and not responding with anger towards others, or ourselves, is no small achievement. Zingerman's 5 Steps to Handling a Customer Complaint can get you effectively through any interaction in which the other person—customer, coworker, cousin, or community member—is unhappy with what we've done. But while they help us help the person who was complaining to feel calmer and better cared for, I think they probably stop short when it comes to restoring our own energy. I think that Julia Cameron's method for dealing with difficult criticism, described in *The Artist's Way*, is an effective approach to moving emotionally past the problem and get-ting back into a space that we feel good about ourselves and the world.

> From *The Artist's Way*:
>
> Receive the criticism all the way through and get it over with.
>
> Jot down notes to yourself on what concepts or phrases bother you.
>
> Jot down notes on what concepts or phrases seem useful..
>
> Do something very nurturing for yourself—read an old good review or recall a compliment.
>
> Remember that even if you have made a truly rotten piece of art, it may be a *necessary* stepping-stone to your next work. Art matures spasmodically and *requires* ugly-duckling growth stages.
>
> Look at the criticism again. Does it remind you of any criticism from your past—particularly shaming childhood criticism? Acknowledge to yourself that the current criticism is triggering grief over a long-standing wound.
>
> Write a letter to the critic—not to be mailed, most probably. Defend your work *and* acknowledge what was helpful, if anything, in the criticism proffered.
>
> Get back on the horse. Make an immediate commitment to do some-thing creative.
>
> Do it. Creativity is the only cure for criticism.

17. Tina Seelig, executive director of the Stanford Technology Ventures Program, says, "Lucky people take advantage of chance occurrences that come their way. Instead of going through life on cruise control, they pay attention to what's happening around them and, therefore, are able to extract greater value from each situation . . . Lucky people are also open to novel opportunities and willing to try things outside of their usual experiences. They're more inclined to pick up a book on an unfamiliar subject, to travel to less familiar destinations, and to interact with people who are different than themselves." What lucky pennies are you leaving laying around that you could pick up and benefit from?

18. The anarchists occasionally wrote about the idea of continuous improvement. Here's what Gustav Landauer had to say about one of the men he admired most, Detroit-based anarchist Robert Reitzel: "Nothing about [him] ever seemed finished. He was always in a state of becoming and of recreating himself." Brilliant 20th century anarchist Murray Bookchin professed, "Immobility would be death ... We must always be on a quest for the new, for the potentialities."

19. The John Buckland Wright quote comes from the amazing, limited edition book *To Beauty*, by his son, Christopher Buckland Wright, published by Fleece Press in 2006. It details the friendship and artistic interaction between anarchist printer Joseph Ishill and Buckland Wright, along with beautiful woodcuts from the artist. Check out Ishill's amazing hand-printed books by looking up the early- to mid-20th century works of his Oriole Press.

20. While I was working on this book, I had the honor of spending some time with two amazing women, both of whom, I think, are evidence of how powerfully positive good work can be, and how much living in harmony with the Natural Laws really is likely to yield great life results. On a trip to New Orleans for our annual partner offsite in January of 2011, we had dinner at Dooky Chase, the restaurant over which Leah Chase, now 90 years old, continues to actively preside. Dooky Chase is a New Orleans institution, started in 1941 in the Treme district of the city, by Mrs. Chase's in-laws. It's one of the best examples of classic Creole cooking, with a beautiful display of African American art on the walls. In the middle of the 20th century, it was the only restaurant in the city to regularly serve meals to integrated groups.

On a visit a year earlier, she'd shared her belief with me that in order to be more financially viable after decades of serving lunch only, the restaurant needed to begin opening in the evenings. Her only worry was whether she could find enough good people to work the new shift. When we were there on the visit in 2011, Mrs. Chase had just gotten her birthday gift from the staff at the restaurant—they started opening for dinner service on Friday nights. Mrs. Chase's energy is as positive, grounded, and engaging as I can imagine. She still works more than many younger people—very clearly she loves what she does.

The next night we drove out to the small town of Galliano on Bayou Lafourche to have a meal cooked for us by Alzina Toups. Mrs. Toups has no restaurant but for the last 35 years she's been cooking in "her kitchen" for private parties that book her small hall. She too loves her work, is passionate and energetic about getting up early, making food from only simple, great ingredients, turning them into the full-flavored traditional Cajun foods she grew up with. At age 85, her commitment to Cajun culture and cooking couldn't be stronger. She's very focused on serving her guests, her family, and even her suppliers. And her food, like Mrs. Chase's, is fantastic. You can see more about Alzina in Joe York's short film at www.southernfoodways.org/alzina-toups-keeper-of-the-flame/.

Lo that I should get to be that age and still be as passionate and firm in my resolve to do good work as these women. To make marvelous food that people will come a long ways to eat and talk about for a long time to come, and to serve others I care about, striving still for improvement, and contributing positively to those around me.

Secret #37

21. "Time," Harriette Arnow explains about that era, "was often measured by flowers, especially among the storytellers; 'It was dog-wood blooming time' or 'the pretty-by-the-nights were open but it was too early for the whip-poor-wills or dew.' ... The morning glories disappeared, bindweed came instead; love vine became dodder, and so it was with many of our old flower names—farewell-to-summer, old maid, bridal wreath, candle sticks, snow-on-the-mountain, and others are now become ageratum, zinnias, and such."

22. If you want to experience the excellence of Irish butter, look for the Kerrygold brand in American specialty food shops. It's made only with cream from cows that are grazing in open pastures (no silage feeding barns). I'm particularly fond of the silver-foil-wrapped version, which is an old-style cultured butter. As was commonly done before the 20th century, the cream is allowed to ripen for a day or so before being turned into butter. The resulting cultures make for a much more flavorful butter. Email me at ari@zingermans.com and I'll send you an essay I did on the subject.

23. A lot of this is about the way we relate to time. Take folk historian Charles Joyner's synopsis from *Albion's Seed*: "New England Puritans held that time was money, and New England time ways were characterized by efforts to improve time, such as the invention of such things as the alarm clock and daylight savings time. Delaware Valley Quakers condemned haste. They sought not to improve time but to redeem it, to sanctify it and make it less worldly. Virginians sought neither to improve time nor to redeem it, but to kill it. They developed the unique idea of killing time. Time was hierarchy in Virginia. A servant's time was not his own, but a Virginia gentleman put his declaration of temporal independence on public display. If New Englanders improved time, if Quakers redeemed it, if Virginians killed it, backcountry settlers placed great value on passing the time as they had passed the time in the British borderlands."

24. One of my favorite fascinations with this sort of scheduling was the "Republican Calendar" in France that was adopted after the French Revolution. In an effort to escape the old religious- and monarchical-centered timescapes, the French New Order organized a completely different calendar—new measures, new names, new everything. It was in use for only a brief time—from 1793 to 1805. Amazingly it took the National Assembly only a month to approve it, but I guess things move more quickly in times of revolutionary change than they can in our own era. Anyways, the Republican calendar was designed to make time management easier to understand, more egalitarian and secular. There were still twelve months in a year, but each was divided into three ten-day weeks. There were ten hours in each day, a hundred minutes

in an hour, a hundred seconds in a minute (for which clocks were actually manu-factured and circulated for a few years). I can only imagine the change management required to put this sort of thing in place. And not only that, but the names of all the days and months were changed to be more in synch with nature. The fall started with Vendémiaire (coming from the Latin *vindemia*, for "grape harvest"). The first month in winter was Nivôse (from the Latin *nivosus*, or "snowy"). July, which had been named for the Roman emperor Julian, was shifted to Fructidor, from the Latin "fructus" for fruit. You have to admit it kind of makes sense. The ten days of the week were simply named for numbers—the French equivalent of "first day," "second day," etc. And instead of the Saints' Days that were associated with the old calendar, the Republican model tied in food, tools, plants, and minerals. Instead of a birthstone, you might have had a vestigial vegetable. As best as I can calculate, my birthday—November 3—was on the 13th day of the month of Brumaire (from the root of "foggy" in French), the day assigned to the Jerusalem artichoke.

One of the other interesting facts of history is that of the advent of railroad time. Yeah, I know you've most likely never heard of it, nor are you likely to again. But 150 years ago, advocacy for railroad time caused quite the controversy. Today, if we were to travel west from Ann Arbor, we'd wait til we get to the Illinois border to fall back an hour, from eastern time to central time. But back in those days there were no time zones. In fact, every city had its own time, a few minutes earlier or later than its neighbors. Remember that because the sun moves westward across the sky, as you drive that way, each city must, by definition, lie at a slightly different spot on the clock's continuum. In truth, town times were probably more accurate than the time zones we're used to today. As one traveled one would regularly adjust one's watch to the local time.

Imagine then, for a minute, what it was like to write a railroad schedule. Not only did you need to take into account how long it took the train to go a particular distance, but then you also had to adjust again, taking into account the local time in the towns at which the train would stop, which was of course rarely the same as the time in the town from which it left. Even the idea of it starts to stress me out, though I suppose if we used town-time today, it would be a veritable treasure chest for app-designers.

Schedule screw-ups, of course, couldn't help but cause collisions. After a major rail accident in New England, it was acknowledged that something had to change. You can imagine what happened—the engineers of two trains using the same track had different times on their watches and disaster followed. The push for railway time followed—leaving the time the same for longer distances to cut back on consumer and conductor confusion. In essence, railway time was the beginning of the time zones we now take for granted. But like all changes, many resisted it at first.

The idea of time zones resolved this problem. In a nutshell, those in charge of "time management" divided the world's 360 degrees of longitude by the 24 hours in the day and came up with two dozen time zones, each roughly 15° of longitude across. Adjustments were made for existing communities, national boundaries, state lines, etc. At first some clocks in Britain (where all this got going) had two minute hands on each clock face—one to show the time in the town, the other the time in London. Eventually, in England, they settled on the time in the town of Greenwich as the starting point, and over the years, Greenwich mean time has become THE standard for ships and others moving quickly around the globe. The second minute hand, as you know, fell away a long time ago.

25. If you write schedules, annual budgets, or any of that sort of thing in your work, take note that the way we now organize the calendar and each day on it is not how it's always been. To the contrary, humankind has changed its constructs regularly over the centuries. There are countless examples to look at. For a long time, for instance, "days" started at sunrise and ended at sunset. Hour lengths were frequently felt to be different at different times of the year—there were twelve hours of daylight regardless of season, which means that ʰours in the (Northern Hemisphere) winter were much shorter than the "same" hours in the summer.

26. "Time Management for Anarchists" probably would have been a terrific name for Secret #37, but that title has already been taken—and beautifully so—by a very creative guy up in Canada named Jim Munroe. He's done a short comic book on the subject. Jim's also put out a fun little film clip that effectively covers the basics of his approach. Emma Goldman and Mikhail Bakunin are transformed from their original 19th and 20th century anarchist identities into 21st century cartoon characters: graphic designers living in Toronto. Jim argues, as I do, that being an anarchist isn't at all at odds with wanting to be good at time management: "Anarchists have to be more organized than average if they don't want to depend on power structures." See Jim's great work at nomediakings.org.

27. There are those who struggle with what's been called Shiny Object Syndrome: the tendency to run after every exciting new idea, while seeing few, if any, of them, through to fruition. Learning to stick with things until they're finished, or at least fairly well implemented, is no small achievement if your mind is used to moving more quickly than completion is likely to come. But it can have a hugely positive impact on our sense of achievement, the contribution we make to others around us, and our self-esteem and vibrational energy.

28. "Samoans Sacrifice a Day." That *New York Times* headline, which happened to show up in print while I was working on this piece, had nothing to do with any ancient religious ceremony. Instead, it had everything to with time, and the way the modern world has tied it to politics and economics. The sun over Samoa will continue to set each evening as it always has, but as of December 30, 2011, the calendar shifted. In the interest of enhancing trade dialogue with Australia and New Zealand (at the cost of the now more awkward schedule for communication with North America), Samoa shifted from one side of the International Date Line to the other. According to the *Times*, "In this giant-step version of daylight saving time, the island's 186,000 citizens, and the 1,500 who live in Tokelau, will go to sleep on Thursday and wake up on Saturday. The government has decreed that those who miss a day of work on Friday will be paid all the same. Samoa has been out of alignment with its Asian-Pacific neighbors since 1892, when American traders persuaded it in 1892 to shift from the western side to the eastern side of the International Date Line to facilitate business with the West Coast of the United States. That earlier shift took place on American Independence Day so that the Samoans could celebrate July 4 twice.

"This shift took place at the stroke of midnight, so that two minutes after 11:59 p.m. on Dec. 29, 2011 it became 12:01 a.m. on Dec. 31. The new time zone set

Samoa 3 hours *ahead* of eastern Australia rather than 21 hours *behind* it, and 22 hours ahead of California, instead of 2 hours behind it." Regardless of one's views on the shift, it's an exceptionally clear example of how economics has become the primary frame through which political bodies now relate to time.

Secret #38

29. Just to take you into the deep corners of my mind, I'll toss in this other tidbit from Bruffee that makes me smile. "If thought is internalized public and social talk," he posits, "then writing of all kinds is internalized social talk made public and social again. If thought is internalized conversation, then writing is internalized conversation externalized." Which means that I, shy, party-averse introvert that I am, am basically just having a serial party with one person at a time, then bringing them all together in my head where no one can see them, and finally putting the whole thing back out in the form of odd essays like this one!

30. Servant Leadership guru Robert Greenleaf said it well: "To be a lone chief atop a pyramid is abnormal and corrupting. None of us are perfect by ourselves, and all of us need the help and correcting influence of close colleagues."

Secret #39

31. From what most everyone tells me, the school system may not be helping much. The belief that there is always a "right" answer, the mindset that the "teacher knows best," is the opposite of the out-of-the-box thinking that we want to have in our organization. Sir Kenneth Robinson, author and expert on creativity and education in the UK, says that the traditional school system is "stifling some of the most important capacities that young people now need to make their way in the increasingly demanding world of the 21st century—the powers of creative thinking." Michigander Edward Davis, whose book *Lessons for Tomorrow*, about the contemporary education system I highly recommend, writes that "we are failing to educate because we fail to bring out what is within. Knowledge has become an increasingly exterior phenomenon … we humans would be so much more resourceful and powerful, our potentials and dreams unbound, if only education would cooperate." As Emma Goldman wrote a century ago, "No one has yet realized the wealth of sympathy, the kindness and generosity hidden in the soul of a child. The effort of every true education should be to unlock that treasure."

32. I did indeed teach my first class on "Creating a Creative Organization" at the American Cheese Society in August, 2013, and the first one here at ZingTrain in September, 2013, a few months before this book went to the printer. I look forward to teaching many more.

33. Taking a more in-depth anarchist look at this issue, here's what Alexander Berkman wrote in 1927: "Free to exercise the limitless possibilities of his mind, to pursue his love of knowledge, to apply his inventive genius, to create, and to soar on the wings of imagination, man will reach his full stature and become man indeed. He will grow and develop according to his nature. He will scorn uniformity, and human diversity will give him increased interest in, and a more satisfying sense of, the richness of being. Life to him will not consist in functioning but in living, and he will attain the greatest kind of freedom man is capable of, freedom in joy."

34. Sometimes we inadvertently get great results by *not* paying attention to a particular goal. I'm not recommending this as a life strategy, but it often seems to turn out that the less we try to get some good outcome, the more it seems magically to appear. This was certainly the case for us when we described the Zingerman's Community of Businesses for the first time in our vision of Zingerman's 2009 (written in 1994) Building creativity into our business model was the last thing on our minds, but we clearly created one anyways. This concept is nicely explained in John Kay's book *Obliquity: Why Our Goals Are Best Achieved Indirectly*.

Epilogue

35. The obituary I wrote for Daphne touched on all the formal details of her adult career. "Over the years she'd served as a board member of the American Cheese Society and did formative work as the chairperson of the organization's annual judging. She was a co-founder of the Cheese of Choice Coalition, an advocacy group dedicated to the preservation of raw milk and artisan cheeses. From 2002 to 2005, she played a lead role in selecting and maturing more than 300 cheeses in the Artisanal Premium Cheese Center's pioneering affinage cheese caves in Manhattan. She lectured, moderated, and presented at the American Cheese Society's annual conference. She taught thousands of professional and avocational students and, in the process, helped significantly improve the quality of cheese and the state of cheese mongering in this country. In 2006, Daphne founded the Essex Street Cheese Company, which still imports a small selection of cheeses from Europe. In 2011, together with her business partner, Kiri Fisher, she and her husband, artist Brad Brown, purchased The Cheese School of San Francisco. In August of 2012, a month after she died, Daphne was the recipient of the 2012 American Cheese Society's Lifetime Achievement Award."

36. Coming back to Bob Wright's words in the foreword about looking in our own mirrors, I think of Massimo Pigliucci's reflection in *Answers for Aristotle: How Science and Philosophy Can Lead Us to a More Meaningful Life*: "Aristotle's opinion was that friends hold a mirror up to each other; through that mirror they can see each other in ways that would not otherwise be accessible to them, and it is this [reciprocal] mirroring that helps them improve themselves as persons."

37. We arrived at the cemetery shortly after a funeral had finished. Daphne got me a taste of the *koliva*, the traditional Greek funeral food, made from boiled wheat berries, sesame, spices, and nuts. I found out later from her sister that she'd always loved it. It's funny that our first day together took us to that spot, admiring the beauty of death in rural Greece. Two decades down the road, I ate koliva served in her memory.

Time to Eat!

38. On the business of cookbooks, Tamar Adler notes, "No matter how well a cookbook is written, the cooking times it gives will be wrong. Ingredients don't take three or five or ten minutes to be done; it depends on the day and the stove. So you must simply pay attention, trust yourself, and decide."

Appreciations

Here at Zingerman's we end every meeting with five minutes or so of appreciations. It's nothing fancy, but it's a positive way to return to our daily lives when the discussions end. The only structure to it is that we always set aside the time to do them, and that we use that time for appreciations. Anyone can appreciate anyone that comes to mind. So here, at the end of this book is a list—as always, incomplete—of the people I appreciate for their assistance and support through the process of putting this book together.

I'll start things off by appreciating Paul Saginaw. We've been at it for over thirty years now—a long time for any relationship, let alone a modern-day business partnership. His support, insight, patience, guidance and good will have contributed more to my life than I can convey. Without him, quite simply, there would be no Zingerman's.

Thanks to all of the now thousands of people who've been a part of Zingerman's over all these years, from Marci Fribourg and Ricky Cohen who worked the first day the Deli was open on Detroit St., to Sara Woods who was the last person hired before this book went to press. What you experience when you come in to eat, work, or learn is a collaborative project—everyone who's worked here has left their own unique imprint on our organization.

Thanks to everyone who's worked on making this book a book—*migwetch* to Meg Noodin for great editing, insight, and support; to Deborah Bayer for her always gentle and enormously insightful editing; to Polly Rosenwaike for her fine line editing, Ann Grahl for copyediting, Suzanne Fass for proofing, Mike White for recipe input, and Liz Lester for layout and design. Great appreciation goes to Pete Sickman-Garner for supporting the book project throughout its life, Nicole Robichaud for great design, and Ian Nagy and Ryan Stiner for the amazing illustrations. Well-designed appreciation also to Betsy Bruner, Billie Lee, Hannah Metler, Sara Richardson, Joanie Hales, Brad Hedeman, Courtney Suciu, Gauri Thergaonkar, and Erica Bertram for helping to make Zingerman's such a hotbed of creative energy.

Thanks to all the Managing Partners at Zingerman's for collaboratively constructing an organization great enough that I could actually write a book about it: Frank Carollo, Amy Emberling, John Loomis, Grace Singleton, Alex Young, Rodger Bowser, Allen Leibowitz, Charlie Frank, Rick Strutz, Steve Mangigian, Mo Frechette, Tom Root, Toni Morell, Aubrey Thomason, and last but most definitely not least, Maggie Bayless; I'm pretty sure that without ZingTrain, very little of what's in here would exist, at least not in such a teachable, explainable, and put-to-usable way, and without Maggie there would be no ZingTrain. Bo Burlingham has said to me that he thinks that most people at Zingerman's will never fully appreciate just how much ZingTrain has altered—for the better—our organization. I probably wouldn't have either, except that I've been far more mindful of the impact since he imparted that insight on me a few years ago.

Special thanks for Stas' Kazmierski, recently retired as the Co-Managing Partner at ZingTrain, who taught me the vast majority of what I know about visioning and organizational change. His influence is all over this book and our Community of Businesses.

Thanks to Ron Maurer, our one and only Vice President of Administration, whose hiring in the year 2000 is certainly one of the best moves we've ever made.

Huge thanks for friendship, advice, insight, and good emails to Lex Alexander, Molly Stevens, Randolph Hodgson, Daphne Zepos, Rob Pasick, Rich Sheridan, Karen Pernick, Marifer Calleja, and Lea Chansard. Additional appreciation to Wayne Baker, Majid Mahjoub, Dean Tucker, Edgar Schein, Jack Stack, Chip Conley, Sam Keen, Gary Snyder, Heather Porter Engwall, Rick Price, Robert Greenleaf, Peter Block, Skip LeFauve, John T. Edge, Jay Sandweiss, James Scott, Seth Samuels, Walter Sowden, Ram Mahalingam, Tamar Adler, Tricia Gatza, John Abrams, and a fair few other folks who I'm sure I'm forgetting. Thanks to Patrick Hoban for his generosity, friendship, good leadership, dialogue, and ongoing elbowing. Especially big appreciation to Tammie Gilfoyle for love, encouragement, patience and putting up with me throughout the many months of working on this book.

Thanks to professors William Rosenberg, Arthur Mendel, Roman Szporluk, and Carl Proffer for teaching me history many years ago.

A few thousand freely-given thanks to all the anarchists who've leant their words, insights and ideas to the world. Emma Goldman, Alexander Berkman, Mikhail Bakunin, Peter Kropotkin, Voltairine de Cleyre, Nestor Makhno, Rudolf Rocker, Étienne de La Boétie, Murray Bookchin, Paul Avrich, Joseph

Ishill, Gustav Landauer, Élie and Élisée Reclus, Ammon Hennacy, Errico Malatesta, Buenaventura Durutti, and all the other insightful anarchists who were writing about this stuff so long ago. Thanks to Julie Herrada at the Labadie Collection for all her help in tracking down relevant anarchist writing. Special appreciation to Bo Burlingham, another modern-day lapsed anarchist, for insight and inspiration. Thanks to Jo Labadie, the peaceful and inspirational Michigan anarchist who donated his archive of books and pamphlets to the University of Michigan in 1911. Thanks to Agnes Inglis, who worked for many years to make the Labadie Collection a living archive that people like me could access. And thanks to Carlotta Anderson for sharing her anarchist books with me.

Special thanks to Bob Wright, both for sharing his knowledge and insight, for being willing to write a foreword, and for connecting me with the father I really didn't know.

Thanks too to all those I've forgotten to appreciate. Given the Theory of Relevantivity (see page 379), there are thousands of people I've never knowingly met who've had a positive impact on me, on Zingerman's, and on this book. Even if I've neglected to note your contribution, it counts just as much as I've I'd mentioned it. And I appreciate all the help I've gotten from all the coworkers, customers, writers, musicians, professors, pets, and poets who've helped me process all that ideas, experiences and approaches that are outlined in the book.

Special thanks to Marsha Ricevuto for all the work that makes it possible for me to focus so much time and energy into things like writing books.

Super special thanks to Jenny Tubbs for keeping tabs on, and leading, the behind-the-scenes work that has made it possible for you to be holding this book in your hands.

Perhaps the biggest thanks for what's in this book go to Richard Kempter and Marge Greene for imparting much of the wisdom that underlies what's in here and for helping me to make my leadership work way more effective and my life far more fun and much more rewarding.

And, of course, thanks to you for reading!

Ari

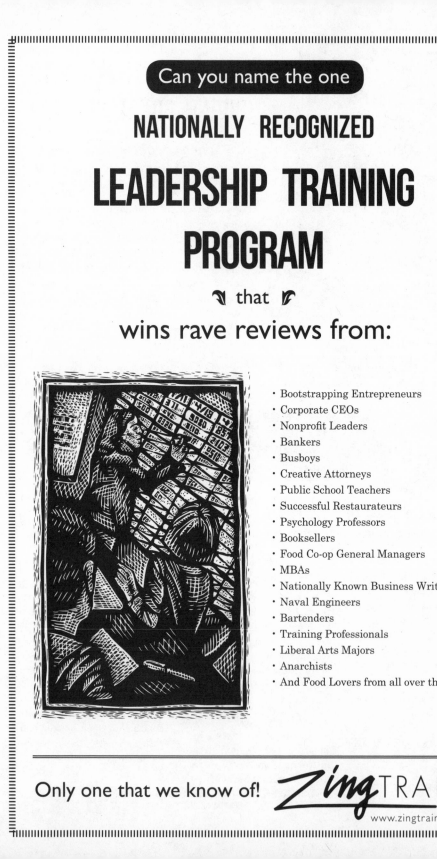

notes

notes

1999

Led by managing partners tom root and toni morell, zingermans.com goes online.

as demand for zingtrain seminars and workshops continues to grow, stas' kazmierski joins zingtrain as maggie's co-managing partner.

2000

amy emberling, one of the original bakers and founder of the pastry kitchen, returns to zingerman's bakehouse as co-managing partner.

2005

the birth of the zingerman's candy bar! zzang!® bars coming out of the bakehouse are quickly named "the ultimate handmade candy bar" by "chocolatier" magazine.

2004

deli retail manager grace singleton takes the reins as deli managing partner.

zingerman's roadshow, ann arbor's hippest drive-up coffee counter, opens in the parking lot of zingerman's roadhouse.

2006

bake!, ann arbor's hands-on teaching bakery and cake!, a showroom worthy of the imagination-defying creations from the bakehouse cake designers, open at zingerman's bakehouse.

for the first time, produce from alex young's cornman farms highlights the roadhouse's annual harvest dinner.

2008

zingerman's coffee company manager steve mangigian joins allen as co-managing partner of the business.

zingerman's is featured on oprah's sandwich episode and #97 Lisa c.'s boisterous brisket is oprah's favorite, rating an "11" on a scale of 1-5.

2009

zingerman's candy manufactory, a wholesale candy maker creating old-fashioned american sweets by hand, opens with charlie frank as managing partner.

zingerman's "guide to better bacon," ari weinzweig's tome on pork (featuring bacon history, recipes and lore) is published.

zingerman's coffee company opens its retail and café space on plaza drive down the walk from zingerman's bakehouse and creamery.

2007

deli restaurant manager rick strutz joins grace singleton as co-managing partner at the deli.

zingerman's launches our 2020 vision charting the course for the zingerman's community of businesses for the next 13 years.